# BEING JOHN LENNON

# BEING JOHN LENNON

## A RESTLESS LIFE

## RAY CONNOLLY

WEIDENFELD & NICOLSON

First published in Great Britain in 2018
by Weidenfeld & Nicolson

1 3 5 7 9 10 8 6 4 2

A CIP catalogue record for this book
is available from the British Library.

HB ISBN  9781474606806
TPB ISBN 9781474606813

Typeset by Input Data Services Ltd, Somerset

Printed and bound by CPI Group (UK) Ltd, Croydon, CR0 4YY

Weidenfeld & Nicolson

The Orion Publishing Group Ltd
Carmelite House
50 Victoria Embankment
London, EC4Y 0DZ

An Hachette UK Company

# CONTENTS

# AUTHOR'S NOTE

On the afternoon of Monday, 8 December 1980, I got a call in London from Yoko Ono, wanting to know why I wasn't in New York. 'We thought you were coming over,' she said. 'The BBC has been here this weekend.' My reply was that when, a few weeks earlier, I'd suggested going to interview her and John – although, in truth, I'd mainly wanted to talk to John – she'd put me off by saying, 'The time isn't right.' I didn't know whether that meant that her readings of the numbers weren't good, because I knew that Yoko was into Numerology, or that there was some other reason. But now with *Double Fantasy*, the first John Lennon album in five years, in the shops, apparently the time *was* right, and Yoko was insisting I go to New York immediately. 'The sooner the better,' she urged.

So, I telephoned my editor at the *Sunday Times,* the newspaper for which I was doing some freelance writing at the time, and a ticket was booked for me on an early flight to New York the following morning. That night, as I played *Double Fantasy* and reread the lyrics, I was full of anticipation. I'd known John since 1967 when I'd been reporting on the Beatles as they'd filmed the *Magical Mystery Tour* in the west of England. After that, having been accepted into the Beatles' coterie, I'd then watched John work at London's Abbey Road recording studios, been with him at the Beatles' Apple office in London and interviewed him several times at his home, Tittenhurst Park, in Berkshire, as well as accompanying him in Canada and then New York.

It was while we'd been in Canada just before Christmas in 1969 that he'd given me potentially the biggest scoop of my life as a journalist when he'd told me that he'd left the Beatles, before adding: 'But don't write it yet. I'll tell you when you can.' So, I didn't.

Four months later when newspaper headlines around the world were screaming 'PAUL McCARTNEY QUITS BEATLES', he was very grumpy. 'Why didn't you write it when I told you in Canada?' he demanded when I phoned him that morning.

'You asked me not to,' I replied.

'You're the journalist, Connolly, not me,' he snapped, angry because, in his eyes, as he'd started the Beatles, when in their embryonic form they'd been called the Quarry Men, he thought he should be known as the one who had broken them up – as indeed he had.

Sometimes you just couldn't win with John. But that was John, as changeable as the Liverpool weather.

What would he be like when I got to New York the next day, I was thinking that night in 1980 as I packed my Sony cassette player into my bag. Since his last letter to me four years earlier we hadn't been in touch, as I'd written a couple of novels and some television plays and he'd retreated from the public gaze to, he would say, bring up his second son Sean, and become a house-husband. I'd read his recent interviews with *Newsweek* and *Playboy* in which he'd talked about enjoying domesticity, but I really couldn't see him having done much child rearing or baked much bread, as they'd reported. Possibly he'd got flour on his hands once or twice, I thought, but what else had he been doing for the past five years? I hoped I would soon find out.

Before going to bed at around midnight, London time, I called the Lennons' home in the Dakota building in Manhattan to let John know the time that I would be arriving in New York the next afternoon. An assistant answered, saying that John and Yoko had gone down to the studio to mix one of Yoko's tracks; and that his instructions were to tell me to go straight to the apartment when I got in, that John was looking forward to seeing me again.

I was woken at four thirty in the morning by the phone beside the bed. In the darkness my first thought was that it must be someone calling to tell me that the cab to take me to the airport was on its way. It wasn't. It was a journalist on the *Daily Mail* apologising for waking me, but he'd just been told from the *Mail*'s New York office that John Lennon had been shot.

For a second or two I didn't quite follow, and he had to repeat what he'd said. Was John badly injured, I asked, when I gathered my thoughts. The man from the *Daily Mail* didn't know.

Those were pre-twenty-four-hour news days, so, getting up, I went downstairs and tuned the radio in the kitchen to the BBC World Service.

The headline I was now fearing came as the 5 a.m. news headline. John Lennon was dead, murdered outside his home on New York's West 72nd Street as he had returned with his wife, Yoko Ono, from the recording studio. He was forty.

Ten years earlier John had told me he was going to have to slow down if he didn't want to drop dead at forty. As we'd smiled together at the thought of one day being as old as forty, he'd then asked me: 'Have you written my obituary yet?'

I told him I hadn't.

'I'd love to read it when you do,' he'd replied.

I cancelled my flight to New York that morning of 9 December 1980. I had an obituary to write.

# FOREWORD

John Lennon didn't fit into any neat classification because he never stayed the same John Lennon for very long. He was a labyrinth of contradictions. As a singer, he disliked the sound of his voice so much he would increasingly disguise it on record; as a rock and roll purist, he also came to consider himself an avant-garde artist; and, as a born leader, he would sometimes find himself being very easily led.

By the end of his life he was a bohemian multi-millionaire who still liked to romantically consider himself a working-class hero, although he had been brought up comfortably off in a roomy home in a pleasant and green suburb outside Liverpool. In truth there was never anything working class about him. Not once in his adult life did he have to do any kind of work other than that of being an entertainer or writer.

But it was in his attitude towards the Beatles that he showed his contrariness, and, perhaps, foresight, most fully. Having started and then helped build the group into the most loved musical and cultural ensemble of the twentieth century, he then merrily turned himself into the iconoclast who destroyed them. In so doing he broke hundreds of millions of hearts.

That the Beatles had to break up at all would become a debate among fans that lasted for decades, but, viewed in retrospect, it was probably the best thing that could have happened to them. By killing them at or near their peak, John was, albeit unknowingly, preserving them, freezing them in time before their music began to be received with a lessening of enthusiasm, as would inevitably have happened had they stayed together.

I was as shocked as anyone when it happened, but perhaps I shouldn't have been. Because John had already become a master of reinvention as he cast off one persona and pulled on a new one. The bookish little boy, who enjoyed nothing more than staying in his bedroom drawing cartoons and rereading *Alice In Wonderland*, would turn into a thieving little devil when outside the house with his school friends. The truculent, rock-mad art student, who would become the clowning, most sharp-witted Beatle, was unrecognisable when he metamorphosed into the late Sixties psychedelic guru, who in turn gave way to the angry, anti-war crusading, feminist John Lennon of 1971. The changes would continue into the Seventies as, almost overnight, he went from being an occasional but famously out-of-control public drunk on what he would later call his eighteen-month 'lost weekend', to becoming a reclusive new father hiding in his New York apartment.

John Lennon was all of these people and more besides. But, most importantly, he was a clever songwriter and a pithy sloganeer who had an ear for the murmurs of his time long before they became the shouts of the multitude; and, who, with others, helped capture that time in song.

He could be whimsical, hyperbolical, cruel, untruthful, self-mocking, occasionally even violent and often impatient and unreasonable. But, never able to sidestep a joke if he could see one coming, he was also often very funny and always imaginative. Had he been born a couple of decades later he might easily have made a living as a stand-up comic. 'Part of me would sooner have been a comedian,' he once said. 'I just don't have the guts to get up and do it.'

He wasn't always very nice, and could be unreasonable and diffi-cult to live with, as his first wife, Cynthia, his second, Yoko Ono, and his mistress May Pang would have agreed. But, jealous and generous in equal measure, he was both well-mannered and sharp-tongued. In truth there seemed to be no constant thread throughout him, other than that in everything he did there was always a restlessness, a desire to be doing something else, to wish, perhaps, to be different from the person he was.

Before the Beatles, popular entertainers were almost universally deferential towards their managers, diplomatic in their utterances to newspaper writers and polite to radio and television interviewers. Most of them took care to be uncontroversial in their political views, too. John Lennon didn't. He was direct and spoke his mind, perhaps sometimes when he wasn't fully informed and when it might have been easier, and perhaps wiser, not to have done. Always he showed a broad streak of the nonconformist in whatever he did, not necessarily in an aggressive way, at least not in the early Sixties, when his barbs were usually delivered with a smiling, jokey insolence. On many occasions, though he might not have been being deliberately rude, his sardonic answers would give interlocutors pause for thought. He had, it could be said, attitude – an air which, although it could irritate and cause suspicion among older detractors, resonated among many of those of his own age.

But why was he like that? Where did that attitude come from? Where did the need for continual reinvention begin? What made John Lennon the person he was? The fractured relationship of his parents must have helped shape the first few years of his life. But, like all of us, John Lennon the man would become the sum of many different contributory factors as well, from the time and place of his birth onwards. The time was the Second World War, and the place was the unfashionable port of Liverpool in the north-west of England.

# 1

*'Soon I forgot about my father. It was like he was dead'*

Had he ever been told, he would have liked the idea that he was conceived on the kitchen floor of a terraced house in the Penny Lane area of Liverpool one January afternoon in 1940 – just a few hours after his father's ship had docked. That, according to a memoir written by his father, Freddie Lennon, was John's beginning. But, like much of what Freddie Lennon said, it might or might not have been entirely true. John was a war baby, for sure, but how could his father have known the exact moment of conception, since he would be at home and sleeping with his wife, Julia, for several more weeks? He didn't say. It was, however, a good story to tell about the origins of a son who was to become one of the most famous men of the twentieth century – and Freddie (sometimes known as Alfred – 'the ignoble Alf', to John – but, more usually, as Freddie) span a good yarn – as one day would his son. Whether or not the tale is true doesn't really matter, other than that it tells us something about the circumstances of the couple involved.

Freddie Lennon was sixteen when he first met Julia Stanley in 1929, just a few weeks after he left Liverpool Blue Coat School. He had been placed there as a semi-orphan at the age of seven on the death of his father, when his mother had been unable to provide for him. Now that he had a job, he was living at home again.

Julia, who had also just left school, was fifteen. Freddie, who had suffered from rickets as a child, was a little fellow, never more than five foot three inches tall. Wearing the new bowler hat he'd just bought to go walking, as teenagers then did, in Liverpool's huge and splendid Victorian Sefton Park, he looked ridiculous. So Julia told him, anyway, when Freddie tried to get off with her. He wasn't offended by the remark. He'd caught this pretty girl's eye, and, in a cavalier gesture of devil-may-care, he threw the hat into the boating lake. That amused Julia, and that day they began a nine-year, on-and-off courtship.

In a city of tribes, Catholic and Protestant, and narrow gradations of status, Freddie was not only of the wrong religion, his family being nominally Catholic, but also a couple of steps down the social ladder from Julia. His father, Jack Lennon, had been born in Dublin and had enjoyed a career in America singing with a troupe of Kentucky Minstrels – white guys who blacked-up, which was the fashion in those days; think only of Al Jolson. But Jack had been back in Liverpool working as a lowly shipping clerk when Freddie had been born – one of six children. It was rumoured that their mother couldn't read, a state not that uncommon in 1912.

Julia's family consisted of five daughters, the eldest being Mary, who would forever be known as Mimi by her nephew, John. Julia was the second youngest, an auburn-haired, headstrong girl who liked going to the pictures so much that she became, for a time, a cinema usherette. It seemed a glamorous job to her. The rest of the Stanley family thought of themselves as working-class posh, in that their father, who, like Jack Lennon, was also involved in shipping – as were the men in many Liverpool families at the time – had become an insurance investigator after a career at sea. More to the point, eldest daughter Mimi was determinedly aspirant middle class, and, like her father, was always dead set against Freddie Lennon. 'We knew he'd be no use to anyone, certainly not Julia,' she would later say.

For nine years, however, as all three other sisters, Elizabeth, Anne and Harriet, married sensibly and left the family's small, bow-fronted terraced house at 9 Newcastle Road, Wavertree, Julia withstood the sidelong looks and criticisms from her parents and Mimi whenever Freddie was mentioned. She must have seen something in the apparently unsuitable, harmonica-playing, pub-singing young man. Not that she and Freddie spent much time together. Within a year of their meeting, he had given up his office job to go to sea as a bell boy on one of the Cunard liners that in those days sailed from Liverpool.

Freddie, like his son, would become a keen letter writer, describing to Julia all the places he visited. But Julia never wrote back, or even, according to him, went down to the docks to meet his ship when he returned home. In Freddie's account, and we only have his word for it, he seems to have been the keener of the two. So, when in 1938 Freddie was in Liverpool between ships and Julia dared him, as a lark, to put up the marriage banns, he did so the very next day. Keeping it a secret from their families, the two met outside Mount Pleasant Register Office on 3 December 1938, and, with a couple of friends as witnesses, became man and wife. For their honeymoon they went to the Forum cinema to see a Mickey Rooney film about an orphanage, before parting at the end of the evening to go to their separate families to break the news. The following day Freddie went back to sea for three months, his marriage to Julia still, he would say, unconsummated.

For the following year Julia stayed in her parents' home, to which Freddie would return when he was, infrequently, back in Liverpool. She was still there in October 1940 when, with Freddie away at sea again, Britain at war and Liverpool under almost nightly bombing from the German Luftwaffe, she went into labour. Her baby was born on 9 October 1940 at the Liverpool Maternity Hospital during a lull in the attacks, and named John Winston Lennon – Winston, after the wartime prime minister, Winston Churchill. Intended as a joke by Julia, the middle name of 'Winston' would be one the grown-up John Lennon would never enjoy, and which he would eventually jettison.

It was an uncertain world in which to make an entrance. Not much unbalances family life so much as wartime, and, as a little family, Freddie and Julia Lennon and their baby never really got started. According to his log book, between August 1940 and January 1944 Freddie Lennon spent a total of only three months at home in Liverpool.

Of course, the absences might not have been so long had Freddie not gone AWOL while in the United States, and then been arrested and held in New York's Ellis Island for desertion; then, on release, sent back across the Atlantic and jailed again in Algeria for three months for stealing a bottle of whisky. Freddie would have his explanations when he finally got home, but his greatest offence was probably sheer foolishness. Maybe the drink helped there a bit, too.

But, for much of this time, Julia had no idea where he was, only that the part of his pay that she would collect from the Mercantile Marine Offices in Liverpool for her and John's upkeep had been stopped when Freddie had disappeared. For all she knew he could have been dead; and it should be remembered that the Merchant Navy in which Freddie served lost over a quarter of its members to enemy action during the Second World War. His had become a dangerous career.

Not that it was only the war that got in the way of this marriage. As friendly and social as both parents appear to have been, neither seems to have had much ambition other than to enjoy life and amuse themselves. Freddie liked to go drinking and singing in pubs, while Julia wanted to go out dancing when he was away. 'She never took anything seriously,' big sister Mimi, who took everything seriously, would say. And when Freddie finally came home and Julia wanted to continue going out, the couple, not surprisingly, fell out.

John, living with Julia and her parents, was too young to have been consciously aware of any of this; or to understand anything other than that he was safe and loved by his mother and grandparents. Later in life he could vividly picture his first home in Newcastle Road as being made of red brick, with a front room that was never used – a common custom then – and in which the curtains were always drawn.

Aunt Mimi, who was also now married, but childless, and who lived with her husband George Smith, just a couple of miles away in Woolton, South Liverpool, was a constant visitor to Julia and John. From his earliest days, Mimi doted on the child, as much as she despaired of her youngest sister's behaviour. Julia, though, was the one who amused John. She was, John would remember, 'a comedienne and a singer . . . not professional, but she used to get up in pubs and things like that'.

For the first four years of his life, the war was all around John, but, shielded from it by adults, he would hardly have been aware of it. The air raid sirens, rationing and shortages in a city first aflame and then scarred with blackened, blitzed, burnt-out buildings and bomb sites where urchins, some bare-footed, would play in the rubble, wasn't a world he knew. Nor would he ever have been told that in 1943 father Freddie, in the 'live for today, tomorrow may never come' spirit of wartime, suddenly had a change of heart and advised Julia: 'While I'm away . . . get out and enjoy yourself.'

Julia was doing that, anyway – like lots of other girlfriends and wives who had boyfriends and husbands overseas during the war. Unfortunately, when her husband next came home eighteen months later, she was pregnant.

At first, Julia told him she'd been raped by a soldier called Taffy Williams. So Freddie, accompanied by his younger brother Charlie, who was also at home on leave, went to an army gun site in Cheshire to see the young man involved. The upshot, according to both Freddie and Charlie Lennon, was unexpected.

His story differed from hers, Charlie would delicately recall in a letter to this author four decades later. There had, the soldier protested, been no rape, but he was in love and prepared to marry Julia if Freddie would divorce her. Julia, however, didn't want Taffy. Nor did she now want Freddie. Her baby, a girl, was born the following March and adopted by a Norwegian seaman and his wife.

The Lennons' marriage had, in effect, been finished for a year and a half. For the next few months, John would appear to have been passed between Julia, Mimi and her husband George, and Freddie's elder brother, Sydney, and his wife.

Then in 1946 Julia met the man with whom she was to spend the rest of her life. His name was John (usually known as Bobby) Dykins. He was at the time a door-to-door salesman, and, while Freddie was back at sea, Julia and John, who was now five, moved into his one-bedroomed flat in Gateacre, a Liverpool suburb. This was too much for the very respectable Mimi. After rowing with Dykins about the unsuitability of the situation in which a little boy was sleeping, not only in the same room but also in the same bed as Julia and her lover, she complained to what would now be the child welfare department of the Liverpool City Council.

On a second attempt she won the day. A representative of the Council interviewed both Julia and Dykins, and John was put into the care of Mimi and her husband.

The chaos of John's young life must have seemed to Mimi to be at an end. But there was one more chapter to be played out.

Freddie, who was now dabbling, like many other men, in the black market by selling nylons, suddenly turned up at Mimi's house suggesting he take his son out for the day. Mimi agreed, only for Freddie to abscond with the boy nearly sixty miles to the seaside resort of Blackpool. A friend, Billy Hall, lived there with his middle-aged parents, all three of whom were planning to emigrate to New Zealand. Perhaps he and John should also go to New Zealand and make a fresh start, Freddie began to think, as he and the little boy moved in with the Halls.

Back in Liverpool Mimi and Julia were desperate. No one had any idea where Freddie had taken John. They'd simply disappeared, with Freddie deliberately making no contact with his wife or her sister.

For several weeks, during which Billy Hall's parents took on the role of carers when Freddie would go off to Southampton furthering his black market racket, John stayed in Blackpool. Eventually, discovering Freddie's whereabouts by enquiring at the 'pool office' of the Merchant Navy (the organisation which kept a record of all seamen who were available for work), Julia turned up at the Halls' front door. She'd come to take John back to Liverpool, she told Freddie. Dykins remained outside in the street as they talked.

How traumatic the negotiations over John's future between Freddie and Julia were that day is open to different interpretations. Billy Hall would tell Beatles chronicler Mark Lewisohn that there was no 'tug-of-love' scene and 'no raised voices'. But it does appear that John, aged five, was asked to choose between his parents – and that, after some confusion in which he went to his father, he changed his mind and ran to his mother. Too young to understand the long-term implications of his decision, John may have been old enough to later remember that whichever parent he chose would mean a rejection of the other.

The choice made, Freddie Lennon then watched as John, holding his mother's hand, and with Dykins alongside, walked down the road away from him. It was 1946. He wouldn't see his son again until 1963. That night he went to a pub in Blackpool and sang an Al Jolson song. It was called 'Little Pal'. That was how he would remember it in his memoirs, anyway.

Julia might have recovered John and taken him back to Liverpool, but it was not so that he could live with her. Soon after they arrived he was returned to Aunt Mimi, and from then on there would be no more to-ing and fro-ing. It was settled. Mimi and husband George could and would offer the child a secure environment in which to grow up. 'Every child has a right to a safe and happy home life,' Mimi would often say. From that moment, John would have little contact with the Lennon side of his family.

When John would enquire about his parents, Mimi would refrain from her usual description of Freddie as a 'fly by night'.

'She told me that my parents had fallen out of love,' John would remember. 'She never said anything directly against my mother or father. Soon I forgot about my father. It was like he was dead.'

\*

Forty years later when Mimi was nearing the end of her life at the bungalow John had bought her on the Dorset coast of southern England, she is alleged to have told a nurse that she was afraid of dying because she'd once 'done a very wicked thing'. If she did say that, was she, as Cynthia, John's first wife wondered, thinking about the time she had insisted that John be taken from his mother and handed over to her? 'You're not fit to be a mother,' she had once raged at Julia. Childless herself, taking care of John was what she had wanted, probably from the moment he'd been born.

As for John, how much long-term effect did the chopping and changing of guardians and minders during the first five years of his life have on him? Did it leave him with a subconscious need for security? How much had he witnessed of the rows between Freddie and Julia, which, Freddie would admit, had turned violent at least once? And had he been aware and puzzled by what would almost certainly have been going on sometimes between Julia and Dykins when they all slept together?

He was certainly loved by whomever he was living with. But in uncertain times his situation was more fragile than that of most small children.

'I just wanted to protect him from all that,' Mimi told Beatles biographer Hunter Davies in 1967. 'Perhaps I was over-anxious. I don't know. I just wanted him to be happy.'

# 2

*'I was aggressive because I wanted to be popular.
I wanted to be the leader'*

The Second World War scarred everywhere it touched, but Great Britain had prevailed and out of the struggle a new national attitude was emerging. In the previous thirty years there had been two world wars, and an economic depression bringing mass unemployment. But by 1945, as the troops began to return home to take up their lives again, the British people were demanding a fairer future for themselves and their children, a feeling which was quickly expressed in a General Election landslide for a Labour government. Lasting reforms to the social fabric of Britain were quickly put into place, changes that, arguably, would help make John Lennon's generation the most fortunate ever. Born five years earlier, his life would have been very different.

One of the most important reforms had already been agreed with the 1944 Education Act, a piece of legislation that provided free education to children, with the right academic qualifications, all the way to university level. It wasn't a perfect system, in that ability was measured at the age of eleven when a free scholarship to a grammar school creamed off the brightest, meaning that two-thirds of the country's children, inevitably including many late developers, were deemed failures before they'd even reached their teens. But it did ensure that those who passed the 11-Plus scholarship, as it was later called, would be given opportunities that their parents, or even their older brothers and sisters, could hardly have imagined. And no parent, or in this case, guardian, would have been more aware of the possibilities for the future of the child in her care than Mary (Mimi) Smith of Mendips, 251 Menlove Avenue, Woolton, Liverpool.

Mimi was an abrupt, sharp and intelligent woman, who read voraciously and who made a point of never suffering fools gladly. She had met her husband, George Smith, in 1931, when he'd delivered milk from his small, family-owned dairy to the Woolton Hospital in

South Liverpool where she'd been a trainee nurse. She would go on to become the matron of a ward, before, after another long courtship in the Stanley family, she and George married, somewhat unromantically in 1939. She was, therefore, already forty when John went to live permanently with her and husband George in their solid, large, four-bedroomed semi-detached house, just across the road from the grounds of Allerton Municipal Golf Club.

Although George's family's lands had been requisitioned by the government towards the end of the war and his dairy business closed down, the Smiths were relatively well-off. It might not fit with the general public perception of Liverpool as a rough and raucous working-class place, but there had always been a large managerial, professional and well-heeled merchant population in and around the city. There had to be, to administer the seven miles of docks and all the ancillary businesses that shipping generated.

Woolton had, until the end of the First World War, been a small village outside the city, a place where detached Victorian mansions lay in large wooded gardens on narrow lanes alongside eighteenth- and nineteenth-century cottages. The expansion of the city in the Twenties and Thirties, and the building of Menlove Avenue as a dual carriageway to provide a central area for tramlines, had turned the area into a suburb. But when John went to live there in 1946 it still maintained a distinctly village-type atmosphere.

'I was a nice, clean suburban boy,' John would admit in 1967. 'We owned our own house, had our own garden . . .' complete with two lawns which as a teenager he had to mow every week in the summer – Mimi turning a deaf ear to his complaints. He never would like physical work; and would get through his life rarely doing any.

They also had a phone, which was a real status symbol in the Forties, and enough room on the side of the house for a car, although they never bought one. Not many people had a car in Liverpool in the Forties and Fifties.

Until John went to live in Mendips, Mimi had been working as a secretary, a job she immediately gave up as she wanted to be at home when her nephew got back from school in the afternoons. So, the new situation would have meant some financial sacrifice, compounded when, with the loss of the dairy, George, at forty-two, eventually found himself taking work in security at a nearby factory built on land where, pre-war, he had once grazed his cows. That must have been a social come-down, but Mimi would never have let it show.

To make ends meet, the family finances were helped out by the letting of the front bedroom of the Smiths' house to a succession of lodgers, who were always young male veterinary students from Liverpool University. Here again, Mimi's ambition and view of herself and her family showed. She didn't want any random lodgers. They had to be educated, which would be good for John, too.

Mimi was a snob. Always well-dressed, with strict rules of behaviour and an insistence on good table manners, she believed herself and her sisters to be a cut above most other people around her, such as those living on the new council estates that were being increasingly erected as the city continued its invasion of Woolton. 'Everybody's common except you, Mimi,' John would tease her when he reached his teens.

Julia was cuddly, but Mimi's way of demonstrating her love for the boy she believed she'd rescued, and whom she now treated as though he were her own son, was by endlessly encouraging him academically. Education would be the key to his success, and she was determined that John would have every opportunity in this new and changing Britain. It was, therefore, important that he speak without a working-class Liverpool accent, generally known as Scouse, which in Mimi's eyes would be a disadvantage later in life.

'I had high hopes for him,' she would remember. 'I knew that you didn't get anywhere if you spoke like a ruffian.' With many boys there might well have been some truth to that in class-bound England. As it turned out, a Scouse accent never hurt John Lennon. In fact, when fame reached him, he would delight in purposely exaggerating it, just to aggravate Mimi.

All in all, it's easy to see that, once John arrived at Mendips, the house tended to revolve around what was good for him . . . whether he liked it or not. And never for a minute was he ever made to feel that his presence was an imposition. Quite the reverse: Mimi made sure he knew that it was his home, too. Decades later when he was rich and famous John pleaded with her not to sell the house. It was the place where all his childhood memories were stored.

John's bedroom was directly over the front door and hall, giving him a view from his window along Menlove Avenue. Until he was eight, trams would still run up and down the tracks in the grassy central reservation of the dual carriageway, and he would kneel at his window watching them, spotting Uncle George or Mimi coming home. On some days he would see his mother arriving, too, when she came on a visit. Buses replaced the trams in 1949, after which the lines were pulled up and replaced with bushes. And kneeling at his window lookout post he would watch the cars go by – not very many in those days.

Uncle George, a mild-mannered man who was under his wife's thumb, behaved quite differently from Mimi in his relationship with John. 'George thought that John had been put on earth purely to amuse him,' Mimi would often joke. But one of John's fondest early memories was when his uncle had taken him out on his float during the war, sitting behind the horse with the crates and large metal urns of milk, as George made his rounds. Always a more tactile person than Mimi, George would later sit John on his lap and help him read the headlines in the local evening newspaper, the *Liverpool Echo*.

Some of the newspaper stories would inevitably have involved football, and most boys living in Liverpool would have shown at least a little interest in the game. It's pretty difficult not to in that football mad city. But, though George would kick a ball around the back garden with John, sport in all forms passed the boy by completely. Instead, as soon as he learned how to write, he would leave little notes asking Uncle George to tuck him up in bed instead of Mimi, or ask him to take him to the pictures in Woolton, which wasn't Mimi's style at all.

More to her liking would be educational family trips five miles into the centre of Liverpool. Rattling along on the hard, wooden benches of the pre-war, double-decker trams, overhead electric lines flashing as they went, they would make their way from Woolton past the shops at Penny Lane and on down Smithdown Road towards the windswept open spaces of the Pier Head.

Once Liverpool had, after London, been the second city of the British Empire, and grand Victorian buildings had been erected on the banks of the River Mersey to administer the docks and the ships that sailed from there. After more than half a century of wind, rain, smoke, smog, neglect and recent war, those buildings wouldn't have looked very impressive to John in the late Forties. But Liverpudlians have always been proud of their city, and for him it would have been exciting to see the water chopped into creamy foam behind the ferries as they made their short crossings of the River Mersey to Birkenhead and New Brighton. While, sometimes, a little further along the dock, there might have been a grand liner waiting to depart for America.

America! The very idea of America, always thrilling and exciting, was lodged in every Liverpudlian heart in that west-facing corner of England. From that waterfront so many migrants had left from all over Europe to make new lives across the ocean, in ships crewed by other Liverpudlians.

John would have been told by his father that his grandfather had left from this very spot to make a living by singing in America. And that he, too, Freddie, had sailed there many times, and that the big buildings here in Liverpool, as towering as they might look to John, were nothing compared with those the Americans had in New York. That was what every other seaman in Liverpool told his children.

But John didn't have to go to America to see Americans. They were right there in Liverpool, and, from his earliest days, he would recognise, by their light cotton uniforms, the US servicemen who would flood into the centre of the city from the nearby US Air Force base at Burtonwood. To small boys of the time, GIs were glamorous. America, ran the repeated subliminal message, was the place to be. And for John Lennon that message was only going to keep growing the older he became.

The Smiths' house in Menlove Avenue, which had been built in 1933, was a cosy home. With elm trees in the back garden, it had mock Tudor exposed beams, leaded windows at the front, a front and side porch and a coal fire around which the family would sit on winter nights – along with a dog and two, then three, cats. Decades later John's first wife, Cynthia, would complain about the smell of fish which 'was always being cooked in the kitchen for the cats', and which, she said, permeated the house. But John didn't mention it. He liked cats, too.

Although he had spent a few weeks at another infant school before being handed over to Mimi, to all intents and purposes his education began at Dovedale Primary, which was down Menlove Avenue towards Penny Lane. Very quickly it was noticed at school that he was a clever but unusual child, 'as bright as a button', Mimi would like to recollect, 'and quick in his movements'. Able to read and write within a few months at Dovedale, this encouraged her to give him a classic book of her own childhood, *Alice In Wonderland*, reading to him at first, and then leaving it up to him. Over the next few years he would repeatedly pore over both it and Lewis Carroll's sequel, *Through The Looking Glass*, with its poem 'The Walrus And The Carpenter'. He loved nonsense rhymes, wordplay and dream world imagery. Twenty years later he would dip into the memories of those books to create the surrealism of 'I Am The Walrus' and 'Lucy In The Sky With Diamonds' in the Beatles' late Sixties era.

'I was passionate about *Alice In Wonderland*,' he would often remember, 'and I drew all the characters. I did poems in the style of the Jabberwocky, too.' He also loved *The Wind In The Willows* and the very funny *Just William* books by Richmal Crompton, stories about an adventurous boy of about ten and his gang. 'I wrote my own William stories, with me doing all the things,' he would say.

Soon, though, it wasn't enough for him simply to read stories, he wanted to create them, too, and by the age of nine he was writing and illustrating his own little books of jokes, cartoons and drawings entitled 'Sport, Speed and Illustrated' by J. W. Lennon. It was a very grown-up title and an adult author's name for a young boy, with the books including an ongoing dramatic serial. 'If you like this, come back again next week, it'll be even better,' he would write at the end of every episode.

He would always like reading and writing, and newspapers, too. And when he became famous he would be friendly with journalists and curious about their jobs. 'I used to think about becoming a journalist,' he would one day tell me. 'Well, I suppose I really wanted to be a writer, but in Liverpool, writing for a newspaper was the only way I thought I could make a living out of it.'

At a time when children made much of their own entertainment, *Children's Hour* at 5 p.m. every weekday on the BBC Home Service gave him a radio snapshot of healthy, worthy, middle-class culture. But it was the nightly fifteen-minute serial *Dick Barton – Special Agent* at a quarter to seven that would bring him running from playing in the garden or reading in his room every night.

In those pre-television days (for the great mass of the people, anyway), radio, with its comedy shows *Up The Pole* and *Life With The Lyons* – a sitcom about an American family living in London – was the national glue. Everybody listened. Later John would remember that there wasn't much music in his house, but in those days a child could get a decent foundation in the popular classics and arias by listening to the BBC's weekly record request programme, *Family Favourites*.

He had inherited a good ear for popular songs from his parents, and, as a little boy, would sing 'Let Him Go, Let Him Tarry', a traditional Irish song that was revived in 1945 by Jean Simmons in the wartime film *The Way to the Stars*, around the house. And, after lending John his mouth organ and seeing how much the boy liked it, one of the lodgers promised him one for himself, if he could learn to play a tune on it by the following morning. John learned two tunes overnight and was given his own new mouth organ for Christmas. 'That was one of the great moments of my life, when I got my first harmonica,' he liked to say. Nor did he leave it at that. Saving his pocket money, he then bought himself a manual on how to play the harmonica. He was already showing intent.

If getting a mouth organ was exciting, one of the more dismal moments of his childhood came at seven when he was taken to the opticians and fitted for a pair of glasses – with very thick lenses. He was fiercely short-sighted. Twenty years later he would make round wire-framed NHS glasses a fashion statement, but that wasn't the way he saw it when he was in primary school and sometimes mocked as a 'four eyes' by the other children. As soon as he was out of class he would whip off his glasses and put them in his pocket, a habit he would continue in public until the mid-Sixties.

Aware of how well he was doing at school, Mimi must have been proud to see her encouragement reaping such immediate rewards, and she and John would sit together at the dining table in the evening, John always writing and drawing, and Mimi reading. Strict as she was in so many ways, they would often laugh together, too. He could always amuse with his made-up words and little boy silliness, and was always good company – probably more in tune with her than was her husband.

But that was John when he was at home. At school he was a different child, as, almost from the start, he became an aggressive little fellow in the playground where he quickly built a reputation for confrontation. 'He wasn't a sit-in-the-corner quiet Harry,' comedian Jimmy Tarbuck who was at Dovedale Primary at the same time re-membered to the *Guardian* newspaper in 2009. 'If there was a bit of uproar he'd be amongst it . . . He wasn't a hard case, but he wouldn't back off anything.'

'I was aggressive because I wanted to be popular,' John would later explain. 'I wanted to be the leader. It seemed more attractive than just being one of the toffees. I wanted everyone to do what I told them to, to laugh at my jokes and let me be the boss.'

Why he wanted to be the leader, and it was a facet of his character throughout his life, he never divulged, or perhaps understood. But, by letting it be known that he was prepared to fight for dominance, although usually verbally more than physically, and getting his retaliation in early, he found the quickest route to getting his own way. With a birthday in October he would have been older than most of the children in his year at school, so that would help him boss his way around the playground, too. But, all through his life, he had a maturity that belied his age. He seemed more mature than he was, and more worldly-wise than his age-mates – with that sing-song deliberate way of talking that suggested sarcasm but which also brooked no argument.

But was there something else? With his school situated further down the road towards Liverpool, there would have been some tough children at Dovedale. John's start in life had been rocky. Did he intuit very early that the outside world could be hostile and that if he was to find and keep his place in it, he would have to stand up for himself, and take on rivals like the rough kids at school? Had he, as Paul McCartney would one day surmise, built a protective shell around himself?

Whatever the explanation, his ever-ready defiance would become a character trait that would stay with him for life. And, just as he could never resist the opportunity to make a joke, he also rarely backed off in an argument, becoming verbally vicious when riled, as some of the people who loved him most would find. He would rarely apologise, though he would often change his mind about people he'd hurt. 'That was just me mouth talking,' he would regularly justify himself, when reminded of something particularly wounding that he'd said.

But saying cruel things was really just another part of being John Lennon.

# 3

*'The sort of gang I led went in for things like shoplifting and pulling girls' knickers down'*

Immediately behind Menlove Avenue was Vale Road, a quiet lane of mainly semi-detached houses where, at the age of seven, John met the best friend of his boyhood, one he would stay close to all his life. He was Pete Shotton, a little blond lad who didn't go to Dovedale but who John would see after school and with whom he would become inseparable. Pete already had his own friends when John arrived in Woolton – Ivan Vaughan and Nigel Walley. But with John included they soon made up a quartet, with John quickly assuming the role of leader.

The friendship was initially based on boys' games of make-believe escapades as they acted out John's latest crazes in their back gardens, the disused wartime air raid shelter behind Pete's house, and the many green areas of woods and parks around Woolton. Pete didn't notice it at the time, but decades later, while reflecting in his memoirs on their boyhood together, he realised that John always had to have a special partner in his adventures, and especially those which involved mischief. 'John desperately needed the supportive presence of who-ever he felt closest to at the time,' he would write.

Pete would be the sidekick when the two boys went pinching apples from neighbours' trees, but, later, there would be other part-ners for John as the need for a like-thinking companion became a necessity. In this way, from Lennon and Shotton as boyhood scamps, it developed into Lennon and McCartney as songwriters, and then on to John and Yoko – with a couple of shorter-lasting duos interspersed along the way.

At first, the biggest trouble John would get into would be stealing bubble gum from the local sweet shop with Pete alongside to join in the fun. The scrapes continued when he and Pete became cub Boy Scouts, and, even more unlikely, choirboys at the local Woolton parish church, St Peter's. Attending Sunday school together, John's misdemeanours, such as pressing his chewing gum into the hand of the choir teacher when ordered to 'hand it over', always had to be done with Pete giggling behind him. It was more amusing for him that way.

But, although singing as choirboys at weddings provided a handy little Saturday income, as well as marking the first time John ever sang in public, neither he nor Pete stayed in surplices for long. Both were expelled from the choir for stealing the fruit at the harvest festival.

John's aim at that stage was mainly to amuse himself, rather than to be seriously defiant. But a pattern was set. It would amuse Uncle George who, when his nephew told lies to get out of trouble, would say to Mimi, 'Well, he'll never be a vicar.'

Mimi wasn't smiling, though, when she realised that John had stolen some money from her purse. It was the only occasion that she ever smacked him, she would say. 'I must have taken too much that time,' John would later reflect. She hadn't noticed all the other occasions.

With Pete, Ivan and Nigel becoming his first admiring audience, John quickly began to realise that he shone in front of a crowd. 'I was the King Pin of my age group,' he told Hunter Davies. 'I learned lots of dirty jokes very young. There was this girl who lived near me who told me them . . . The sort of gang I led went in for things like shoplifting and pulling girls' knickers down . . .' Other boys' parents disliked him, and warned their children not to play with him. According to Rod Davis, whom he'd met at the church choir, even before John was ten he was known in the neighbourhood as 'that John Lennon!!'

Those were the great days of Western movies, with films like *Colt '45*, *Red River* and *Rio Grande* hugely popular, and despite Mimi's strictures, Uncle George would take John, and sometimes Pete, to the Woolton Picture House. Like all small boys at the time, John loved Westerns, invariably playing a Red Indian as he and his gang re-enacted their battles with the cowboys and the US Army. 'That was typical of John . . . supporting the underdog,' Mimi would say, laughing at the memory. Of course, because he was leader of the gang, history would have to be reversed and the Indians always won the battles, with John wearing a head-dress of pheasant feathers that Mimi had made up for him. 'He loved it. He never took it off,' she would say. 'I can see him now in the garden, dancing around Pete Shotton who was tied up to a tree.'

Even playing cowboys and Indians, John always had to be in charge. And when he said the other boys in the game were dead, that he'd got them with his imaginary bow and arrow or make-believe rifle, they had to act dead. 'Pretend you're dead properly,' he would shout at them.

Those early years with Mimi and Uncle George were the most settled and happy of John's young life. And, like other middle-class children, he would be taken on outings to pantomimes at Christmas, one of which was to see the ukulele-playing singer George Formby at the Empire Theatre in Liverpool. Then there would be trips to the sandhills at Formby, or the Tudor mansion Speke Hall, which was just a short bus ride away, as well as summer days out to the local resorts of New Brighton and Southport.

In Woolton a favourite walk would take the family along Menlove Avenue and then around the corner and up the hill to a Victorian mansion, Strawberry Field, with its overgrown wooded grounds. Once it had been the grand home of a nineteenth-century Liverpool merchant, but, when John lived nearby, it had been turned into a Salvation Army children's orphanage, where every summer there would be a garden fete. 'As soon as he could hear the Salvation Army band starting to play,' Mimi would say, 'he would jump up and down shouting "Come on, Mimi, we're going to be late".' And he would rush her off along the road and through the big wrought iron gates of the estate.

Not everyone could afford a summer holiday away in those days, but, from the age of nine, John would always go to Scotland for a week or two to stay in Edinburgh with Mimi's sister Elizabeth (who was always known as Aunt Mater) and her husband, Bert. At first Mater's son Stanley Parkes, who was six years older than John, would come for him, but John was soon allowed to travel there on his own. On one occasion he played his mouth organ so much on the journey that the coach driver told him to come to the bus company's lost property office in Edinburgh the following day. When he got there, he was handed a new harmonica which had been lying unclaimed for months.

The time spent in Scotland would become a highlight of his year, and especially the week in a croft that the Parkes family owned in Durness in the north-west Highlands, to which they would drive every August. Later, at his senior school, when asked what he would like to do in life, he replied: 'Salmon fishing.' It seemed ridiculous at the time, but he meant it. He liked to be near water. He always would.

Despite Mimi taking over John's upbringing, she and Julia remained close, as did all the Stanley sisters, who would regularly congregate at Menlove Avenue, particularly Aunt Harrie and her daughter Liela, who was three years older than John. Harrie's first husband having died, she and her second husband and Liela lived in the Woolton cottage at the old dairy that Uncle George had once owned.

George would also be at the get-togethers, although not Julia's partner Bobby Dykins, but when later John talked of those days, as he often did, it was as though he was remembering a matriarchal society with Mimi at the top of the pyramid. The Stanley sisters, he would tell interviewers, 'were five strong women', and all his life he would be attracted to strong women. Women who couldn't stand up to him would get hurt.

Was Julia a strong woman? Not in Mimi's eyes. But she'd been unlucky, too, and, although technically still married to Freddie – they would never divorce – she put her life together when she met Dykins. With him she had a daughter in 1947, also called Julia, while another daughter, Jacqui, would follow two years later. How happy Julia was with the situation and with her life is impossible to know. But when she arrived at Mendips one day 'wearing a black coat and with her face bleeding', as was John's memory of the moment, her son didn't believe that she'd simply been in an accident. Nor, though, did he ask her who had hit his mother. Instead he went into the garden, not wanting to be involved.

His father, meanwhile, hadn't quite given up hope of seeing him again. According to Freddie's account, which would be published after his death, he wrote to Mimi in 1949, enquiring about John, who was now eight. But, as he had just spent six months in jail for kicking in a shop window in London's West End while drunk, Mimi was not going to see all her efforts on John undone. Freddie, she is said to have replied, had 'made a shambles' of his life and 'brought shame' on his family. Then she added that, should he ever try to become involved in his son's life again, she would tell John that his father was a jailbird.

Freddie got the message. There was no way back for him. Unable to return to sea because of his criminal record – petty though it was – and finding it difficult to find any other regular employment, he took to the road.

John's behaviour might have been edging towards occasional minor delinquency with his and Pete's shoplifting, but, to no one's surprise, at the age of eleven he passed the 11-Plus exam. 'That was the only exam I ever passed,' he would remember. His reward was a brand new, three-speed, green Raleigh bicycle – the customary 11-Plus present from parents who could afford it.

For John's next school, Mimi considered the Liverpool Institute, the most highly thought of school in Liverpool. But it was in the middle of the city. So, she settled for the local Quarry Bank High School for Boys, which, on the far side of Calderstones Park, was only a pleasant mile and a half away in a quiet, middle-class area. It, too, was an excellent school. She must have been delighted with the way things were turning out. But just as pleasing for John was the fact that his friend Pete had also passed the exam and would be joining him there.

One of his other friends, Ivan Vaughan, would, however, not be with them, his parents choosing the Institute for their boy – precisely because 'that John Lennon' would be going to Quarry Bank. Ivan was clever. They didn't want to risk him being led astray.

One consequence of the decision to send Ivan to a different school could never have been imagined. But five years later it would completely change John's life . . . and eventually the lives of millions of others.

# 4

*'I'm either a genius or I'm mad. But . . . I can't be mad because nobody has put me away.*
*Therefore, I must be a genius'*

Like all eleven-year-old boys on their first day at senior school, he was intimidated. It was 4 September 1952 and the sheer muscularity of over six hundred youths converging on the imposing, Edwardian-style Quarry Bank High School in leafy Harthill Road to begin the new term was daunting. The presence of little girls had softened the atmosphere at his primary school, but a single-sex institution of hormonal teenage boys was going to be something different. 'I thought, Christ, I'll have to fight my way through all this lot . . .' he would often remember. It was reassuring then that Pete was alongside him and that they were even put together in the same class. Rod Davis, the boy he'd met in the choir at St Peter's, was also there. There was security in numbers.

School, however, would be different from now on. Grammar schools took their ambitions seriously. Quarry Bank might only have been built in 1922, but, with an Old Etonian for a headmaster and a Latin inscription on the school crest, *Ex Hoc Metallo Virtutem*, which translated as 'Out of this quarry cometh forth manhood', its ethos was firmly that of the traditional British public school. Socially structured around the house system, which dated back to when boys actually boarded in different houses on the school premises (no one boarded at Quarry Bank), the curriculum included Latin and French, and the teachers wore gowns to indicate their academic status. Founded as a fee-paying school for Liverpool's better-off sons, its remit was now to take some of the brightest boys from all backgrounds and to educate as many as possible towards careers in the professions.

Seeing John off on his new bicycle, wearing his new school uniform of black blazer and grey flannels, school cap on his head, with Pete on his bike alongside him, must have pleased Mimi. All her plans were coming to fruition. John was a creative, artistic boy, maybe not so good at maths, but good enough, and he was brilliant at English. He could do anything he wanted if he put his mind to it, she had been told by his previous headmaster. Surely the discipline of a grammar school, where, in those days, most headmasters still believed in the maxim 'spare the rod and spoil the child', would dampen his mischievous spirit and he would make the most of this golden opportunity.

She could hardly have been more wrong. Quarry Bank's traditionalism didn't suit every boy. And it didn't fit John Lennon. While his behaviour in his first year was unremarkable, and he still spent most of his free time in his bedroom reading, by his second year, as he moved into his teens and he and Pete became ever more disruptive in class, his concentration began to fail him. 'For some reason he just hated authority . . . hated being told what to do,' his friend Rod remembers. Increasingly school became one long joke for him – and, therefore, for Pete, too. Because, whatever John did, Pete always followed.

At around this time the radio comedy programme *The Goon Show*, which was mainly written by Spike Milligan and starred Harry Secombe, Michael Bentine, Peter Sellers (before he became famous in films) and Milligan himself, had become compulsive listening for young people, and John rarely missed an episode. Having begun in 1951, it was already turning into the most original comedy radio show the BBC ever produced, sowing the seeds that would one day bring forth *Monty Python's Flying Circus*. And, with its constant mockery of authority, it was unlike anything ever heard before on the radio.

John loved its absurdist situations and eccentric characters, all of which soon began to influence his own cartoons and jokes. He had already begun to draw in the style of the *New Yorker* cartoonist James Thurber, whom Mimi much admired, but now a darker side to his humour began to emerge, as he would create grotesque, wart-covered, misshapen creatures, and draw cruel, though recognisable, cartoons of his teachers.

With *The Goon Show*'s surrealism and catch phrases in his head, and always encouraged by Pete, his antics in class quickly graduated to the downright rebellious. Not surprisingly, he and Pete eventually found themselves summoned to the headmaster's study for punishment. Even here John couldn't resist being the comedian. Going in first for a caning, he came out crawling on his knees in what, to the waiting Pete, looked like agony. Only as Pete opened the door to what he thought was the headmaster's office did he realise that there was a short corridor before a further door led to the headmaster. John had only dropped to his knees after he'd had his punishment. Amused by this, Pete went into the headmaster's office still smiling at John's joke, only to get an additional whacking for having the cheek to look amused.

More canings would follow for both of them, but to no avail. The dye was now cast, and for the rest of John's school life there would be more jokes than application. The contradictions in his personality were plain to see. He knew, as did all the teaching staff, that he was intelligent. His masters mentioned it in his end-of-term reports – when they weren't criticising his attitude. John, who never lacked for a high opinion of himself, would later tell me: 'I used to think I must be a genius, but nobody had noticed. So I thought, I'm either a genius or I'm mad. But then I thought, I can't be mad because nobody has put me away. Therefore, I must be a genius.'

When he wasn't drawing caricatures, there were some elaborate pranks. On one occasion he persuaded the rest of the class to put white strips of cardboard around their necks, like the dog collars that vicars wore, for the moment the teacher of religious knowledge entered the classroom. The poor man had to be amused, as were the class when, having being asked to write an essay about St Paul's epiphany on the road to Damascus, John is said to have written: 'On the road to Damascus a burning pie flew out of the window and hit St Paul between the eyes. When he came to, he was blind forever.'

All this made John the popular boy he wanted to be (and a flaming pie would be an image he would use later in a jokey reference to the origins of the Beatles), but therein lay the problem. As he moved through the school and his confidence and notoriety grew, he was falling increasingly behind with his work.

By the fourth year, when he was fourteen, he and Pete had been moved down to the C stream, the lowest level. This embarrassed him, because he was now with boys whom he considered to be less intelligent than himself. Not that that made him work any harder. Deadpan gags came more easily. When he'd first begun living with Mimi the worst punishment she could inflict on him had been to ignore him. 'Don't 'nore me, Mimi,' he would beg. 'Don't 'nore me.' Now his overactive desire for attention and constant clowning made some teachers' lives a misery. Not all of them put up with it. One was so angry at the pupil's insolence that, Rod Davis says, he physically lifted John off the ground by the lapels of his blazer. Others, while secretly amused by his cartoons, despaired of the way this bright boy was wasting his time, their time and his classmates' time. Perhaps his headmaster summed him up best when he wrote: 'He has too many of the wrong ambitions and his energy is too often mis-applied.'

Looking back on his schooldays, John would be unrepentant: 'I was never miserable. I was always having a laugh.' As to why he was so disruptive, he never offered a serious explanation, other than to blame the school for not recognising his talent. 'I've been proved right. They were wrong and I was right,' he would say, before admitting, 'although I think I went a bit wild when I was fourteen.'

It has to be possible that his later reflections were post-rationalisations to cover up his embarrassment at his school failures. It wouldn't be the only time he would reinterpret events to suit his view of his own history.

Like many boys who become difficult during their teenage years, John was bored with school and hated science and maths – in which in one exam he got just 17 per cent. But there was no questioning his ability in other subjects. He was so good at art he would sometimes do Pete's art homework as well as his own.

He made, however, no effort to fit into the school regime. 'He would get what we used to call "black marks" all the time,' Rod Davis remembers, 'which would lead to detentions. And then sometimes while he was doing a detention, he'd get another black mark, therefore a double detention, for having given cheek or some such offence. He just didn't care.' A school punishment ledger shows that John Lennon was punished for 'making silly noises during an exam', on one date, and for 'bad behaviour' on the same day. While the following day he got another black mark for 'sabotage' (of what it doesn't say), and yet another for 'fighting in class' a little later.

'He'd realised early on there was nothing anyone could do to him, so he was just going to enjoy himself and make everyone laugh,' Rod Davis says. 'He and Pete were once suspended for a week. John loved it. Quite simply, no one could make him do anything he didn't want to do.'

He was perfectly capable of doing his homework, but only if it interested him. He always enjoyed English. 'When I was about fourteen they gave us this book in English Literature,' he liked to recall. 'It was Chaucer or some guy like him . . . and we all thought it was a gas. . . After that I started to write something on the same lines myself. Just private stuff for friends to laugh at.'

That something turned into 'The Daily Howl', his own newspaper which appeared in a series of exercise books, and which he would spend his evenings creating when he should have been doing his schoolwork. Carefully laid out and very neatly written, his newspaper would be filled with little nonsense stories, jokes and poems, all illustrated with cartoons – many depicting several of his teachers in unflattering poses, and even some of those he quite liked.

Where did the obsession with drawing ugly people come from? He never explained. Probably he never knew, though he would continue drawing them into adulthood. For a fourteen-year-old, the skill and observation in the cartoons was clear. At that stage, allied with his mordant sense of humour and interest in current affairs, a career as a cartoonist might not have seemed unlikely.

It wasn't perhaps surprising that he would be the first of his gang to take up smoking and become interested in sex. Both occurred when he was thirteen, by which time, incidentally, 'fucking' had become his most used adjective when among friends. When Mimi discovered an obscene poem that he'd hidden under his pillow, she demanded an explanation. His excuse was that another boy had asked him to write it on his behalf. 'I'd written it myself, of course,' he would later admit. 'I'd seen those poems around, the sort you read to give you a hard on. I wondered who wrote them and thought I'd try one myself.' Uncle George would have been amused. He knew about boys and wasn't beyond telling John and Pete the odd mildly dirty joke. But Mimi, brought up solely among girls, would have disapproved. Even if, secretly, she didn't, she would have pretended she did, because that was the role she'd chosen to play with John.

Had she known about the erotic cartoon that he drew at school and that got passed around the class before it was confiscated, she would have been mortified. It might not matter to John what people thought of him, but it would always matter to Mimi.

So, sex and girls were much on his mind from a very early age. But soon something else of importance happened. From about the age of fourteen he began to see more of his mother. Julia had regularly visited Mendips, but now, accompanied by his older cousin, Stanley, who was down from Scotland, he went to visit her for the first time at her home in Blomfield Road in Garston. Stanley gave him the address.

He was surprised when they got there. He'd had it in his head that Julia lived some distance away, maybe on the other side of Liverpool completely. But her house was in fact only a couple of miles from Mendips, a fifteen-minute walk across Allerton Golf Course. He'd had no idea that she was so close. Did he wonder why she hadn't invited him to go there earlier? Or why she'd kept the proximity of her home a secret from him? He must have done. It had to have hurt, to see her in her three-bedroomed home with his two half-sisters.

He didn't tell Mimi where he'd been or who he'd seen on that occasion. It would, he knew, have upset, and possibly worried, his aunt. At first, his further visits to his mother were occasional, but gradually over the next couple of years they would become increasingly frequent.

Visiting Julia wasn't, however, like going to see a mother, so much as calling in on a big sister. That was how Julia behaved towards him, and he loved it. Although she was now forty, she was still an attractive, young-at-heart, amusing woman, and she made him and his friends welcome – especially when Bobby Dykins, whom John would unkindly refer to as Twitchy because of a nervous tic, was absent. The day she wore a pair of knickers on her head for fun amused all of John's friends. Mums didn't do that sort of thing. Like her son, Julia was an attention seeker.

The difference between Mimi and Julia was still as marked as ever. While Mimi was unbending in her determination that John would make something of himself by hard work, Julia remained easy-going. The 'Julia' of whom John would later sing on the Beatles' *White Album* was a dreamy idealised version of her. She was probably more dizzy than romantic. But he enjoyed being at her house where the rules of Mendips didn't apply. One school report when he was fifteen shows that he was absent for almost all of the end-of-term exams. 'He would probably have been sagging off school [playing truant] going round to Julia's,' Rod Davis believes.

In effect, John was receiving conflicting messages. It was natural that an adolescent boy would be drawn to the zany, more permissive world of his carefree, modern-thinking mother who had been the first member of his family to get a television. To John she represented the exciting new world he was growing up in. Mimi, who had taken on the serious job of caring for him, was traditional and unbending. His loyalties must have been strained.

But there was something else about Julia that chimed with him, something that Mimi couldn't offer. While the only music Mimi wanted played in her house belonged in the Liverpool Philharmonic Hall, Julia liked pop songs. She still liked to sing, too, and even had a record player. When John once suggested to Mimi that perhaps they should get a piano, her reply, knowing the kind of music he would want to play, was instantly discouraging. 'Oh no, we're not going down that road, John,' she said. 'None of that common sing-song stuff in here.'

As usual John went up to Scotland during the summer of 1955 and was therefore away when Uncle George suddenly collapsed on the stairs. A long-time lodger at Mendips called Michael Fishwick was downstairs with Mimi at the time and immediately called for an ambulance. George died the following day in Sefton General Hospital of a non-alcoholic liver disease. He was fifty-two. John only found out when he got back from Edinburgh.

'I think John was very shocked by George's death, but he never showed it,' Mimi would later say. He may not have shown it to her. Instead he and his cousin Liela went up into his bedroom and giggled hysterically, neither understanding why, but both feeling guilty afterwards. John was hiding his true feelings. The shell that he'd built around his emotions saw to that. He would never let the cracks show in public. Fifteen years later he would remember George to me fondly as 'a kind man', before bleakly adding: 'I've had a lot of death in my life.'

# 5

*'Nobody was fighting and dancing in the aisles . . .
It must have all been done before I got there. I was all
set up to tear up the seats, but nobody joined in'*

He would always claim that 'in our family the radio was hardly ever on, so I got to pop music later, not like Paul and George who were groomed in it coming over the radio all the time'. But when he did discover it and its potency, it wasn't enough for him to simply listen to it, as most other boys did. He wanted to play it, to write it and to perform it – to be at the very centre of it. Mimi thought this was just another craze.

Every era has its own popular music, and the early Fifties had its hits. There'd been Guy Mitchell singing songs that sounded like sea shanties, such as 'The Roving Kind'; and Frankie Laine had put blood and guts into pop with the ballad from the film *High Noon*, 'Do Not Forsake Me, Oh My Darling'. Then there was Tennessee Ernie Ford's deep 'Sixteen Tons' and Johnnie Ray's cover of the Drifters' 'Such A Night' – which the BBC banned on the grounds that in between the gasps and sighs something carnal was being intimated.

So, mainly the hits of John's early teens were elaborately orchestrated numbers sung by big American stars who would tour Britain every year, and sell out for a week at the Liverpool Empire. John would see their photographs in the *Liverpool Echo* and hear their records played on the BBC – although not very often. Wartime rationing of food and sweets might have ended in 1954, but old habits were dying hard at the BBC in regard to popular music. 'The less of that stuff the better' was the policy there. Only on Radio Luxembourg at 208 metres on the Medium Wave could British fans find the music they wanted to hear. The signal wasn't very clear, especially in the summer, coming all the way from the little principality between France and Germany; but, intermittent though it was, the records Radio Luxembourg played brought a new kind of stardust to a still down-at-heel Britain and a 40-watt Liverpool.

At that stage in his life, John liked music, but that was all. He didn't know very much about it, other than that all the singers and records he liked seemed to come from America. Naturally enough, Mimi disliked Americana in general and popular music in particular. But she couldn't shield John from what the boys at school were talking about, and the records he would hear in their homes.

Changes were coming in the Fifties, and not only in music, with the new demographic of 'the teenager' causing much interest among academics and advertisers alike. For the first time, young people, as distinct from children and adults, were being targeted by manufacturers, analysed by social psychologists, and, inevitably, criticised by newspaper pundits. The angst of this new generation had even been made into the subject of a bestselling novel by J. D. Salinger – *The Catcher In The Rye*.

Nor did Hollywood want to miss out on the new market. The James Dean films *East Of Eden* and *Rebel Without A Cause* caught the fashion for misunderstood youth to perfection, while a more provocative film, *Blackboard Jungle*, captured grittily the modern problems of an inner-city New York high school. It was good, but little remembered now other than for a moment of inspiration when its producers laid a record by Bill Haley and the Comets called 'Rock Around The Clock' over the opening sequence.

'Rock Around The Clock' wasn't a particularly interesting song. It had been a forgotten flip side of a minor hit until rescued by Hollywood – and it would never be one of the hundreds of songs that the Beatles would later perform during their careers. John never liked it. 'When Bill Haley records came on the wireless my mother used to like them okay. But they did nothing for me,' he said.

Rock and roll had been struggling to break out of the R&B market in the US, where it was classified as 'race music' and played mainly on black radio stations. But when sung by a chubby white man in a plaid jacket, it reached mainstream America, and Britain wouldn't be very far behind. Something else, however, was also happening in the UK at that time.

Just a couple of months after 'Rock Around The Clock' had been recorded in New York, in April 1954, a guitar-playing Scot called Lonnie Donegan had gone into a London studio with a hepped-up Leadbelly blues song called 'Rock Island Line'. Like 'Rock Around the Clock', it also took over a year to become a top ten hit. But when it did, it created a whole new movement – skiffle.

Requiring only a cheap acoustic guitar, a lusty voice, an old washboard, which every mother or grandmother then owned, and a bass made from a tea-chest, a broom handle and a length of string, just about anyone could put together a skiffle group. And just about anyone did. No musical experience was required to scrape a washboard, and there were no frets on a broom handle. As for the guitar, a knowledge of three chords was all it took.

At the beginning of 1956, fifteen-year-old John didn't know even one chord, nor did he have a guitar. But boys at Quarry Bank, like schoolboys all over the UK, were suddenly talking about Lonnie Donegan and skiffle, and John was intrigued enough to buy 'Rock Island Line' to play on his mother's record player. He liked what he heard and what he was seeing of Lonnie Donegan on television. Skiffle looked easy.

At first, he borrowed a guitar from a school friend, Eric Griffiths, but then Julia bought him one of his own from a mail order firm. 'It had a label on the inside that said "guaranteed not to split",' he would remember. 'I suppose it was a bit crummy, but I played it for a long time and got in a lot of practice on it.'

Julia, who could play the banjo, was ever encouraging and showed him how to play the few chords of Fats Domino's 'Ain't That A Shame'. Her method 'was by using only the top four strings and forgetting about the other two – because banjos only have four strings,' Rod Davis recalls. It was a start. As John would say, 'Most of our stuff then was just twelve bar blues boogies . . . nothing fancy.'

Although John always gets the credit, it hadn't originally been his idea to form a group. It was first suggested by another boy whose name has been forgotten, but who, in the end, wasn't invited to join.

From the start, John's enthusiasm, bossiness and sheer nerve determined that he would be the singer, front and centre. No one disagreed with him. That was the way he was. Pete Shotton, who was unmusical, would have to be in the group, of course, as John's best friend. He could play the washboard. That didn't require any talent. Rod Davis was invited to join, too. He had a banjo.

John might not have done much homework, but over the next few months he thrashed his new guitar until his fingers bled, as gradually the little band of schoolboy skifflers began to expand – although not exclusively with other Quarry Bank boys. A boy called Len Garry, who was with Ivan Vaughan at the Liverpool Institute, was added on tea-chest bass, with Ivan sometimes helping out if Len didn't turn up. Meanwhile Nigel Walley, another of John's Woolton gang, decided that he should be the manager – although there wasn't anything yet to manage. According to Pete Shotton, it was his idea to name the group the Quarry Men – partly after his and John's school, but also because there were several overgrown quarries around Woolton hill.

By the spring of 1956, the Quarry Men were becoming relatively adept at copying other Lonnie Donegan recordings, like 'Maggie May' and 'Stewball', especially after a drummer called Colin Hanton joined the band. Colin wasn't at Quarry Bank High School either. He was, in fact, already working as an apprentice upholsterer, which meant he had money in his pocket – not much, but enough to have bought himself a set of drums. Lots of boys had guitars, but a boy with a set of drums was someone to be sought after. Primitive though their sound might have been, the Quarry Men were now complete. And it was just in time, because John was already seeing wider horizons.

Elvis Presley's 'Heartbreak Hotel' had been released in Britain in March 1956, and immediately put on the 'restricted play' list by the BBC. They didn't like the sound of it. John did. 'This boy I knew at school, Don Beattie . . . his mum bought him records,' he later told me. 'He showed me the name "Elvis Presley" in the charts in the *New Musical Express*, and he said it was great. I thought it sounded a bit phoney . . . "Heartbreak Hotel". But then I heard it on, I think, Radio Luxembourg, and it was the end for me.'

Actually, it was the beginning. 'Before Elvis there was nothing,' he would very famously say later, which was a little bit of Lennon hyperbole. But, for John, the arrival of Elvis and rock and roll was an epiphany. He was fifteen. 'It was the only thing to get through to me . . . Rock and roll was real. Everything else was unreal.' He now began to realise what he wanted to do, who he wanted to be. Lonnie Donegan had provided the initial spark, but it was Elvis – who, inci-dentally, had started out, like Donegan, singing a rocked-up version of a blues song – who mostly fired John's ambition.

Since he'd been a little boy, he'd dreamed about writing *Alice In Wonderland*, or, rather, a book like it. But, looking back on that period in his life, he would tell me: 'I wanted to write *Alice In Wonderland* and be Elvis Presley.' He saw no problem in putting the two together, not allowing that some may see Lewis Carroll as high culture and Elvis as something else. To him there was no conflict. They fitted together. It was a belief he would always hold.

That year he began to buy records in earnest to play at Julia's home, with 78 rpm versions of Elvis Presley's 'Blue Suede Shoes', 'Don't Be Cruel' and 'My Baby Left Me' following 'Heartbreak Hotel'. Then there was Gene Vincent's 'Be-Bop-A-Lula'. He bought a comedy record, too. It was the nonsensical 'Ying Tong Song' by the stars of his favourite radio programme, *The Goon Show*. It was an exciting time. 'The Daily Howl' and John's wacky insolence had made him famous – well, notorious – at school, he was starting his own skiffle group, and now Elvis was in his life. Then along came Little Richard singing 'Long Tall Sally'. This was almost too good to be true.

'When I heard it, it was so great I couldn't speak,' he told me and other journalists. 'You know how you are torn. I didn't want to leave Elvis . . . I didn't want to say anything against Elvis, not even in my mind. How could this be happening in my lifetime. *Both* of them.'

Then someone told him that Little Richard was black. It hadn't occurred to him until then. 'So . . . Elvis was white and Little Richard was black. There was a difference between them.' That meant he could love them both without being disloyal to Elvis. 'I thought about it for days at school, about the labels on the records. One was yellow [the American Specialty label of Little Richard's record], the other was [His Master's Voice in the UK] blue. I thought about that . . . yellow and blue.' These were the memories of a nerdy teenage boy he would tell and retell all his life, luxuriating in the passions recalled.

Naturally when a film with Little Richard, *The Girl Can't Help It*, which also starred the pneumatic Jayne Mansfield, was shown in Liverpool, John went to see it, as he had also been to see the rock exploitation movie *Rock Around The Clock*. The experience of both was not quite as he had been led to expect.

When any rock and roll film was shown in the UK in the mid-Fifties, there were newspaper stories of riots, fighting and dancing in cinema aisles, which then sparked copycat incidents around the country, and which, in turn, triggered further newspaper headlines. The culprits were said to be Teddy boys (and their girlfriends), gangs of working-class youths whose fashion was to wear Edwardian-style outfits of narrow trousers and long jackets, and to grow long side-boards under quiffs of greasy duck-tailed hair. Like hormonal youths the world over, some Teddy boy gangs liked to fight with other gangs, the result being that in Britain they were considered, at least by the tabloid newspapers, a menace.

As a suburban schoolboy in a blazer and tie, John steered well clear of them. 'I was never in any street fights or gangs,' he would remember. But he was intrigued by the reports of riots in the cinemas.

'I was most surprised,' he would often say, comically deadpan about going to see *Rock Around The Clock*. 'Nobody was fighting and dancing in the aisles like I'd read . . . It must have all been done before I got there. I was all set up to tear up the seats, but nobody joined in.'

The notion that rock and roll drove young people crazy because of its 'jungle beat' (rock's early detractors really used to say that) might have been a myth built around the behaviour of a few over-energised and aggressive show-offs. But, because of the newspaper coverage, by the late Fifties rock and roll had become firmly associated in the public's mind with the uneducated and unsophisticated. It would take the Beatles, eight years later, to eventually change that.

John was sixteen in October 1956. It was the beginning of his last year at school and by now it wasn't only rock and roll and the Quarry Men that was obsessing him. There was sex, too. And when at weekends he and his gang would ride their bikes as a squad to nearby Calderstones Park for a secret smoke and a chat, there would often be girls hanging about, trying to attract his attention. He wasn't the best-looking boy in his group, but girls always liked him, and one day, out cycling in the park with Len Garry, they met a couple of new faces. John fancied the pretty fair one with the pony tail, but, at first, she preferred Len. Her name was Barbara Baker and she was fifteen. A little later, in the way these teenage things go, she transferred her affections to John. Len didn't mind. And, off and on, for the next eighteen months, Barbara and John would become a couple, going off on cycle rides, or to the pictures, or to the homes of friends when their parents were out. He even wrote her love poems, enjoying the security of having a steady girlfriend, although he was rarely steady himself – expecting her to be available when he wanted her, but happy to be with the Quarry Men when he didn't.

'I was a very insecure male,' he would one day tell *Playboy*, 'a guy who wanted to put his woman into a little box, lock her up and then bring her out when he feels like playing with her. She's not allowed to communicate with the outside world, outside of me, because it made me feel insecure.'

Not surprisingly, Mimi was cool towards this new development in her nephew's adolescence, but Julia liked Barbara and would welcome the pair into her home.

For the best part of his last year at school, Julia, Elvis, the Quarry Men and Barbara defined the boundaries of John's life. No one, other than he, saw the Quarry Men as anything more than a craze, but the rehearsals, which were usually in the homes of the other members of the group (Mimi didn't want them disturbing her lodgers' studies, and would make John practise his guitar outside in the side porch), were fun, if haphazard. But when Julia allowed them to use her bathroom for practice, because the tiled walls gave the best approximation of the echo effect heard on Elvis's records, she endeared herself to everyone.

None of the group was, of course, even close to being a musician, so the playlist for the Quarry Men's earliest unpaid appearances at the St Peter's Youth Club in Woolton depended on the few songs they knew. And playing some of them didn't come easily, as Rod Davis remembers. 'When another skiffle song, "Freight Train" by Chas McDevitt and Nancy Whiskey, entered the charts a few months later, we were all wondering what to do because you needed to know *four* chords to play that.' Another limitation was that the lyrics to the songs were often indistinct on the records. John tried to get a vague idea of the words, but, when he couldn't, he just made up new ones as he went along. It didn't matter. No one else knew them either.

The Quarry Men's first proper public appearance, probably in late 1956 (no one can remember exactly), was at a golf club in Childwall, a Liverpool suburb. It had been arranged by Nigel Walley, who had now left school and was an apprentice golf pro at the club. And although the group weren't actually paid, someone passed around a hat at the end of the evening, so the boys shared a few shillings between them.

Julia was there, too, encouraging. Mimi, however, with her mantra, 'The guitar's all right, John, but you'll never make a living with it', wasn't. In her view, her nephew was in danger of throwing his life away, just as his mother had.

But was she also jealous of the increasing amount of time that John was now spending with Julia? She had lost her husband, and although she and John rowed frequently, he was the centre of her life. In her pretend-stern way she doted on him. She would have been too proud ever to admit it, but it must have hurt when John preferred to be with his real mother. If so, that would explain why one day during that first year of the Quarry Men her emotions may have got the better of her.

After yet another row, John had banged out of Mendips and gone to stay at Julia's place, telling Mimi that this time he wasn't coming back. Of course, he did go back. He *always* went back. But when, after a few days, he returned something was missing. His terrier dog, Sally, that his Uncle George had given him when he'd been still in short trousers, was no longer there. Mimi explained that if he wasn't going to be around to look after the dog, she had decided to give her away.

It was, Pete Shotton would recall, the only time he ever saw John with tears in his eyes. It seems unlikely that Mimi had the dog destroyed, as Pete believed. John's cousin Stanley Parkes was under the impression that Mimi simply found another home for Sally. She always preferred cats, anyway. But, knowing how fond John was of his dog, it does suggest an act of spiteful jealousy on Mimi's behalf.

# 6

*'With the toughest-looking face you've ever seen.*
*I'd get into trouble just because of the way I looked'*

If he ever worried about facing the second major academic milestone in his life, his GCE O-levels, John never let it show. But then, all the Quarry Men seemed to have a pretty insouciant attitude towards exams, as, during the spring and early summer of 1957, instead of sitting at home revising, they turned out increasingly for regular bookings. They'd been together for nearly a year, mainly making informal appearances at their local St Peter's Youth Club and friends' parties. But, if their musical progress had been slow, that didn't get in the way of John's ambition. So, when an appearance in a preliminary heat for the Carroll Levis television talent show was offered to Liverpool's skiffle groups, they grabbed it. The audition was held on stage at Liverpool's Empire Theatre which was where all the big American stars appeared, and, though the Quarry Men were immediately eliminated, their confidence wasn't dented. How many other sixteen-year-old South Liverpool boys could say they'd appeared on stage at the Empire? Things weren't going badly at all. They'd even made a guest appearance playing at the sixth form dance at Quarry Bank High School.

To John, all these moments were seen as little victories, but with his vagueness for details, he would later say that his earliest real memory of appearing in public was when the group played on the back of a coal lorry. That was in June 1957, in Roseberry Street, Toxteth, which was a pretty tough area of Liverpool. The occasion was the 750th anniversary of a charter given to the city by England's King John – the famously 'wicked' monarch who was to be bullied into Magna Carta eight years later by the English barons. John would have been told about all that at school, but for him the appearance in Toxteth was memorable mainly because, for some reason, a gang of local Teddy boys in the audience took against him.

Quite why he should have annoyed anyone by simply singing a few songs, in front of his mother and his two half-sisters who were there that day, is puzzling, but throughout his life John would make a habit of rubbing people up the wrong way. Could it be that standing there unsmiling in front of the microphone, he looked arrogant? Certainly, there was always something slightly supercilious about that top lip. Or might it simply have had something to do with his extreme short-sightedness? Refusing to wear his glasses in public, he would stare myopically into the audience as he sang, with the result that anyone in what would have been his line of vision might have thought he was staring challengingly at them.

'I was never really a street kid or tough guy . . .' he would tell *Rolling Stone* years later. 'I was just a suburban kid imitating the rockers . . . with the toughest-looking face you've ever seen. I'd get into trouble just because of the way I looked.' That was probably true, because not everyone liked his attitude – even when he wasn't aware that he was displaying any kind of attitude.

So, amid an undercurrent of threats, he and his schoolboy band cut short their Roseberry Street performance and sought sanctuary in an obliging woman's house until, according to Quarry Men drummer Colin Hanton, 'a bobby escorted us' to the bus stop.

The Toxteth appearance might have been fraught, but the Quarry Men's next gig, two weeks later on Saturday, 6 July, at the Woolton Parish Garden Fete, with its sideshows, balloons, ice-creams, pop, home-made jam tarts and the annual crowning of the local Rose Queen, promised to be more comfortable. John, like most of the members of the group, had been attending the fete behind St Peter's Church since he was six, it being a day that Woolton children looked forward to. So, it was fortuitous that Pete Shotton's mother had overheard neighbours discussing plans for that year's fete while she'd been out shopping, and sharp of her to have quickly suggested that the Quarry Men should be added to the entertainment. Had Mimi, and not Pete's mum, been the one to have overheard the plans for the fete, all kinds of things might never have happened.

But she wasn't. And, as the Band of the Cheshire Yeomanry led a noisy musical parade around the little lanes of Woolton, followed by floats bearing children in fancy dress costumes and that year's Rose Queen, all waving to groups of neighbours who were lining the route, the Quarry Men, again on the back of a lorry, brought up the rear. They'd been asked to play and sing as the procession moved through the streets, but it wasn't easy to make music on the back of a truck that kept stopping and starting. 'I felt a real twat,' said Pete.

The Quarry Men's performance was on a raised platform in the field next to St Peter's cemetery in the late afternoon, and John was wearing a check shirt given to him for his stage appearances by his mother. As usual, the majority of the group's songs were skiffle standards, but there were some Elvis hits, too, including one of John's all-time favourites, 'Baby, Let's Play House'. Then there was 'Be-Bop-A-Lula' and a song by the American doo-wop group the Del-Vikings, 'Come Go With Me'.

As the microphone on stage was attached to the fete's tannoy system, John's voice could be heard all around the grounds, and soon a familiar face appeared among the crowd in front of the stage. It was Mimi, pushing her way through the teenagers and children, gaping at her nephew. Years later she would say: 'I couldn't take my eyes off him. There was this big grin all over his face. Then he saw me and his expression changed a bit.'

So did the lyrics to 'Cumberland Gap'. *'Here's Mimi coming down the path'* John sang instead of *'seventeen miles from the Cumberland Gap'*. In truth, he can't have been particularly surprised to see her, as she always went to the fete. And she might not have been quite as amazed to see him as she professed, since the Quarry Men's appearance was advertised on the posters and the programme. But as she had taken absolutely no interest in the group, it must have been a shock for her to realise how competent and confident John was on stage.

Mimi wasn't the only one to be surprised that afternoon. John didn't know it, but someone else was watching from the crowd. It was a fifteen-year-old school friend of Ivan Vaughan's – the boy whose parents had purposely sent their son to the Liverpool Institute when he was eleven in order to get him away from 'that John Lennon'. The boy's name was Paul McCartney and he'd cycled across the golf course from Allerton specifically at Ivan's invitation. Ivan, who had continued to see John locally sometimes, knew that Paul was keen on pop music, too.

It wasn't until the Quarry Men had finished their set and moved into the church hall for a break, leaving the ground free for the City of

Liverpool Police Dogs to begin their annual display, that Ivan was able to introduce Paul to John. With nearly a two-year age gap between the two, which is a lot in mid-teens, the meeting was at first awkward. Paul, however, said all the right things. He would later remember that he'd been impressed that John had sung the Del-Vikings' song. To him that showed seriously good taste. 'Come Go With Me' would never be a hit in Britain, and not many groups would have covered it. He had also been impressed by the way John improvised lyrics for those he didn't know. That took guts, he felt.

As a musician what was puzzling Paul, however, was that John had been playing banjo chords. He didn't understand that. And, asking permission, he picked up John's guitar and played and sang the Eddie Cochran hit 'Twenty Flight Rock'.

John was impressed. But he was also instantly jealous. Not only could the boy play and sing, he looked good, with his black hair slicked back, 'a bit like Elvis', he thought. There was more to come. Eventually putting the guitar aside, Paul went across to the piano and played and sang 'Long Tall Sally' – full-throated.

As Paul had noted John's version of the Del-Vikings song, now John admired Paul's take-off of Little Richard. He probably knew more than anyone else there how good an impersonation it was.

Eventually the kid ended his impromptu audition, although that hadn't been what he'd thought he was doing, and went back to Ivan's house to pick up his bike and cycle home across the golf course.

John had some serious thinking to do. Paul was obviously talented and knew more about playing the guitar than he or anyone in the Quarry Men. It was impossible to ignore him. Should he ask him to join the group? he asked himself. But what if he did and Paul wanted to be the lead singer and lead guitarist and then began to take over? That was a risk. Besides, did he really want to share the singing with Paul? Apart from the Everly Brothers, rock and roll bands only ever had one singer.

Of course, Paul might not want to join, but if he did, he would obviously be an asset. 'It went through my head that I'd have to keep him in line,' John would later recall. 'But he was worth having.' It was a big decision, but in the end, music made the choice for him. Paul's inclusion would inevitably 'make the group stronger'. The Quarry Men would be different with two singers. It would prove to be the best decision he ever made.

A couple of weeks later, Pete ran into Paul when the younger boy had cycled over to Ivan's house only to find that he wasn't in. 'I've been talking to John,' Pete said, 'and we thought maybe you'd like to join the Quarry Men.'

According to Pete, Paul was very cool about the offer. After thinking about it for a moment he simply said: 'Yes, all right.' Then, having explained that he couldn't start playing with them for another few weeks as he was leaving for a Boy Scouts camp the very next day, which would be followed by a week at a Butlin's holiday camp with his brother and father, he cycled off home.

As for John's acceptance that Paul would benefit the group musically, this is what he would reflect to me in 1970, a few months after the Beatles broke up. 'I learned a lot from Paul. He taught me quite a lot of guitar really. He knew more about how to play than I did and he showed me a lot of chords. I'd been playing the guitar like a banjo so I had to learn it again. I didn't write much material early on, less than Paul, because he was quite competent on guitar. I started to write after Paul did a song he'd written.'

Nothing feeds ambition so much as competition, and from that very first day, as close as John and Paul became as friends and colleagues, continually helping each other musically, they never lost their mutual competitiveness. By virtue of complete serendipity the two boys, who would become the most successful songwriting partnership of the second half of the twentieth century, lived just a mile and a half from one another.

That afternoon has become one of the most celebrated days in rock history – the moment that Lennon met McCartney. But for one of the Quarry Men, it turned out to be a swansong. Rod Davis would never play with the group again. A skiffle purist, he'd never been keen on rock and roll, and, with John leaving school, while Rod was staying on to go eventually to Cambridge University, the two just drifted apart. 'I was replaced with Paul McCartney,' he says now, smiling. 'I wasn't kicked out. I just stopped playing with them. It was always very friendly.'

Indeed, Rod hadn't been forced out. But, had he still been there, his presence with his skiffle banjo might have eased the group's reception when, while waiting for Paul to join them, the Quarry Men played at a new jazz club in Liverpool's city centre in early August.

It was called the Cavern, and was housed in three barrel-ceilinged cellars under a fruit and vegetable warehouse in an alleyway called Mathew Street. To be playing in a grown-up venue close to the Pier Head was a real thrill for the group, even though John was swiftly handed a note by the management to 'cut out the bloody rock and roll'. The traditional jazz purists there could just about tolerate skiffle because it was considered authentic American folk music. But rock and roll . . .? That was beyond the pale.

Characteristically John ignored the order, but he would never forget the put-down, professing ever after to hate the snobbery of jazz. 'Jazz never gets anywhere, never does anything, it's always the same . . .' he would complain. 'We'd never get auditions because of jazz bands.'

But he'd seen the way the wind was blowing. The absence of a banjo would make it easier for the group to begin the full transition from being a skiffle group to becoming a rock and roll band. The skiffle craze had been fun, but by the middle of 1957 it had pretty well run its course. A washboard and a tea-chest bass in a band screamed '*Amateurs!*'

Mimi had been fully aware that John hadn't been putting any effort into his school work, but, as the regular difficult phone calls from the headmaster's office at Quarry Bank had grown fewer in his final year (probably because the teachers had given up on him and didn't care if he played truant), she may have been hoping for a miracle when the exam results arrived in August. She didn't get one. John had failed every subject. All nine of them.

She just couldn't believe it. *Every single subject?* John had spent half of his boyhood reading, surely he'd passed English? He hadn't. But he *must* have passed art? He drew all the time. He hadn't. When he'd been asked in the art exam to compose something about travel, he'd drawn a 'hunchback with warts all over him', he would later wryly remark.

For Mimi the results were the bitterest of disappointments and she was seriously worried. John cared, too, at least about English and art, but he wouldn't have shown that in front of his aunt.

But, what was he going to do? He couldn't stay on at Quarry Bank. They didn't want him. Ever determined, Mimi set off to the school.

'So, what are you going to do with him?' mused the headmaster, Mr Pobjoy, when confronted.

Straight-talking Mimi wasn't having that. 'No,' she would say that she replied. 'What are *you* going to do with him? You've had him for five years.'

The headmaster might have retorted that it was hardly the school's fault if John had refused to learn. But, as it turned out, a solution was already at hand. A young English teacher, Philip Burnett, had been both impressed and amused by an edition of John's mock newspaper 'The Daily Howl' that had been making its way around the staff room. Showing it one night to a girlfriend who was teaching at Liverpool College of Art, he asked her if she, too, thought it was clever and funny. And, if so, was it possible that John Lennon, with his off-the-wall humour, might fit at an art college? She thought he might.

Further education at an art college was not, in the Fifties, considered the best destination for a bright pupil at a high-achieving grammar school. Although only 4 per cent of British schoolchildren would at that time go to universities, scholastic snobbery still marked art a good few ranks further down the academic ladder in that largely non-visual age.

Not that John was particularly interested in art college, anyway. 'I thought it would be a crowd of old men,' he would later say. So, instead, like his father, he tried to join the Merchant Navy, even filling in the forms. Then Mimi found out and put her foot down. After the experience Julia had had with her 'worthless' seafaring husband, Mimi was determined that John was definitely not going to sea.

To her, Liverpool College of Art was a godsend. 'Any port in a storm,' she announced, as she so often did. Lacking any other ideas, and absolutely not fancying the idea of getting a job, John decided, as he later put it in words that were probably Mimi's, to 'try to make something' of himself.

He didn't admit that there may have been another inducement. An older boy he knew, who had gone to the College of Art, told him how one afternoon a week there would be a life class, during which students would have to sketch a naked woman. That didn't sound too bad.

So, as Mr Pobjoy, over at Quarry Bank, wrote a not completely damning reference for his most difficult pupil – 'He has been a trouble spot for many years in discipline, but . . . I believe he is not beyond redemption and he could really turn out a fairly responsible adult who might go far . . .' – at Mendips, John took Uncle George's best suit from where Mimi had left it hanging in the wardrobe. Then, putting on a tie, he got on the bus to the centre of Liverpool. At least he would look relatively smart for his interview, Mimi must have thought, as she committed herself to paying for her nephew's upkeep for a further two years.

*'What's so sad about the past is that it's passed.'*

Everything about him demanded 'Look at me!' when on 16 September 1957, John Lennon made his way unenthusiastically along Hope Street to the entrance of Liverpool College of Art. It was a grey Victorian building, with echoing stone staircases and light classrooms, just behind Liverpool's vast and still unfinished Anglican cathedral – the one they'd been building since 1904.

Obviously, he'd known there would be girls at college, but, until he got there, he probably hadn't appreciated the difference they would make to his every day. Despite its wooded setting, all-boys Quarry Bank High School had been knee-deep in testosterone, but now, wherever John looked, there were pretty shampooed girls whose very presence seemed to soften the atmosphere. Confident, exotic looking creatures in self-made outfits were studying fashion, studious young ladies were bent, lips pursed, over their lettering, and serious, arty-beatnik types wearing black were there, too, and not taking any nonsense from loudmouths like him.

When lessons began it would be the first time he would be sitting next to a girl in class since he'd been eleven. Some boys from a similar background might have had initial difficulties with that, but not John. Those 'five strong Stanley sisters' who had helped bring him up had seen to that. He was comfortable with women of all ages. There would, he saw immediately, and despite Barbara back in Woolton, be quite a few girls to pursue at the art college.

Unlike school there was no compulsory uniform to wear, but on that first day of college, determined that eyes would be upon him, he chose to wear his old school blazer with the Quarry Bank crest unpicked from the breast pocket by Mimi, a ruler-thin tie, and a pair of tight-fitting drainpipe jeans. Already trying to grow sideboards, his hair was Fifties long, which meant not very long at all, and sported a casual quiff on top. Perhaps a dab of Brylcreem helped keep it in place. It was said later, by those who first encountered him, that he'd turned up looking like a Teddy boy, a species that would have been a rare sight then in a place of further learning.

If that was the case, it probably wasn't what he'd intended. Real Teddy boys, who went to some expense to dress the way they did – and which involved money that John didn't have – were at the bottom end of the educational spectrum, usually working in low-skilled jobs, and were not a group with whom he would have wished to identify. It seems more likely that he was trying to look like a moody young rocker, an English Elvis.

Whatever he looked like, with his admirers from Quarry Bank High School now scattered, and his best friend Pete talking disquietingly about joining the police force, he was, he knew, going to have to gather together a new gang. Notoriety was always a short cut to that, and could be quickly achieved by being loud, funny and outrageous. He was good at all of those.

His first few days were spent finding his way around and sorting out like-minded people. A tall, burly and eccentric mature student of twenty-five from Manchester called Jeff Mahomed, whose father was Indian and mother Italian, became one of his first friends. Sharing with him little interest in anything the art college wanted to teach, Jeff would be John's first 'grown-up' friend. Not that mature behaviour, or indeed blinding talent, was much in evidence in either student, which meant that, instead of John being considered the next Pablo Picasso, his first year at college would be almost as onerous as his last at Quarry Bank.

The exception was the life class, when twenty-seven-year-old model June Furlong would, naked though she was, keep a sharply disapproving eye on teenage gigglers like John, who regularly appeared every first term. When he finally stopped mucking around, he and June would get on very well.

All teenagers love an excuse to get out of the classroom, and the afternoons when the staff thought it would do their students good to go out and appreciate what they had around them showed John a city he really didn't know. It would stay lodged in his mind for the rest of his life.

He had come from a suburb, but Liverpool 8, which was the postal address of the art college, with its cobbled streets and terraces of once grand but now crumbling Georgian and Regency houses, was the most interesting and historic corner of Liverpool. The rich had once lived there when Liverpool was growing as a port and trading centre – including the slave trade. But with the lofty terraced houses now divided into flats and bedsitters and inhabited by artists, musicians, actors, eccentrics, the occasional prostitute and students from the nearby Liverpool University, the area had become the city's bohemian quarter. And, with its West Indian and Chinese population in nearby Toxteth, it was also Liverpool's melting pot. Less than half a dozen miles from village-like Woolton, it was as different an environment as could be envisaged – exactly the place to feed a capricious imagination. Studying there, John would love for the hurly burly of city life that would never leave him.

There was also something else that was of particular interest in Liverpool 8. It was the building that was immediately adjacent to the art college, just around the corner in Hope Place. It was the Liverpool Institute, where Paul McCartney, now the newest member of the Quarry Men, was at school. With only a brick wall and an open door between them, it meant they could see each other every day if they wanted to. They did want to.

Paul had returned from his summer holiday at the end of August, after which the Quarry Men had soon got together to rehearse at drummer Colin Hanton's parents' house, and again in Julia's bathroom. Soon, however, John and Paul were meeting separately from the rest of the group.

Paul had been brought up in a musical home, with his father Jim McCartney having played trumpet in a traditional jazz band when he was younger. His mother, Mary, had been a nursing sister in a hospital, and, ambitious for her family, had believed, just like Mimi, that success could only be achieved through education. But she had died suddenly while having surgery for breast cancer in 1956, leaving Paul and his younger brother, Michael, to be brought up by their father. The shock of her death hadn't only devastated the family, it had, Paul would come to believe, driven him deeper into the music that he had already begun creating.

Now, thrown together by chance, John began visiting Paul's house in the empty hours after classes and before Jim McCartney got home from his job as a cotton salesman. There, in the McCartneys' little kitchen in Forthlin Road, Allerton, John would lean over his guitar and listen carefully to what Paul, also with a guitar, had to teach him. And gradually, over the weeks, the two found a way of working and then playing and singing together.

Often Michael McCartney, who was thirteen and also at the Liverpool Institute, would watch them, intrigued by his brother's new friend. 'There were never any compromises with John,' he would remember. 'He was very simple, yet complex, if you know what I mean. He was like a young, hungry animal.' At college John would play the tearaway, forever being funny and making sick jokes. With Paul, he was more serious and keen to learn.

The first couple of gigs with the new member were at a Conservative Club in nearby Norris Green, and immediately a difference could be seen in the group. As well as his musicianship, Paul brought an element of professionalism that the Quarry Men had never had before. Both he and John now wore light-coloured jackets, stringy ties and black jeans, and stood together up front at the two microphones while Len, Eric, Pete and Colin, in white shirts but without jackets, were behind them. Financially, all five band members were sharing whatever 'manager' Nigel Walley managed to get for them, if they were paid at all. But it was clear that there were now two classes of Quarry Men – John and Paul, and the rest.

As it happened, the autumn of 1957 was like one long masterclass in rock and roll, as almost every week new classic records were arriving from America for them to listen to and study. There was Jerry Lee Lewis with 'Whole Lotta Shakin' Goin' On', Chuck Berry's 'School Day' and the Everly Brothers, in close harmony, with 'Bye Bye Love' and 'Wake Up Little Susie', unknowingly demonstrating how John and Paul (and Simon and Garfunkel, too) might sound when they sang together. But most important of all was Buddy Holly in his horn-rimmed glasses, who, with the Crickets, sang 'That'll Be The Day', and then, as a solo artist, 'Peggy Sue'. Holly was more than special. He not only wrote the songs, but played lead guitar and sang them. Elvis almost never played lead guitar on a record, using his instrument just to strum the rhythm. And he certainly didn't write hit songs.

Buddy Holly could do everything. And, with those glasses, he didn't look, or even try to look, like a rock star. His success was entirely due to the music he made. After him it should have been acceptable for a lead singer to wear glasses, but it would be years before John had the nerve to wear his in public – and he would still take them off as soon as he'd finished reading anything.

Perhaps more important was the other message that Holly was sending, which both John and Paul picked up on. It was that people of talent anywhere could write songs and maybe one day make records, too. Holly didn't come from New York or Los Angeles, or even Memphis or Nashville. He was from Lubbock, Texas, which was a long way off any beaten track John or Paul knew about. And he'd made it.

So, invigorated by the very idea of Buddy Holly, the two spent hours listening to the shape of 'That'll Be The Day', learning how to master the opening riff. Could they one day write something like that, they wondered, a song for guitars, bass and drums built around an everyday catchphrase?

By 1958 the Quarry Men were improving, but being a member of the group was no longer the merry lark it had been – certainly not for Pete Shotton and his washboard. And when a young school friend of Paul's, a fourteen-year-old called George Harrison, who didn't say much but who could play the guitar better than any of them, began to tag along, Pete could feel his position slipping. A rock and roll band didn't need a washboard.

'Being John's friend I didn't want to say I was getting fed up and that I wanted to leave,' Pete would write in his memoirs. 'But my contribution was totally non-musical. I just went along to make wisecracks and help carry the gear. I never liked going on stage. It gave me the willies.'

John must have realised this, but he wasn't going to push his best friend out of the group. Instead he waited for Pete to make the decision himself. It came after the Quarry Men had played at a wedding reception when they had both had too much to drink, and Pete plucked up the courage to say he was leaving.

He thought John would be upset. But John had obviously been struggling to tell Pete that he didn't want him in the group any more. 'Anyway,' Pete remembered, 'he suddenly picked up my washboard and hit me over the head with it.' It broke and ended up around his neck.

'Well, that takes care of that problem, doesn't it?' John said.

'So that was it,' Pete remembers. 'We then just laughed until the beer rolled from our eyes . . .'

It was an inevitable turning point that they had both recognised. But John hadn't dropped Pete until he had a new partner in Paul. For years, as the two had roamed Woolton together, it had been Lennon and Shotton. Now it would be Lennon and McCartney – a very different kind of relationship.

Years later, reflecting on his friendship with Pete, John would say: 'I ruined Pete's education, just as I ruined my own.' But Pete never complained, not then, nor later.

Jim McCartney was not happy about his son Paul's new friend. Jim, then fifty-five, was the nicest of old-fashioned men and held great hopes for his sons. He had been thrilled when Paul had shown early promise at music, but then disappointed when the boy had quickly given up on piano lessons. So, he'd bought him a trumpet, the instrument that he used to play himself in the Jimmy Mac Jazz Band. But Paul couldn't play the trumpet and sing at the same time, and Paul always liked to sing. The trumpet had, therefore, gone back to the shop to be replaced with a guitar. Jim didn't mind skiffle – it was, after all, tolerated by jazzmen like Chris Barber – but he wasn't sure about rock and roll. And, following a path already trodden by the parents of children at Dovedale Primary School and teachers at Quarry Bank High School, he was especially not sure about John Lennon.

To Jim, the ideal path for Paul would have taken him from school to university and on to a good professional career. He was a clever boy and, having been accelerated at school, had taken his Latin and French O-levels a year early. Unfortunately, distracted by his guitar playing – although the loss of his mother might have contributed to a lack of focus – Paul had failed both. For Jim, music was fine as a hobby, but education was what mattered, and now he was afraid that Paul was being led astray by this wise guy Lennon. 'He'll lead you into trouble, son,' Jim would warn.

Paul disagreed. He could see qualities in John that eluded most parents. John was bright and funny. Musically, he and John were absolutely on the same wavelength, and playing music was what he wanted to do far more than pass exams. The afternoons when they went back to Forthlin Road to play together, or to try writing a song, or maybe just to listen to records, were the best part of the week for both of them. When he hinted to John that his father wasn't happy, John's automatic response was to encourage him to rebel. 'Tell him to fuck off,' he advised, although that was something he would never have dared say to Mimi.

Paul didn't say it to his father, either.

Some other people who didn't like John Lennon – and by the time he was seventeen there was quite a queue – were the parents of his on-off girlfriend, Barbara. All the time they'd been going out, John's world had really been a boys' only gang, in which girlfriends were expected to be pretty, admiring, as sexy as any girl dared to be in those pre-Pill days, and content to play a minor role. Even before he'd gone to art college, he had never been a very loyal boyfriend, and there had been other local liaisons – one of the not inconsiderable benefits of being a lead singer in a group. According to him, he'd lost his virginity before any of his friends while still at school, but, knowing his talent for over-dramatising situations, the details of a comical tryst he'd enjoyed with a girl on top of an ancient, flat gravestone in a cemetery one night might not have been entirely reliable.

As for Barbara, the final parting of the ways came after some months at art college – no doubt to her parents' delight. He hadn't treated her well and had often been off pursuing other girls with lusty intent, although he'd be beside himself with jealousy if Barbara went out with another boy. In the end their relationship, like many when one partner goes off to college, had simply petered out. And, although, many years later, Barbara was invited to talk about their days together, she almost never did.

John would never forget Barbara or that period of his life when the world and new possibilities were beginning to open up for him. Twenty years later he reminisced about her in an American radio interview, wading, at first spikily, back into the few years of normality he had enjoyed before fame had engulfed him. 'Barbara, where are you? Fat and ugly? Fifteen kids? Years of hell with me should have made you ready for anything.'

But regrets and nostalgia quickly followed the more he thought about her. 'What's so sad about the past is that it's passed,' he ruminated, before ending the reverie with a jokey reference to a song lyric from his childhood. 'I wonder who's kissing her now.'

# 8

*'George looked even younger than Paul, and Paul
looked about ten with his baby face'*

It had begun as just another hobby, like acting out the characters in
*The Wind In The Willows* when he'd been ten, or writing and drawing
'The Daily Howl' at fifteen. But now, what he enjoyed doing more
than anything was singing and playing rock and roll. Rock music had
taken over his life, and already he was becoming a semi-detached art
student. When criticised by an irate tutor for his lack of effort he was
angrily unembarrassed. 'I don't need all this,' he shouted back. 'I'm
going to be a rock star.' That had become his sole ambition, and he
was determined that it would be his destiny. The only problem was in
working out how he was going to achieve it.

Since his meeting with Paul McCartney, and his realisation of how
little he and the other Quarry Men knew about music, one thing was
becoming very clear. Friends though the original group were, they
were not going to be with him on his journey, as Pete had already
discovered. For John to get to where he wanted to be, he would need
talented musicians around him, not half-hearted part-timers who
sometimes didn't even turn up for rehearsals.

For the time being, though, his job was to keep playing and learning; and to hold the group together while boy manager Nigel Walley
arranged occasional appearances in church halls. It was at such a
date that he first became seriously aware of George Harrison. John
didn't pay him much attention at first, not even when Paul told him
how good a guitarist George was. In John's eyes, the kid was just too
young.

George, however, was also very determined. While both John and
Paul lived their lives under constant adult warnings about the dan-
gers of throwing their opportunities away, George received nothing
but encouragement from his family, particularly from his mother,
Louise. And, by sheer force of will and practice, and complete neglect

of homework, he'd learned to do things with a guitar that not even Paul could do. He could, for instance, play 'Raunchy'.

'Raunchy' was in 1958 a big American guitar instrumental hit that had followed Elvis, Carl Perkins, Jerry Lee Lewis and Johnny Cash out of the Sun recording studios in Memphis and straight to the top of the US charts. Rock guitarists loved its twangy riff, and by mastering it, George was considered in his tiny circle to be something of a self-taught prodigy. 'Raunchy' was his passport to membership of the Quarry Men.

'We asked George to join us because he knew more chords, a lot more, than we knew,' John would often say. 'So we got a lot from him. And every time we learned a new chord, Paul and I would write a song around it.'

Outside the Quarry Men, John wasn't, however, prepared to so-cialise with George – as evidenced when, on one occasion, believing himself to be now in the gang, George arrived at Mendips and sug-gested that he and John go to the cinema together.

Immediately John made an excuse and sent him away. He didn't want to be seen hanging out with a fourteen-year-old, no matter how good a guitarist the kid was. He would later sum up the problem to me with his usual exaggeration. 'George looked even younger than Paul, and Paul looked about ten with his baby face. George used to follow me around like a bloody kid, hanging around all the time.'

Mimi probably applauded John's behaviour on that occasion, if not for the kindest of motives. George's winkle-pickers, drainpipe jeans, jazzy shirt and masses of grease-coiffured hair, allied to his thick Liverpudlian accent, had revealed him to be a very working-class boy. 'He's a real whacker, isn't he! You always seem to like lower-class types, don't you, John,' she would snipe, with an undisguised implied dig at her nephew's ne'er-do-well absentee father, Freddie.

She would tolerate Paul, though. Paul thought she even 'quite liked him', which she probably did, although she would patronise him whenever she answered the front door to him by calling up to John in his bedroom saying: 'Your little friend's here, John.' She had a twinkle in her eye as she said that, Paul would remember, but she was making a point. He was slightly in awe of John's smarter, more comfortable home, the prominent collection of books by Winston Churchill that Mimi had on show in a bookshelf in the sitting room, and Mimi's long cigarette holder.

As far as Mimi was concerned, Paul was, just about, all right. His accent was less pronounced, and his manners and diplomatic skills more mature than those of George, whom she knew to have a Saturday job as a butcher's boy. She didn't see a butcher's boy delivering sausages, liver and lamb chops on a bike as the right company for her college-educated nephew.

Not that Paul could get around her. When he turned up with his guitar, she always chased John and him from the house, making them practice out in the front porch. As it happened, they preferred to play and sing there. Like Julia's bathroom, the porch had a better acoustic, and John's bedroom was too small for them to practise in, their arms bumping into each other's, sitting on the bed as they played together. Instead, when they were there, they would just put John's 45s on the record player he now owned – two teenage boys sharing their obsession.

Sometimes for a change they would go to see Julia and play her records, too, as she lived quite near to Paul's home. The relationship between John and Julia left a lasting impression on the younger boy. 'I'd lost my mum, that's one thing. But for your mum to be actually living somewhere else and for you to be a teenage boy and not living with her is very sad,' Paul told his biographer friend Barry Miles. 'Julia would be very nice but when we left there was always a tinge of sadness about him . . . Being John, he didn't admit to it much unless it was a very quiet or drunken moment . . . He loved his Aunt Mimi, I know he did. But she was always the surrogate.'

Pete had already left, but George's admission into the Quarry Men presented John with a problem. Four guitars in a six-man group made it, to say the least, unbalanced. So, he suggested to Eric Griffiths that he put aside his acoustic guitar and buy one of the new electric bass guitars and amplifiers that were then just becoming available in Liverpool.

Not seeing the danger looming, or that making an expensive investment in a bass guitar might be his way of staying in the group, Eric turned the idea down.

At this point it would have been politic, or even kind, to have explained to Eric that he was being replaced by George. But John didn't do that. Instead the group held a rehearsal at Paul's home without Eric, and, in the end, Nigel Walley was sent to deliver the sacking.

Eric was upset. John was his friend and Eric had been a founder member of the band.

It wouldn't be the last time that John would leave it to someone else to impart bad news.

Most groups were content to copy the records that were arriving from America, and almost everything the Quarry Men played in public was a cover of an Elvis, Buddy Holly or Carl Perkins record. But what made Lennon and McCartney different was that, from the beginning, years before they knew that the big money in popular music was to be made in its writing and publishing, they decided, like Buddy Holly, to write their own songs.

Paul had already written his first song, 'I Lost My Little Girl', when he met John. So, spurred on, as he always would be, by rivalry, John then wrote one. That was the way the working partnership evolved – as friends, rivals and perhaps most importantly, as contributors to and editors of each other's ideas. Most of the songs they wrote in that period were lost because, as neither boy could write music or had a tape recorder to save what they'd written, there was no way of re-membering what tune they'd come up with. This didn't worry them. Although Paul would diligently copy the name and lyrics of every song into an exercise book, as 'Another original by John Lennon and Paul McCartney', if they couldn't remember the tune, that must have meant it wasn't any good. So they forgot about it. A few though, like one of John's first songs, 'One After 909', hung around for years – before eventually appearing on the *Let It Be* album in 1970.

Now and then Nigel Walley would hear of somewhere new for the Quarry Men to play, and off they would go to brave the local gangs who would watch with suspicion if they thought their girlfriends might fancy them too much. A couple of times, carrying their guitars, they had to run for the bus to escape the wrath of the locals – which was another good reason not to be the drummer in a band. You couldn't run very quickly when hauling a drum kit on and off a bus. Mainly, though, their performances were met with friendly indifference and small audiences, the main benefactors being the Quarry Men them-selves who regarded gigs as practice time.

John might no longer have been a schoolboy, but he was still depend-ent on Mimi, who, brought up among girls, and with her husband

George now dead, had little idea of how to handle a truculent teenage boy. So when she found a packet of condoms in her nephew's pocket she sought the advice of one of her former lodgers, Michael Fishwick, who had now returned to stay at Mendips while writing his PhD at Liverpool University. His advice to Mimi was that it would be better if she didn't mention the condoms to John. This was wise counsel. But there was something ironical about the whole situation. Mimi and Michael Fishwick, who was half her age, had, over the past few months, become lovers. As John was now spending more and more time at Julia's home, it's quite possible that he was never even aware of it. Certainly he never talked about it.

Of course, there was no reason why a widowed landlady of fifty shouldn't have been having a relationship with her unmarried young lodger. But since the day John had moved into Mendips, Mimi had always presented herself as being the living spirit of dignified behaviour. What would have been his reaction had he known that she was now having sex with her student lodger in the bedroom next to his? He would have been astonished, for sure. But would he have been shocked, appalled, hysterically amused or . . .? Mimi couldn't tell.

As it happened, at around the same time, John found himself having to reassess his mother's love life when, arriving at Julia's house one afternoon, he wandered into her bedroom only to interrupt her giving her partner, Bobby Dykins, oral sex.

Being John, he couldn't keep it a secret, and told his best friend Pete. He couldn't keep it a secret either.

Meanwhile at Liverpool College of Art, academic history was repeating itself. Just as he had failed at school, John was continuing to disappoint at college. This time, though, the problem wasn't just that he was lazy and not interested, although he was certainly both. It was that he simply didn't have the appropriate talents and temperament for the course on which he found himself.

Arthur Ballard, one of his tutors, a tough, no-nonsense former army boxing champion, had, unlike most of the staff, a soft spot for him, and was happy to let him invite Paul and George into his classroom at lunchtime to practise together. But Ballard was blunt about John's abilities as an artist. 'I think he felt frustrated, though he would never admit it,' he said. 'There he was, surrounded by people who had some talent with art, and I think he felt a bit in over his head. He would act in a daft manner to distract people . . .' probably to hide the fact that 'he wasn't as good an artist as they were'.

John had an excuse for that. 'I should have been an illustrator or in the painting school because it seemed groovy. But I found myself in lettering. I didn't turn up for something so they put me in that. They were neat fuckers in lettering. I was never neat. They might as well have put me in sky-diving for the use I was at lettering. I failed all the exams.'

Again, what he seems to have been unprepared to admit, not even to himself, was that he wasn't good enough to be in the painting school. That was why he hadn't been chosen. It was the same complaint he'd had at Quarry Bank – that the school hadn't recognised his genius. His high opinion of himself could blinker him sometimes.

Only when Arthur Ballard accidentally came across a notebook of John's caricatures did he revise his opinion of the boy. They were, he thought, 'the wittiest thing I'd seen in my life'. *That*, he told John, was what he should be doing.

'He would act the fool,' Ballard told me years later, 'but underneath all that I could see that he was a thinker.'

Other people at college were discovering the same thing. While some fellow students were appalled when John would revel in saying the unsayable, such as his loud comment when passing a one-legged man in the street, 'Some blokes will do anything to get out of the army' – and with two world wars having occurred in the last forty years, they were not an uncommon sight – others were discovering a more thoughtful side to him.

One of them was a dark-haired boy called Bill Harry who'd had a tough Liverpool upbringing, and who saw art college as his big opportunity in life. Sitting with John at lunchtime in Ye Cracke, a faux ancient pub a couple of streets away from the college where the two would drink beer and eat chips, Harry discovered that, when he could get the class joker away from his little mob of admirers, he was articulate and well read. Eventually Bill brought a slight, pale, good-looking boy called Stuart Sutcliffe into their company.

Reckoned to be the most promising student of his generation at the college, Stu Sutcliffe was, at seventeen, the same age as John, but a year ahead in his course. Clever, quietly spoken, talented and hard-working, he had grown up in Prescot, a small town about nine miles east of Liverpool. His parents were Scottish and his mother had spent some years as a novitiate in a convent intending to be a nun before realising that she didn't have a vocation. This was the sort of detail that fascinated John, as did much of Stu's conversation. While the teaching staff failed to hold his attention with their art history lectures, Stu fascinated him by talking about existentialism – which he may only just have got to know about himself. Most probably Stu – whose image of himself led him to frequently wear sunglasses, even in cloudy Liverpool – was the sort of talented student John would like to have been. For his part, John's whimsical conversations and the generally restless anarchy of his daily life found a ready admirer in his new friend.

Opposites attract. John might not have been able to paint very well, and lettering bored him, but what he *could* do was talk, and a part of him began turning into a student intellectual. Conversation with Stu made him feel clever. And, to cap it all, Stu loved rock and roll, just as much as he did Kandinsky and Dali, Duchamp and Dadaism. Arthur Ballard summed up Stu's influence on John in a single line. 'Without Stu Sutcliffe, John wouldn't have known Dada from a donkey.'

But something more than that was involved. John's friendship with Stu would initiate the way he would begin to think of rock music as an art form. A synthesis of rock and art would, in a few years' time, be occurring at other colleges all around Britain, but for John it started one lunchtime in a pub in Liverpool.

All the Quarry Men had read how Elvis had begun his career by simply going into Sun Records in Memphis in 1954 and paying four dollars to make a record of himself singing. So when one of them heard that there was a studio in Kensington in Liverpool where they could do the same thing, they booked a session.

By this time the group was down to John, Paul, George and drummer Colin Hanton, but a school friend of Paul's called Duff Lowe sometimes played piano with the band and was invited along to the session. It took place, according to John, 'in the front room of some guy's house that he called a recording studio'. It was apparently all over in about half an hour, after which they were handed a single copy of the specially cut 78 rpm shellac record to take home. What they considered to be the A-side was a cover of 'That'll Be The Day', while the B-side was an early composition by Paul and George (who wrote the guitar break) called 'In Spite Of All The Danger', the melodic shape of which leant somewhat on Elvis's 'Trying To Get To You'.

'I sang both sides,' John would remember to a US radio interviewer in the mid-Seventies. 'I was such a bully in those days. I didn't even let Paul sing his own song.' Paul's contribution, as well as on guitar, was to add a strong harmony in the style of Phil in the Everly Brothers – shades of things to come.

Making a record meant that for the first time the Quarry Men had been able to hear what they sounded like, and it was, therefore, a big moment for the band. So after the session, they all chipped in to pay the seventeen shillings and sixpence cost (about £20 in today's money) and agreed to share the disc, passing it, one to the other, for a week each. Duff Lowe, being outside the group, got the record last . . . and would accidentally keep it for the next twenty-five years.

# 9

*'The copper came to the door . . . It was just like it's supposed to be, the way it is in the films . . . asking if I was her son'*

By the end of his first year at college, John was spending more and more nights with his mother and her family. When he was there, his two half-sisters, Julia and Jacqui, would sleep together in one room, while he was given Jacqui's bed. He was there on Saturday, 15 July 1958, watching television with the girls and Bobby Dykins when, at about seven in the evening, his mother announced that she was just going out to see Mimi. Dykins may well have had an inkling of what that might have been about, but John wouldn't.

Over the years there had been times when Mimi and Julia hadn't got on, but they had remained devoted to one another. And if John was a problem, it was one that they both now shared. Optimist that she was, Julia was sure things would turn out well for him; realist Mimi could only hope.

It was about John that Julia needed to talk to Mimi that night, and it can't have been easy for her. The problem was, she explained, he was spending so much time at her house that Bobby, who had just lost his job, was complaining about the cost of feeding him. That may just have been an excuse. John wasn't his son. It wouldn't have been surprising if Dykins, who was now unemployed and at home much more, simply resented John's frequent presence around the house.

Julia loved having John there, but she now suggested to Mimi that perhaps Bobby could be assuaged if her son visited a little less often. That wasn't unreasonable, and Mimi agreed to have a diplomatic word with her nephew when he returned to Mendips. With that settled, the conversation moved back to other matters. Then, at around a quarter to ten, Julia said goodbye to Mimi, and set off to catch her bus, running into Nigel Walley at the front garden gate as she did.

Nigel had been about to call at Mendips to see if John was at home.

But, as he wasn't, Julia and he chatted as they walked a little way along Menlove Avenue together, before they reached the junction with Vale Road. There they bade each other 'goodnight', Nigel turned up the hill to go home, and Julia crossed the first part of the dual carriageway.

Nigel hadn't got very far before he heard a loud screech of car brakes and a heavy thud. 'I turned to see her body flying through the air,' he told Beatles chronicler Mark Lewisohn. 'I rushed over. It wasn't a gory mess, but she must have had severe internal injuries. To my mind she'd been killed instantly.'

Inside Mendips, Mimi had heard the sound of the brakes too, and rushed out, followed by lodger Michael Fishwick. Julia's body was lying several feet in front of the car, a Standard Vanguard. She looked quite peaceful, Fishwick would later say. An autopsy would reveal that she had died as a result of a fractured skull. She was just forty-four.

John's memory of the night was told to the Beatles' biographer, Hunter Davies. 'The copper came to the door to tell us about the accident . . . It was just like it's supposed to be, the way it is in the films . . . asking if I was her son . . . It was the worst thing that ever happened to me. We'd caught up so much, me and Julia, in a few years . . . I thought, "fuck it, fuck it, fuck it! That's really fucked it. I've no responsibilities to anyone now . . ."'

He and Bobby Dykins took a taxi to Sefton General Hospital. 'I talked hysterically to the taxi driver all the way and ranted at him, the way you do.' When they got there, he refused to go in to see his mother's body. Dykins did. He broke down.

Pete bumped into John in Woolton the following day. He'd heard the news from Nigel. He told John how sorry he was.

'I know,' John replied. That was all.

They never discussed the subject again. 'It was like when a master beat him at school, he never gave anything away,' Pete would say. 'His exterior never showed his feelings.'

The funeral was held nine days later after which Julia was buried at Allerton Cemetery. Tea and sandwiches followed at Aunt Harrie's house in Woolton, where cousin Liela, who was now a medical student, sat with John's head in her lap. Neither spoke. There was nothing either could say. The one person John did want to see and talk to was his old girlfriend Barbara. Julia had always been kind to her. After the funeral he went over to her house and the two went for a walk in the park, where he talked and talked.

At the inquest it was revealed that the driver of the car had been an off-duty policeman, who shouldn't have even been driving unaccompanied as he didn't have a full driving licence. The verdict was 'misadventure' and he was banned from driving. He later resigned from the police force. A distraught Mimi is said to have shouted out 'Killer!' when the verdict was announced.

John would tell me that his mother was killed by a 'drunk driving, off-duty cop on a Saturday night', but the 'drunk' part may well have been his own embroidery of the facts. It's most likely that Julia simply stepped out from behind the bushes that separated the dual carriageway without realising how close was the oncoming car.

The favour that Julia had hated having to request of Mimi earlier that evening needn't now be carried out. John wouldn't be going to stay at Blomfield Road any more.

Julia's death changed the lives of several people. As Julia and Dykins were not legally married, her two daughters, then aged eleven and eight, were taken to Scotland the following day to stay with Aunt Mater. They were told that their mother was in hospital. Only several months later when they returned to Liverpool to live with Aunt Harrie and her husband Bert in Woolton did they learn that she was dead. Having lost their mother that night in July, they couldn't go home and would never live with their father again. Dykins, who also had children by an earlier marriage, took the death of Julia very badly. On a couple of occasions John would take Paul to visit him, sitting in the loneliness of Dykins' new flat and playing the records that Julia had liked.

Mimi's plans were also affected. She had inherited some money a few months earlier and was secretly considering going to live in New Zealand with Michael Fishwick. It may only have been the vague, unlikely, romantic dream of a middle-aged woman, which would never have come to anything, but that thought ended with Julia's death.

'I couldn't leave John now,' Mimi would later say. 'He had nobody.'

# 10

*'The underlying chip on my shoulder that I already had, got really big then'*

By his own admission John's behaviour deteriorated after the death of his mother. For the next two years he was, he would say, angry with the world. As his tongue and temper grew increasingly vicious he began to drink a lot, spending longer in Ye Cracke at lunchtime – and not now for the conversation. Throughout his life he would never be good with alcohol, often becoming cruel and unpleasant when he drank.

'It was mainly one long drinking session,' he would later tell *Rolling Stone*. 'But when you're eighteen or nineteen you can put away a lot of drink and not hurt your body so much . . . I was pretty self-destructive . . . smashed phone boxes . . . a little violent . . . It made me very bitter. The underlying chip on my shoulder that I already had, got really big then.'

One of his college girlfriends at that time, a pretty, dark-haired Liverpudlian called Thelma Pickles, identified his problem with one deadly accurate line when after being berated by him she eventually snapped back: 'Don't take it out on me because your mum's dead.'

His friendship with Paul helped. He didn't want to talk about Julia's death, as Paul didn't discuss losing his mother. But, though unspoken, it was something they shared as they continued to play and write together. Paul believes it may have drawn them closer together.

'We had a bond there that we never talked about,' he told Keith Howlett. 'I know he was shattered, but at that age you're not allowed to be devastated . . . We had private tears . . . but we knew we just had to get on with our lives. I'm sure I formed shells and barriers in that period that I've got to this day.'

It was a quiet time for the Quarry Men, with Len Garry having been taken ill with viral meningitis during the summer. And although

John and Paul visited him in hospital, his tea-chest bass had already become an anachronism. By the time Len came home from hospital, nine months later, the group had moved on. He wasn't needed any more.

Because drummers were still hard to find, Colin Hanton hung on in the original Quarry Men line-up for the longest, but even his grip was slipping. Having had less education than John or Paul, who were both not beyond flaunting their grammar school erudition, he was never close to either, and would become irritated when Paul would criticise him for playing his drums too loudly. Furthermore, rehearsals had been regularly held at Paul's home on Sundays, but, after complaints from the neighbours, Jim McCartney banned drums from his home, which meant Colin's weekly get-together with the others ended.

The end came for Colin in a drunken row on the top deck of the bus after an appearance in a club in the Norris Green suburb of Liverpool, when, as he told Hunter Davies, John began imitating the way deaf mute people spoke. It was part of John's sick, show-off routine, and on this occasion the adolescent Paul also joined in.

'It annoyed me because I had a couple of deaf and dumb friends,' Colin, who by then was almost twenty, remembered. 'It wasn't quite a fist fight. Just a lot of shouting and arguing . . . I got so pissed off by how they were behaving that I stood up, even though it wasn't my stop, collected my drums, left the bus, and left them. I never contacted them again. They never contacted me.'

All of which meant the Quarry Men didn't have a drummer.

As it happened, John soon didn't have a guitar, either. After two years of being hammered by him, the acoustic Gallotone instrument his mother had bought him had become unplayable. That meant that when John, Paul and George did get the occasional booking, they would sing with just two guitars as accompaniment. Nor were they still appearing under the name of the Quarry Men. On some nights the three of them would call themselves the Rainbow Boys because of their colourful shirts, while later on they would become Johnny and the Moondogs.

John always liked that name and it was the one they were using when, in late November, they made the thirty-mile train journey to Manchester to audition once again for the Carroll Levis amateur talent TV show. This time, despite their lack of instruments, but now with Paul, they were much more confident and professional. And, judging by the Manchester Hippodrome's audience reaction when John sang Buddy Holly's 'Think It Over', with the other two Moondogs on either side of him with their guitars, they did well.

Whether they would be wanted back to appear in a further heat, they didn't know, as they were to be informed by post. But as they were leaving John did something that could have ruined it for all of them. Without a guitar of his own, and spotting one leaning against a wall, he stole it and took it back to Liverpool. To him it was probably just a bit of teenage devilry – made more exciting by the presence of Paul and George as an audience, as he had once enjoyed petty shoplifting with Pete. But it was a dangerous and mean-spirited thing to do. Had he been caught, Johnny and the Moondogs would, at the very least, have been kicked out of the competition. The police might even have been called and John charged with stealing. Luckily for him, none of that occurred. But in the fun of the moment, didn't he wonder about the boy who owned the guitar, who might have been still paying for it on hire purchase, and who might not have been able to perform when his turn came in the competition?

This was a side of John Lennon that Colin Hanton, and others, disliked and that Jim McCartney feared. In many ways he was generous and welcoming. But there was a selfish streak there, too. As John would say of himself, he could be a real bastard.

As it happened, Johnny and the Moondogs did get through to the second round. And they returned to Manchester a few weeks later – without the purloined guitar, in case anyone should recognise it. Introduced on stage by Jackie Collins, before she became a famous author – and of whom John was overheard to comment admiringly, 'Look at the tits on that' – they sang another Buddy Holly song. Unfortunately, they had to leave before the end of the show to catch the last train back to Liverpool, so they never found out how well they'd done. But, no one ran after them with a contract to sign . . .

At college John was distracted and further drifting. Spending his lunch breaks talking to Stu Sutcliffe, he would then go round to Stu's nearby flat after classes, to put off the time when he had to return home to Mimi in Woolton. 'I never saw two teenage boys as close as those two,' tutor Arthur Ballard would remember. Other students would puzzle at the friendship the two shared, but Stu was helping fill a new vacuum that had appeared in John's life. Julia's home had been a friendly, lively place for John to go. He missed it.

Sometimes he would take Stu home to Mendips to meet Mimi. As might have been expected, she liked the other boy's polite, middle-class manners, and his accent, which was northern, like hers, but not the 'common' Liverpudlian Scouse of some of John's other friends. Stuart was, she would tell journalist Ray Coleman, 'the nicest of all John's friends'.

John was halfway through his second year at college when Buddy Holly was killed. The news reached Britain on the evening of 4 February 1959. Holly, along with the Big Bopper, the disc jockey who had made a hit out of the song 'Chantilly Lace', and seventeen-year-old Ritchie Valens who'd had a million seller with 'La Bamba', had decided to take a private flight after appearing at Clear Lake, Iowa, while on a winter tour of the US Midwest. The small plane in which they were travelling had crashed shortly after taking off from Mason City airport, killing all three as well as the pilot.

The newspapers, radio and TV duly covered the story, with a photograph of the little Beechcraft Bonanza plane lying wrecked in a snow-covered field after the bodies had been taken away. But Buddy Holly had belonged to a new culture that wasn't readily understood by middle-aged editors, and there was little appreciation of how innovative and influential he'd been. There would, therefore, be no long, earnest obituaries published, because there were no dedicated rock writers to file them. Some of the popular papers gave Holly a few showbiz columns, listing his hits and the fact that he had recently married a Puerto Rican girl. But there were bigger stories fighting for space that day, such as the American Airlines flight from Chicago that had crashed into New York's East River killing sixty-five passengers, and the results of a referendum in Switzerland that had overwhelmingly banned women from voting. The death of a pop singer, along with two others who were not as well known, was tragic, but it didn't dominate the news for very long.

To young rock and roll fans, however, Holly's death was more than shocking. It seemed inexplicable. Young rock stars didn't die in those days. Rock was new. Nothing like this had ever happened before. There was no internal memory by which fans could deal with it.

For John and Paul, as surely as for thousands of boys who were starting out with their own groups, the news was numbing. Holly had been only twenty-two, but, as a songwriter and guitarist, he'd been showing the way. When John next saw Paul and George, they could talk of little else, reminding each other of information they all knew, and how when Holly had appeared for one night only at the Liverpool Philharmonic just eleven months earlier, they, for some now regretted reason, hadn't gone to see him. What they had done was study his performance when he'd appeared earlier on ITV's *Sunday Night At The London Palladium*.

'That was the big occasion, to watch his fingers,' Paul would later tell a BBC interviewer. 'To see what guitar he had, to see if he played the chords right . . . to see if he used a capo . . . all the various technical things.'

For John, it had been the first time he'd seen a Fender guitar played while the singer sang. What Buddy Holly did with three chords made a songwriter out of him, he would write in a letter to a Holly fan in 1974.

And now the teacher was gone. The Quarry Men had been incorporating many Holly songs into their act for two years, but the songwriting lessons he'd unknowingly given John and Paul would serve them for life.

For a boy who spent so much of his time in all-male gangs, it was important to John to always have a steady girlfriend. There had been various liaisons at college but the longest-lasting would be with Thelma Pickles. Thelma was brave and clever, and streetwise enough not to take any verbal clatterings from him – and there were several – without sticking up for herself. Good friends rather than star-struck lovers, they just got on. He made her laugh. It wasn't a serious relationship, and when it reached its natural breaking point, they remained friends. They were never in love, simply, for a few months, a pair of like minds in a gang of young Liverpool students who were starting out in life.

Thelma's successor would be altogether different.

# 11

*'It was terrible. I couldn't stand being without her'*

Her name was Cynthia Powell, and, because she didn't have a strong Liverpool accent, she was thought by the other students to be 'a bit posh' – an inaccurate assumption, but one that had been reinforced when, during her first year at college, she'd turned up every day wearing a tweed twinset and with her brown hair permed. She lived in Hoylake, which was on the Wirral peninsula on the other side of the Mersey – 'over the water' in Scouse-speak, and she was shy and quite different from all the self-confident city girls around her. By the beginning of her second year, however, she'd learned how to present herself as an art student. The twinset had been replaced with a pair of black velvet pants, and her hair had been dyed blonde. Looking like this, John couldn't help but notice her.

The great fantasy woman for boys at the time was French actress Brigitte Bardot, who, with her pouty lips, had bared all (albeit in frustratingly gloomy shadow) in Roger Vadim's film *And God Created Woman* – which John had been to see. Obligingly, the weekly tabloid newspaper *Reveille* had then published a free life-sized photograph of Brigitte in a state of mild undress, for which John had sent off, and which, despite Mimi, he had then stuck to the ceiling above his bed. By the summer term of 1959, as far as John was concerned, Cynthia Powell was his Brigitte Bardot fantasy made flesh and blood in Liverpool 8.

John's abrasive confidence had seemed threatening to a girl from Hoylake, so the two had never spoken in their first year. But then John found himself relegated to the dreaded lettering class. Sitting behind her, he would call her 'Miss Hoylake', and ask first for a pencil, and then a rubber, because he never seemed to have either with him. Then he would mock-scold other boys with the warning, 'No dirty jokes in front of Miss Powell.' It was John's way of showing her that he was interested.

Cynthia fancied him for his sheer attitude. She would later say that, in his drainpipe jeans and his uncle's old overcoat, he looked like a bohemian, Teddy boy and comic all at once. And she didn't know how to respond to a big-headed, loud-talking comedian.

He often took his guitar to college, and one afternoon while he was fooling around with it after class he jokily began to play and sing the old song 'Ain't She Sweet' – looking directly at her. He could see that she was embarrassed, but also that she was enjoying it. They got together just before the summer term ended when a group of students were given permission to hold a party in the college. Couples were already jiving and smooching when John got there – late. Jeff Mahomed, who was going out with one of Cynthia's friends, was encouraging: 'She likes you, you know.' Of course he knew.

Never much of a dancer, at some point John indicated the floor. 'Do you want to go out with me?' he shouted above the music.

Cynthia was taken by surprise. 'I'm sorry, but I'm engaged to a fella in Hoylake,' she replied. In truth she and a window cleaner called Barry weren't actually engaged, but, after going out together for a couple of years, their relationship seemed to be heading that way.

Seeing it as a rejection, John immediately bit back. 'I didn't ask you to fucking marry me, did I!' They danced on.

That was the start of their romance. When the party finished, some of the students made their way to Ye Cracke. Cynthia went with her girlfriends. At first, biding his time, John purposely ignored her. So Cynthia chatted to her pals, had a Guinness and a glass of cider, and, finally, assuming that John had been put off her, turned to leave.

He stopped her at the door with a joke about her being a nun, bought her another drink, and eventually took her outside and kissed her. 'Stu has a room,' he told her. Then, taking her hand, he led her down the street to buy some fish and chips, before they went along to the Georgian house in Percy Street where Stu shared a flat with several other students. John was, he would later say, 'exultant at having picked her up'.

Cynthia would remember Stu's home as a large room, with no curtains, no bed, and just a mattress on the floor which was surrounded by clothes, art materials, empty cigarette packets and books.

They made love for the first time that night. Then, getting dressed again, John hurried her down to the station for her to catch the last train back to Hoylake. He was in love.

A decade later, after they had divorced, he would deny that he'd ever felt that way about her, but his many love letters to her give the lie to that. His denials were just John, rewriting his own past. He was actually besotted with her. Everything important that he did in life, writing, playing, drawing his cartoons, love and hate, was done with an urgent, impulsive passion, as he lived, in his words, 'on the spur of the moment', and Cynthia was his new passion.

That they should have got together at the very end of the summer term was frustrating for both of them, because it meant they were soon going to be separated. Cynthia was going away with her mother to stay with relatives in the south of England, and, for the only time in his life, John was about to do some physical work.

For months he had been begging Mimi to help him buy a new guitar – the one that he had stolen in Manchester being of dubious quality – and finally she agreed. But only up to a point. He would have to do his bit, too, she insisted, by getting a summer job to help pay for it. So, when a college friend told him that there was work available for the two of them labouring for his father on a building site in a little village called Scarisbrick, he took it.

He should have looked at the map before he agreed. Scarisbrick was situated in the middle of the West Lancashire Plain, and to get there involved catching a bus the six miles to the centre of Liverpool, then taking a train from Exchange Station for twelve miles to the market town of Ormskirk. There his friend's father would pick him up and drive him a further four miles out into the fields of Scarisbrick, where the work involved clearing the ground for a new waterworks. Basically, the job was with a pick axe and shovel, and John complained about it every day, praying, he would say, that the train would crash before it reached Ormskirk. He lasted six weeks, before he was sacked, as being 'unsuitable'. He would be remembered by his fellow labourers as the boy who, when it was his turn to make the tea, put the kettle on the primus stove having forgotten to put any water in it. The result was that the kettle had a hole burnt right through its base.

That he lasted so long was extraordinary, but the wages enabled him to drag Mimi down to Frank Hessy's music shop in Liverpool's Whitechapel and buy his first electric guitar on hire purchase. It was a Hofner Club 40 semi-solid model and cost about £30 (that's around £660 in today's money). Mimi signed as his guarantor, insisting that John would have to pay all the instalments himself. Since he was usually short of money and the weekly allowance that Mimi gave him hardly covered his cigarettes, beer and bus fares, it seems unlikely that he always did.

The new guitar came just in time. The rump of the Quarry Men, John, Paul and George, had scarcely played together for months, in that a group without a drummer was hardly a band in the eyes of potential bookers. But an opening had just occurred at a Victorian mansion in the suburb of West Derby owned by Indian-born Mona Best and her husband Johnny – a well-known boxing promoter in Liverpool. As John would soon discover, Mona was a spirited, entrepreneurial woman who had struck on the idea of turning the basement of her home into a youth club called the Casbah Coffee Club, where her sons' friends might meet. One of her sons was a good-looking, quiet boy called Peter.

It was George's connections that led John and Paul to the Casbah. He'd now left school and was employed as a trainee electrician at a Liverpool department store, and, with no gigs for what remained of the Quarry Men, he'd been playing with other bands. One of them had been booked by Mona for the opening night of the Casbah, but the band members had fallen out, and now Mona needed another group quickly. George had the answer.

Naturally, Mona wanted to meet the replacements before they played, whereupon, learning that John was an art student, she instantly detailed him, Paul and George to finish off painting her new basement club. Their decorations of stars, a dragon, rainbows and a beetle, along with a profile of John drawn by Cynthia, are still there in what is now an English Heritage-listed building.

Joined by yet another guitarist who had his own amp, and without which the band couldn't perform, the Quarry Men played at the Casbah almost every Saturday night for the next couple of months. Paul would remember those weeks as when 'the Beatles really got started' – although they didn't yet call themselves the Beatles.

The Casbah often gets overlooked in the Beatles' story, but it provides a snapshot of late Fifties teenage Britain – of how a big suburban home that had once been owned by the local Conservative Association became a club where two hundred teenagers, some arriving on their bikes, could go and listen to a local band . . . and where there was no alcohol and no drugs, just a frothy coffee machine, bottles of pop and crisps on sale. And where, if the Quarry Men weren't playing, the

Searchers or Gerry and the Pacemakers might be.

It was also the place where John and the other Quarry Men would first get to know Mona Best's son, Pete.

Back at college in September, John and Cynthia resumed their relationship. She'd broken up with the 'fella in Hoylake' as soon as she'd become involved with John, but she was a pretty girl and inevitably other boys fancied her. That was something John couldn't tolerate, and when, at a college dance, another student asked her to dance, he attacked him and had to be dragged away.

It was all very intense, as though, having won her, John was terrified of losing her. He had a phrase he liked to use as a joke – 'I'm jealous of the mirror'. But his degree of possessiveness wasn't a joke. As he was scared of the possibility of her being unfaithful with another boy, he was also jealous of her past with Barry, wanting to know every detail of everything she'd done with him.

Cynthia was a sweet young woman and extremely likeable who, while she never appeared to be particularly interested in rock music, would always defer to John's opinion, intelligence and talent. But, as she would later wonder, was she some kind of emotional substitute for the mother he had so recently lost?

'I was hysterical,' John would say in 1966. 'I was jealous of anyone she had anything to do with. I demanded absolute trust from her . . . I was neurotic, taking out all my frustrations out on her . . . There was something wrong with me.'

At one point his insecurities went too far. One night, Cynthia and a friend accepted a lift home in a car with a couple of boys. It was all innocent enough, but she made the mistake of telling John about it the next day. He followed her down the stairs at college into the Ladies and hit her, catching her face so hard that her head hit a wall.

She broke up with him immediately, and began avoiding him at college, although his eyes would find hers in class and in the canteen. The separation lasted for three months, until in the end he telephoned her, told her how sorry he was and begged her to come back to him. She did. He was still difficult, and his anger could, she said, be terrifying. But he was never, she told me, physically violent to her again during the years they were together.

'It was terrible,' he would admit of their time apart. 'I couldn't stand being without her.'

More than ten years later, after undergoing primal therapy, he would reflect on how many of his songs had been unknowingly autobiographical. A consideration of one of the earliest songs he ever wrote, 'I Call Your Name', might have been revealing. On the surface, it is an anguished, self-recriminatory lament about the loss of a girlfriend. Most boys understand that feeling. But might he have recognised that the lyrics were a reflection of his own desperate mood when Cynthia left him? 'Was I to blame for being unfair?' he asks in the song, as he details how he can't sleep at night or carry on without his girlfriend.

Cynthia, like John, had recently lost a parent, her father having died from lung cancer a year earlier. So she understood the ache of loss. She also knew what she was getting into with John. 'I fell in love with a bad boy, whom I knew to be a bad boy,' she told me. 'John wasn't the best, but he wasn't the worst. But if my father had still been alive, he wouldn't have got past the front door of our house.'

As it happened, when John did visit her house in Hoylake – which, despite her apparent poshness to Liverpudlians, she would describe as 'a modest semi about half the size of Mendips' – her worries that John would upset her mother proved unfounded. He was charm itself. Her two older brothers liked him, too.

Her own visit to meet Mimi was more fraught. 'She was friendly but cool,' she said. 'Regal, almost,' although she served them chips and egg for their evening meal.

'Don't worry about Mimi,' John told her as he took her to the bus stop after her first visit. 'If I like you, she'll like you too.'

Cynthia wasn't so sure about that. Later on, though, she came to see that Mimi's froideur hadn't been personal. Mimi just 'didn't think any girl was good enough for her boy', she said.

The heat often goes out of teenage relationships after a couple of months. But it didn't with John and Cynthia. He would make up love poems about her, send her love letters, and draw funny little cartoons all through the next term and for years after.

Traditionally the art college ended the autumn term with a pantomime, and in 1959 it was *Cinderella,* in which John made, not only his writing debut, as one of the play's two authors, but his acting one as well. Cast as the Ugly Sisters, and dressed in a pair of pink corsets, a blue velvet dress, a straw hat and blue feather decorations which had been given to them by life class model June Furlong, he and Jeff Mahomed mugged their way through some cod Chaucerian dialogue.

And then it was Christmas, and John drew a card for Cynthia that was festooned in hearts and kisses. 'Our first Christmas,' he wrote, and then added, 'I love you, yes, yes, yes.'

As Cynthia would later realise, with a change of pronoun and a more casual vernacular, it was a message that four and a half years later he would turn into one of the Beatles' biggest hits.

# 12

*'Paul could have gone to university. He could have become,
I don't know, Dr McCartney . . . I ruined his life!'*


John moved out of Mendips and into a flat with Stuart in January 1960. 'I feel like a baby living at home,' he had told Mimi. Not surprisingly, she didn't like the idea but he'd got around her by promising he would go home once a week – although it was double-edged in that it gave him the opportunity to take her his washing and get a decent cooked meal. She complained, but went along with it. One night a week was better than him not going home at all. When things were bad between them, there would be much shouting and arguing. But in better times it would be Mimi affecting despair at what she saw as his silliness and sloth – while being still amused by his joking. He could always make her laugh. When he was in the mood, he could make everyone laugh. He was an entertainer.

Stu's new flat was the first floor of a house in Gambier Terrace, an imposing 1830s street of grand homes, the front room of which overlooked Liverpool Cathedral. No students could afford to live there today, but in 1960, although the front door was between two Doric columns, and the hall, stairs and rooms were vast, the entire building was in a crumbling state of disrepair. John didn't notice that. Going home to sleepy Woolton after classes had made him feel more like a commuter than a student. Having his own place – well, a part of a room he shared with Stu – in the heart of Georgian Liverpool, unchained at last from Mimi's strictures, was pure freedom. Paul and George liked it, too, sometimes staying over on a Saturday night and sleeping on the floor after an all-night party. As well as Stu, the flat was occupied by three other students, two of whom were girls. In 1960 to be living in a student flat with girls was almost 'permissive', a word that hadn't yet found its place in the vocabulary of most people.

Apart from its convenience, Gambier Terrace also meant that John had somewhere to be alone with Cynthia – the obliging Stuart being regularly asked to make himself scarce for a while. And when Cynthia fibbed to her mother about staying the night with her pal Phyllis and ended up in bed with John instead, Stuart would be accommodating about that, too.

By this time the Quarry Men's appearances at the Casbah had ended after a row over whether the extra guitarist (who owned the amp) should receive his share of the pay for a night when he'd been too unwell to play. Mona Best as the employer thought he should. John, Paul and George disagreed, insisting that his share of the fee should be split between the three of them. Mona made the rules in her club and wasn't going to be dictated to by a mouthy John Lennon. If they didn't like it they could go. They went.

It was a big mistake because for a while nobody else wanted them. The trouble was, they lacked a bass player and a drummer. Reflecting on the Beatles' early years, John would often stress how important it was that three of them had been to grammar schools and one to art college. 'That was what made the Beatles different,' he would say. 'We were pretty well educated . . . Paul could have gone to university. He could have become, I don't know, Dr McCartney . . . I ruined his life!' Which, apart from the joke at the end, was true. The education that the Beatles had, especially John and Paul who would become the main songwriters, did make them different from rival groups of that time – and very different from the working-class early American rockers. But in Liverpool in 1960, that education could also be something of a handicap.

In the years since the skiffle explosion, many Liverpool youths had evolved into good rock and roll bands. But, while skiffle had been acoustic, rock and roll was an electric form of music that relied upon amplifiers, electric guitars and bass and a decent set of drums.

Most boys in rival groups had left school at sixteen and taken jobs to fund their musical aspirations. A group that included a schoolboy and a penniless student couldn't hope to compete with the expenditure on instruments and equipment that was now necessary. Over the months several of John's college friends had been offered the chance of joining the band, if they would buy and learn to play an electric bass. But none had taken him up on the chance, either because they weren't musical, or because they couldn't afford to buy a bass.

Then one day, Stuart had a stroke of luck. In the autumn of 1959, he had entered a painting in the John Moores Liverpool Exhibition at the Walker Art Gallery, only to discover that millionaire philanthropist John Moores himself, the owner of Littlewoods Pools and over fifty department stores, had bought it for £65. That would be about £1,400 in today's money. It was a fortune, and John, aided by Paul and George, knew exactly how Stu should spend some of it – either on a set of drums or a bass. The choice was his.

Stu couldn't play either instrument, or indeed any instrument, but the bass seemed the easier choice. So, accompanied by John and George, he was walked to Frank Hessy's shop where he bought a large Hofner 333. When he confessed that he didn't know if he could ever learn to play it, John was scornful. 'Of course you can,' he insisted. 'Anyone can play the bass. It's only got four fucking strings.' Perhaps what John should have said was that anyone who was 'naturally musical could learn to play the bass'. There's a difference. But the deed was done. Stu was in the band whether he could play or not.

Quite what the group he had just joined were even called had been uncertain for some time, when John suggested a new name. He'd been musing over what a great name 'The Crickets' had been for Buddy Holly's band, and had been going through friendly insects like ladybirds (obviously unsuitable), spiders and grasshoppers, when . . . 'The idea of beetles came into my head. I decided to spell it BEAtles to make it look like beat music as a joke,' he would remember. So, the Beatles was the name by which the ex-Quarry Men, ex-Rainbow Boys, ex-Johnny and the Moondogs, would become known.

Now they had a new name and a bass; what they didn't have was an amplifier that could take more than one guitar. The college entertainment committee solved that when Stuart and Bill Harry convinced them that an amp was essential for dances. As the Beatles were the only band to play at such evenings, they very soon appropriated it for themselves . . . and, in the piratical environment of nascent rock and roll, never bothered to give it back.

The admission of Stuart into the band may have seemed a simple solution to an ongoing problem, but it also created a new tension. John didn't have a monopoly on jealousy. Paul could be jealous, too. Once it had been John and Pete Shotton, inseparable friends and partners, and, as Pete had noticed, John always needed a partner. Then Paul had replaced Pete, and Lennon and McCartney had been born. Over months that friendship had grown into something more than the swapping of chords and lyrics, and the high harmony that Paul would sing over John's lower voice.

In fact that Easter of 1960 John and Paul would even sing as a duo, when they hitch-hiked to Caversham in the south of England where a friend was running a pub. For a week, John and Paul, who had to sleep together in the same single bed, would entertain the regulars under the name the Nerk Twins. They were best friends and there was a mutual admiration between the two. While John would always recognise Paul's greater gift for melody and musical craft – no matter what he might sometimes say years later – Paul admired John for his unalloyed bravery in speaking his mind, and his ability to summarise a thought in a single, often witty, line.

There was more. When John had been living at Mendips, Paul would sometimes go over on his bicycle to find him at a typewriter in his bedroom composing a nonsense piece. Or, perhaps, it might have been a poem that John was writing – something that played with words and images in the style of Dylan Thomas by way of radio star Stanley Unwin, whose corruption of everyday English turned sentences into clever-sounding nonsense. John liked to call that style gobbledegook, a wartime word he'd picked up from the radio, when presenters poked fun at seemingly unintelligible official documents. Always a great talker, John loved words and slogans and enjoyed bending and reshaping their meanings. And Paul, who was studying English Literature at school, and seeing himself as a culture vulture, was impressed. At one point the two even started to write a play together, before quickly deciding that they didn't know what to write about and that song lyrics were more their metier.

So, with a friendship that was now based on more than music, it was inevitable that, with the introduction of Stuart to the group, Paul began to feel like an outsider. It was hardly Stu's fault that John had dragged him into the band. But feeling increasingly cast aside, the perfectionist in Paul couldn't help hearing the wrong notes the new bassist was playing. John would have heard those wrong notes too, but must have consoled himself with the thought that, given time, Stuart would improve. He would, but he would never be good enough. When the occasion demanded, however, John had an infinite capacity to deny the evidence of his own ears.

When Paul was older he would be embarrassed by his youthful jealousy. 'It was something I didn't deal with very well,' he would admit.

'George and I were always slightly jealous of John's other friendships. He was the older fella . . . and . . . when Stuart came in . . . we had to take a bit of a back seat.'

It wouldn't be the only time that Paul felt his partnership with John was being put under pressure by a newcomer.

John grew up a lot during those months in Gambier Terrace. In his overcoat and jeans, he enjoyed being the eccentric art student, while the beatnik ethos of the time, with its romance of the hip artist, would stay with him for life.

Parts of central Liverpool, drab during the day, would come alive at night, and a coffee bar called the Jacaranda, which was down the hill towards the centre of Liverpool, had recently become a focal point for students. It was an exotic place, which had been recently opened by thirty-year-old, bearded Allan Williams, the son of a local dance promoter, and his eye-catching Chinese-Liverpudlian wife Beryl.

Initially, John had gone there at lunchtime with his college friends, where they had dreamed magnificent futures for themselves in which they turned their city into a cultural beacon. But now that he was living in town, he and Stuart, often joined by Paul and George, would hang out in the evenings in the Jacaranda's cellar, which had been converted into a small nightclub.

He wasn't there the night that 'beat poet' Royston Ellis turned up. Ellis had come to Liverpool to give a talk at the university. But, being disappointed with the students' reaction, he'd made his way to the Jacaranda, where he fell into conversation with George Harrison. Intrigued by this almost-famous poet, George quickly invited Ellis back to Gambier Terrace.

Of all the group, John was the most impressed by Ellis. He had never met a real poet before, and the idea of fusing rock music with poems (which Ellis would do later with guitarist Jimmy Page in the musician's pre-Led Zeppelin days) captured his imagination. But particularly interesting was Ellis's advice on how to get high by chewing the Benzedrine cardboard strips which were then to be found inside Vicks nasal inhalers. Setting aside alcohol, this would be the first time John tried any kind of drug. It was, Ellis told the Beatles, the fashion in London.

But when Ellis then read them a poem about a homosexual act (then still a crime in Britain) and told them that one in four men was probably homosexual without knowing it, they were nonplussed. Paul probably summed up all the Beatles' reactions best in an interview in 1997 when he remembered: 'We looked at the group. "One in every four." It literally meant one of us was gay. Oh, fucking hell, it's not me, is it!!!'

The Beatles didn't know very much about homosexuality. In those days it wasn't much talked about in their circle. It was sex with girls that was never far from John's thoughts, but, in those pre-Pill times when pregnancy always loomed, that, too, was a subject that usually came wrapped in code and euphemism. So, John would talk about 'edge of the bed virgins' to describe girls who would say 'no' at the crucial moment; while the uniquely Liverpudlian phrase 'getting off at Edge Hill' described coitus interruptus, Edge Hill being the small station where long-distance trains would stop to let suburban travellers alight, immediately before terminating in Liverpool Lime Street. Finally there was the ultimate act – 'going for a five-mile run', John would say, which was what a boy and a girl did when she didn't say 'no'. As a figure of speech it may have been a little bit of Lennonesque, John's explanation being that it came from something he'd read, probably in the *Reader's Digest*. For years 'a doctor' would regularly write there about the dreaded perils and occasional medical benefits of sex – one of the few pluses being that the physical effort expended during intercourse was the equivalent of going on a five-mile run, and therefore good for the heart. John had never been one for long-distance running (in fact he'd got into trouble at Quarry Bank for skiving off during a school cross country) but he would always be an enthusiastic partaker in a metaphorical five-miler.

History would show that the Jacaranda was a fortunate choice of meeting place for the Beatles, because not only was its owner Allan Williams keen on rock and roll, he was also a fledgling promoter with growing connections. And in 1960 he made one very big connection with Larry Parnes, then the most famous pop manager in London.

Hearing that Williams had been asked by Parnes to find a backing group to tour with Liverpool star Billy Fury, every local band put their names forward. Included among them were the Beatles, although, since Williams knew them as the Silver Beetles, that was the name they would be booked under.

To no one's surprise the Silver Beetles failed the Fury audition, as did all the other local groups. There was, however, a consolation prize on offer. If they could find a drummer, they could go on a nine-day tour of Scotland backing a second-division Parnes singer called Johnny Gentle. They found one. He was, by day, a forklift truck driver called Thomas Moore – Tommy to his mates.

The tour was a surprise, and a big moment in all their careers, but it had come at an awkward time. Paul should have been preparing for his imminent A-levels, but managed to convince his father that the break would do him good; George took time off from his apprenticeship, and John and Stuart simply skipped college and final exams. And while Cynthia finished off John's course work for him, Mimi was never even told.

A tour of ballrooms and church halls in remote towns in Scotland wasn't much, but at £18 each it was the first tour the group had ever done. At last they were being employed as professionals and travelling around Scotland in a Dormobile was, for the first couple of days, a lark. After that, however, the claustrophobia of being locked in together began to fray the nerves, with John unable to resist teasing the stand-in drummer.

Why would John pick on the outsider, especially as the drummer had taken time off from his job at a bottle works to accompany them? It's difficult to understand. Had it begun as a defence mechanism in his broken childhood? Or had he simply been born with an impatient and mean streak that meant he didn't suffer fools gladly, nor anyone else who didn't have the wit or the devil in him to fight back?

Nor was it only Tommy whom he picked on. Stuart may have been his room-mate, but on the road, the newcomer to the group came in for it too – and not only from John. Paul and George, encouraged by their leader, joined in the sniping as well. 'We were terrible,' John would remember. 'We'd tell Stu he couldn't sit with us. We'd tell him to go away, and he did . . . It was all stupid but that is what we were like.'

The journey from Liverpool to Inverness is 375 miles, after which there was much to-ing and fro-ing between little Highland towns. So, the Silver Beetles were hardly hitting the high spots. But this was something new for them. John got on well with Johnny Gentle, whose real name was John Askew, an apprentice carpenter also from

Liverpool, and to whom he gave a few lines for a song that Gentle later recorded; while Paul and George found themselves being asked for their autographs for the very first time. Even Stuart seemed to enjoy the tour. Only Tommy Moore absolutely regretted it, particularly after the Dormobile collided with a car and he was thrown against the band's equipment, losing two teeth, being concussed and taken to hospital.

If things weren't bad enough for him, that night John turned up at the hospital with the tour organiser, and, despite Tommy's concussion, insisted the drummer get out of bed and go and play with them. According to Tommy, he had to play with a bandage around his head, with John constantly glancing back at him in amusement.

'That John Lennon has a fucking perverse sense of humour' was something John would grow used to hearing about himself.

# 13

*'We knew this guy who had a drum kit. He could keep one beat
going for long enough, so we took him to Germany'*

Despite Tommy's misfortunes and opinion of him, John could at last
see that the future was beginning to look just a little less opaque.
The Beatles had played every night for over a week and he'd enjoyed
his first proper glimpse of show business. The band had developed,
too. Instead of either he or Paul singing the lead, they would increasingly now, on some songs, sing together in a basic harmony.
It didn't happen all the time, but when it did they both enjoyed it.
Other groups didn't do that. The fashion then was for there to be
one lead singer and a backing band. They were two lead singers. But
they didn't sound like the Everly Brothers, who sang in such close
harmony, with such similar voices, that they sometimes sounded as
though they were singing in unison. John and Paul didn't ever sound
the same. They had two distinct voices when they sang together.

Meanwhile, now that they were back in Liverpool, Allan Williams
was finding the Beatles more work. Much of that meant crossing the
Mersey and risking the wrath of rival Teddy boy gangs from Wallasey
and Birkenhead. A band could get caught in the middle of a turf war
there if it didn't take care, and for some reason the Beatles' version of
the Olympics song 'Hully Gully' would often be the spark that lit the
fuse for mayhem to begin.

With Tommy Moore having returned to his regular evening shift
at work, Paul, much against his will, stepped in on the drums, using
his brother Michael's rarely used set. Competent drummer as he was,
he didn't enjoy it. He was proud of his rendition of the Ray Charles
song 'What'd I Say', but it wasn't easy to sing with much passion in
a sitting position while hitting the drums at the same time. On top
of that, it bugged him to see Stuart, who was still struggling with his
bass, up there at the front of the stage with John, while he was stuck
at the back.

All the same, those appearances in ballrooms around Liverpool were rarely less than exciting as, with new confidence as well as new hire-purchased amplifiers, the Beatles were learning how to turn up the heat on rock and roll.

Less boisterous was an afternoon that Williams arranged for them to back a striptease artiste called Janice in a small club in Liverpool's Upper Parliament Street. It was a bizarre gig in that when the Beatles arrived, Janice presented them with the sheet music for 'The Sabre Dance' and 'The Gipsy Fire Dance'. That was the music she liked to strip to.

None of the Beatles, however, could read music. Could she hum the tunes, they enquired. Apparently not. In the end, with Paul on a tom-tom, they improvised by playing Duane Eddy's 'Ramrod' and John's interpretation of the 'Harry Lime Theme Cha-Cha' as, bra by tassel by knicker, Janice took off her clothes.

By mid-summer, Paul could go back to his guitar when another drummer joined them. He was a year older than John and he was good. Unfortunately, hardly had he settled in than he was issued with his call-up papers for National Service, and would soon find himself in the British Army in Kenya fighting the Mau Mau insurrection.

John had mixed thoughts as he watched the drummer go. All his life he'd heard teachers telling him 'the Army will make a man of you', which had seemed a terrifying prospect. But then, like a gift from God, had come the government decision to abolish National Service in 1960. No one born after 3 October 1939 would be called up. John had missed it by just over a year.

Would the Beatles have survived had John, or any of the group, been forced to take two years out of his life at the age of eighteen to become a soldier? It seems unlikely. The Education Act of 1944 had funded grammar schools and art colleges, both of which would have a profound effect on the Beatles and their music. Now, another side effect of government policy further helped create the climate that made some of the Sixties cultural changes possible.

Not that John had any idea of what his future would hold. The only certainty in his life was that, as with Quarry Bank High School, he left art college, having done virtually no work for three years, without a single qualification.

Back in Mendips, Mimi had her say. 'That's very nice, John. So, what are you going to do now?'

Which was pretty well the attitude being taken by Paul's father, who was naturally upset when the A-level results came through. His son had passed in only one subject – English Literature. George was in trouble, too. On returning from Scotland in May, he'd been sacked from his job for taking time off without permission. His parents, usually so encouraging, hadn't been pleased, so, to escape their nagging, he'd moved into Gambier Terrace with Stuart and John. Not for long. Following some bad publicity in a national tabloid Sunday newspaper, Stuart and the other students there had been given notice of eviction.

Once again it was Allan Williams at the Jacaranda who came up with an unlikely solution to their problems. Just as he had linked up with Larry Parnes, Williams had now forged a relationship with a German club owner from Hamburg called Bruno Koschmider. Rock music was rapidly becoming popular in Germany, and Koschmider wanted American-sounding bands who sang in English to play for the US servicemen who would flood into Hamburg when they were on leave. There was a reason for Hamburg's popularity. Having been a port for more than a thousand years, the city had built a reputation for being a place which, with its strip clubs, bars and prostitutes, welcomed single men who were away from their wives and girlfriends. Williams had already supplied Koschmider with the Liverpool group Derry and the Seniors to play in his main club, the Kaiserkeller. Now, spotting a good business, the German wanted another group for the imminent opening of a smaller club around the corner, the Indra.

The Beatles were not Williams's first choice. But the successful Gerry and the Pacemakers, Cass and the Cassanovas and Rory Storm and the Hurricanes were all unavailable. So, who else was there? 'Well,' Williams must have been thinking, 'I suppose there's always the Beatles . . .'

But, once again, the Beatles didn't have a drummer. And a proper rock and roll band had to have a drummer.

They soon found one, back in Mona Best's Casbah Club in West Derby. Mona's son Pete had a brand new set of drums. Quickly an audition was arranged. Pete, they agreed, on hearing him play, was good enough. 'He could keep one beat going for long enough, so we took him to Germany,' John, somewhat snidely, would say of the Beatles' first full-time drummer.

Pete, who had been a promising rugby player at his grammar

school, Liverpool Collegiate, was a year younger than John, quiet and good-looking. Would he fit in with the Beatles? It's unlikely that John gave it much thought. None of the Beatles had passports, and, with less than a week to get them before leaving for Hamburg, such finer considerations were put on hold.

With the exception perhaps of Mona Best, none of the group's parents was happy about the venture. George's father thought his son should settle down and get a proper job, while his mother fretted that at seventeen George was too young to go abroad. Jim McCartney was dismayed that his son wasn't going back to school to retake his A-levels and blamed John. As he'd warned, John was leading his son into trouble. For his part, Stuart didn't have to go to Hamburg. He could have stayed at the art college. But John wanted him to go, so he'd agreed. His mother was distraught that he was walking away from a brilliant career. She blamed John, too, as did lecturer Arthur Ballard. He'd had such high hopes for Stuart. As for Mimi, not for one minute did she believe John when he told her that he would soon be earning £100 a week. She knew, though, that when he wanted something badly enough, he would get it.

Cynthia knew it, too. Mimi was staying with one of her sisters in Birkenhead the night before John left, so he and Cynthia slept together in his single bed at his room in Mendips. Swearing undying love and fidelity to one another while they were apart, they promised to write to each other every day. Cynthia meant what she said about being faithful, and John kept his promise to write her lots of letters.

# 14

## 'I might have been born in Liverpool,
## but I grew up in Hamburg'

They met outside the Jacaranda, where they stuffed their guitars, drums, amps and suitcases into the back of an old Morris minibus. John was the last to arrive, having only that morning managed to obtain his passport from the Liverpool Passport Office. Mimi didn't come to wave him goodbye, but Cynthia was there.

It was a crush in the minibus, because as well as the Beatles, there was Williams, who was driving, his wife Beryl, her brother-in-law, Barry Chang, and Williams's friend 'Lord Woodbine' who led a steel band. They faced a long journey. First were the two hundred miles to London, where, at a stop in Soho, they picked up a German waiter who wanted to go home. That made it ten on the bus, which was then driven a further eighty-five miles out to Harwich on the Essex coast, after which came the one-hundred-and-twenty-five-mile North Sea crossing to the Hook of Holland.

None of the Beatles had ever been abroad before, so everything seemed distant and strange, except perhaps the amount of bomb damage that was still visible as they drove through the Netherlands. Parts of Liverpool, mainly near the docks, had areas of wasteland where whole blocks of houses had been blitzed and then pulled down. But the war had raged street by street right through Holland only fifteen years earlier, and the signs were still everywhere.

Being more than ten years older than most of his passengers, the war meant more to Williams than the Beatles. So, when they reached Arnhem, the scene of one of its most famous battles at the bridge over the Rhine, he insisted they pay their respects at the war memorial. For some unexplained reason John stayed in the minibus. After that, they drove on into the town itself, where, while looking around the medieval streets, John stole a harmonica from a music shop.

It was a strange and risky thing to do, and Alan Williams was not pleased when he found out, as, back on the bus, John began to play his stolen toy. Other than wanting to be the centre of attention and to show off in front of everyone, perhaps especially before new boy Pete Best, it is again difficult to understand John's rationale. Hamburg was the biggest break the Beatles had ever had, but, with twenty-five miles still to go before they even reached Germany, he had deliberately chosen to jeopardise his part in the venture for the momentary thrill of shoplifting. As with his escapades with Pete Shotton when they'd been kids, he only pulled these stunts when he had an audience there to gasp at his audacity.

Everything about Hamburg came as a surprise, and not always a pleasant one. Although John's work permit described his purpose in Germany as being that of 'musical entertainment', it was soon clear that the Beatles weren't going to be treated like professionals. Their living quarters hadn't been negotiated before their arrival, and only when Williams complained did Koschmider arrange for them to be billeted in two very low cell-like storerooms, behind the screen at a soft porn cinema, the Bambi Kino. For sleeping there were four camp beds and a couch and very few, very old covers. There were no cooking facilities and the only water was from the cold tap in the cinema's ladies' toilet down the corridor. With no drawers or coat hangers, they lived out of their suitcases. 'It was a pigsty . . . a run down fleapit,' was John's most polite description of his new home as he, George and Stuart grabbed the slightly larger room and Paul and Pete got the other. Not surprisingly, during all the months that they would be in Hamburg on that first visit, they spent as little time as possible in their rooms.

   One of the first songs John had learned to play had been 'Maggie May', which is about a mythical Liverpool prostitute, and the Beatles were well aware of the girls who patrolled some of the streets of their own city. But the neon-lit Reeperbahn in the St Pauli dockside district of Hamburg, where they were living, was unlike anywhere they had ever seen before. Everywhere they looked, sex was brazenly, guiltlessly, joyfully on offer. Whether it was the half-naked women sitting, somehow simultaneously both provocative and bored, in the upstairs windows of a terrace of houses along Herbertstrasse, or the cheeky girls in the strip clubs – the message was unavoidable. The women they were now going to meet had a totally different outlook on sex from the more cautious English girls with whom they had grown up.

The Indra wasn't a big club, and for the Beatles' first night there, John, Paul, George and Stuart wore a stage uniform of black jeans and lilac jackets that had been specially made for them by a tailor neighbour of Paul's in Liverpool. Unsure of what to play, and what to say to the customers – and not knowing how much English was understood – they were too diffident and not an immediate success. Bruno Koschmider, a formidable-looking guy who had been a circus clown, a fire-eater and an acrobat in earlier life, knew what was missing. If the Beatles were going to draw the punters into his club, they were going to have to do more than just play and sing. *'Mach schau, mach schau'* ('Put on a show!') would be his clarion call, so that was what they did.

'I did Gene Vincent all night . . .' John would recall, 'lying on the floor and throwing the mike around and pretending I had a bad leg . . . We all did *mach schauing* all the time from then on.'

It worked. Things soon picked up, and when they realised that it didn't matter what they played so long as it was rock and roll they did their whole repertoire. They even tried doing a couple of their own compositions, but that didn't work. The club-goers, and they were overwhelmingly male, only wanted the hits they already knew. Interestingly, John and Paul would rarely write any new songs while they were in Germany, the conditions being hardly conducive.

Before they'd left Liverpool, all excited by the promise of £18 a week each, none of them had realised how much they would be expected to work in Hamburg. The hours were punishing – six hours a night Tuesday to Friday, eight on Saturdays and eight and a half on Sunday, with just half-hour breaks for food and drink during the shifts. It was rock and roll on an industrial timetable.

'We'd have to eat and drink on stage,' John would remember. 'And to get the Germans going . . . we really had to hammer . . . The Germans liked heavy rock so we had to keep rocking all the time. That was how we got stomping.'

There was also, however, another purpose to their stamping on stage. It helped keep the tempo going and encouraged their novice drummer, Pete. 'We kept that big heavy four-in-a-bar going all night long,' George would remember. As for Paul, he would sing 'What'd I Say', complete with instrumental breaks, 'for about an hour and a half,' John would add. That was obviously an exaggeration, but it gives an indication of the expectations put on this group of boys who, as John said, 'had never played regularly together for more than about twenty minutes' until then.

'My voice began to hurt from the pain of singing,' he often recalled, 'but we learned that you could stay awake by eating slimming pills . . .' They were Preludin, a kind of amphetamine, which the management was happy to supply, and which would be routinely passed up to the musicians by the waiters, along with free glasses of beer. They called them 'prellies'. Paul was always cautious about what he swallowed, but John would rarely know the meaning of the word 'caution'. Within a couple of weeks in St Pauli he would, he said later, be frothing at the mouth as the prellies kept him singing and playing into the early hours.

The Beatles were obviously being exploited, but, grateful for the chance to play to growing and enthusiastic audiences, they accepted the situation. Besides, they'd all signed contracts written in German, which they'd barely understood. John had a German-to-English dictionary but hardly opened it, and only Pete had studied German at school – a course that was unlikely to have included contract law.

There was, however, a plus to the marathon sessions. With their amps turned up to max they were beginning to knit together as a group in a way they never had in their sporadic gigs around Liverpool. 'We got better and we got more confidence,' John said. 'We couldn't not . . . with all the experience, playing all night long. It was handy them being foreign, too. We had to try even harder, and put our hearts and souls into it.' With so many hours of intense practice on stage, he was also becoming a competent rhythm guitarist. He would never be a virtuoso: never as good as George. He never wanted to be, happily admitting that he 'only ever learned to play to have something to busk along with when I sang'.

They'd played some rough places on Merseyside, but the Teddy boys there had been at worst merely teenage delinquents with a fashion fetish. In Hamburg, the Beatles discovered the reality of violence when professional gangsters would come into the Indra late at night, and call out their song requests . . . demands, more like. There would be seamen from all around the world, too, including some from the Soviet Union and Eastern Europe who would be looking for a good

time. And American soldiers out for a weekend of 'rest and recu-
peration' from their units in other parts of West Germany, where
they might have spent weeks on manoeuvres, or been out all night
keeping watch on the border with East Germany. They would want
fun as well, and girls and drink. In all, the Indra could become a
fiery ferment of too much rival testosterone and booze, and, regularly,
fights would break out.

The staff there could take care of themselves, too. 'The waiters
would get their flick knives out, or their truncheons, and that would
be it,' John would relate. 'I've never seen such killers.' One of Koschmider's minders, Horst Fascher, had once accidentally killed a guy in
a street fight. The Beatles liked Horst. He'd once been a professional
boxing champion. It was good to have him on their side, they thought,
should there ever be any trouble involving them.

There never was, as, watching from the stage, they would be wryly
amused by the violence, until their eyes would sting as police teargas
used to break up street fights seeped into the club. As John would
say: 'I might have been born in Liverpool, but I grew up in Hamburg.'

Not that it was only drunks, sailors, prostitutes and gangsters who
came to hear the Beatles play. Working-class boys and girls who
worked in St Pauli's shops and offices came too, as well as leather-clad
rockers and their girlfriends, thrilled to find the kind of music that,
until then, they'd only heard on American Forces Network stations.

Very soon, as they improved, the Beatles began building up the nu-
cleus of a following, so that within a few weeks Koschmider moved
them down the street to his bigger club, the Kaiserkeller. Derry and
the Seniors had now left and Allan Williams had returned to Hamburg
with yet another Liverpool group – Rory Storm and the Hurricanes,
with whom the Beatles would now alternate every night. The two
groups had hardly known each other in Liverpool, but now they were
in friendly competition. And, almost immediately, the Beatles would
notice what a great drummer the Hurricanes had. His stage name
was Ringo Starr, but his real name was Richard Starkey. They would
always know him as Richie.

The year 1960 now belongs to a bygone age of letter writing, but in
those days, for young people away from home, letters were more
than important, and that applied to the Beatles as much as anyone.
Subsequently letters were the subject of popular songs, and although

they hadn't yet heard the Marvelettes' 'Please Mr Postman', which they would famously revive, Paul had already written a version of 'P.S. I Love You'. So, as they sang about letters, and waited for letters, every one of them frequently wrote home. John and Mimi may have sometimes had a tempestuous relationship, but that didn't prevent him writing to her, or stop Mimi from delivering money to Hessy's music shop that he sent to pay for the instalments on his new guitar.

Most important to John, though, and despite the exciting life he was now experiencing, were the letters that Cynthia would write, telling him how late summer was turning into autumn in sleepy Hoylake and how she was getting on without him. Often they would be accompanied by photographs she had taken of herself in a Woolworths photo booth, which showed her with her bosom pushed out and her eyes half-closed, in an expression that she hoped made her look sexy, as he would always request. She didn't know what was going on in Hamburg but she knew her man and his appetites, so she did her best to please.

His letters in reply, and there were several a week, were detailed and long about everything that was happening to him. Well, not quite everything! They were also loving and affectionate and inevitably 'X-rated', as she would later coyly describe his references to his 'throbber' when he thought about her. 'The sexiest letters this side of Henry Miller,' he would boast later. 'Forty pages long, some of them.'

But there was another element to them. Still insecure, he was always desperate to know that she hadn't found another boy while he was away. 'I love, love, love you,' he would write. 'Please wait for me.' She did.

For his part, however, shortly after he arrived in Germany, he was casually unfaithful with a girl who worked in a bar. Did he ever reflect on the hypocrisy in the devotions he regularly posted to Cynthia? Probably. But it was her fidelity to him that was important; not his to her.

# 15

*'Women should be obscene and not heard'*

The Kaiserkeller was a much bigger place with a floor for dancing and a neon sign outside, and, while walking home one night, a young commercial artist called Klaus Voorman heard some rock music coming from inside. With nothing else to do, he went inside and sat listening as Rory Storm and the Hurricanes were finishing their set. They were enjoyable enough, but then the Beatles came on stage, and, as John went straight into 'Sweet Little Sixteen', Klaus was mesmerised. He went back the following night and the one after that – finally convincing his girlfriend to accompany him. She was Astrid Kirchherr. The Kaiserkeller was not the sort of rough place she would normally go, but when she did, she was fascinated by the energy that the Beatles generated, as John would jokingly berate the audience as 'Nazis' with 'Sieg Heil' salutes. The audience found it funny.

Astrid, a pretty, sophisticated photographer's assistant, had recently graduated from Hamburg's art college. With her black clothes and modish, fairish, short hair, she was the sort of girl you couldn't fail to notice. The hit French film of that year was Jean-Luc Godard's *À Bout de Souffle* (*Breathless* in the UK and the US) and Astrid had the look of the young Jean Seberg. France was the style capital of Europe, and, as a middle-class, educated bohemian, she wanted to look French rather than German. As she and Klaus started to bring their friends to the Kaiserkeller, the Beatles began to realise they were attracting a new kind of audience, a student group, whom John would christen the 'exis' – short for 'existentialists'.

John would always be drawn to intelligent women, girls he could talk to, and he was impressed by Astrid. She was twenty-two, and had such presence that, back in Hoylake, Cynthia was immediately worried as his letters would be full of references to this wonderful, new, fascinating woman they'd met.

Obviously, he fancied her. Astrid was smitten, too, but not with him. Stuart, the quiet artist of the group, with his pimples, James Dean hair brushed up at the front and dark shades clipped on to his glasses, was the one she went for, the one for whom she would break up with boyfriend Klaus.

At this time in their development, girlfriends didn't have much say in what the Beatles did. John's gag that women should be 'obscene and not heard' might have been funny, but, as he would later admit, the Beatles were indeed a very macho band. Their girls were always kept in the background. Astrid, however, who had her own car and her own career, represented a new generation of young, modern women. She was totally unlike Cynthia, who was still trying to please John with a Brigitte Bardot look.

Nor was Astrid shy, and although she spoke no English, very soon she asked, using Klaus as an interpreter, if the Beatles would let her take their photographs. They were flattered. In those days most photographs of pop groups were taken in five minutes with a quick flash from a camera and a cheesy grin from the group. But, showing that she was years ahead of her time, Astrid did the Beatles' first real photo session by taking them in her Volkswagen to a Hamburg fairground, where she shot them against the heavy machinery of a rollercoaster. All her images were in black and white, but it was her portraits of them that were most effective. Three years later a similar half-light monotone technique would be used on the cover of the group's second album *With The Beatles*.

After the photo session, she took them back to her flat which was at the top of the house where her parents and grandparents lived, as well as Klaus, in a middle-class area of suburban Hamburg. It was the first time the Beatles had been outside St Pauli and the free-living elegance of Astrid's home left a lasting impression, not least her bedroom which was painted completely black – with black furniture, black sheets on the bed and black curtains. You didn't get bedrooms like this, or girls like this, in Liverpool. Today we might think that she was trying too hard to show how different she was . . . although everything in black would certainly have saved on the washing. But in 1960, as far as the Beatles were concerned, Astrid *was* different. No wonder John wrote to tell Cynthia about her.

Was he disappointed that Astrid went for Stuart instead of him? Almost certainly. Most boys would have been. But he would never have admitted it. Over the next decades there would be other women who were similarly intelligent and avant-garde in their looks and life-styles to whom he would be attracted. That was John. At least Astrid hadn't chosen Paul. That would have been disastrous. John could live with the idea of Stuart and Astrid, and by November the two were engaged, with Stuart living in the Kirchherrs' house in the room now vacated by ex-boyfriend Klaus Voorman. Apparently, Klaus took it very well.

The Beatles felt that they were old hands in Hamburg by this time, and John loved the nightlife. 'They roll up the pavements at eleven o'clock in Liverpool, but in Hamburg they're just rolling them out at midnight,' he would say. And, confident now in matching black leather jackets and high leather boots worn outside their black jeans, the group walked the streets, looking in on drag acts in clubs or chatting to prostitutes on the pavements. Some mornings, after a late session, they might wander down to the Sailors' Society (also known as the Seamen's Mission – although John had his own interpretation of the 'semen's mission') for some breakfast with Ringo and the other Hurricanes who were, wisely, staying there. At first, they'd been wary of Ringo with his beard, that silver streak in his hair and his Teddy boy clothes. But he was nothing if not affable, and in mid-October John, George and Paul played with him for the first time when they backed one of the Hurricanes in a recording session in a little Hamburg studio.

John was playing another new guitar that day, a Rickenbacker Capri 325 that he'd found in a shop that imported American instruments, and which allowed him to lend Paul his Hofner Club 40. A new, better guitar wasn't just a status symbol or even just a tool of John's trade. To a rock musician a good guitar is a companion, too, something to be nursed and treasured, a friend to turn to in lonely times.

So, with a new guitar, it's easy to imagine that he must, at that point, have been feeling particularly good about himself. Things were going well. And yet . . . he still did crazy, sometimes cruel, inexplicable things. One night, presumably while drunk, he decided to rob a drunken sailor of his wallet, taking Pete along as an accomplice. 'I thought I could chat him up . . . kid him on we could get him some birds,' he would remember. 'We got him drinking and drinking, and he kept on asking, "Where's the girls?" We were trying to find out where he kept his money. We never made it. We just hit him twice in the end, then gave up. We didn't want to hurt him.' In Pete's version of the incident, the venture failed when the sailor fought back with teargas.

Quite why John would want to rob a sailor, who was probably earning less than he was, he never explained, other than hinting that it was just a bit of devilry carried out for no better reason than the fun of it.

After three months in Hamburg the Beatles were having second thoughts about the Kaiserkeller. Every night they could hear how good they'd become, and see how popular they were. They wanted better money and living conditions. And when better was offered to them at a different, bigger venue along the street, the Top Ten Club, they told Koschmider they would be taking it, despite their contract with him. Considering the reputation that Koschmider had for violence, they were taking a risk, and threats of broken fingers were made.

Koschmider had a more subtle revenge in mind, however. George was still only seventeen, which meant that for three months he'd been violating a local by-law that stipulated a curfew of 10 p.m. for everyone under the age of eighteen. He should never have been allowed to play in Hamburg after ten at night in the first place. Now, someone who knew how old he was tipped off the police. George was arrested and questioned, and, the following day, put on a train back to England.

Paul and Pete were the next to fall foul of the law. While collecting their belongings at the Bambi Kino to take over to the Top Ten Club, as a final riposte to Koschmider they set fire to some condoms which they hung in the passageway outside their room. The smell of burning latex in the little cinema was horrible, but apart from a slight singeing of the wall there was no damage, and the pair went off to the Top Ten Club for the Beatles to make their first appearance there – albeit now as a four-man group.

The next morning Paul was walking blithely along the Reeperbahn when he was arrested, locked in a police cell and charged with attempted arson. John and Pete were arrested next, and, last of all, Stuart, who had been with Astrid at her home when the alleged offence had taken place. After being left to sweat for a bit, Paul and Pete were deported.

John hung around Hamburg for a few more days, then he, too, followed. 'It was awful,' he told Hunter Davies. 'I had my amp on my back, scared stiff I was going to get it pinched. I hadn't finished paying for it. I was convinced I'd never find England.'

It was the middle of the night when he reached Liverpool and took a taxi home to Woolton. Mimi was upstairs asleep and didn't hear the bell, so he had to throw pebbles at her bedroom window to wake her.

Of course, when he asked her to pay the taxi for him, she made a fuss and pretended to be cross. But that was just her way. She was delighted, and relieved, to see him home again.

'He had these awful cowboy boots on, up to his knees they were, all gold and silver,' she would remember. 'He just pushed past me and said, "Pay that taxi, Mimi." I shouted after him, "Where's your hundred pounds a week, John?"'

'Just like you, Mimi, to go on about a hundred a week when you know I'm tired.'

Her response was all it took to remind him that he was home again: 'And you can get rid of those boots. You're not going out of this house in boots like that.'

# 16

*'Is this what I want to do? Nightclubs? Seedy scenes?
Being deported? Weird people in clubs?'*

It would be a recurrent feature of his life. Whenever things got difficult, John would go to earth and cut himself off, or perhaps just go to
bed and stay there for as long as he could. After getting home from
Hamburg he needed time to think things through. So, for ten days
he hung around Mendips and played his records, and then bought
some more and listened to them, while making no attempt to contact
the other Beatles, nor even to find out if they had got home safely.
The Great Hamburg Adventure had ended miserably. He had turned
twenty in October; it was time to reassess. 'I was thinking, "Is this
what I want to do? Nightclubs? Seedy scenes? Being deported? Weird
people in clubs?" I thought hard about it. Should I continue doing
it? It had been a shattering experience,' he would tell a friend, Elliot
Mintz, in 1976.

The only person he did want to see was Cynthia, and he went into
Liverpool to meet her after her classes at college. He was wearing the
leather jacket he'd bought in Hamburg and decided that she should
have a leather coat, too. So they went into C&A's department store
and picked out, as Cynthia would write, 'a gorgeous, three-quarter
length chocolate brown one for seventeen pounds. It was my first
present from him and I couldn't wait to show it off.'

They also bought a takeaway cooked chicken and set off back to
Woolton as a treat for Mimi. The encounter didn't go well. According
to Cynthia, when Mimi saw the coat and heard that John had paid
for it, 'she hit the roof', screaming that he'd 'spent his money on a
gangster's moll', and hurled the chicken at him. 'Do you think you
can butter me up with chicken when you've spent all your money on
this? Get out,' she said.

Embarrassed by his aunt's behaviour in front of his girlfriend, John
took Cynthia to the station. 'All she cares about is fucking money and

cats,' he apologised. That wasn't true. All Mimi really cared about was John.

It was almost Christmas when he finally made contact with the other Beatles, by which time Paul, under duress from his father, was working delivering the Christmas post. He, too, had been wondering whether he should pursue another career. But a session at Mona Best's Casbah, where a pal of Pete's filled in on bass, quickly banished those thoughts when the Beatles saw the response they provoked. They had improved so much. Something else happened that night. Neil Aspinall, an acquaintance of Paul's from school, who was also a friend of Pete's and lodging with Mona while he studied for account-ancy exams, was so thrilled by the Beatles that, as Mona tried to get the group bookings in other venues, he began to make and stick up posters for them.

But it was in working-class North Liverpool at Litherland Town Hall on 27 December that the great breakthrough in their home city really happened. With each of the group being paid £6 for their appearance, from the moment they came on stage and Paul went into his Little Richard impersonation with 'Long Tall Sally', the large ballroom came alive. The timing was perfect. With Elvis turning to Hollywood, Buddy Holly dead, Jerry Lee Lewis in disgrace over his marriage to his thirteen-year-old cousin and Chuck Berry in jail, the fashion for groups had recently diluted into the soft rock of Ricky Nelson in the US and Cliff Richard and the Shadows in the UK. Musi-cally, the Shadows were terrific, but with their shiny suits and fancy little choreographed steps they looked like four bank clerks when they appeared on TV.

No bank in the world would have employed the Beatles. Just the volume of sound that they made – and they would always play very LOUD – shocked and thrilled. Wearing their German leather jackets and black T-shirts as they stamped away in their boots, they were punk-like in their arrogance. John's art college friend Bill Harry was astonished at the progress they'd made since he'd last seen them in the summer.

Neil Aspinall's posters outside the hall had billed them as 'The Beatles, Direct from Hamburg', but apart from their Casbah fans who had followed them to Litherland, and who obviously included Cyn-thia and Paul's pretty seventeen-year-old girlfriend Dot Rhone, who worked in a chemist's shop, no one knew who they were.

'Suddenly, we were a wow!' John would say. 'Mind you, seventy per cent of the audience thought we were a German wow. They didn't know we were from Liverpool. They said, "Christ, they speak good English, don't they." That was when we began to think we were good. Up until Hamburg we thought we were okay, but not good enough. It was only when we were back in Liverpool that we realised the difference and that everybody else was doing Cliff Richard shit.'

Not that the Beatles were doing anything original yet. The Lennon and McCartney writing partnership may have already produced several songs, but the Beatles didn't sing anything new that night. It was their full-blooded covers of American rock and roll records that the Litherland audience loved.

It might be imagined that, seeing the audience's response in Litherland and at other Liverpool venues over the next few months, some enterprising promoter would have pressed a management contract into the group's hands. But it didn't happen. Just as the city's evening newspaper, the *Liverpool Echo*, which in those days was seen by over a million readers in the Merseyside area, remained totally uninterested in any of the local groups, no young manager saw himself as the next 'Colonel' Tom Parker. The lack of managerial interest puzzled John, but this was Liverpool in 1961, where there was no culture of pop management and where the pay was rarely more than eight pounds a night per Beatle. Even though they would sometimes play at two different halls in a single night, after Neil Aspinall bought an old van and put aside his accountancy homework to ferry them across Liverpool, it all seemed very precarious. Small wonder that, with the Christmas post finished, Paul took a day job as an apprentice electrician for three months. None of them could yet be certain that there really might be a future in music.

Stuart returned home from Hamburg in mid-January 1961 to apply for a teacher's training course at Liverpool College of Art. John had missed him, the two having written long letters to each other over the past six weeks, and he went immediately to see him the night he got back. Both now accepted that music wasn't going to be Stuart's career. But in the meantime, while he waited for Astrid to join him in Liverpool, Stuart retook his place on bass with the group. And it was after a gig at Lathom Hall, another North Liverpool venue, at the end of January that he became the victim of an attack in the toilets by a group of Teddy boys.

No one knew why Stuart should be the victim, because he was the most inoffensive of all the group. But, whatever the trigger, while the others were loading their equipment into Neil Aspinall's van, Stu was knocked to the ground and kicked in the head. When John and Pete realised what was happening, a melee erupted in which John broke a finger.

Stuart was living at his parents' new home near Sefton Park by then. According to his sister, Pauline, he arrived home still bleeding from the attack, but refused to go to hospital. And when, the following day, the family GP visited him and pronounced that no permanent damage had been done, he resumed his position on bass that night at another venue. John played with a splint around his broken finger.

It was still there when, on 9 February 1961, he and the other Beatles made their debut at the Cavern. John had been there before, of course, in 1957, with the Quarry Men, when he'd been told to 'cut out the rock and roll'. The world had now moved on . . . more or less.

'That's the youngest tramp I've ever seen,' the bouncer on the Cavern door observed as George arrived at 10 Mathew Street in jeans and a leather jacket. He wasn't joking – not much, anyway. It might have been lunchtime but the Cavern still had standards, and right at the top of its prohibited list were 'jeans'. It must have made a kind of sense. Mathew Street was in the city centre. Any fans around there in the middle of the day would be kids who were already working for a living. If they were boys, they were either clerks or messengers in the nearby insurance and shipping offices, and therefore had to look smart when they went to work, which meant a collar and a tie and jacket. To let boys into the Cavern who were wearing jeans would have been to encourage the 'rougher types', the Cavern's owner, Ray McFall, had decided. And he didn't want those fellas in his club. The girls who might attend, and who would mainly be typists or shopworkers or hairdressers' assistants, would be appropriately dressed, too, in their sensible, if drab, skirts for work and back-combed beehive hair. The decade of the Sixties may already have been more than a year old, but the Sixties of fable, that time of colourful teenage fashion, youthful optimism, permissiveness, drugs and rock and roll, wasn't even in sight.

Or was it?

George's appearance at the Cavern door, shortly to be followed by John, George, Pete and Stuart, all similarly dressed, might have given the clue. The barbarians were at the gate and the doorman had to let them in because, jeans or not, they were the entertainment. And, as everyone knows, entertainers live by different rules.

From the outside, in 1961 the Cavern suggested the most unexciting of places – just a doorway in a warehouse in a cobbled alleyway. Not far from the Pier Head, the club's entrance was surrounded for much of the day by trucks and vans disgorging, or picking up, boxes of fresh produce, the essence of which would lace the surrounding atmosphere with the cloying aroma of ripening fruit. Inside, seventeen steps led to three airless cellars, with a couple of smaller ones to the sides where, in the days before anyone worried too much about ventilators or air conditioning, the walls would quickly become damp with teenage perspiration.

It was a former railway clerk called Bob Wooler who in his new talent-spotting role for the Cavern took the Beatles there. Owner McFall would tell him that if he'd seen the Beatles first he wouldn't have let Wooler book them. But then he heard them, after which he would stand at the back of the club watching in total admiration as on stage they would play and sing, and then joke and tease and eat and goon about between songs, all the time keeping a conversation going with the fans who would shout out requests. Somehow, the Beatles had developed the gift of turning the audience into friends. When something went wrong with an amp or a microphone, as it often did, they didn't panic and wonder what to say next. Instead they would simply amuse the fans and maybe have a communal singsong until the problem was mended. Those long hours playing in Hamburg had made them completely at home on stage and with themselves.

Not that any of this would have worked if Hamburg hadn't also turned them into a terrific band, in which John now sang the Shirelles' 'Will You Love Me Tomorrow', blithely overlooking that it's a girl's song as she contemplates losing her virginity. Paul, for his part, went from 'Good Golly, Miss Molly' to 'Somewhere Over The Rainbow', George did his Carl Perkins numbers, Stuart sang 'Love Me Tender', and they let Pete leave his drums to do 'Wild In The Country'. They had an eclectic repertoire.

For this they earned a total of £5 for a two-hour session – a pound each. Their fans paid a shilling (5p) to get in, where they could swap their Luncheon Vouchers, often given to them by their employers, for a Cavern cob (a roll) and a bowl of soup. There was no alcohol, obviously, but a cup of tea cost fivepence (about 2p).

That it would be from this modest, cheap chrysalis of a former wine cellar that the Beatles would emerge, fully formed, less than two years later, seems ever more unlikely the further away in time we get from it.

By March 1961 steps were being made by the Top Ten Club in Hamburg to get the Beatles back to Germany. The group was keen to go. The money, they were now promised, would be much better than at the Kaiserkeller, and there would be accommodation over the club. So, while the Top Ten lobbied the relevant Hamburg authorities, Allan Williams wrote to the German consul in Liverpool explaining that the Beatles were hardly the juvenile delinquents Koschmider had painted them. And, as George was now eighteen, he was therefore legal to work on the Reeperbahn.

While they waited to hear, John would often hang out at the Jacaranda when he was in town, keeping in touch with his college friend Bill Harry. Bill's news was that with a fifty-pound loan he was setting up a bi-weekly music newspaper for the Merseyside area. It would be called *Mersey Beat*, and he now wondered if John would like to write for it.

When John didn't want to do something he was a sloth. When he did, few were quicker. Going home to Mendips he immediately set to work, telling, in a Goon-like allegory, the story of the Beatles' creation. It was very funny, and told in a fairy-tale style how three little boys 'grew guitars and formed a noise', and how the name 'Beatles' had been brought to them 'in a vision' by a man 'on a flaming pie . . .'

The account would appear in the first edition of *Mersey Beat* that coming July with an inspired headline written by Bill Harry himself that read 'Being a Short Diversion on the Dubious Origins of Beatles, translated from the John Lennon'. Harry could forever be justly proud of himself for being the first editor to publish a piece by John Lennon.

But John was proud of himself, too: more than proud. He might not have written *Alice In Wonderland* but he was going to be published, writing in his own style, the one he'd experimented with in 'The Daily Howl' when he'd been at school. He hadn't had to compromise.

He was a writer now, as he'd always wanted to be.

# 17

*'There was a certain type . . . you'd call them groupies now . . .
who went for any performer. They didn't care if it was a comedian or a man who ate glass, as long as he was on the stage'*

In John's eyes, the Top Ten Club was the best place the Beatles had
ever played – because the microphones had a new echo built into
them. Now, when he sang 'Be-Bop-A-Lula' he could sound the way
Gene Vincent did on the record. The boost that the reverb gave him
was immense, covering up for his lack of confidence in his voice, as
his playing the comic on stage was perhaps compensating for his
uncertainty about his looks.

Not everything was perfect about the Top Ten Club, however.
The Beatles were now expected to appear alongside, and live with,
London guitarist/singer Tony Sheridan, meaning there would be six
on stage every night, with Paul now playing the piano. After the show
Stuart would go home to Astrid in the suburbs, while the others,
including Sheridan, would climb up to their narrow camp beds in
an attic room. There would be five in this makeshift dormitory, and,
should Tony Sheridan's German girlfriend, Rosi, join him, six, and
even more if one of the Beatles got lucky. This was where George
lost his virginity with a girl he'd met, believing his companions to
be sleeping until they all cheered, upon his completion of the act.
'At least they kept quiet while I was doing it,' George would happily
remember.

All in all, there wasn't much in the way of privacy for any of them,
as Paul's account of accidentally entering the attic when John was
busy illustrates. 'I'd walk in on John and see a little bottom bobbing
up and down with a girl underneath him. It was perfectly normal.
You'd go, "Oh, sorry," and back out of the room.'

For a rock musician, girls were a perk of the job, and, as many
will testify, one of the abiding reasons why teenage boys took up the
guitar in the first place. A decade later John would tell *Rolling Stone*

about some of the girls who would attend their gigs. 'There was a certain type . . . you'd call them groupies now . . . who went for any performer. They didn't care if it was a comedian or a man who ate glass, as long as he was on the stage.'

When they'd agreed to play at the Top Ten, the Beatles had been promised more money than Koschmider had paid them, but what they hadn't realised was that they would now have to pay tax at their new venue – something their former employer had, probably fraudulently, neglected to do. They were always underpaid wherever they played, but on seeing their tax deductions, they decided to make a saving where they could – by not paying Allan Williams his 10 per cent agent's commission on their wages. This was shabby behaviour, and a bitter Williams immediately 'saw the hand of Lennon' in it. 'He was the leader and the dominant figure among the Beatles,' he would write in his book *The Man Who Gave The Beatles Away* – which John would wickedly rename *The Man Who Couldn't Give The Beatles Away*.

Morally, if not legally, because there had been no contract to breach, Williams had right on his side, and he threatened to black-ball the group when they got back to Liverpool. But he wasn't that kind of guy, as the Beatles surely guessed. He had never been their manager in the usual pop music sense, but he'd done more for them than simply acting as a booking agent. As he reminded them, in a surprisingly conciliatory letter, without him they 'wouldn't even have smelled Hamburg'. It was true, but it didn't help. They still didn't pay him.

During the Easter break from college, Cynthia, accompanied by Paul's girlfriend Dot, arrived in Hamburg. It was the first time Cynthia had been abroad, and John mischievously showed her the sights of the Reeperbahn, as well as introducing her to the staying powers of Preludin. Then at night the two girls would sit in the audience watching their boyfriends on stage, with John sometimes hurrying Cynthia upstairs to the communal room when no one else was there for a quick 'five-miler' in the fifteen minutes between sessions. 'Those weeks in Hamburg were among the happiest times John and I had together,' Cynthia would later write. 'We were free and in love. Life was full of promise and the sun shone.'

Astrid had already given the Beatles their 'look' as a photographer, and now she had a couple more contributions to make. When Stuart admired her new, black, collarless leather jacket and trousers she had a similar outfit made for him. The other Beatles quickly ordered some for themselves, too. But what Astrid did next would be her greatest gift to them. She cut Stuart's hair, combing it forward into a fringe in a style that some of her German friends were copying from the ever-groovy French.

On seeing what she'd done to their bass player, the other Beatles were amused. It looked sissyish, they thought, and stuck to their slicked-back rocker styles. What had been good enough for early Elvis was good enough for them . . . for now.

Neither John, nor any of the others, knew much about Bert Kaempfert other than that he was an easy listening orchestra star in Germany, and that his record 'Wonderland By Night', the sort of slinky trumpet music that ice skaters liked to glide to, had topped the American charts. More intriguing was that Kaempfert had also been involved in turning the German folk song 'Muss i denn' into 'Wooden Heart' for Elvis. Paul would sing it sometimes, partly in German, but John never liked it much, seeing it as further evidence of Elvis's selling out to Hollywood. But when told that Kaempfert had been to see them at the Top Ten and wanted to record them with Tony Sheridan, he was excited.

The Beatles felt confident when, having been up all night high on pep pills, they turned up at Polydor's Hamburg studio ready to show Kaempfert what they could do. 'We thought it would be easy. The Germans had such shitty records, ours was bound to be better,' John would remember.

As it transpired, the cultural collision did no one any favours. Not at first, anyway. Mainly present as backing musicians for Tony Sheridan, who sang 'My Bonnie Lies Over The Ocean', which was an odd choice for a rock singer, the Beatles even had to change their name to the Beat Brothers for the record's release. Kaempfert didn't like the name Beatles.

As for the Beatles, they hated the finished record. 'It was terrible,' John said. 'It was just Tony Sheridan singing with us banging in the background. It could have been anyone.' The one song on which John sang was the oldie 'Ain't She Sweet'. It was one of the first songs his mother had taught him to play, so there must have been some emotion involved when he recorded it. But Julia hadn't imagined it as the marching song that the German producer wanted.

It was the band's first proper recording session, and they were disappointed, but it was already June and their second stay in Hamburg was drawing to a close. By now Stuart had decided that a musician's life wasn't for him, and had already begun studying at the Hamburg College of Fine Art. He cried on his last night as a Beatle, but everyone was emotional, with Paul regretting some of the sharp comments he'd made about Stuart's playing. Musically, he'd been right – Stuart wasn't good enough. But John had enjoyed his company more than anyone else's.

Whether Stuart had been holding back the development of the Beatles, no one has ventured to suggest. But his friendship with John was probably impeding the progress of Lennon and McCartney as songwriters. Feeling left out, Paul's writing partnership with John had dried up. Had Stuart stayed a Beatle, would Lennon and McCartney have become the two most famous songwriters in the world? Or would Paul have eventually given up, tired of feeling sidelined by John, and gone off on a solo career at the beginning of the Sixties rather than at the end of that decade?

By leaving the Beatles, Stuart wasn't just leaving the band. He was abandoning music. George was given his amplifier and Paul was offered his bass. It wasn't welcome. In Paul's eyes the bass was usually 'played by a fat guy at the back', and that wasn't how he saw himself at all. But, if the Beatles were going to be a four-man group, someone would have to play it, and, as John made clear, it wasn't going to be him; and it would have been a waste if George, the best guitarist in the group, played it. So, it had to be Paul.

'I really got lumbered . . .' Paul would say. But for the sake of the group, he got on with it, and, going to the Steinway music shop, he ordered a violin-shaped Hofner 500/1 for a left-handed player. He didn't know it then, but it would signal an inspired change of direction for him.

Paul wasn't the only one whose role was changed by Stuart's decision. He might not have wanted Stuart's bass, but Klaus Voorman had decided that he wanted to be a musician, too, so he took it. A decade later, Klaus would play bass on John's *Imagine* album.

# 18

*'I wasn't too keen on reaching twenty-one . . . I was thinking
that I'd missed the boat, that you had to be seventeen'*

The week the Beatles arrived back in Liverpool the first issue of *Mersey Beat* went on sale with John's history of the group on the second page. For a writer there is little as thrilling as seeing your work in print for the first time, and he was no exception. Collecting together all kinds of poems, short stories and cartoons from his bedroom drawer at Mendips, he took them round to Bill Harry's little *Mersey Beat* office in Liverpool's Renshaw Street. 'Print whatever you like,' he told Harry. And, leaving the pieces with him, he agreed to contribute a column for every issue of the newspaper.

One part of his career was safely off and running. The other quickly resumed as Ray McFall wanted the Beatles in the Cavern at lunchtimes and again one night a week, while Mona Best, and a couple of other promoters, were filling most of their other nights at clubs and ballrooms around Merseyside.

It was an exciting, and yet frustrating, time. Within a few months there would even be a Beatles Fan Club, and they were enjoying their music and gigs like never before. But outside Merseyside, the group remained completely unknown. They needed a manager, but because of their reputation for being difficult, no one was prepared to take them on. Mona Best might have been a possibility, but that wouldn't have worked with her son Pete in the band. Besides, things were delicate at the Casbah. Technically Neil Aspinall, now the Beatles' road manager, was a lodger at Mona's house, but, at twenty-one, he had also become the lover of Pete's extremely attractive thirty-eight-year-old mother who was separated from her husband.

For their part, the Beatles would continue to play at the Cavern at lunchtimes and loaf around town all afternoon, maybe in the Grapes pub or the Kardomah café in Stanley Street. Best of all, though, was when they would squeeze into a booth at the NEMS record shop around the corner in Whitechapel and play both sides of the new American releases – sometimes arguing with one another about who would sing what. In this way John laid claim to Ben E. King's 'Stand By Me', which he would finally record himself over a decade later on his solo *Rock 'n' Roll* album.

Some gigs would be better than others, and, along with other Liverpool groups, an all-nighter of a Riverboat Shuffle on the *Royal Iris* as it sailed out of the Mersey into Liverpool Bay in late August was a favourite. John enjoyed these sessions when musicians from several different bands would all join in. 'Sometimes we'd go on with fifteen or twenty musicians and play together, and we'd create something that had never been done on stage by a group before,' he would say years later when such co-operation began to be a regular occurrence at rock charity shows.

It was all very ad hoc, but, as pleasant as it was, it wasn't leading anywhere. Something new had to happen.

That summer Cynthia's widowed mother had gone to Canada to stay with relatives and their house in Hoylake had been let, so it had seemed a good idea for Cynthia to become another of Mimi's lodgers. It was actually a terrible idea. When John was living at home, Mimi would always wait up for him, and she didn't take kindly to now finding Cynthia also waiting . . . and in her nightdress, too, which, overlooking her own secret liaison with one of her past lodgers, she deemed provocative.

According to Cynthia, Mimi was a demanding landlady, but this uneasy situation went on for several months, with Cynthia working at Woolworths during breaks from college, and going to wherever the Beatles were playing in the evenings. Obviously, there would be no opportunities for any hanky-panky at Mendips, not when Mimi was at home, anyway. It was a difficult time all round.

John was going to be twenty-one on 9 October 1961. In those days a young man of that age was considered old enough to be taking on responsibilities, and not, as Mimi would never cease to tell him, 'touting around stupid dance halls for £3 a night! Where's the point in that?'

Despite himself, he did listen to her. 'I wasn't too keen on reaching twenty-one,' he would say. 'A voice in me was saying, "Look, you're too old." I was thinking that I'd missed the boat, that you had to be seventeen. A lot of stars in America were kids. I remember one of my relatives saying to me, "From now on, it's all downhill."'

It's unlikely that the doom-mongering relative was Mimi's sister Aunt Mater or Uncle Bert, because in an act of great generosity the two presented John with a coming-of-age birthday present of £100 – the equivalent of over £2,000 in today's money.

There were several things John could have done with £100. He could have deposited it safely in a savings account at the bank where it would have accrued interest. Or he could have paid off his hire purchase debts on his guitar and amplifier. He also might have taken Cynthia away for a romantic few days. He did none of those things.

Instead he planned a month's holiday hitch-hiking to Spain with Paul. In the event they only got as far as two weeks in Paris and they went by train. Cynthia was upset, but was too timid to complain. But George and Pete were furious, and not just because they'd been excluded – although George would have felt that strongly. The Beatles had several appearances already booked for the time when John and Paul were away, and it was left to George and Pete to apologise to the clubs that their two colleagues had let down.

Through his letters to and from Stuart in Hamburg, John knew that a German friend, Jürgen Vollmer, was now living in Paris, where he was working as a photographer's assistant. So, having booked into a small hotel in Montmartre, John and Paul quickly hooked up with him. As they'd realised in Hamburg, Vollmer was an evangelist for French style, and, as they toured the sights, they probably fell in love ten times a day as they passed a never-ending array of the beautiful, sophisticated young women of Paris. As John would tell *Playboy* in 1980, and as poets had been discovering and rediscovering for hundreds of years, Paris breathed romance. 'All the kissing and holding . . . it was so romantic the way people would just stand under the tree kissing. They weren't mauling each other, they were just kissing. To be there and see them . . . I really loved it.'

When they'd arrived in France in their black leather jackets, black jeans and quaffed greasy hair they'd looked like a couple of bikers from Liverpool, and, dressed like that, they found themselves invisible to the self-regarding bohemian girls they fancied. One look at Jürgen showed them their problem. Jürgen, like Astrid and now Stuart, combed his hair forward in the French style. So now John and Paul wanted their hair cut like Jürgen's, and in his small hotel bedroom the photographer's assistant became a style-creating hair-dresser. It wasn't his idea, because he liked the Beatles' rocker look. But they reckoned that with a haircut like his, 'they'd have more chance with the bohemian beauties on the Left Bank,' as Jürgen told Beatles chronicler Mark Lewisohn. As they never told whether their new hairstyle worked as they'd hoped, it probably didn't. But it would come to the aid of millions of other boys in a couple of years' time.

There were some sniggers when they got back to Liverpool, but George quickly joined them and combed his hair forward. Only Pete couldn't be persuaded. He was the best-looking of them all and he liked the way he looked – 'Liverpool's answer to Jeff Chandler', as *Mersey Beat* described him.

Poor Pete, unclubbable and unassuming, he never really fitted in. It wasn't so much that the others left him out when they were off stage, as he didn't necessarily want to be included. He was just different from them, and now his hair looked different, too.

# 19

*'Brian Epstein looked efficient and rich.*
*We were in a daydream till he came along'*

John would never be able to recall the precise moment he saw Brian Epstein for the first time. Had it been in the NEMS record shop? As Brian was the manager of this branch of his family's firm, he was always there, so John might have been at least peripherally aware of him as he browsed through the records. Or had he spotted him standing at the back of the Cavern on 9 November 1961? If he had, Brian in his expensive suit would have stuck out among the lunchtime crush of kids. Most likely John and the other Beatles only fully realised Brian's interest when, a littler later, Bob Wooler announced his presence over the tannoy system and asked the Cavernites, as the fans were now calling themselves, for a big hand for him.

'And what brings Mr Epstein here?' George is reputed to have asked the young shopkeeper in that smiling, slightly insolent style that he had picked up from John.

Brian Epstein didn't tell him. He hadn't decided yet. He was nervous. The Beatles were a pretty intimidating gang to approach. He needed to make some enquiries. A few days earlier a fan, possibly called Raymond Jones, had walked into his shop and asked for the Beatles' recording of 'My Bonnie'. The Beatles may have been disappointed with the recordings they'd made with Tony Sheridan in Hamburg, but Stuart had sent them a copy of 'My Bonnie' and they couldn't help but talk about it. It *was*, after all, their first appearance on a proper record. After that, word had inevitably got around.

Most record shops would have sent Raymond Jones away telling him that 'My Bonnie' hadn't been released in Britain, and that he would have to go to Germany to buy it. And that would have been that. But Brian Epstein, or 'Mr Brian' as he asked his staff to call him, had, in the last few years, built up his business by meticulously noting and pursuing every customer's request. And when a couple of days later he received two more requests for 'My Bonnie', he was intrigued enough to ask Bill Harry for a little more information on these Beatles. Bill had pointed him towards the Cavern.

In the small world culture that was pop music in Liverpool, Brian had met Bill when the ex-art college student had approached him for financial backing for *Mersey Beat*. He hadn't given it, but he had agreed to sell copies of the newspaper in his shop, to compile a 'Liverpool Top Ten' based on record sales at NEMS, and to write a record review column. He had grown up as a lover of classical music, but his job was inevitably drawing him ever closer towards pop.

The legend is that he'd never heard of the Beatles before the Raymond Jones enquiry. But, not only were there regular advertisements in the classified columns of the *Liverpool Echo* for the Beatles' appearances around Merseyside, *Mersey Beat* was now also regularly publishing John's column on one page and Brian's own pop reviews on another. So, he could hardly have been totally unaware of them. That said, the world that Brian inhabited was much different from that of the Beatles.

To John, Brian seemed at first to be an uncomplicated, posh, rich young man who owned a top-of-the-range Ford Zephyr Zodiac, and who, in his conservative suits, ties and polished shoes, was an uncool-looking twenty-eight years old. But when, over the next few months, more aspects of Brian's life were revealed to him, it became increasingly clear that 'uncomplicated' was nowhere near a valid description. Brian Epstein was, in fact, a very complicated man.

Brought up in a Jewish family in the comfortable suburb of Childwall by his father, Harry Epstein, and mother, Queenie, he had one younger brother, Clive. Privately educated, he went unsuccessfully through seven different schools, before at sixteen he'd given up on education without any qualifications. Initially his ambition had been to become a dress designer, but his father thought that wasn't a very manly job. So he was sent to work in one of the Epstein family's furniture shops as a salesman and window dresser. National Service had broken into that when he was eighteen, until, charged with impersonating an officer, he was examined by psychiatrists, found to be psychologically unsuitable to live a soldier's life and kicked out of the army. A year at the Royal Academy of Dramatic Art in London had followed, before he'd decided he didn't like the social life of drama students. Back in Liverpool, he was given a family job and put in charge of the record department at NEMS in Whitechapel. He never missed a performance of the Royal Liverpool Philharmonic Orchestra, and lived with his parents.

The Beatles were culturally a world away from him, but, from the first time Brian made his way down the steps into the fug of the Cavern, he was mesmerised by them. Some have surmised that his interest in the group was sexual, that he saw in them, and in John in particular, rough trade. That has to be possible. In an age when homosexual acts were illegal and could be punished by imprisonment, he might have been turned on by a group of unruly boys in black leather jackets. He did like good-looking working-class boys, and he had the scars, mental as well physical, to show for his pursuit of some of them.

But, it's more likely that it was the Beatles' spark, humour and cheek that attracted him. Up on the stage they seemed to be having such a good time together, as they sang and played and bantered with the audience. And, unlike him, they appeared to be supremely confident in who they were. He may have been quite well off, but he wasn't happy, trying to hide his homosexuality behind a going-nowhere relationship with a girlfriend. Selling records had, for the past five years, been his only success in life, and, at a time when pop was beginning to boom, he had indeed been successful. But now his job was beginning to bore him. He needed something bigger.

Then, there they were, the group that no one wanted to manage. Could *he* manage them, he wondered, as he brought friends and colleagues to see them? Could he even be a manager? He wasn't sure. It took him a month to decide what to do, and to enquire of others what a manager actually did and how he did it. Allan Williams was never one to mince words. 'My honest opinion, Brian, is don't touch them with a fucking barge pole.' The Beatles would let him down, as they had let Williams down.

Brian listened, but just kept going back to the Cavern. It wasn't simply that he was in love with the Beatles. He wanted to have their recklessness, their *joie de vivre* and enthusiasm for the music they played, their couldn't-care-less backchat with the fans, and their arrogance at being in a very special gang.

By the end of the month he'd made up his mind, and he invited the group to a meeting in his office above his shop. For some reason, the Beatles, possibly drunk after an afternoon in the Grapes, were being silly and nothing was decided. Nevertheless, Brian persevered. Calling another meeting with them on 3 December, he became cross when Paul didn't turn up. Paul, he was informed, was taking a bath.

'This is disgraceful. He's going to be very late,' he complained.

'Late. But very clean,' countered George, deadpan.

Eventually Paul did arrive and Brian nervously made his pitch, admitting candidly that he was new to management, to which, according to him, the Beatles jokily replied that they were, too. He was surprised when he discovered that they were splitting only £15 a gig between the four of them, and promised he would get them more. And they were surprised when he, as manager, said he would want 25 per cent of their income. It seemed a lot, but, he was so keen, they accepted it. The only thing that concerned them was the music. Would he interfere in what they played? No, he replied, he would not. But their stage act would need to be tidied up if they were going to get on to television. That meant no eating, chewing gum, smoking or swearing on stage and no repartee with the first couple of rows of fans, because the kids at the back couldn't hear and felt left out.

John would later put it this way. 'Brian was trying to clean our image up. To us, Brian was the expert . . . Fucking hell! It was a choice of making it, or still eating chicken on stage. We respected his views.'

As in all the big decisions, the other Beatles deferred to John. And he made his mind up instantly. 'All right, Brian, manage us,' he said. At which Brian took them across the road to a pub to celebrate their new partnership. When, later, Brian came to assess the difference between John and Paul, he would shrewdly write: 'Paul has the glamour. John has the command.'

Talking to *Rolling Stone* in 1970, John would say this of the meeting. 'It was an assessment. I make a lot of mistakes, characterwise, but now and then I make a good one . . . and Brian was one.' Not that he didn't have some misgivings about having to wear a suit *and a tie* when on stage. This amused Mimi enormously. 'John came home in a right old mood, banging around,' she would remember. 'I thought, "Ha-ha, John Lennon, no more scruffs for you."'

John would later come to reflect, almost bitterly, on how he had been turned, in his phrase, 'into a performing flea' and how 'we became famous by compromise'. They were 'playing the game' in order to get ahead. But at the time he embraced the game with little outward rebellion. He wanted to be rich. 'All right,' he would say to himself, 'I'll wear a suit. I'll wear a fucking balloon if someone's going to pay me.'

Having reached an agreement with the Beatles, Brian set to work getting their parents onside, which was necessary as three of them were still under twenty-one and needed an adult to sign their contracts. Jim McCartney was very pleased, being from a generation that reckoned that all Jewish people must be good at business. He even had a piano bought from NEMS in his front room. For her part, Mona Best was canny enough to see that Brian could do more for her son and the Beatles than she could. She and Pete had been taking care of the Beatles' Liverpool bookings in, according to road manager Neil Aspinall, a primitive, ad hoc way, with dates scribbled down in a diary or on the back of an envelope, and pay divided, cash in hand, at the end of every gig. So, it was probably a relief to hand that part of the business over to Brian, who would prove a demon at meticulous organisation. But Mona had another reason for stepping back – something that was soon going to be occupying her life more than somewhat.

As always, George's parents wanted whatever was best for their boy, so it was only Mimi whom Brian really had to charm, and he quickly discovered that she was as forthright as her nephew. As she would admit later to biographer Hunter Davies, at first she worried that Brian would 'have finished with them in two months' time and gone on to something else, while John and the others wouldn't even have got started'. Brian promised her that he would 'look after John'.

Then he told her that he thought John was very talented and that the Beatles were going places, 'I was flabbergasted,' Mimi would remember. 'I thought the only place John was going was the Labour Exchange.'

Had Brian's efforts been unsuccessful, that might well have been John's destination, but, unlike any other possible manager in Liverpool, Brian had, by virtue of his shop, contacts with the big record companies in London. He wasn't just thinking about managing a popular Liverpool band. He was dreaming on an altogether bigger scale.

In truth, the union of Brian Epstein and the Beatles at that moment was a marriage made in heaven. George Harrison summed up their situations perfectly in *The Beatles Anthology*: 'We needed somebody to elevate us out of that cellar, and he needed somebody to get him out of that hole he was in. It was mutually beneficial.'

Brian described his side of the agreement almost gratefully when he was interviewed by Kenneth Harris in the *Observer* two years later. 'My own sense of inferiority evaporated with the Beatles because I knew I could help them and that they wanted me to help them and that they trusted me to help them.'

EMI didn't show any interest when he approached HMV and Columbia, the two big labels there. But Decca got back quickly, sending a representative, Mike Smith, up to Liverpool to see the Beatles in the Cavern. Smith liked what he heard and saw, and in mid-December confirmation arrived that the Beatles had been booked for an audition at Decca in London on 1 January 1962.

After so many years believing that they were invisible to the London music powerbrokers, the Beatles were thrilled to bits. The year was ending on another high, too. Bill Harry had privately told John that the Beatles had beaten friendly rivals Gerry and the Pacemakers in a *Mersey Beat* readers' popularity poll, and would be named, on the front page of the next edition in the New Year, as the top group on Merseyside.

It didn't matter that the Beatles had bought dozens of copies of *Mersey Beat* so that they could vote for themselves. Gerry and the Pacemakers had probably done the same.

# 20

*'I was the closest to Brian – as close as you can get to somebody who lives a sort of fag life, and you don't know what they're doing on the side'*

They drove down to London on New Year's Eve in a van specially hired for the trip by Neil. London was two hundred miles away by busy, winding roads, roundabouts and traffic lights, and it was snowing heavily as they travelled south. Somewhere in the Midlands they got lost, and when they did arrive at their hotel near Russell Square in the Bloomsbury area of London it was already nine in the evening. Brian had travelled down by train in a first-class carriage, but the Beatles had to bring their instruments and amplifiers with them, so rail hadn't been an option. Brian had paid for the hire of the van. As John would remember, they were all terrified about the forthcoming audition, but they were hungry, too. So, setting off through the snow again, they went with Brian into a restaurant, only to be asked to leave when they complained too noisily about the cost of the soup. Brian was probably embarrassed by the behaviour of some of them.

It's impossible to emphasize how strange and yet enticing London looked to the Beatles that night. All their lives they'd been told that London was where everything happened, and now this little gang of musicians who were so sure of themselves in Liverpool felt awkward and overawed, aware that they didn't belong here, but desperately hoping they soon would.

Finally finding something to eat that they could afford in Soho, they then made their way down Charing Cross Road and gazed in a shop window at some black ankle boots with Cuban heels. They all agreed they liked the look of those. The shop was Anello and Davide, and they made a mental note of the name. Then, on they went, to Trafalgar Square to join the New Year celebrations, and watch as drunken and hardy revellers fulfilled an annual tradition by getting themselves soaked in the fountains. No one did that in Liverpool.

There weren't any big, fancy fountains there.

They arrived early at the Decca studios in West Hampstead the following morning and carried their amplifiers from their van into the studio – only to be told they wouldn't be needed as they'd be using the company's own equipment for the audition. Brian was already there, fussing a little when the technicians were late. It *was* New Year's Day – although not then, as now, a public holiday in the UK. Presumably the Decca crew had been celebrating the previous night.

All the group were on edge. George would later say that the red light which came on when they were recording put him off, and Paul, usually so confident when performing, found his voice cracking under the strain. For once there were no jokes from John; no playing to the gallery. He would always be concentrated when he was most tense, although he did snap at Brian when he thought the manager was interfering in how they were playing.

Then, very professionally, they set to work. What, in their innocence, they didn't realise was that even before they'd left Liverpool they'd made an enormous mistake. Brian had many qualities – issuing neatly typed military-style movement orders to road manager Neil, telling him where they would be playing and at what time precisely, was one; and suggesting that the Beatles cut the ends off the strings on their guitars because they looked untidy was another. But Brian was a Sibelius fan, a Philharmonic habitué, not a rock and roller. That he should have suggested that they audition by performing a variety of numbers to demonstrate their versatility, comedy included, only demonstrated his naivety.

'The Sheik of Araby' was a comic interlude, which, with John goofing about on stage as George sang, might have amused Cavernites as the former got his voice back after singing 'Money', but it didn't work on record. Nor did 'Three Cool Cats' or the Latin-flavoured 'Besame Mucho', pleasantly Latin as it was. Yet nearly half of the fifteen-song audition tape they made that day consisted of odd middle-of-the road numbers.

This wasn't the Beatles that had knocked the German spivs off their chairs in the Top Ten Club or caused a crush in the Cavern. What those song choices did was to demonstrate that Brian was a rookie manager who didn't yet know which way to pitch his group. And nor did they. Though John sang the Chuck Berry song 'Memphis, Tennessee', and Paul and George harmonised with him on the Teddy

Bears' 'To Know Her Is To Love Her', the Beatles' stage magic didn't transfer to tape. Apart from the three Lennon and McCartney numbers, 'Hello Little Girl', 'Love Of The Loved' and 'Like Dreamers Do', they could have been any competent group of the time. Interestingly, usually shy about singing their own songs on stage, as the fans in the ballrooms only wanted to hear hits, the fact that they included three that morning showed their intent.

Had they done enough? John wondered as the session ended. 'We didn't sound natural,' he worried, self-doubt never far away.

By mid-afternoon, they were back in the van and driving north again. Mike Smith had told them he would let them know what his superiors thought, and, in the meantime, Brian had already booked them for twenty-nine more gigs to play in and around Liverpool before the end of the month.

The changes that Brian was insisting upon didn't come at once, but soon, as the Beatles were measured for new Italianate mohair grey suits with tight trousers, and dates at venues outside Liverpool were arranged, including a big one at the Floral Hall up the coast in posh Southport and another in Manchester, his influence became increasingly evident. And, going along with it, John was soon hurrying back to see Bill Harry at *Mersey Beat* to ask for the return of a couple of his most pornographic poems. Brian wouldn't have wanted to see those in print. John even agreed to do little smiley bows to the audience after every song. He later thought of it as 'selling out', but the Cavernites didn't care whether the Beatles bowed, or chewed or argued onstage, or even wore the poncy new Anello and Davide boots they'd ordered from London. They were still their Beatles.

From the moment Brian had first seen the Beatles he'd been struck by how much the young girls in the audience loved them, how much his boys had become romantic fantasies for them. That was good. But, it seemed to him that to keep it that way, it would be better if Cynthia and Dot weren't seen with John and Paul so much, so that all the Beatles would appear to be romantically unattached. That was said to be the way the Colonel handled Elvis's busy love-life, thus making him available for every girl's longings.

Some girls might have been cross at being told to stay away from the Cavern, but Cynthia, and apparently Dot, too, weren't about to make trouble for their boyfriends. As Cynthia would later admit, if it helped make the Beatles a success, she was ready to take a back seat. John might have argued on behalf of his girlfriend, but he chose not to. Actually, Cynthia's absence suited him rather well, and when he would be chatting up a new girl after a gig, he would ask the watching fans not to tell Cyn what he'd been up to. Before long he would have a couple of new regular girlfriends on the side – girls Cynthia didn't know about.

Not everything that Brian suggested would be met with such obedient compliance. While the Beatles had been in Germany, John had taken to occasionally mimicking the mentally handicapped while on stage, sometimes seeming to claw with an inane smile on his face, while at other times mindlessly swinging his leg backwards and forwards while Paul was trying to introduce the next song. It was part of a scene-stealing routine, or what John would call his 'spazzie' act – which was short for 'spastic'. Quite why he behaved like that – even giving his behaviour the wrong name, since his actions aped the traditional idea of the mentally challenged rather than someone with a muscular disorder – was something else he never explained, though it was in line with his cartoons of misshapen people and enjoyment of sick humour.

Today it would be unthinkable that an artist would get laughs out of pretending to have learning difficulties, but John grew up in a time when there was a very famous music hall act on radio and television in which a gossipy comedienne, Hylda Baker, would be accompanied on stage by a very tall, mute, unsmiling stooge. 'She knows, you know,' the comedienne would tell the audience, to roars of laughter as the stooge remained expressionless. So, John was following in a well-trodden, cruel path at mocking the handicapped. But why?

In George's opinion, John was simply 'allergic to cripples'. Interviewed for *The Beatles Anthology* he said: 'You can see it in the home movies. Whenever you switch a camera on John, he goes into his interpretation of a spastic.'

It was something Brian had spotted from the beginning at the Cavern, and, finding it distasteful rather than funny, he asked John not to do it. John ignored the request. The spazzie moments stayed in the act for now. What was going on in his mind?

Whatever it was, it doesn't appear to have turned Brian off him. He was always in the manager's thoughts. Paul put it this way: 'I'm sure Brian was in love with John. We were all in love with John, but Brian was gay so that added an edge.'

John would later agree: 'I was the closest to Brian – as close as you can get to somebody who lives a sort of fag life, and you don't know what they're doing on the side.'

In contrast, Paul's relationship with Brian was more distanced from the beginning. Whether this was once again a touch of jealousy because he felt another person was coming between John and himself, as Stuart had, only he would know. It's a common enough human trait, but Brian had to tread carefully to keep Paul as well informed as John on all developments.

As John and Brian lived fairly close to each other in South Liverpool, Brian made sure he visited Mimi and got to know her well. She took to him straight away with his middle-class manners and charm. In return, John would sometimes go over to the Epsteins' house to make Beatle plans and talk; and John did love to talk. He might have liked to think of himself as a rocker, but he would always be attracted to sophistication, something that Brian's conversation always suggested. He was flattered when Brian told him how much he liked his column in *Mersey Beat*, and fascinated when Brian told him about his year in London at drama school. He would later boast that he introduced his manager to the amphetamine-like Preludin to get him to talk. 'If someone's going to manage me I want to know him inside out,' he said. So it was to John that Brian would admit his homosexuality. It hardly came as a surprise.

For weeks Brian had tried to keep up the fiction to the Beatles that he wasn't gay, as he did at home with his parents. But the Beatles weren't fooled for a moment. They didn't care. Sexual inclination just didn't matter to them.

Decca didn't keep them waiting very long. At the beginning of February 1962, Brian was invited down to lunch in the Decca boardroom, where Dick Rowe, the head of artistes and repertoire, told him that he would not be signing the group. Brian was astonished. Having been summoned all the way from Liverpool he had, quite reasonably, assumed he would be hearing good news. Nor could he understand it. But these boys were going to be 'bigger than Elvis', he later said he told Rowe. If he did say that, Rowe must, also reasonably, have thought he was mad. Brian would later write bitterly in his autobiography that when he asked Rowe for a reason, he was told that 'groups of guitars are on their way out . . . The boys won't go, Mr Epstein. We know these things. You have a good record business in Liverpool. Stick to that.'

Dick Rowe would later deny that that was an accurate report of his conversation, and it does sound extraordinarily blunt. But, although an alternative independent deal was apparently discussed, at the end of the day, Decca chose to sign instead a North London group, Brian Poole and the Tremeloes, who were obviously more conveniently based. Poor Dick Rowe would forever be labelled as the man who turned down the Beatles.

John, Paul and George were in the habit of waiting in the Punch and Judy snack bar at the entrance to Lime Street Station in Liverpool when Brian was returning from London with news for them. So it was probably there that they heard about the rejection.

John immediately blamed it on a London prejudice against everything northern . . . 'Oh, yes, Liverpool on the banks of the Khazi,' he is said to have retorted, as though Londoners considered Liverpool to be somewhere far away in the African jungle. There may have been some truth in that attitude, because Liverpool was by no means a fashionable place then, and certainly a very long way from Big Ben.

'We really thought that was the end,' he would remember. 'We didn't think we were going to make it . . . They always said we were too bluesy, too rocky . . . I think they expected us to be all polished . . . They should have seen our potential.'

They should, and the depth of the Decca wound could be measured years later by the way John would so often bring it up. But Decca weren't the only culprits. And, as Pye, Philips, Ember and Oriole also turned them down, the Beatles' faith in their new manager began to slip. 'Brian would come back from London and he couldn't face us . . .' John would recall. 'He was terrified to tell us.'

The single piece of good news in those first months of 1962 was an audition on the only BBC radio programme that gave an opportunity to first timers. It was called *Teenager's Turn,* and was produced in Manchester. This time the Beatles stuck to what they did best. They sang rock and roll songs – Roy Orbison's 'Dream Baby', the Marvelettes' 'Please Mr Postman', and Chuck Berry's 'Memphis, Tennessee', adding John's composition 'Hello Little Girl' for good measure. They passed that audition. They were learning.

Despite the odd ungrateful comments from his four disappointed clients, Brian never gave up. But it didn't help that he was hawking a reel-to-reel tape recording of the Decca audition to play to record companies, instead of demo records. So, when he learned that EMI offered a little tape-to-disc service above their HMV record shop in London's Oxford Street, he went in to get a few private acetates of the Decca session cut as demos.

It was another serendipitous moment. The disc cutter there, a man called Jim Foy, became interested in the Lennon and McCartney songs he was hearing on the tapes as he worked. 'I asked whether they had been published,' he would tell Beatles chronicler Mark Lewisohn. When Foy learned that they hadn't, he suggested Brian talk to a man called Syd Colman, who was the head of EMI's music publishing company, Ardmore and Beechwood, which just happened to be on the floor above in the same building.

Going up the stairs, Brian played Colman the songs. The music publisher liked them. So Brian made him an offer. If Colman could help get the Beatles a recording contract, Ardmore and Beechwood could publish the songs.

For two years the Beatles had been playing and singing cover versions of their rock heroes' work that had turned them into a terrific band. But it was the songs that John and Paul wrote that proved to be the key that would unlock the door to the recording studio for them. And it had taken a humble disc cutter to spot the talent that the record makers had missed – the songs of Lennon and McCartney.

# 21

*'I looked up to Stu. I depended on him to tell
me the truth . . . and I'd believe him'*

Throughout all these months John and Stuart wrote regularly to each
other – as John had a crisis of confidence after the Decca rejection,
and Stuart began telling of mystery headaches that he was suffering.
Then in mid-February 1962 Stuart came back to Liverpool for a few
days. His mother was recovering after an operation and he wanted to
see her. But it was Stuart who didn't look well.

With the Beatles now playing two venues on most days, there was,
however, hardly any time for John and Stuart to get together and
talk, and, after seeing the band a couple of times at the Cavern, Stuart
returned to Germany. There would be better opportunities for them
to catch up when the Beatles went back to Hamburg for another
season in a few weeks' time, they told each other. John was looking
forward to it.

For the Beatles' third Hamburg visit, Brian handled the negotiations, which meant that they flew there. But because George had
contracted German measles and wasn't quite recovered, John, Paul
and Pete went out to Germany, via Amsterdam, on 10 April. The following day, they got up late and returned to Hamburg airport to meet
Brian and George who were coming out to join them. Almost the first
people they saw at the airport were Astrid and Klaus Voorman. That
was a surprise.

'Hello, where's Stu?' were John's first words. Then he saw Astrid's
expression.

'Stu's dead, John.'

For a moment the three Beatles were mute. It didn't seem possible.
Then John broke down, shaking in shock and grief. Astrid and Klaus
had assumed that John would have been informed by Brian, Klaus
having telephoned him the previous day. But for some reason, and
in those days news travelled far more slowly, the message hadn't

reached the three Beatles who had been en route to Germany.

John had known that Stuart was unwell. He'd never been a strong boy; sometimes it was his stomach that troubled him, and at other times Stuart had thought he had a grumbling appendix. Then the headaches had begun. At first doctors in Hamburg had put them down to exhaustion from painting into the night; or perhaps it was nervous strain. So Stuart had taken time off college. Tests had found nothing unusual. Later, however, Astrid would tell of how Stuart had become increasingly difficult in that the blinding pain in his head would affect his personality, and he had become convinced that she was seeing another boy. She wasn't.

Then the previous afternoon, Stuart had gone into convulsions. An ambulance had been called, but it was too late. Stuart had lost consciousness and died while on his way to hospital. He was twenty-two. Astrid and Stuart had been living together and planning to marry later that year. Now she was an unmarried widow.

Momentarily out of control at the airport, John quickly managed to put away his tears. He would never want to show grief in public. But when Brian and George's plane arrived, bringing with them Stuart's mother, Millie Sutcliffe, whom Brian had collected in his car that morning, he didn't know how to face her. She had blamed him for getting Stuart involved in music and taking him away to Hamburg. And now she had come to take her son's body home.

John's friendship with Stuart hadn't been forged in the mill of shared ambition like his with Paul. There was never any competition between them. Privately they would admit to each other their worries about not being good enough at what they wanted to do, and they encouraged each other when doubts arose. Stuart was impressed by John's original mind, and John had admired Stuart's artistic talent, his intelligence and his honesty. 'I looked up to Stu,' he would one day reflect. 'I depended on him to tell me the truth . . . He would tell me if something was good and I'd believe him.'

It wasn't only John who was devastated. George, too, had burst into tears when told of Stuart's death. Pete remembered how ill Stuart had looked on his visit to Liverpool a few weeks earlier, and now he sat in the airport crying. Young people never expect to encounter the sudden death of one of their own.

Nevertheless, thirty-six hours later the Beatles were back on stage in Hamburg, professionally hiding their loss in their music. 'You have to decide if you want to die or go on living,' John would tell Astrid when he went to see her. He would have been telling himself the same thing. That was John, grim-faced and angry at the loss of his best friend, but, once sufficiently recovered, restoring the armour he'd built around himself, ever determined not to let sentiment control him, or at least to allow it to show. Other than when Astrid asked him if there was anything of Stuart's he would like by which to remember him, and he chose Stu's navy blue and cream striped college scarf, only once did he let his mask of stone slip. Having insisted that Astrid went to see the Beatles at the Star-Club one night, he sang 'Love Me Tender' – the song Stuart had always sung when he'd been a Beatle.

Stuart's funeral took place in Huyton Parish Church, just outside Liverpool. The Beatles were still in Hamburg, so they didn't attend. Cynthia went. An autopsy would reveal that Stuart had died from a cerebral haemorrhage leading to bleeding into 'the right ventricle of the brain'. The cause was unknown, but a small dent in one side of Stuart's skull was also noted. It would later be speculated, by Stuart's sister, Pauline, that the dent may have been caused by the kick to the head that her brother had received at Lathom Hall in 1961 from a group of Teddy boys after a Beatles gig. Whether that injury was the original cause of the haemorrhage, no one will ever know.

What we do know is that John's behaviour in Hamburg now became more self-destructive than ever. From going on stage pretending to be a cleaner, or with a lavatory seat around his neck, or gabbling incoherently as amphetamines and beer bent his consciousness, sometimes he became violent, often he was sick, and frequently he had sex with different girls he picked up. The fabled permissive society of the Sixties had arrived early in the red-light area of the Reeperbahn, and, although his letters still pleaded with Cynthia to 'wait for me', he made no attempt to be faithful to her: quite the opposite. Was he behaving that way simply because he could? He probably never knew himself.

Back in Liverpool, Cynthia was still living unhappily at Mendips. Then one day, Mimi came across a love letter that John had written to his girlfriend, and read it. She was apoplectic. It was, she stormed to Cynthia, 'pornographic'! That would certainly have been John's intention when he wrote it.

It was the end for Cynthia with Mimi. They'd never got on. Soon after that, she moved in with an aunt, and then went on to have a bedsit in the same house as Paul's girlfriend Dot.

The first time the Beatles had heard the name 'George Martin' had been when Brian had returned from London in March 1962 with what looked tentatively like good news. His meetings with the disc cutter and the music publisher had led him to Martin's office at Parlophone Records, which, as music labels went, was the mongrel runt at EMI. Specialising for years in Scottish country dance Jimmy Shand jigs, light orchestral pieces and comedy records featuring the *Beyond The Fringe* satirist team and Peter Sellers, Parlophone was something of an oddity, almost an experimental corner of the record business save for the smooth voice of Matt Monro. Some rock musicians might have been affronted to be told that Parlophone was vaguely (no more than that) interested in them – but the Beatles weren't. At least Parlophone wasn't Embassy, the Woolworths budget label that John had half-jokingly suggested that Brian might try next.

What neither the Beatles nor Brian knew was that George Martin, the thirty-six-year-old head of Parlophone, was looking for a singer or a group that could deliver him the youth market. All the other EMI labels – Columbia, Capitol, HMV and MGM – had regular top ten records from rock stars, and it irked him that over on Columbia, Norrie Paramor had enjoyed four years of regular UK number one hits with Cliff Richard. Martin's lack of success in finding anyone young and suitable probably wasn't helped by the fact that he was a classically trained musician not a rock fan, who had never got Elvis Presley. 'Rock and roll,' he would later admit to me, 'was alien to me.'

He knew he had to find someone, however, so when the very polite Brian Epstein from Liverpool had turned up in his office with a demo record of Paul singing 'Like Dreamers Do', and the boss of EMI's publishing arm, Ardmore and Beechwood, wanted to publish one of the Lennon and McCartney songs, the least he could do was give these boys a listen. An alignment in the fortunes of several people was approaching.

There was no hurry, however, so George Martin took his time. Then, towards the end of May, with the Beatles approaching the end of their Hamburg season, they received a telegram from Brian in Liverpool: 'CONGRATULATIONS BOYS. EMI REQUEST RECORDING SESSION. PLEASE REHEARSE NEW MATERIAL.'

The Beatles had been dismayed when Decca had turned them down. But Dick Rowe had unwittingly done them an enormous favour with his rejection, in that he'd saved them for someone far more suited to discover them – George Martin. The Beatles knew everything there was to know about rock and roll, Martin knew hardly anything. But he knew a great deal about all kinds of other music. They would teach him and he would teach them. They would make the perfect match.

# 22

*'Cyn's having a baby. We're getting married tomorrow.*
*Do you want to come?'*

In the early evening of 6 June 1962, Neil Aspinall drove his van through the opened gates of EMI Recording Studios in Abbey Road, St John's Wood, and parked on the gravel that had once been a rich family's large front garden. The early nineteenth-century London mansion that faced the Beatles as they climbed from the van didn't look anything like a modern recording studio, but, as they soon discovered, the house was only a facade, with the studios having been built on to the back of it over the previous forty years. Getting instructions from the EMI sound engineers, in their white laboratory coats, Neil and the Beatles carried their guitars and equipment through the tradesmen's entrance at the side of the building and into the large Studio Two. Dressed up in their new stage suits for the big occasion, and with their hair combed forward, the EMI staff who greeted them were amused. 'Well, what have we got here,' one was heard to say.

The plan was that Ron Richards, George Martin's thirty-three-year-old assistant, would start the session by getting the group to set up and play a few songs while Martin was in the canteen having his evening meal. The Beatles had got as far as 'Love Me Do' when a message was sent to the canteen that Martin should come and take a listen. Unknown to them, the producer then approached the studio up the back stairs to the control room and sat at his console watching the four very nervous boys below him as they also went through 'Ask Me Why', 'Besame Mucho' and 'Hello Little Girl'. Nothing he heard excited him particularly, but although he considered 'Love Me Do' as 'not much more than a riff', it seemed the most likely of their songs, and he liked John's harmonica playing. It reminded him of the guitar and harmonica blues of Sonny Terry and Brownie McGhee.

Paul had written 'Love Me Do' a few years earlier and he and John had always quite liked it; but *only* quite liked it. 'It was the first one we dared do of our own,' John would say. 'It was quite a traumatic thing because we were doing such great numbers by Ray Charles and Little Richard and all of them. So, it was quite hard to come in singing "Love Me Do". We thought our numbers were a bit wet.'

The problem had been that the original arrangement they'd played in the clubs had lacked something. Then Bruce Channel's 'Hey Baby' had been released. It was a good record, but what made it a great record was the way the singer sang a duet with a harmonica played by a man called Delbert McClinton. John loved it. He hadn't often taken out his own harmonica – the one he'd shoplifted in Arnhem on the Beatles' first visit to Germany two years earlier. But its moment had now arrived and the stolen harmonica's bluesy sound would haunt its way through 'Love Me Do'.

Before the session George Martin had been puzzling over whether it was John or Paul who was the lead singer, whether it would be 'John Lennon and the Beatles' or 'Paul McCartney and the Beatles' on the record's label. But the realisation that there were two and sometimes even three lead singers when George Harrison was given a chance only fully dawned on him when he noticed that John, who was singing the lead of Paul's song, couldn't quite finish the line 'love me do-oo' at the end of every verse, because he had to then immediately play his harmonica. So, it was agreed that Paul would step forward to sing that bit. With the Beatles it wasn't going to be one or the other. This was something quite new, a group who worked as a whole and shared singing and playing responsibilities.

After their stipulated three hours, the session in the studio finished, and Martin invited the boys up into the control room to get to know them better. Having first played the results of their evening's work, he then gave them a good talking to, in what to them sounded like the posh accent of a young public school housemaster. None of them, he would remember, uttered a word in reply. So, finally, he asked if there was anything they didn't like.

At first there was another silence until George drolly, and ultimately famously, said: 'Well, I don't like your tie.' It was challenging and slightly provocative, a typical Liverpudlian rejoinder, going off on a tangent, but said with a smile.

George Martin laughed. The ice was broken. Instantly, with the exception of the determinedly silent Pete, all the Beatles were laughing and joking and talking at once. 'We liked each other,' Martin would tell me. 'They were charismatic. I thought that if they could charm the pants off me, they could charm the pants off an audience. And if I could find them a hit song, I'd have a hit group.' In other words, secretly, he was by no means convinced of their songwriting abilities.

As the Beatles left Abbey Road that night they were feeling pleased with themselves. George Martin and assistant Ron Richards, however, knew there was a problem to be overcome. That first recording of 'Love Me Do' wasn't good enough. It would need to be recorded again, and the next time with a better drummer than Pete Best. As Martin firmly told Brian Epstein when he explained the problem, it wasn't unusual for record producers to use different musicians on record from those who appeared in the clubs. What was acceptable in a dance hall, wasn't when the record was heard on the radio.

This was an opinion Brian didn't want to hear, but one which, having overheard the conversations between John, Paul and George, he'd seen coming. It didn't mean that Pete had to be immediately replaced. But the moment the Beatles had been putting off was approaching. For John, it was particularly difficult, as he and Pete had regularly gone out drinking together in Hamburg. And although Pete may not have been on the same mental wavelength as the other three, he was pleasant enough company. None of them ever disliked him. That, however, wouldn't be enough to save him.

'We were always going to dump him when we could find a decent drummer,' was John's memory. 'But by the time we got back from Germany we'd trained him to keep a stick going up and down – four to the bar. He couldn't do much else. He looked nice and the girls liked him.'

Years later John would talk about how the Beatles were 'bastards' in their determination to succeed, and so it would prove in their dis-posal of Pete, when they were wily, conspiratorial and, at the end of the day, two-faced. Through all of June, July and half of August 1962 they played dozens of gigs with Pete at the Cavern and all over Merseyside as Brian secretly plotted with lawyers about how to edge Pete out – all the time suggesting other drummers to the Beatles. He was wasting his breath in that respect. George had been pushing John and Paul to bring Ringo Starr into the group since they'd first played with him in Hamburg. 'Ringo was a star in his own right before we even met him . . . a professional drummer,' was John's opinion, 'the best drummer in Liverpool.'

But that wasn't Ringo's only attraction. Having taken up playing the drums while in a long-stay children's isolation hospital for tuberculosis, he'd missed much education, but had made up for it with a street wisdom, a quirky gift for jokey malapropisms and a disarming honesty. Brought up in a particularly poor area of Liverpool, he could also make people laugh, but not in John's often snide way. For Ringo to be 'so aware having had so little education' was, John would later conclude, 'rather unnerving to someone who's been to school since he was fucking two years old onwards'.

The Ringo manoeuvres all had to be worked out very delicately. But, meanwhile, totally unaware of what was going on behind his back, Pete was faced with an unusual situation at home, when his mother Mona gave birth to a baby boy. The baby's father was the Beatles' road manager Neil Aspinall, Pete's close friend. And although John, Paul and George wanted Pete out, they definitely wanted to keep Neil in. He was a rock of common sense. All of which meant they couldn't tell Neil what they were planning to do to Pete. It was becoming an ever more tangled web.

Since John had been home from Hamburg, Cynthia had been living in a bedsit in South Liverpool. It wasn't ideal as not only was she now being discouraged from going to the Cavern, 'gentlemen guests' in her new home were not allowed to stay the night. So John and she would get together in the afternoons or whenever he wasn't playing.

One day, early in August, Cynthia had two pieces of news when he arrived. The first was that she'd failed her final exams at college and couldn't now become a teacher. The second was that she was pregnant.

Cynthia would remember that John sat silently for some moments as the implications sank in. 'There's only one thing for it,' he said at last. 'We'll have to get married.' Getting married was the last thing he wanted to do. But . . . 'I didn't try to fight it,' he would recall.

Actually, for a boy from his background, marrying Cynthia was the only decent thing he could do. Abortion was illegal in the UK in 1962, and if a boy got a girl pregnant it was universally considered his duty to marry her. Cynthia would always insist that not for one moment did he try to get out of it.

'I thought it would be goodbye to the group,' were his first thoughts, but he didn't share them with Cynthia, as he joked: 'I'll make an honest womb of you.'

Perhaps the most surprising thing about the pregnancy was that it hadn't happened sooner. In the two and a half years that John and Cynthia had been lovers they had never used any kind of contraception. The birth control pill had only very recently been invented and was definitely not available to young unmarried women in the UK, the general attitude being that if it were it would inevitably lead to much promiscuity. But condoms were readily available. John had just never bothered to buy them.

The first person John told of the new complication was Brian, who immediately and calmly took it on himself to organise the marriage licence and the register office. John, meanwhile, had to tell Mimi. Knowing what her reaction would be, he put it off.

One of the first people Cynthia told was her neighbour, Paul's girlfriend Dot. She chose a bad time. Paul had just been to see Dot to tell her that although he loved her, as he didn't want to get married, they would have to break off their relationship. And that was that.

It was a busy time for Brian. Putting John's problems to one side, he turned to the drummer situation, and, after a Cavern gig, asked Pete to go to see him the next day. Pete assumed it was to discuss a business matter and took Neil with him.

On arriving at Brian's office, Neil waited outside. Inside, Pete noticed that the manager was very nervous.

Finally, Brian came to the point. 'I've got some bad news for you, Pete,' he said. 'The boys have decided that they don't want you in the group any more, and that Ringo is replacing you.' Then he added the excuse that producer George Martin didn't think Pete was a good enough drummer.

Pete was devastated. Other possibilities were offered to him, but that afternoon he went home and cried.

'We were cowards,' John would later tell me, opening a hitherto guarded vein of guilt. 'We got Brian to do our dirty work for us.' But he never had much time for sentiment when it interfered with his ambition. Life was for living and getting on with. 'If we'd told him to his face that would have been much nastier. It would probably have ended in a fight.'

Neil Aspinall was upset for his friend and considered giving up his job with the group. Mona's advice was for him to stay with them. She was, understandably, angry and hurt for her son, as she let Brian

Epstein know. But she was a realist, too.

With Ringo having agreed to join the Beatles, a record deal signed and Granada TV about to film a performance by the group at the Cavern, everything was falling into place. And, eight days after Pete's sacking, with Ringo now behind the drums, the Beatles were filmed for the first time. What Neil Aspinall would describe as 'the chain' was now complete. John had found Paul; Paul had introduced George; and now George had brought Ringo into the band.

Wearing white shirts, black waistcoats and ties, along with their black Anello and Davide Chelsea boots, the group played and sang 'Some Other Guy' for the TV cameras with John and Paul singing together at separate microphones. Although at the time the performance wasn't televised, that strip of film was a scoop for Granada TV, and has been seen since then by hundreds of millions of fans.

With his wedding for Cynthia planned for the following day John couldn't keep the secret from Mimi any longer. That night when he got home from the Cavern, Mimi was, as always, waiting.

John's recollection of the encounter would be: 'I said, "Cyn's having a baby. We're getting married tomorrow. Do you want to come?"'

Mimi reacted as he had expected. 'She let out a groan . . .' before saying with much anger all the things he already knew. 'You're too young,' she shouted, almost certainly with the image of her feckless sister Julia arriving home to tell the family that she'd just married the ne'er-do-well Freddie Lennon in her mind. She would not, she declared, be going to the wedding. Later she would tell biographer Ray Coleman that John cried that night.

The following morning Brian picked up Cynthia in a chauffeur-driven car and drove her to the Register Office in Liverpool's Mount Pleasant. John was waiting, accompanied by Paul and George, all wearing suits and ties. John didn't know it, but this was the office where his parents had married in 1938. Unable to afford anything new for her wedding, Cynthia was wearing her best purple and black checked suit and had put up her hair in a French pleat. John, she would later write, immediately told her how beautiful she looked. There were no bridesmaids, nor had Ringo been invited, because, although he was now a Beatle, John didn't know him well enough to be sure he could be trusted to keep the marriage a secret. And secrecy would now be the order of the day. The only other guests were

Cynthia's brother Tony and his wife Marjorie, for whom it was their lunch hour.

Throughout the short ceremony a road drill was hammering in the back yard of the building behind the register office, making it difficult for the couple to hear what the registrar was saying, and forcing them to shout their responses. John found this funny. And when the registrar asked the groom to approach and, by mistake, George stepped forward instead everyone began to giggle. Then, as the rain began to pour down outside, John Lennon and Cynthia Powell became man and wife. There was no one there from John's family, not even his half-sisters. Most probably Mimi hadn't told anyone, and no one had any idea where his father might be.

If he was hurt by Mimi's absence – and he probably was, because, despite her irascibility, he loved her – he didn't let anyone see. Instead he hid behind jokes. 'It was all a laugh. But I did feel embarrassed walking about married. It was like walking around with odd socks on or with your flies open . . .'

No wedding reception had been planned, and, because Cynthia's brother Tony and his wife had to get back to work, Brian suggested that the three Beatles, Cynthia and he went for lunch to the nearby Reece's café. Again, history was repeating itself. That was where John's parents had gone for lunch after their wedding twenty-four years earlier. As it was more of a cafeteria than a restaurant, the little wedding party had to queue for soup, chicken and trifle, and, because Reece's had no licence, glasses of water were raised to toast the newly-weds.

Did John still love Cynthia at that stage? Probably, in his way, and certainly more than anyone else. Years later he would say unkindly that their son Julian was 'born out of a bottle of whisky on a Saturday night'. But that was untrue and unworthy of him. He had loved Cynthia very much when they'd first got together in the year after his mother had been killed.

Brian was a solicitous manager. He didn't have to do it but he very kindly decided to lend John and Cynthia a little flat, which, unknown to his parents, he had secretly acquired for himself not far from the Liverpool College of Art in Falkner Street. It was somewhere he might meet friends of whom his parents might not approve, but he happily gave it up for John and his new bride.

'Well, Mrs Lennon, how does it feel to be married?' John asked

Cynthia that afternoon as he returned from Menlove Avenue with some of his belongings.

That evening Brian's Ford Zodiac was at the front door to pick John up. The Beatles had a gig in Chester that night. Cynthia wasn't invited. She stayed at home. In fact, great efforts would be taken to make sure that she would not be seen anywhere with John over the next few months as her pregnancy began to show. It would be a lonely life.

'We didn't keep the marriage a secret,' John would fib later. 'It was just that when we came on the scene nobody really asked us. They weren't interested in whether we were married or not. The question they used to ask was, "What sort of girls do you like?" . . . I wasn't going to say, "I'm married . . . "'

# 23

*'When the dirty work came, I had to be the leader . . .*
*When it came to the nitty gritty, I had to do the talking'*

As the pace began to accelerate, with dates being booked increasingly further afield and the Cavern gigs becoming ever more packed, the Beatles' support group began to expand, too. A friendly giant of a fan called Mal Evans, who was twenty-six, married with a wife and child, gave up his job as a Post Office telephone engineer to assist road manager Neil; and a true Cavernite called Freda Kelly moved into Brian's NEMS office to eventually run the Beatles Fan Club. 'It was my dream job, but at first I couldn't understand why the Beatles should even have a fan club because to me they were just a Liverpool group,' she would remember. A young woman of great devotion, she was as loyal to them as John was unfaithful to Cynthia. 'John was seeing a girl who I knew and I was dying to tell her that he was married, but I couldn't because I'd promised not to,' she would admit decades later. 'I felt torn. It was awful.'

With its docks and many suburbs, Liverpool might seem a big city, but for rock groups the centre of town was more like a village where the musicians would get off with girl fans. Thus, Thelma Pickles, with whom John had had a relationship when he was at college, went out with Paul for a short time, while Maureen Cox, who would become Ringo's first wife, had previously had a couple of dates with Paul.

It was a cosy place and an exciting time, but what none of the Beatles could possibly have realised was that the summer and autumn of 1962 would be the last time any of them would enjoy anonymity before fame took over their lives.

They had expected 'Love Me Do' to be released in July, but it was postponed, and then at the end of August, Brian received a demo copy of a new song from George Martin. It was 'How Do You Do It?' and had been written by a young London songwriter called Mitch Murray.

Part of the job of a head of artistes and repertoire in those days was to find suitable songs for the artists under contract, and to Martin this sounded much more like a hit than 'Love Me Do'. So, accompanying the demo was a terse order that the group arrange and rehearse the song and prepare to record it at the beginning of September.

The Beatles didn't take kindly to their producer's instructions. Not only was 'Love Me Do' obviously going to be relegated to a B-side, which meant it would probably never be heard on the radio, but they hated 'How Do You Do It?'. It was commercial, but it just wasn't for them. But what could they do? George Martin was the boss. If they wanted to get a record out they would have to do what they were told.

They did. Returning to London they recorded it, as professionally as they could. But then, at the urging of the others, John went to work on Martin. 'When the dirty work came, I had to be the leader,' he would later say. 'Whatever the scene was, when it came to the nitty gritty, I had to do the talking.' So now he put it to Martin that 'we can do better than this'.

Martin was unimpressed. 'When you write something as good as that song, I'll let you record it. Otherwise that's the song that's going out.'

It looked like an impasse. But, as Beatles chronicler Mark Lewisohn has unearthed, there was, unknown to the Beatles, another pressure on Martin. This time it came from EMI publishers Ardmore and Beechwood, who had delivered the group to Parlophone in the first place. As the publishers of 'Love Me Do' they, too, wanted the Lennon and McCartney song to be the A-side. In the end, Martin had no choice but to back down and, a week later, set about making a better recording of 'Love Me Do'.

John reckoned, with his usual exaggeration, that he must have sung it 'about thirty times' before Martin was satisfied. On some of the takes Ringo played, and on others it was a session drummer called Andy White, who had been brought into the studio in case Ringo was no better than Pete. But at last the Beatles' first record, 'Love Me Do', with Andy White on drums (although Ringo's version would go on their first album), was ready for release. It had taken a lot of work, and George Martin would never regard it highly. (He was, however, to be proved right about 'How Do You Do It?'. A few months later Brian Epstein would begin to manage another Liverpool group, Gerry and the Pacemakers, and 'How Do You Do It?' would become their first number one.)

Martin had challenged the group to write a better song, and John soon had one in mind. It was called 'Please Please Me' and the producer's first reaction was to suggest a change to the tempo as it sounded like a dramatic Roy Orbison piece. John took that on board and went back to Liverpool to work on it. He now had an added inducement. With 'P.S. I Love You' scheduled to be the flip side of 'Love Me Do', that meant that the two songs on the first Beatles record would have been written mainly by Paul. The competitive instinct in him was stirred. It would be his turn next.

Before any of that could happen, however, all four Beatles were asked to sign a five-year contract with Brian Epstein and NEMS. Despite their reservations, they agreed that Brian would take a management share of 25 per cent of their earnings, with the other 75 per cent being shared equally between all four Beatles – Ringo having joined as a full partner. This arrangement only covered records and public appearances, however, and as John and Paul were now going to have their songs recorded and therefore published, an additional arrangement was now necessary to formalise their relationship as songwriters. Accordingly, a separate, secret meeting was held at the Falkner Street flat where John and Cynthia were living.

The two Beatles hadn't until then considered themselves serious songwriters. It was just something they did on the side, and they knew nothing about song publishing. What they did know was that a lot of the American hits they played were written by songwriting duos, such as Pomus and Shuman, and most recently husband and wife Gerry Goffin and Carole King. So they decided, with little discussion, to become either Lennon and McCartney, or McCartney and Lennon, depending upon who was the main instigator of the song, and to share equally in credits and income any song, written either by both of them or by one or the other.

As an agreement it was a fine testament to their working friendship as well as an acknowledgement that they were already a songwriting team who needed each other to get the very best results. But, while it was good for Brian Epstein, who was to act as their songwriting agent and who would take 20 per cent of their royalties, it was to prove short-sighted for them – as events would eventually show.

For John and Paul, the immediate positive side was that it locked them ever closer together. But for George and Ringo there was a negative aspect, in that they were left out of this side deal – which irked

George particularly, because he was a songwriter, too. He would never be as confident a singer as John and Paul ('I used to scream at him to open his mouth and *sing*,' John would later tell me. 'I encouraged him like mad'), nor as prolific a songwriter. But, then, he had no writing partner, John and Paul deciding that a trio might be too cumbersome, and that they would work better as a traditional twosome. Eternally optimistic as George had been when times had been bleak, he was still the youngest, as he would increasingly discover after the older boys sewed up the songwriting between them, making them, quite clearly, the first two among equals.

'Love Me Do' went on sale on 5 October 1962, and Mimi's opinion was typically straightforward. 'Well,' she told John, 'if you think that's going to make you your fortune, you've got another think coming.' Unfortunately, her judgement seemed to be shared by Parlophone, who gave the record little more than minimum exposure on their sponsored programmes on Radio Luxembourg – which was just two plays a week for three weeks. Even so, it was a giant step forward for the Beatles, and they would get Neil to stop the van so that they could listen to it on the few occasions their record *was* played. Naturally, BBC radio ignored it completely at first.

Brian, meanwhile, was relishing his new life in pop management. As the Beatles played every night and most lunchtimes, plugging their record, he was also trying his hand at being a rock promoter, booking no less a star than Little Richard to two headline Liverpool shows – with the Beatles co-starring of course. John later summed up his manager's thinking: 'Brian used to bring rock stars who were not making it any more . . . like Little Richard, and he would put us on the bill with them. So, we'd use them to draw the crowd. It's hard for people to imagine just how thrilled the four of us were to even *see* any great rock and rollers in the flesh . . . We were almost paralysed with devotion.'

For Little Richard's second Merseyside show Brian even took over the Empire Theatre and treated some of his staff to seats in a box with him. Freda Kelly, whose main job was sending out the first publicity photographs of the group and taking the Beatles' wages to wherever they were playing on Friday nights, was flattered to be included. 'I'd never been in a box before,' she remembers. 'And when the Beatles came on stage and Paul sang "A Taste Of Honey", I couldn't believe it! The Beatles at the Empire! The biggest theatre in Liverpool!' She'd bought a copy of 'Love Me Do' on the day it came out, even though she didn't have a record player. 'Lots of Liverpool fans did that,' she explains. 'Out of loyalty.'

Such support was not evident in London, where on a tour of Britain's pop music newspapers they were met with indifference, and the general feeling that 'Beatles' was a funny name for a band. 'We were treated like provincials by the Cockneys,' John would say afterwards, before adding a typical exaggeration: 'They looked down on us like we were animals . . .'

They returned to Liverpool disappointed, aware that another problem was approaching. The release date for 'Love Me Do' had been arbitrarily decided by Parlophone, but the Beatles were under contract to return to the Star-Club in Hamburg for the first two weeks of November. This meant they would be away when they should be promoting their record. John and Paul had had enough of Hamburg and didn't want to go back.

'If we'd had our way we'd have copped out of the engagement because we didn't feel we owed them fuck-all . . .' John would admit. 'But Brian made us go back to fulfil the contract.' That was Brian, ever the honourable man. So, off the Beatles went, back to a Hamburg they'd now outlived, cursing their rotten luck – although, as usual, John would have a girlfriend waiting there to soften the blow.

Then a curious thing happened. In the Beatles' absence their record began to sell, not in prodigious quantities, but enough for it to slowly begin to climb the charts. All the Mecca dance halls around the country had been sent copies, and some were now playing it, as were some of the clubs. The BBC even put it on *Two-Way Family Favourites*, a record programme that linked British soldiers serving in Germany with their families and girlfriends back in the UK. Tens of millions of homes were tuned to the show every Sunday at midday, so millions of young people must have heard it.

Although, over the next few weeks, it reached the top of the local chart in Liverpool, where the sales were so big that a rumour emerged that Brian had bought ten thousand copies – he hadn't – it would never get higher nationally than number seventeen. But it sold steadily over several weeks, and by the time the Beatles returned to Liverpool in mid-November the mood towards them had changed. Brian's phone at his office in Liverpool's Whitechapel was now beginning to ring,

TV producers and tour promoters wanting to talk. The 'Beatles' had stopped being just a funny name to Londoners, and Liverpool didn't seem quite so far away any more.

Having a hit, even if it was only a small one, meant that George Martin was now keener, too. And on 26 November in Studio Two at EMI's Abbey Road, John showed him what he and the other Beatles had done with 'Please Please Me'. Years later John would remember how he had started writing it in his bedroom at Mendips, and that he could still picture the pink bedspread there as he had played around with lyrics from an old Bing Crosby hit that had started 'Please, lend your little ear to my pleas'.

John had always enjoyed doodling with words, and the double use of 'please' intrigued him. Now, after work with Paul and George, the main inspiration for the song had gone from being Roy Orbison's 'Only The Lonely' to the Everly Brothers' 'Cathy's Clown'. The effect was immediate. In popular music terms 'Please Please Me' was a masterpiece of attention grabbing, from the guitar and harmonica opening, to the call and response passage of *'Come on, come on, come on, come on'*, which had been picked up from American R&B records, and which built excitement for the leap into falsetto in the chorus *'Please, please me, oh yeah, like I please you'*.

John sang most of it pell-mell, with Paul harmonising a third higher, and George also coming in for the refrains. It was as though they knew they were finally on the cusp of stardom and were hurrying to get there.

It was such an obvious hit that, even before the end of the session, George Martin was congratulating them somewhat portentously: 'Gentlemen, you've just made your first number one record.'

The Beatles just laughed. They knew how good it was. What they didn't know was how big a turning point it would be in their lives. Years later, John would often talk nostalgically about the great days of playing the Cavern and the Liverpool ballrooms before he'd been famous. 'We were the best bloody band there was,' he would tell me. 'When we played straight rock . . . there was nobody to touch us. Basically I'm just a rocker, and that's the way I've always been.'

He might have liked to say that, but it wasn't true. He was a cultural magpie who took from whatever he came across, be it Bing Crosby, *The Owl And The Pussy Cat* or the Everly Brothers by way of Roy Orbison.

*

Neither he nor Paul had ever given much serious thought to music publishing. From seeing sheet music and the names of publishers on records, they knew that such companies existed, but they had no idea of how large a part publishing played in the music business. But they'd seen little effort by Ardmore and Beechwood to promote 'Love Me Do', which gave them cause to wonder what exactly those publishing guys did, apart from owning the copyright of a song and taking 50 per cent of the royalties from records and radio plays. And then they met a music publisher called Dick James.

Luck had taken Brian to George Martin, and now Martin's friendship with James opened another door. Unlike Epstein and Martin, James, at forty-two, was already middle-aged when he first heard the Beatles. But after twenty years in show business, first as a singer with the Geraldo and Henry Hall bands, he knew a good song when he heard one and had become a small-time music publisher. On top of that, to use one of his own favourite expressions, he was 'hungry'. The son of Polish immigrants, and born Leon Isaac Vapnick, he was an East End boy always hungry for songs he could publish from his little West End office in London's Charing Cross Road. At Martin's suggestion, Brian went to see James, who, after one hearing of 'Please Please Me', agreed to publish it, and the record's flip side 'Ask Me Why'. But there was more. After so many years in the business, he knew who to phone, and he immediately got the Beatles booked on to *Thank Your Lucky Stars*, a nationally networked pop music programme, for the week of the record's release in January 1963. He was a new ally in London for the Beatles and a very influential one. Some years later John would, perhaps with some justification, be critical of him. But in those heady days of anticipation, as Dick James became Brian's experienced guiding hand through the maze of necessary promotion, all the Beatles, and especially John and Paul, had reason to be grateful to him.

There were just eight weeks between the recording of 'Please Please Me' and its UK release on 11 January 1963, fifty-six days when, so confident were the Beatles of success, that they found themselves impatiently saying goodbye to one life as they waited to begin their new one.

Earlier in the year Brian had been offered a hike in money for them

John, aged about 10, with his mother Julia.

▼ John, aged 11, wearing the uniform of his new school Quarry Bank High School For Boys. That cap was rarely seen on his head after this photograph was taken.

▲ John's father, Alfred Lennon. 'He looked as unkempt and down at heel as a tramp . . . but, alarmingly, he had John's face,' said Cynthia Lennon on first meeting him.

John's 'Auntie Mimi' Smith, in the front room of her house,
Mendips, on Menlove Avenue in Woolton, south Liverpool, in 1965.

Quarry Bank High School for Boys which John attended from 1952 to 1957.
'I was never miserable. I was always having a laugh,' John would say of his
time there. But he didn't do much work either.

John's childhood home, Mendips. From his bedroom window above the front door, John would watch the cars going by.

On their first visit to Hamburg, the Beatles and party stopped at the war memorial at Arnhem, the scene of a major World War II battle. John is not in this photograph, either because he was holding the camera, or, as some believe, because he couldn't be bothered to get out of the minibus in which they'd been travelling

The Beatles as they were at the Cavern in February 1961, with Pete Best on drums – and when they were still wearing their black leather rocker suits. By the end of the year they would be managed by Brian Epstein and the leather would have to go if they wanted to get on television. As it turned out, Pete would have to go, too.

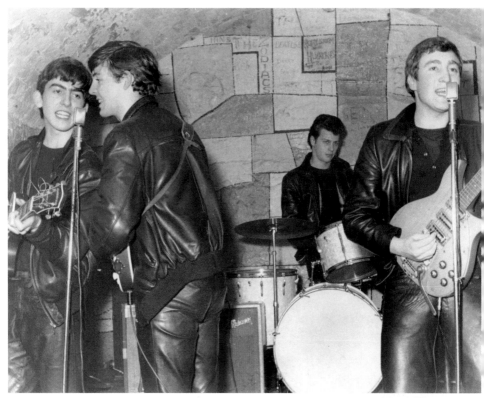

▶ John's friend from Liverpool Art College, Stuart Sutcliffe. His relationship with Stuart made Paul and George jealous.

▼ John and Cynthia in 1963. A rare photograph of John wearing his hated horn-rimmed glasses.

◄ The young, clean-cut Brian Epstein in 1962, the year he signed the Beatles to Parlophone Records. At that time he was still managing the record department in one of his family's shops.

▼ Mal Evans drives the Beatles away from a gig during Beatlemania. Starting as an assistant road manager, loyal Mal attended every gig and recording session the Beatles ever played. Tragically, he would be shot to death by police in Los Angeles during a misunderstanding.

▼▼ Producer George Martin working with the Beatles at an early recording session at Abbey Road Studios.

◄ John never enjoyed having to wear what he saw as a 'Beatle uniform', so he bought this leather cap in a little act of nonconformity. He was first seen wearing it at Heathrow Airport when the Beatles were on their way to play in Paris in January 1964.

▼ 'Never in a million years did we think anything like this,' John would say in astonishment at the fan pandemonium when the Beatles began appearing in America in February 1964.

The Beatles after being presented with their MBEs by the Queen at Buckingham Palace in October 1965. John didn't want his, so he gave it to Aunt Mimi who put it on her mantelpiece.

▲ Music publisher Dick James with the Beatles in 1965 on one of his few visits to one of their recording sessions.

What John called his 'Hansel and Gretel house' – Kenwood, the home he bought for his first wife Cynthia, their son Julian and himself in Surrey stockbroker country in 1965. He was never happy there.

The Beatles, with their manager Brian Epstein, set off on one of their last tours in 1966. Playing live to hysterical fans had long ceased to be enjoyable.

to play a final fifth season in Hamburg for two weeks at the end of December, and, not knowing how quickly events would change, he had accepted it. It meant that for the first time in their lives all four boys would be away from home for Christmas, and that John and Cynthia would be separated during their first Christmas of married life.

Relations had now been somewhat repaired with Mimi, and Cynthia had returned to live at Mendips during her pregnancy, but it was a bleak and lonely time for the first Beatle bride. John would phone home regularly, but, according to Cynthia, Mimi would always be the first to the phone, chatting happily with her nephew, while his secret, pregnant wife waited to grab a few words with her absent husband. Already it wasn't much of a marriage.

# 24

*'We'd sung for twelve hours, almost non-stop. At the end of the
day all we wanted to do was drink pints of milk'*

It began snowing on Boxing Day, with blizzards raging the length
of the country. After that came the big freeze. Northern Europe and
large parts of North America are familiar with months of snow and
ice, but the weather across Britain during those first two months of
1963 was something new for a country generally used to mild but
damp winters. It was so novel that it was thrilling in its severity, as
schools stayed closed, the North Sea froze on the beaches, and roads
were blocked by snowdrifts in the coldest winter of the century.

John probably didn't find it quite so exciting, however, as the Beatles' new nationwide touring schedule took them first up to and around
Scotland, and then five hundred miles down to Kent, before returning
the two hundred and fifty miles back to Merseyside the following day.
Travelling in their van on icy, treacherous roads, with Neil driving,
the lucky Beatle in the passenger seat and the three others crammed
in the bench seat behind, with three amplifiers, two guitars, a bass,
and a drum kit shifting about behind them, it was hardly glamorous.
Unable yet to afford hotels they stayed in boarding houses around the
country, John sharing a bedroom with George, and Paul with Ringo,
before driving on to the next venue the following day.

Inevitably there were arguments and bitching at each other, and
disappointment with the sound equipment at the halls in which they
played – where often there would only be one microphone. Then
there was their slot on the bill, which usually gave them only twenty
minutes to sing five or six songs. Compared with the hours played in
Hamburg and the Cavern, that was hardly even an audition. But that
was what a pop group with a new record to sell and a reputation to
build did in 1963, and night by night, week by week, they would see
that the crowds were getting bigger and noisier.

Then, on their few brief nights back in Liverpool to relax and reflect, and when John would remember that he had a wife, they couldn't be unaware that a new spirit was adrift across the country – one of fun, wit and youthful irreverence.

Towards the end of the previous year a new late-night satirical television programme called *That Was The Week That Was* had been launched on Saturday nights on the BBC, on which Prime Minister Harold Macmillan and his Conservative government were routinely mocked along with Members of Parliament, the clergy, trade union and military chiefs, and an assemblage of foreign leaders. The show's target was the establishment in all its forms, and no one was sacred or safe from the clever jesters, not even the Queen and the Royal Family.

Unsurprisingly there were immediate gales of protest from older generations who saw satire on the BBC as a display of rank disrespect. But, for those who had grown up after the war, the programme's firing of darts into the pompous and self-regarding was both aston-ishing and liberating. Among those young people were, inevitably, the Beatles, especially John, because what was *That Was The Week That Was* if not a more sophisticated TV version of his schoolboy 'Daily Howl'? Not that he was able to see much of the programme, in that the Beatles were invariably on stage somewhere on Saturday nights. But, always a keen newspaper reader, he followed the consternation about it with glee as the indignation and resultant headlines grew.

This was the background against which 'Please Please Me' was re-leased on Friday, 11 January – Britain, a frozen country but one on the brink of change. With the economy thriving, new jobs in newspapers, television, advertising, fashion, finance and business were, for the first time, becoming available for the young and better educated from all classes. Cheeky working-class photographers with their youthful chat and dazzle were beginning to de-gentrify the stiff and aristo-cratic images in *Vogue*, new and ambitious fashion designers, straight from art colleges, were opening boutiques in Chelsea and Carnaby Street, and one of the most popular West End theatre tickets of the day was *Beyond The Fringe*, a satirical revue written and performed by five Cambridge graduates in their early twenties. The old order was changing in all manner of ways and the Beatles were arriving just in time to join that change. Not that it must have seemed very likely on the nights when they would have to huddle up close together in the van in order not to get frostbite.

Back in London, in his centrally heated office at EMI, very pleased with the overwhelmingly positive reception that 'Please Please Me' was getting in the UK, George Martin had wasted no time in sending off a copy to Capitol, which was owned by his EMI employers, in America. This, he was sure, was the recording that could break the Beatles big in the States.

He was swiftly disabused of that notion. Like 'Love Me Do' before it, 'Please Please Me' was turned down for US release. Capitol, whose big seller then was Frank Sinatra, didn't think, like Decca, that guitar groups were the coming thing.

But there was something else that reputedly troubled them – the lyrics to 'Please Please Me'. Surely they were about sex, weren't they? A plea from a boy to his girlfriend for her to, at the very least, join him in pleasuring each other with some mutual heavy petting? What else could the words mean? *'Please, please me, like I please you'* – coming immediately after those increasingly urgent pleas to *'Come on, come on, come on, come on . . .'* Would American disc jockeys even be allowed to play such a song?

In London this interpretation was met with astonishment. The record was soon at number two in the UK charts (at number one in some), was being played on *Housewives' Choice* and *Children's Favourites* on the BBC Light Programme and had been voted a resounding hit on television's *Juke Box Jury*. No one in Britain had suggested for a moment that it might be about sex. Teenagers at school weren't sniggering to each other about its 'secret meaning'. It hadn't occurred to them that it might have one.

Was it possible that John had written some smutty lyrics that no one had noticed? Or was it just a case of some over-cautious American executives reading meanings into the words that had never been intended?

Nearly half a century later, when I asked George Martin if he'd ever thought 'Please Please Me' was a song about sex, he replied, 'Not for a minute.' Then he smiled. 'But I dare say it crossed the boys' minds.' He would always call the Beatles 'the boys'.

As it happened, 'Please Please Me' did get released in the US, as did 'Love Me Do', but not, at that time, by Capitol Records. The small label Tollie took 'Love Me Do' and Chicago's Vee-Jay licensed 'Please Please Me'. Both flopped on their initial US releases.

The Beatles were obviously aware of their American turn-down, but it would have registered only as a minor blip. Because their lives were very rapidly improving as they left their van and began travelling by bus with other musicians as support for sixteen-year-old Helen Shapiro.

She, as an established star, was in a limousine, but, although she'd had five top ten hits in the previous two years, it must have been a chastening experience for her. The plan was for the Beatles to play just four or five numbers in the first half of the show, and for Helen to close it. But her appeal was already struggling against that of the Beatles. By the time the tour reached Southport in Lancashire, just up the coast from Liverpool, the calls for the Beatles to come back on stage drowned the young star's performance. Plum Balmforth, then an eighteen-year-old Beatles fan from nearby Ormskirk, couldn't help feeling sorry for her. 'It was terrible. The entire cinema was calling for the Beatles to come back on, and she just had to carry on singing and smiling her way through it all.'

The excitement wasn't hysterical, and wouldn't be for several more months, but it was an early indication of the way things were going. The Beatles weren't just a popular band. There were lots of those around. They had something more than that. They were capable of communicating directly with an audience, of instantly conveying a sense of friendship to the kids in the seats, and of arousing a mass shared emotion of genuine good-time happiness. They made an audience feel good. With their strange collarless suits, copied from a Pierre Cardin style, and their hair combed defiantly forward, they were special from the very beginning.

Helen Shapiro would never again have a top twenty record . . . but she probably missed one. Throughout the tour John and Paul were still writing new songs for their first long player – or LP, as twelve-inch albums were called in those days. One of them was 'Misery'. John got on well with Helen and, as 'Misery' was only ever going to be an album filler for the Beatles, he suggested to Dick James that the song might suit her. An approach was duly made, but Helen's management turned it down without even telling her. It was felt that it was too bleak a subject for a young girl to sing. That was a mistake. A self-obsessed lament like 'Misery' was exactly the kind of song for a teenager to sing.

Considering how George Martin had dawdled over the recording and re-recording of 'Love Me Do', he was quickly off his marks when, just a month after the release of 'Please Please Me', he demanded that the Beatles get back down to London to record their first album. There was no time to lose. And on 11 February, the group took a day off from the tour to go back into the studio. EMI already had four tracks available from the first two singles, so *all* the Beatles had to do now was to record ten new ones to make up a fourteen-song album. It was a monumental undertaking for which they chose songs that were already in their repertoire, covers of American favourites like the Shirelles' 'Baby, It's You', with its Burt Bacharach melody, and 'Boys', which actually only made sense when a girl group sang it. They gave that one to Ringo to sing. John was never keen on Paul's predilection for 'A Taste Of Honey', but the girls at the Cavern liked it, so that was in. And then there was the Carole King/Gerry Goffin song 'Chains', and 'Anna' by Arthur Alexander – the R&B songwriter who also wrote 'Need A Shot Of Rhythm And Blues', as well as 'You'd Better Move On', which the Rolling Stones would soon make their own.

But it was the Lennon and McCartney songs that made the album extraordinary. The previous October, Paul had left behind the car he'd bought himself in Liverpool and hitch-hiked to London for a couple of days with a new girlfriend, Celia Mortimer. While there, he'd come up with 'I Saw Her Standing There'.

Was he thinking about Celia when he wrote it? Possibly, or maybe not, because in his first version of the song the second line was 'never been a beauty queen' – and Celia was a very pretty girl. John didn't like the line, anyway, when later they sat together at Forthlin Road polishing it. So he offered 'you know what I mean' as an alternative. That was better, slightly risqué and almost sexy, suggesting that this girl had all the bloom of youth, yet is suddenly a young woman . . . you know what I mean?

It was chosen to be the opening track of the album, with the count-in *'one, two, three, four . . .'* by Paul left on the front of the song. Why it wasn't put aside and kept as the Beatles' next single is hard to fathom, because, with its 'When The Saints Go Marching In' derivation hardly showing, it was certainly strong enough. It's now considered a Beatles classic.

Probably the second best of the new songs was John's 'There's A Place' which, borrowing its title from the first line of the *West Side Story* song 'Somewhere', isn't about anywhere physical at all. Instead it's a secret place in John's mind into which he can withdraw when he's unhappy. Sung as a breakneck duet with Paul, its style would appear to militate against its theme. But its depiction of the imagination as a location, so early in John's development as a songwriter, is already pointing us back towards *Alice In Wonderland* – albeit in a rock and roll format. It's difficult to imagine any other rock band of the time defining a corner of the mind in song in such a way.

He'd been playing around with 'Do You Want To Know A Secret?' for a couple of years before finishing it at the little flat that Brian had loaned him and Cynthia. It had been inspired by a song in a Walt Disney film he'd seen as a child, but when it came to recording it, he gave it to George to sing. 'If they were lousy we gave them to George or Ringo,' he would tell me later. But this wasn't a lousy song, so, on this occasion, he was probably following the Beatles' golden rule that at least one track on the album should be sung by the guitarist. A year later, it would, when released as a single in America, go to the second spot on the Hot Hundred, having already been separately a big British hit for Billy J. Kramer. John didn't know it then, but he was already writing future hits. 'Hello Little Girl', which the Beatles had used as an audition song at Decca but since abandoned, would soon become a UK top ten hit for another Liverpool group, the Fourmost. John had always liked that one 'because it was the third or fourth song I ever wrote'.

It took the best part of twelve hours for the Beatles to record nine of the songs chosen for the album, but George Martin wasn't yet happy. He needed, he said, one more rousing rock and roll number. It was over a break in the canteen as the clock ticked past ten at night, and when everyone was exhausted, that *New Musical Express* journalist Alan Smith, who was then close to the band, suggested the Isley Brothers song 'Twist And Shout'. Alan, who, like John, wrote for *Mersey Beat*, had seen how the song was almost impossible to follow when they performed it at the Cavern. After weeks of touring and having been singing all day, John wasn't sure that he could manage it. Reluctantly, he agreed to make one last effort – and it's that version that appeared on the album, with John feeling as though he was ripping his vocal cords as he forced himself through the song.

'It nearly killed me,' he would remember. 'My voice wasn't the same for a long time after . . . Every time I swallowed it was like sandpaper.' Nor was he satisfied with the take. 'I was always bitterly ashamed of it because I knew I could sing it better than that . . . But we'd sung for twelve hours, almost non-stop. At the end of the day all we wanted to do was drink pints of milk.'

His voice may have been hurting but John couldn't deny that he was proud of the album. George Martin had tried to capture the sound of the Beatles live, and the record was the nearest thing to what audiences in Hamburg and Liverpool would have heard. 'You didn't get the atmosphere of the crowd stomping on the beat with us,' John would say, 'but it came close to what we sounded like before we became the "clever" Beatles.'

The following day the Beatles rejoined the Helen Shapiro tour in Sheffield, before, three weeks later, they were summoned back to London to record their next single, 'From Me To You'. It went to number one in the charts within two weeks of going on sale.

'Paul and I wrote this together while on the tour bus . . .' John would tell me. 'We were travelling from York to Shrewsbury, just fooling about on the guitar, when we began to get a good melody line . . . I think the first line was mine and we took it from there . . . We nearly didn't do it, because it was too bluesy. But by the time we'd finished it and George Martin had scored it with harmonica, it was all right.'

Actually, it was more than all right. The lyrics may have been slight boy/girl stuff, but it was John and Paul working eyeball to eyeball, offering phrases and guitar chords until they were both satisfied. And once again there was that trademark falsetto at the end of the middle eight. The use of the falsetto was fashionable on Four Seasons and American doo-wop records, but was rarely heard from British groups.

The flip side of 'From Me To You' was 'Thank You Girl'. 'We knocked that off as a B-side,' John would later say. 'In those days we used to write songs around catch phrases like "tip of my tongue" or "lift up your leg".'

Later in his career he would be embarrassed by some of the lyrics in the earlier songs, as he would be ambivalent about the teenybopper audience which the group were starting to attract. But, at the time, he was just grateful that he was able to write songs and make records.

It would have been surprising if during those first few weeks of the year music publisher Dick James, who used to say, 'I used to think of myself as a bit of a songwriter until I met Lennon and McCartney', hadn't been congratulating himself. Not only had he published two huge hit songs, he had also made sure that their two writers wouldn't leave him, as they had left Ardmore and Beechwood after 'Love Me Do'.

By formalising his agreement with them in a shared publishing company, Northern Songs, in which he held 50 per cent of the shares, John and Paul 20 per cent each and NEMS the remaining 10 per cent, he had guaranteed their loyalty. From his point of view, it had been an inspired move. At the moment, it looked good to the young John and Paul, too. But they wouldn't always see it that way.

# 25

*'The holiday was planned. I wasn't going to break it for a baby.
I just thought, what a bastard I was, and went.'*

Cynthia went into labour at four in the morning of Saturday, 6 April
1963. Her college friend Phyl was staying with her at Mendips at the
time and called an ambulance. Still wearing a nightdress and with
curlers in her hair, Cynthia was rushed to Sefton General Hospital,
where it took until the early hours of the Monday for her baby to
be born. Her mother was still in Canada, and no one came to see
her as she waited, Phyl assuming, wrongly, that Mimi would visit.
John was away with the Beatles on a second tour of the year with
American stars Tommy Roe and Chris Montez in Portsmouth, and
wouldn't get home to visit her until the Beatles played Birkenhead
on the Wednesday. By then he (or Brian probably) had organised for
her to be moved to a private room, partly so that he wouldn't be seen
there, thus keeping up the lie that he was still single. Cyn was happier
there. With no visitors, she'd felt like an unmarried mother when
she'd been alone on the public ward.

John was, Cynthia would later say, genuinely thrilled when he
saw the baby. 'Who's going to be a famous little rocker like his dad,'
he said as he held his son. They had decided to call the child John
Charles Julian, after John, Cynthia's father, and John's mother Julia
– although John had worried momentarily that Julian might sound
like a sissy's name.

He didn't stay long at the hospital, but soon Cynthia's room was
filling with flowers and cards from the other Beatles and their friends
who were in the know. Brian immediately offered to be a godfather.
The nurses, of course, quickly guessed that John was the father, but not
a word appeared in the newspapers, where there was still little interest
in popular music. The Beatles may already have had two hit records
and been causing considerable excitement wherever they played, but,
with one exception, Fleet Street was still blind and deaf to them.

The exception was an interviewer from the London *Evening Standard* called Maureen Cleave who had been intrigued when told by a Liverpool friend about the excitement the group generated on Merseyside. She would later become very close to John and would one day write one of the biggest John Lennon stories of all.

For now, though, the rest of Fleet Street's finest were wearing blinkers as Cynthia took her baby home to Mendips and John rejoined the Beatles in London for the *New Musical Express* Pollwinners Concert. They weren't yet famous enough to be among those collecting prizes, but just to have been invited to appear alongside the nation's favourites, Cliff Richard and the Shadows, about whom John had never hidden his contempt (until he met and liked them), was more than flattering.

Having been either on the road or in radio or recording studios since they'd arrived back from Germany in January, it was time for the band to have a break. Most new fathers might have gone home to help with a three-week-old baby, but that kind of domesticity wasn't for John. And while Paul, Ringo and George flew to Tenerife to join Klaus Voorman, whose parents had a holiday home there, John went off for twelve days in Spain with Brian.

Whichever way it's viewed, that was an odd thing to do. Setting aside John's neglect of Cynthia, John and Brian were hardly best friends. It was John who had first begun to call Brian 'Eppy', which Brian didn't like, and John could be brutal when he thought the manager was getting in the way. 'You just take care of your percentage and leave us to worry about the music,' he is reputed to have said when Brian began fussing at the first EMI recording session. Despite that, John chose to spend twelve days in Spain with his manager at a crucial time in his married life.

Loyally, Cynthia would later write that John asked her if she minded if he went and that she'd told him that she didn't, and had given her husband her blessing. But was she, once again, accepting a situation that she knew she couldn't change, that there was every chance that John would go whatever she said? Later John would admit it: 'The holiday was planned. I wasn't going to break it for a baby. I just thought, what a bastard I was, and went.'

Undoubtedly he must have been exhausted, but his Spanish break showed another side of John. When something got in the way of what he wanted to do he could be callous. Although, he had done the 'decent thing' by marrying Cynthia, that had been before he'd begun appearing on television, before Beatles records had topped the record charts . . . before he was a star. His world had now changed, and he knew that the girl he had once worshipped could hold him back if he let her.

Cynthia knew that, too. So, she stayed at home at Mendips with the baby, and John and Brian went to Torremolinos, where John would tease Brian about being gay. 'I watched Brian picking up boys and I liked playing it a bit faggy . . . We used to sit in a café looking at all the boys and I'd say "Do you like that one? Do you like this one?"' But, of course, the person Brian fancied most of all was John himself – something John had been very well aware of when Brian had suggested the holiday.

In his book *John Lennon: In My Life*, John's childhood friend Pete Shotton would write that John had told him that, eventually worn down by Brian's entreaties while in Spain, he allowed Brian to masturbate him. It's highly unlikely that Pete would have made that up. He wasn't a fantasist. What's more, John also told a journalist friend about the episode.

But was John telling the truth? It was well known to those around him that he was keenly heterosexual. But he loved to shock, too. Did he invent a homosexual experience for the fun of it, or, perhaps, did he just exaggerate the incident after Brian made a pass at him? Both are possible. But, equally, as all his life he would be eager to experience anything new, was he curious about homosexuality? When Brian came on to him, did he simply want to know what it was like to be touched by another man?

In public he always denied that anything sexual had happened. As he told *Rolling Stone:* 'It was almost a love affair, but not quite. It was not consummated, but it was a pretty intense relationship.'

Back in England and off on a third tour in three months, this time with Roy Orbison ('I knew we were successful,' John said, 'when Roy Orbison asked us if he could record two of our songs'), any gossip about the Spanish holiday was quickly forgotten, only to be reopened at Paul's twenty-first birthday party in June.

The celebration took place in the large garden at the home of Paul's Auntie Gin in the Liverpool suburb of Huyton, and, as befitting a young man whose first album was at the top of the charts, it was quite a do. All of Paul's family and friends were invited, along with singers Gerry Marsden and Billy J. Kramer, who in the wake of the Beatles were now also part of Brian's growing Merseyside caravan of talent.

It should have been a terrific party, and was at first, as Paul introduced his new girlfriend, actress Jane Asher, to his old friends ('posh but really nice', was the general view). Then, a rather drunk Bob Wooler, who had announced the Beatles at the Cavern for the last two years, made a silly, jokey comment: 'Come on, John. Tell us about you and Brian in Spain . . . We all know . . .'

Without warning, John exploded. Lashing out, he began to batter Wooler's face and body with both his fists and a stick. He was never good when he'd been drinking, and the other Beatles had seen him become violent in fights before. But his reaction to Wooler was of a different magnitude. He went berserk, to the extent that when he was pulled off Wooler, the inoffensive and much older man had to be quickly driven to hospital by Brian, where he was treated for bruised ribs and a black eye.

According to Cynthia, John was still livid with Wooler, muttering that 'he called me a queer' when, the party ruined, they got home. Pete Shotton, who with his girlfriend was also among the guests, had a different recollection. According to him, John carried on drinking and eventually the two got into a drunken conversation about wife swapping, which had recently been the subject of a Sunday newspaper exposé. 'What about that then, Pete? Fancy swapping wives?' John asked.

'You mean you want to swap the girls for the night?' Pete asked incredulously.

'Yeah! Yeah! Great. Let's do it.'

Pete, however, was having none of it.

John backed off. 'Only kidding,' he said, and dropped the subject.

Pete didn't believe him. As far as he was concerned John, who, he said, was always happy to try anything once, had been serious. Cynthia almost certainly never knew.

The following day, when he had sobered up, John agreed with Brian to send a telegram to Wooler apologising for the attack. Although it bore his name it was written by Brian together with the Beatles' new press officer, Tony Barrow. It read: 'REALLY SORRY BOB. TERRIBLY WORRIED TO REALISE WHAT I HAD DONE. WHAT MORE CAN I SAY?'

Had he gone to see Wooler, John might have been able to say quite a lot more. But he chose not to. Privately, he may have been reflecting on the motives that had spurred the attack, thinking how any hint of homosexuality, no matter how untrue, could ruin his career and the Beatles' future. That was the way it was in 1963.

John's memories of the night, given just a couple of days before his death in 1980 to the BBC's Andy Peebles, were that he'd been frightened by his own anger. 'I must have had a fear that maybe I was homosexual to attack him like that. But I was very drunk . . . I hit him and I could really have killed someone then. And that scared me.'

Wooler could have sued, but instead he accepted a £200 ex gratia payment from Brian Epstein – which would be about £3,500 in today's money. Had it happened a few months later, the incident would have been front-page news. But the only coverage of what was described as a 'brawl' was in the *Daily Mirror*, with no mention of the comment that had caused the attack.

It might seem bizarre that most Fleet Street editors were still not paying attention to the Beatles, but perhaps there were extenuating circumstances. Since the spring, rumours of a growing web of intrigue linking the British Minister for War, John Profumo, with a Soviet spy, by way of a very pretty goodtime girl and two of her West Indian lovers, had been fascinating newspaper readers. Day by day over the weeks, and libel lawyers allowing, new pieces were being regularly added to a jigsaw of sex in high places. The lady's name was Christine Keeler, and she, and her attractive friend Mandy Rice-Davies, were, it appeared, being pimped around upper-class circles by Mayfair osteopath Stephen Ward. It was career-wrecking stuff for Profumo, who, after denying any adulterous impropriety, had to resign from the government, but it was a festival of hilarity and hypocrisy for readers as unsubstantiated rumours of High Court judges, royalty and government ministers attending upper-class orgies were reported, or hinted at, by the press. Nor did it end well, when Stephen Ward committed suicide in August.

But that wasn't all. Parallel with the Profumo Affair was a notorious divorce that had been making its way through an Edinburgh court, involving the adulterous and aristocratic Duchess of Argyll, which included as evidence a photograph of the lady giving sexual relief to an unnamed man whose head was out of shot. Once again rumours danced around the country: 'Who was the headless man?' the tabloid newspaper demanded to know. And once again a government minister, Mr Duncan Sandys, had to resign. As it happens, he was not the gentleman in the photograph, but, having enjoyed the lady's favours on a previous occasion, he hoped by giving up his job to escape their association being made public. That was not to be.

Nothing ever sells newspapers so much as a posh sex scandal, so perhaps Fleet Street had some excuse for overlooking the story that, out of their eyeline, just kept growing and growing.

# 26

*'I'm John. I play a guitar, too. And sometimes I play the fool'*

For the Beatles, 1963 was passing in a blur. Their work load was intense. They had all grown up lying in bed at the weekend, listening to disc jockey Brian Matthew presenting *Saturday Club* on the BBC Light Programme. Now they were stars on it themselves, appearing ten times during 1963 alone. Between joking with Matthew ('I'm Ringo and I play the drums'; 'I'm Paul and I play the bass'; 'I'm George and I play the guitar;' 'I'm John. I play a guitar, too. And sometimes I play the fool'), they would dig out songs they couldn't now perform in the restricted stage time they had while on tour. Then there was another radio programme called *Pop Goes The Beatles* and more and more TV appearances, usually where they simply mimed to their hits. Back on the road again, in that year alone they played over two hundred gigs across the length and breadth of Britain, as well as recording two albums and four singles. And when they weren't doing that, John and Paul would be locked together writing new songs for themselves or for other Brian Epstein protégés. Former cloakroom girl at the Cavern Priscilla White metamorphosed into Cilla Black and got one. Billy J. Kramer got four.

The Beatles never stopped working. It might have seemed like overkill, and, with any group less charismatic, it might have been. But for them it was the opposite. Brian Epstein, as much by good luck as good management, was cementing them in the nation's mind. The work load meant, of course, that none of them had any meaningful kind of home life. To all intents and purposes Cynthia was a single parent, pushing her baby in his pram around Woolton, and waiting for John to call. She was always waiting.

On 3 August the Beatles made their last appearance at the Cavern. Although the cellars were packed and celebratory there was grieving, too. The fans realised they were being left behind. For Cynthia it was another night when she was asked to stay away.

*

By the Sixties most families in Britain who could afford to would go away to the seaside in the summer, to stay, perhaps, in a boarding house and to hope that the sun shone. And it was for them that the Beatles performed during July and August during week-long seasons in resorts around the country, before finishing close to home, in Southport. Fittingly it was while they were there, and at last able to spend more than a couple of nights in their own beds, that the record that would become their biggest UK hit was released. It was 'She Loves You'.

John and Paul had written it back in June in a hotel after an appearance in Newcastle, and had then grabbed a day off touring to record it. It was quite different from anything else in the charts, or anything they'd done before. From its opening drum announcement by Ringo, to the three-part harmony in the final chord which sounded strangely jazzy to some people, it was instantly arresting. Constructed as a message being passed to a friend, it suggests that Paul, who liked to write little stories in his songs (as Buddy Holly had sometimes done), was mainly responsible for the overall theme. But the descending 'Three Blind Mice' notes in the oft repeated refrain of *'Yeah, Yeah, Yeah'* was absolutely John Lennon. John didn't know it yet, but he would develop a knack for writing memorable phrases and slogans into songs, and the one in 'She Loves You' was so infectious that soon groups of teenagers were chanting it, and football fans were singing it in support of their team. *'We love you, yeah, yeah yeah . . .'* they roared on the terraces, while across Europe the Beatles soon became known as the Yeah-Yeahs.

With 'She Loves You', the British national press finally saw what had been under its nose for months. And as the Beatles continued their odyssey around the country, now travelling in a huge black Austin Princess, just like the one that would carry the Queen, reporters hurried after them.

What they found often astonished them. Traditionally, most pop stars had been meek-working class lads who did what their manager told them. The Beatles weren't like that. While Paul was usually helpful, and John could be funny or grumpy, depending on his mood, their confidence in themselves and with their new situation often strayed into arrogance. For a reporter, catching up with them as they waited before going on stage in a new hotel in yet another new town must sometimes have been not unlike stepping into a play by Beckett or Pinter.

American journalist Michael Braun captured their bored, deadpan conversation to perfection when he followed the group on tour in a fly-on-the-wall account for his book *Love Me Do*.

> John: 'One more ciggy, and I'm going to hit the sack . . . "Hit the sack" being an American thing . . . I never liked "sack". It's something you put potatoes in over here.'
>
> Paul: 'The whole thought of hitting the sack . . . It's so dirty and can mean a lot of things.'
>
> John: 'You can sack Rome. Or you can sack cloth. Or you can sacrilege, or saxophone, if you like, or saccharine.'
>
> Ringo: 'Or sacrifice.'

This wasn't the sort of banter that show business reporters were used to hearing from pop stars. But the Beatles were daring to be different. And on the nation's most popular TV variety show *Sunday Night At The London Palladium* on 13 October, they shook their just-shampooed mop-top hair in unison as they hit the falsettos. It was a joke, almost against themselves, and John had been laughed at when he'd first suggested the head-shaking. But it worked. The entire country, all generations, was falling in love with these cocky nonconformists who were making all previous rock stars look old-fashioned. Now the popular newspapers ran stories about boys being sent home from school for having Beatle haircuts, or about cut-price Beatle-style jackets going on sale, or fans queuing all night to get tickets for Beatle appearances. In the midst of this, 'She Loves You' sold a million copies (the first single to do so in the UK), and, as the wave of excitement spread into Europe, the group went to Sweden for four days of concerts there.

Only when they flew back into London from Stockholm and saw thousands of fans awaiting their return at Heathrow airport did the group begin to fully comprehend the enormity of their success.

Four days later, on 4 November, came the final British hurdle when they appeared before the Queen Mother at the Royal Command Performance. In those days to be asked to perform for royalty was considered the greatest compliment that could be bestowed on an artist, and even the Beatles were on edge. As always, on big occasions it was John the group turned to as their onstage spokesman.

'I was fantastically nervous, but I wanted to say something to rebel a bit,' John remembered. So, squinting out at the overwhelmingly middle-aged and well-heeled establishment audience, and with a nod towards the tiaras in the royal box, which without his glasses he couldn't see anyway, he said: 'For our last number I'd like to ask your help. The people in the cheaper seats, clap your hands. And the rest of you . . . if you'd just rattle your jewellery.' And off he went: *'Well, shake it up, baby, now . . . twist and shout . . .'*

Some commentators saw that night as the birth of Beatlemania, but, if so, it had been in the delivery room since August, with the word creeping increasingly into the English language to describe the bedlam and hysteria the group was provoking. From newspaper reporters, television presenters, radio disc jockeys and magazine picture editors to workers in offices, students at universities, nurses in hospitals, staff in shops, farmers in fields and old people in care homes . . . almost everyone in Britain, it seemed, wanted to be involved or associated with the Beatles. There had never been anything like them before. They weren't just loved by teenagers. By being seen to smile and applaud, the Queen Mother, with 26 million people watching – that is, around half the population of the UK – had given the group a token royal imprimatur. The Beatles were the sound and face of modern Sixties Britain.

Quite what John's feelings were as he bowed low, almost in a mock gesture of fealty to the Queen Mother's party, we can only imagine. He was, once again, 'playing the game'. He had no embarrassment about telling anyone who asked that his ambition was 'to be rich and famous'. If it meant bending a knee before royalty, he was happy to do that, albeit with his fingers metaphorically crossed behind his back.

Inevitably there were those who were dismissing the Beatles as a passing fad, but they were ignoring the evidence of not only their own eyes, but their ears. Because, while the hysteria had been building in public, in hundreds of private hours of work in hotel rooms and snatched days back at Abbey Road, the Beatles' creative engine had never stopped. Already a new album and single were waiting for release just in time for Christmas.

*

When the Beatles had first met George Martin, they'd felt like school-boys in the presence of someone whose accent suggested that his social background was several cuts above theirs. Over the past year, however, their relationship with him had changed. As he amused them by talking about his work with Peter Sellers and his experiences as a young officer in the Fleet Air Arm section of the Royal Navy at the end of the Second World War, he also apprised them of his child-hood. He hadn't been born to educated, well-off parents, as they had assumed. On the contrary, his father had been a machine carpenter in London's working-class Holloway Road, and, during the Depression, his mother had gone out to work scrubbing floors to make ends meet. Neither of his parents had been musical, but for some reason they had always owned an old piano, and, as a child, George had taught himself to play. When, later, he took piano lessons, he discovered that he'd been born with perfect pitch.

'But what about your posh accent, George?' they wanted to know.

So, George had explained. When he was sixteen he'd decided to make a private recording of a Debussy-like piece of music for the piano that he'd composed, and had gone to a little private studio. It had all gone well, until he listened to the playback, and for the first time heard his own speaking voice as he'd announced what he was about to play. Only then did he realise that he had a strong Cockney accent.

From that moment on, he told them, he realised that if he was to get anywhere in music he would have to change his accent, and speak like a BBC presenter – which he finally did. If the Beatles were impressed by his confession, history doesn't record.

Martin had been born in 1928, so was from an earlier generation than them, and in a managerial position where accents were important. It was different for the Beatles. To Mimi's despair, John would now exaggerate, rather than try to diminish, his Scouse accent, especially when he was on television. Indeed, throughout his career he would remain militantly determined not to lose the way he spoke, or his allegiance to his working-class origins – imaginary though they were. 'We were the first working-class singers that stayed working-class . . . and didn't try to change our accents . . . which were looked down on in England,' he would insist. It would be more accurate to say that he had turned himself into something of a professional Liverpudlian.

Ironically, by the end of 1963, the Beatles' influence was beginning to redefine how a Scouse accent was viewed across Britain. Within a few more months it would be almost fashionable to come from Liverpool.

*

If the greater part of the Beatles' first album had been recorded in a single day, their second, *With The Beatles*, spent six months in development and was altogether a conscious and considered step forward. Right from the cover, photographed by Robert Freeman the previous August, and showing, in Astrid style, the monochrome four faces of the group in the natural half-light of a hotel corridor, style predominated. The cover for their first album had been a snatched job taken on a staircase at EMI headquarters in central London; but, from now on, current art student fashion would be applied to everything the group touched. Having set the musical trend, they were now defining the visual way records were marketed – with styles that would be immediately copied by rival rock groups. Already they were emerging as leaders of a new popular culture.

Musically, half the songs for the second album were covers of their favourite American R&B hits, with John choosing to sing the Marvelettes' 'Please Mr Postman', Barrett Strong's 'Money (That's What I Want)' and, best of all, the Miracles' 'You've Really Got A Hold On Me', leaving George to sing Chuck Berry's 'Roll Over Beethoven'. But the style of recording had changed, as George Martin showed them how effective double-tracking could be on a single voice. 'We double-tracked ourselves to death on that album,' was John's memory of the sessions.

Apart from being their producer, George Martin had another contribution to make. He might never have cared for rock and roll, but in the presence of the Beatles he turned himself into a real boogie-woogie man at the piano. There may have only been four Beatles but there were five musicians present on a third of the songs on that second album.

None of the six new Lennon and McCartney songs was chosen to be a single, although Paul's 'All My Loving', yet another of his letter-writing songs, would become one of his biggest ever hits when recorded by many other artists. For John, 'It Won't Be Long', with its call-and-response sequence, was familiar territory, while 'I Wanna Be Your Man' was a throwaway song that he and Paul first gave to Ringo to sing, and then, in a moment of rock comradeship, also to the Rolling Stones. They'd met the Stones at the Crawdaddy Club in Richmond after they'd finished making a TV appearance at nearby Teddington Studios. So when, while riding in a taxi through Central London, they spotted the Stones' manager Andrew Loog Oldham, they'd jumped out and followed him to Trident Studios in Soho where they found the Stones struggling to come up with anything for their second single. 'I Wanna Be Your Man' wasn't quite ready, but after a brief discussion the two Beatles finished the lyrics and left the Stones to it. It would become the London group's first top twenty hit in the UK.

John always got on well with the Stones, particularly Keith Richards and Brian Jones, in spite of the fact that they would soon be seen by fans as the Beatles' rivals. But John wasn't a fool. He didn't like the Stones enough to give them one of the Beatles' better songs.

*With The Beatles* was released on Friday, 22 November 1963. They were playing at Stockton-on-Tees that night, and just before they were due on stage, news filtered through that President John F. Kennedy had been assassinated while on a visit to Dallas.

Later that evening all four Beatles, together with members of the other groups who were with them on tour, gathered around a television in the lounge of the hotel where they were staying. As in many other places that night, no one had very much to say.

A week later, with 'She Loves You' still near the top of the charts after an unprecedented three-month run, 'I Want To Hold Your Hand' was released. John could be vague when talking about the writing of many of his songs, but he remembered this one. He liked it. He'd been living in a hotel in London's Russell Square at the time, and had gone over to work with Paul at Jane Asher's parents' house in Wimpole Street, where Paul was now staying. 'We were downstairs in the cellar [it was probably known as the basement in the Asher household] playing on the piano . . . and we had the line, *"Oh you, got that something"*, and Paul hits this chord and I turned to him and said, "That's it! Do that again." In those days we really used to absolutely write like that . . . both playing into each other's noses.'

For a writer who could be so deliberate with words, 'I Want To Hold Your Hand' was almost infantile in its lyrics about adolescent love – so perhaps it wasn't surprising that it was often jokily referred to more realistically as 'I Want To Hold Your Gland'. But, for the moment, words didn't matter. It was the impact of their records that was important. Interestingly, while the doo-wop, three-part harmony of the flip side, 'This Boy', with its contrasting attitudes of two boys towards a girl, was much more thoughtful, when I asked John about it seven years later, he said that he couldn't even remember writing it.

To fans, that might seem strange, but there were so many songs then, with so much praise raining down on the heads of Lennon and McCartney, that sometimes even major moments in their careers failed to fully register. And, sometimes, that praise came from the most unlikely sources.

By 1963, *The Times* newspaper had for over a century been regarded as a sober and responsible pillar of the British establishment. So when its chief music critic, William Mann, in the spirit of the moment gave his column over to a review of the Beatles' new album, he caused more than the light-hearted amusement in music circles that he had envisaged. Writing about 'their flat, submediant key switches . . . chains of pandiatonic clusters' and the 'Aeolian cadence at the end of "Not A Second Time" (the chord progression which ends Mahler's "Song Of The Earth")', he opened the gate for, at first, ridicule, but then more serious consideration of Lennon and McCartney songs.

John was still talking about it, in his usual robust way, in 1970. '"Not A Second Time" . . . that was the one that fucking idiot from *The Times* was talking about,' he told me. 'It was the first intellectual bullshit they wrote about us. It was really just chords like any other chords. Still, I know it helps having bullshit written about you.'

# 27

*'This isn't show business. It's something else'*

John watched the ever-growing waves of Beatlemania with a mixture of astonishment, glee and incomprehension. The Beatles might have been at the centre of the whirlwind, but, as John would say, most of the time it felt as though it was happening to something else called the Beatles – not to John, Paul, George and Ringo. They had been a very good rock and roll band, but now, as the screaming grew ever louder, and the press followed them wherever they went, the excitement was puzzling as much as flattering.

Of course, there were advantages. 'What success does for you is give you a real feeling of confidence in yourself. It's an incredible feeling, but once you've had it, you never want it to stop,' John would say. But he was becoming aware, too, that success on this scale brought problems he'd never anticipated. Recently he'd been appalled to discover that his Scottish cousin, Stanley Parkes, whom he'd known all his life, now looked on him, he said, as 'some kind of God'.

Like everyone, he could see that Beatlemania was a sociological phenomenon, and he was particularly tickled to read the attempts by pundits and social psychologists to explain the mystery of it all in the quality Sunday newspapers. But no one *could* quite explain it – not the screaming, anyway, other than to agree that the uproar when the Beatles went into falsetto was an expression of shared joy, all part of the ritual of going to see them. For young female fans there wasn't much point in seeing a Beatles concert unless you were going to enjoy a jolly good scream along with everybody else.

Even the Beatles themselves couldn't agree about the reasons for their appeal. In one edition of the BBC's *Juke Box Jury*, when the Beatles comprised the whole panel, Paul suggested that the fans liked them because they were 'like the fans themselves'. At which point, John virtually snorted, saying that most of the Beatle fans were thirteen- or fourteen-year-old girls. 'You mean, you're like them?' he teased.

Paul looked embarrassed to be shown up on national television. But he needn't have been. John didn't have any better explanation to offer, other than to say on another occasion, as he came off stage leaving behind a bedlam of screaming: 'This isn't show business. It's something else.'

It was. And whatever that something was, everyone agreed, from Brian, to EMI and to the Beatles themselves, it should be exploited for all it was worth before the magic wore off.

So, in the festive spirit of traditional British pantomimes, Brian booked his four young magicians into an eleven-day, twice nightly *Beatles' Christmas Show* at the huge Astoria Theatre in North London's Finsbury Park. With a few comic sketches inserted between the songs it was a family outing – definitely not something the Beatles would have even contemplated in their leather-jacket Hamburg days.

John never enjoyed the shows. 'It didn't seem natural seeing old people out there in the audience looking at us,' he said. 'They should be at home, doing the knitting.'

For the past few months Cynthia and baby Julian had been living in Hoylake with Cynthia's mother, and although the Beatles flew back to Merseyside on Christmas Eve, the focus of their careers was inevitably now in London. Brian already had a NEMS headquarters in Mayfair, Paul was living in Jane Asher's parents' London house and George and Ringo were sharing a flat just north of Hyde Park. So, John and Cynthia went house-hunting in London, and, at the suggestion of photographer friend Robert Freeman, rented a flat at the top of a very grand, if rather gloomy, house at Emperor's Gate in South Kensington. Freeman lived with his very pretty model wife Sonny on the ground floor.

John liked Freeman. He was intelligent, Cambridge-educated (rare for a photographer), and good to talk to – the sort of intelligent so-phisticate, with experiences far outside popular music, to whom John would always be drawn. Living above the slightly bohemian, artistic Freemans in the faded Victorian grandeur of South Kensington was perhaps a glamorous reflection of the student life he'd once enjoyed with Stuart in Liverpool's Gambier Terrace. It had its drawbacks, though. A top-floor flat up six flights of stairs was hardly ideal for a young mother, baby and pram.

Not that John would have been particularly aware of the problem. He was hardly at home. Live performances were where the instant money was, and as soon as the Astoria season finished, Brian whisked the Beatles off to Paris for three weeks. And it was there, at the Paris Olympia, starring alongside French favourite Sylvie Vartan and Trini ('If I Had A Hammer') Lopez, that, for the first time since fame had found them, Les Beatles flopped. The sound system was bad, the French didn't seem to get them and the French critics were mocking.

After the opening night there was some consternation in the Beatles headquarters at the plush Hotel George V. But John didn't care. He'd spent the rest of the evening sitting in a café talking to his journalist friend Maureen Cleave.

'The French haven't made their minds up yet about the Beatles,' a Paris-based BBC reporter asked him the following day. 'What do you think of them?'

'Oh, we like the Beatles. They're gear,' John deadpanned back.

In truth, if the Paris opening had been a disappointment, it hardly mattered. Any country where Johnny Hallyday was considered a serious rock star didn't have much taste, the Beatles laughed to each other as, holed up in their hotel, they played a new album that Paul had been given by a French journalist. It was *The Freewheelin' Bob Dylan*, the tracks of which included 'Don't Think Twice, It's Alright', 'Girl From The North Country' and 'Blowin' In The Wind', and its effect on all the Beatles, but mostly on John, would be far-reaching. They'd scarcely even heard of Dylan until that album, but his message was clear: this is what could be achieved if songwriters paid more attention to the lyrics of their songs.

Discovering Dylan wasn't the only distraction in Paris. As always, there was more studio work to be done, and George Martin joined them to re-record 'She Loves You' and 'I Want To Hold Your Hand' in German for the German market. Then there was a new song that Paul had just written called 'Can't Buy Me Love'. The hit songs just kept coming and coming.

America, was, of course, the big prize. After reading about Beatlemania in Britain as cover stories in *Time, Newsweek* and *Life*, and a year of sending polite rejection notices back to London, Capitol's resistance had broken.

'I Want To Hold Your Hand' had been released across America during the last week of December 1963, amid a blitz of hype. This had included five million 'The Beatles Are Coming' stickers for telegraph poles, washrooms and walls across the country, and Beatles records to every disc jockey in the nation, none of which the independent labels had been able to do for the group's earlier single releases. And, now, as reports reached Paris of massive airplay across the States, the Beatles began to realise that, far from the magic running out, it was gathering potency. America was surrendering, too.

On 25 January 1964 Brian got a phone call from New York. 'I Want To Hold Your Hand' had leapt to the top of the *Billboard* Hot 100. 'It just seemed ridiculous,' John would remember thinking. 'I mean, the idea of having a hit over there. It was just something you could never do . . . We didn't think we stood a chance. We didn't imagine it at all. Cliff Richard had gone to America and died.'

But Cliff Richard had gone to America without a number one hit record. That had been something the Beatles had been determined not to do.

It was time to celebrate. So Brian took them all out to an upmarket but somewhat louche restaurant he'd heard about where there were sponge-covered breasts stuck on the walls and, according to George Harrison, where 'the bread rolls were shaped like penises and the soup was served out of chamber pots'.

John had always thought Brian's rule that Cynthia must be confined to the shadows to be silly and unreasonable, so when the call came to go to New York, he insisted that she be among the accompanying party. That she was John's wife wasn't a secret any more anyway, the tabloid press having printed the story two months earlier, to no discernible dip in the Beatles' popularity. So, for the first time in their marriage, Cynthia wasn't left behind as Pan Am flight 101 took off from Heathrow on the morning of 7 February 1964 to a crescendo of screams from thousands of young girls watching from the viewing terrace of the Queen's Building.

For the Beatles themselves it was obviously an exciting moment, but, so much had they become part of the daily national conversation, it was thrilling for an entire generation of young Brits, too, who now identified with them. And as the jet set out across the Atlantic that morning, flying with it, along with reporters, photographers, TV film-makers and businessmen hoping to cut a Beatle franchise deal with Brian in mid-air, was a newfound youthful pride in simply being, like the Beatles themselves, British.

# 28

*'We're just walking through it like watching a film . . .*
*as though it's happening to somebody else'*

America was the place to go. From boyhood John had wondered about it, marvelled at its seeming zest and creativity and loved its music – not just rock and roll, but some of the Broadway show tunes, too. But as Pan Am 101 lowered its undercarriage to touch down on the runway of the newly renamed John F. Kennedy International Airport, he was feeling nervous. He and Cynthia had sat together on the flight, during a journey when the tension had gradually been rising for the Beatles – and all their party. They might be top of the US charts, but what if that was a one-off fluke? What if America didn't like the look of them? Bill Haley had been a big star in England, until he'd appeared there, after which his career had gone into terminal decline. Had that been an omen? 'We can always turn around and go home again if no one likes us, and say we'd only come to buy some LPs,' he'd joked during the flight. But then, as the plane taxied to a halt, laughs of relief broke out around the first-class compartment. Capitol Records had done their job well. Down there at the foot of the steps to the plane was a small army of photographers and newsreel cameras.

What none of them had known while they'd been travelling was that music radio stations all over New York had been priming the pump of expectation, playing Beatles records one after the other. WINS had even been giving the time as '8.30 a.m. Beatle-time', and the weather report as 'fine, sunny, 32 Beatle-degrees'.

The Beatles got off the plane first. Leaving Cynthia still sitting in her seat, as Brian had insisted, John pulled on the jaunty leather cap he had decided to wear and joined the others as they stepped out of the door and smiled hello to America for the first time – the country that would one day become his home.

From that moment, Americans took the Beatles to their hearts and kept them there. It had taken nine months for the Beatles to conquer Britain, but America's devotion was instantaneous. Perhaps there's some truth in the theory that it was, in some part, a mass reaction after the national trauma of the assassination of President Kennedy that had occurred less than three months earlier. America, the thinking goes, needed something feel-good to help it recover, and the fun of the Beatles was a means of catharsis. With their songs, and jokes, and what looked like silly hair, they brought a kind of wholesome joy to a recovering nation. Of course, the hysteria would become bigger and noisier in America, but then everything was bigger and noisier in America.

The press conference that followed the group's arrival has since become a part of rock folklore, with the four Beatles at their irreverent best, wisecracking answers to dumb questions. It was easy for them. They'd done it hundreds of times before – never taking any of it seriously. 'Will you sing something for us?' asked a reporter.

'No. We need money first,' came back John. Everyone laughed.

'What about the movement in Detroit to stamp out the Beatles?'

'We have a campaign of our own to stamp out Detroit.'

'Do you hope to take anything home with you?'

'The Rockefeller Center.'

And so it went on. Everyone present wanted to be amused, and, when necessary, the Beatles could be an effective comic turn, as they tried to make each other laugh, too. As George would say: 'Everyone in Liverpool thinks they're a comedian . . . We've had that born and bred into us.'

After meeting the press, the four Beatles were then driven into Manhattan in four separate Cadillacs, with their records coming at them from whichever radio station their car radio was tuned to. This hugely impressed John. Before arriving in America he'd been thinking, 'If we could just get a grip, we would wipe them out.' They already had that grip.

A year earlier, their beds for the night had often been cheap hotels in small English towns as they toured up and down the country, and they'd survived on a diet of egg and chips in transport cafés. Now they were staying in the Plaza, New York's smartest and most traditional hotel, in four separate suites that opened out on to a large central room, from where they could stare out at the thousands of fans in Central Park below. It was a kind of celebrity prison, but it was thrilling, too, as a documentary film crew tried to capture the moment.

For the next two days, when the Beatles weren't doing interviews, they tried to enjoy New York, sneaking out of the Plaza Hotel one night to visit the Peppermint Lounge, where Ringo doffed his usual lugubrious demeanour and manically danced the twist. Then there was a drive around the periphery of Central Park, which, if he'd known, would have given John his first sight of the Dakota building. But their real purpose in New York was to announce their arrival and sell records, so on the Sunday afternoon they were driven to the CBS TV Studio 50 on West 53rd Street for *The Ed Sullivan Show*.

And, just as the Queen Mother had given the Beatles her blessing in Britain, now Ed Sullivan did the honours for the United States. Aided by a telegram from Elvis and the Colonel, the TV host welcomed the group before 73 million Americans – at least some of whom might have been otherwise engaged robbing houses or cars, a dip in crime statistics for the hour of the show would later suggest. Reckoned at the time to be the biggest audience for any TV show in history, 'The Beatles on Ed Sullivan' became a life-punctuating moment for many, and life-changing for others.

Like their television appearances in the UK, their performance was pretty standard stuff. Dressed in dark little suits, ties and Chelsea boots and their hair just shampooed and pageboy floppy, Paul opened with 'All My Loving', while John, who sounded as though he hadn't been plugged in, looked happily around as though he didn't really care. In truth, he couldn't see very far.

Altogether, his attitude throughout that first weekend in New York was one of bemusement. 'Never in a million years did we think anything like this,' he would say over and over in amazement at the pandemonium going on around him. 'I've never seen anything like it in my life . . . We're just walking through it like watching a film . . . as though it's happening to somebody else.'

Meanwhile, Cynthia was trying not to be photographed, and diverting her eyes from where, across the room, her husband was being flirted with by the Ronettes, and any other girl who could wangle her way into the inner circle – as pretty girls often did.

The Beatles had expected some snide comments from the press about their debut, and they duly got them the following morning. 'Seventy-five per cent publicity, twenty per cent haircut, five per cent lilting talent,' came the *Herald-Tribune*; 'a sedate anti-climax', read the *New York Times*; and 'laughable lunacy', reckoned the *Daily News*. John liked that line. It was 'lunacy'. But the obsession with their hair was becoming wearyingly boring.

The following day the entire party took the train through a snow-storm down to Washington DC. So far the Beatles had been playing up the cuddly, zany image that Brian had been cultivating for them. But that wasn't who they were, and John could only be pushed so far. The cliff edge was reached when, after a performance with the Chiffons, Tommy Roe and a then little-known group called the Beach Boys at the Washington Coliseum, they were invited to a charity ball at the British Embassy by the ambassador, Sir David Ormsby-Gore. He was a charming, trendy aristocrat, but some of his young staff at the embassy were about to forget their manners. Having joined the party with Lady Ormsby-Gore on his arm, John had just waded through the crowd to get a drink when a pushy embassy official said: 'Come on now, do your stuff.'

'I'm not going back through that crowd,' John replied. 'I want to finish my drink.'

'Oh, yes you are,' replied the official firmly, to be immediately joined by a smart young lady in a ball gown, who tried to chivvy John along.

The Beatles hadn't found themselves being patronised or pushed around by a bunch of toffs before, and they didn't like it. To John, the British class divide was still 'as snobby as it ever was . . . people like us can break through a little . . . but only a little'. He decided to leave. Just then, however, a British debutante walked up to Ringo, produced a pair of nail scissors from her handbag and snipped off a lock of his hair – his *Beatle hair!!*

John blew up. Brian Epstein might have been signing contracts the whole weekend to get images of the Beatles stuck on to all kinds of memorabilia from lunch boxes to T-shirts, shoes, chewing gum, candy bars, toy guitars and cuddly toys, but the Beatles themselves weren't cuddly toys. 'People were touching us as we walked past . . .' John would remember. 'Then some bloody animal cut Ringo's hair. I walked out . . . swearing at all of them.'

Lady Ormsby-Gore apologised as they left. But it wasn't her fault. Everyone was over-excited. But, as the ball had been filled with jour-nalists following in the Beatles' wake, the row inevitably made the newspapers on both sides of the Atlantic the following day. Some

# 29

*'A Hard Day's Night was a comic strip version of what was actually going on . . . But the pressure was far heavier than that . . .'*

There had never been a welcome like it at Heathrow airport when, just under two weeks later, the Beatles came home from America to find thousands of fans waiting for them. Everything they'd done while they'd been away had been reported – the concerts at Carnegie Hall, the holiday in Florida where, accompanied by photographers, of course, they'd visited Muhammad Ali in his training camp . . . But now it was immediately back to work.

Before Christmas, Brian had agreed with Walter Shenson, an American movie producer who lived in Britain, that the Beatles would star in a quickie exploitation film packed with their own songs. The financial deal that Brian agreed was dreadful, in that the Beatles didn't even get a royalty on a movie that is still earning over half a century later. Big mistake.

Brian, however, had other qualities, one of which was style. This wouldn't be just another terrible pop film with a clichéd script, and, to make sure, an award-winning Liverpool-born playwright, Alun Owen, was asked to write a semi-documentary screenplay about the Beatles themselves. Furthermore, it would be directed by a quirky American who had made his home in England, Dick Lester. From the start, Lester got bonus points when John realised that he had directed a Goon film.

The Beatles' task now was to record six new songs in time to start shooting at the beginning of March. And three days after getting off the plane they were back at Abbey Road. 'We'd managed to get a couple written while we were in Paris, and three more completed in Miami while we were soaking up the sun in Miami Beach,' John explained. The speed with which Lennon and McCartney could produce good new songs never ceased to astonish.

The first song they recorded wasn't even for the film, as George Martin was also demanding material for their next single. It was 'You Can't Do That', and would be seen later as one of John's first confessional songs, in that it dealt with his fits of jealousy.

'*I can't help my feelings I go out of my mind*,' he anguished as he sang, which was something Cynthia would have recognised from their days at art college. He was very proud of it and put it straight into the stage act as soon as the Beatles were on tour again. 'It was my first attempt at being Wilson Pickett,' he told me, 'but it was a flip side because "Can't Buy Me Love" was so fucking good.' That had been Paul's song.

Within five days the Beatles had recorded eight new tracks, including some classics, including Paul's 'And I Love Her', John's 'If I Fell' and 'I Call Your Name' (another of his favourites), and then, towards the end of filming, the movie's title song. And this would be when the rivalry between John and Paul really showed.

Ringo was noted for muddling up phrases in malapropisms, and the way he would often say 'it's been a hard day's night' at the end of a day's work always amused everyone. Then one evening after filming, director Dick Lester wondered to John whether they should call the still-untitled film *A Hard Day's Night*.

John needed no further encouragement, but he knew he had to act before Paul did. Going straight home, he set to work on the title song and presented it to the others the following morning. It was almost perfect for playing over the movie's opening titles, and it became absolutely perfect when in the studio George Harrison played the extended opening chord that would soon echo around the world. 'Basically, it's what musicians would call an F with a G on top,' Paul later told me. 'After you hear that, everyone knows what's coming.'

In comparison with the race to have the songs ready on time, the filming of *A Hard Day's Night* was almost a holiday. Naturally all the Beatles were nervous – 'the director knew we couldn't act and we knew it, too,' said John – but, shot in black and white (the way most people saw television news then, at least in the UK), and with its running, hiding and chasing, it captured the zany innocence and high-energy intensity of the time.

'It was a comic strip version of what was actually going on,' was John's verdict; '. . . a good projection of one facade of us on tour . . . But the pressure was far heavier than that . . .'

Nor was that pressure eased when, during shooting, *Billboard* announced that all top five positions on their US charts were held by the Beatles, with seven other Beatles records further down the Hot 100. No other artist or band had ever achieved anything approaching this level of instant cultural domination. And, as far as America was concerned, the Beatles had only just begun.

It was a frenetic time, but for John, life was about to get even more complicated. Shown a copy of the *Daily Express* one day, he found a photograph of his long-absent father staring out at him. It wasn't a complete surprise. He'd always suspected that Freddie would turn up again one day. All the Beatles' backgrounds were being picked over by the tabloid newspapers, and John's runaway dad was a good story.

But it wasn't good for John. All he felt was bitterness that only now that he was famous had his father wanted to see him again. Little by little, over the next few weeks, details reached him from Mimi and his Uncle Charlie, Freddie's younger brother, of his father's vagabond life.

Freddie had never got to New Zealand as he had planned. Instead, John learned, he'd spent the years since saying goodbye to his son roaming the country, sometimes as little more than a tramp, in better times as an itinerant worker, a kitchen porter in a pub here, a dishwasher in a hotel there. Freddie's career had been the kind of life that Mimi had dreaded John might follow without her stabilising hand, and her sharp tongue hadn't been idle when it came to criticising her miscreant brother-in-law.

At first, John resisted Freddie's efforts at a reunion. Not only had he absolutely no desire to see his father again, he knew it would upset Mimi if he did, and it really wouldn't be worth the aggravation it would cause. Nevertheless, neither Freddie nor Fleet Street gave up, and a meeting was eventually negotiated, during a break in filming at London's Scala Theatre, by *Daily Mirror* reporter Don Short, whom John happened to like.

'It wasn't what you would call a happy reunion,' Short remembers. 'John didn't exactly throw his arms around his dad's neck. It was very tense.'

'What do you want then?' John snapped, first off the mark as his father entered the room.

For ten minutes, Freddie then sought to reassure John that he wasn't after any money, and that he only wanted to explain to his son how circumstances had come between them. Then, after sharing a few mutual vague memories of their stay in Blackpool, John, assuming he would now hear no more from his father, went back to filming; while Freddie left with the reporter to pick up the large cheque he'd been promised for his part in the story.

The reunion had been a classic tabloid stunt, but John would later tell his friend Pete Shotton that he'd found it impossible to dislike his father. That wasn't perhaps surprising. Freddie might have been a hopeless father, but he wasn't a bad man, nor, despite the havoc of his life, was he devoid of charm.

Before John had wanted to become a rock star, his ambition had been to be a writer, and just a few days after the end of filming that dream was realised, too, with the publication of his first book, *In His Own Write*.

Pop stars were not then known for having hidden literary ability. It's impossible to think of any others. But Michael Braun, the journalist who was following the Beatles for his own book, had become intrigued when he'd seen some of the little poems and stories that John would be continually tapping away at on his portable typewriter, and the cartoon characters he was drawing while on tour. Braun had, therefore, mentioned the jottings to a London publisher friend, who had rushed to claim his company's share of Beatlemania.

John had no illusions. He knew very well that it was only his sudden fame that had propelled him to become a published author. 'There was never any real thought of writing a book,' he admitted at the time. 'If I hadn't been a Beatle I wouldn't have thought of having the stuff published,' he told Cliff Michelmore on the BBC-TV programme *Tonight*. He would, he added, have just been 'writing it and throwing it away . . . crawling around, broke. I might have been a "beat" poet . . .' That was a joke, because he was almost embarrassed to think of himself as an author.

But, beyond the jokes, he was thrilled just the same. *In His Own Write*, the cover of which was designed by his friend and neighbour Robert Freeman, validated him, he believed, as a creative force beyond popular music, and, spurred by its critical success, he would continue to write for his own amusement for the rest of his life. Supplying a short author's biographical note for the cover of the book, he wrote:

'I was bored on the 9th of October, 1940, when, I believe, the Nasties were still booming us led by Madalf Heatlump (who only had one). Anyway, they didn't get me.'

The book was a collection of his sometimes grotesque cartoons, nonsense stories and poems in which he deliberately mixed the wrong words with archaic phrases of English, modern-day references and occasional mangled Biblical quotes to puzzle and amuse.

Liverpool readers who had read his pieces in *Mersey Beat* – where several of the stories had previously been published – were familiar with his style, but the black comedy came as a surprise to most.

The story of 'No Flies On Frank', for instance, is that of an ordinary man who, when waking up to discover that he has grown 'twelve inches more tall heavy' overnight, clubs his wife to death. 'She shouldn't see me like this . . . not all fat and on her thirtysecond birthday', Frank thinks, then takes her body, 'covered in flies', to her mother's house, where he is disappointed when he isn't offered a cup of tea.

The world's teenyboppers who had bought 'She Loves You' must have been confused by *In His Own Write*, but, on its rushed publication, fans and students everywhere immediately drove it to the top of the bestseller lists. 'There's a wonderful feeling about doing something successfully other than singing,' said the author, drawing a deliberate line between himself and the other Beatles. 'Up to now we've done everything together, and this is all my own work.'

The sales were unsurprisingly massive, but it was the literary reviews that surprised him, as the word 'genius' was banded around, and perhaps over-generous comparisons were made with the work of his childhood literary hero, Lewis Carroll. Perhaps more important to him was that Mimi told him she liked it, that it had made her laugh.

When asked to explain what the stories were about, though, he just smiled disarmingly. 'It's about nothing. If you like it, you like it. If you don't, you don't. That's all there is to it. There's nothing deep in it, it's just meant to be funny. I put things down on sheets of paper and stuff them in my pocket. When I have enough, I have a book.'

But, when invited to be a special guest of honour at a Foyles literary lunch, packed with critics and writers, probably for the first time in his life, nerves got the better of him.

He had assumed that he would just have to say a few words and make the odd joke, and hadn't therefore planned anything. Realising too late that he was expected to make a proper speech, and with television cameras bearing down on him, his mind went blank. Standing up, he just said: 'Thank you all very much. It's been a pleasure.' And then sat down again.

Clear disappointment, and even a murmur of boos, could be heard from the six hundred other diners who had paid to be present at the expensive event. For someone who could, and usually did, talk about anything and everything, it was an uncharacteristic mistake. The sophistication of literary London had unnerved him.

Even Beatles need a holiday sometimes, and after a pulverising eighteen months, John and Cynthia flew off to Tahiti, leaving baby Julian in the care of Cynthia's mother. It was the first proper holiday they'd ever had together, the first opportunity they'd had to spend much more than a couple of days alone in their married life. But they didn't go alone. Accompanying them were George and his new girlfriend Pattie Boyd, a model the guitarist had met when she'd been cast as one of the schoolgirls in *A Hard Day's Night*.

A few months earlier they could have gone just about anywhere in the world without being much noticed. But, now, only on a boat in the South Pacific could they be sure not to be followed, or even mobbed. John enjoyed the sailing and the feeling that they could go in any direction. But there was a crew on board to take care of all that. So, he read everything on board that he could find that was in English, and after finishing a collection of Conan Doyle's Sherlock Holmes stories, he began writing a pastiche of one. He called it 'The Singularge Experience of Miss Anne Duffield', with a character called Shamrock Womlbs doing the investigating.

Cynthia would remember 'a lovely, fun-filled holiday', but, although John didn't disagree, he seems to have missed the whole point of the break. 'I don't give a damn about the sun. You go out to these places and you waste your time lying on the beach,' he grumbled, slightly tongue-in-cheek, when he got back. 'We were as brown as berries and it had all gone the next day, so what's the point. I didn't feel any healthier . . . I was dead beat.'

While the Beatles' lives were now changing beyond recognition, so was that of Brian Epstein. Still only thirty, he was becoming an international celebrity. With a home in London's Mayfair, in addition to managing the Beatles he was now also running a management company that looked after a host of other chart-making artistes – most of whom were benefiting from a seemingly inexhaustible supply of cast-off songs from Lennon and McCartney. The kind and sensitive young man who had struggled at RADA and in the British Army, and who had become bored managing a record shop, was now the show businessman of the moment. So when he, too, was asked to write a book, he was immensely flattered, only to have that joy quickly punctured when he unwisely asked the Beatle he was closest to for suggestions for the book's title.

'Queer Jew,' came back John without hesitation.

Once again John had twisted the knife. He must have known how hurtful that would be to Brian, of whom he was very fond. But that didn't stop him. The casual cruelty of his tongue was always there.

As for Brian, fame and success weren't the panacea for his insecurities. To John and the other Beatles, he was a supremely confident businessman. Only he knew about the mistakes he was regularly making on their behalf, and his sense of loneliness when he was excluded from their lives. And only he knew about the pills he was starting to regularly take to hide his insecurities.

# 30

*'The idea of being a rock and roll musician sort of suited my talents and my mentality'*

For much of the rest of 1964 the Beatles would be on tour. John, like the others, was excited to be visiting so many other countries, and he even took Aunt Mimi along when the Beatles went to New Zealand – she had relatives there she wanted to see. But he didn't take Cynthia. Being a Beatle was a man's job, and, at the time, neither he, nor anyone else, saw why a wife or a girlfriend would be invited along when a fella went to work.

And it *was* work, a hard grind, day after day. Slogging from one country or city to the next. During the year, the Beatles would perform before thousands of screaming fans at 123 shows in 80 towns and cities across Europe, Hong Kong, Australia (where an estimated 300,000 people turned out to greet them in Adelaide), New Zealand, the United States and Canada. Usually they would now only play for thirty minutes at a time, singing a dozen or so songs, but their presence would give fans the chance to say, 'I was there. I saw them.' And that alone would sell millions of records when the tour had moved on.

They'd quickly accepted the wall of sound that now greeted them and largely overwhelmed their music, in that the primitive equipment they found in many venues hadn't been designed to combat mass hysteria. And at first they were amused by the screaming more than annoyed. 'There's no point in doing a show if they're just going to sit there listening,' John would joke. 'I like a riot.' At the same time, to have become the objects of what was now a global fascination took some getting used to.

Back in London in July, John was puzzled that the streets were filled with people as he and Cynthia were being driven to the premiere of *A Hard Day's Night*. 'Is it a Cup Final or something?' he innocently asked, only to be genuinely surprised when told by Brian that the crowds were there because they were hoping to see the Beatles.

Obviously, it was fun, for John as much as for any of them. It had to be, as each new peak of popularity was overtaken by a bigger and better one. How could it not be? What could be more flattering for a young man than to be met by screams of devotion from teenage girls whenever you flew into an airport or appeared on a stage?

Even the film critics seemed to bow in supplication when *A Hard Day's Night* was released, although their constant references to the Beatles as latter-day Marx Brothers slightly irritated – John seeing no similarity between the two, other than a few one-liners and that Harpo Marx had combed his hair forward.

When he realised that none of the Beatles would share financially in their film's huge box office success, having each been paid a flat fee of £8,000 for their appearances, he, along with the others, would be a little narked. But with the movie in cinemas around the world, it was a terrific piece of promotion for the soundtrack album, which, as he and Paul wrote all the songs, would profit them both enormously as it immediately became another worldwide number one.

Everything that was happening was good. But John was a realist. The popularity of rock stars was usually fairly brief. Chuck Berry, Little Richard, the Everly Brothers and even Elvis weren't selling records in the quantities they had. That was the nature of the job. Why should the Beatles be any different? So, it was always in his mind that this kind of fame couldn't go on for ever. Best to keep his sense of humour and earn as much money as possible before the fire went out.

Only when the Beatles went home to Liverpool for a civic reception before the premiere of *A Hard Day's Night* did he begin to understand that this particular fire would not be going out any time soon. As the Beatles stood on the balcony of the Town Hall and looked out at the ocean of faces on Castle Street, John knew that nothing could ever be the same again.

Somewhere in the two hundred thousand faces below him were his uncles and aunts, half-sisters and cousins, friends, ex-girlfriends, schoolmates and college pals – all the people with whom he'd grown up. They would always stay the same to him, but in their eyes he would now always be different from them. Massive fame had set up barriers between him and people and places he'd known and loved as a boy. He would think about them often, he liked to talk about them, and sometimes to sing about them. But, though he always planned to go back, he would rarely visit Liverpool again.

*

The Beatles had played a few hastily arranged New York and Washington concerts during their Ed Sullivan visit in February, but it was during their first North American tour in the summer of 1964 that they began to feel at home in the US. John liked to say: 'The idea of being a rock and roll musician sort of suited my talents and my mentality.' But rock and roll was an American music form, and there was much else about the United States, with its energy and speed and restlessness, that suited his talents and mentality.

With Elvis's former bassist's band, the Bill Black Combo, together with the Righteous Brothers on the bill, the Beatles' first American tour opened in San Francisco. After which, off they flew in a hired plane as they went looking for America in a 22,000-mile zig-zag of twenty-six of the largest towns and cities. It was an odyssey, not just for them but for the pack of reporters who were accompanying them, too, a time when the Beatles learned a lot about America; and one during which the accompanying reporters learned about self-censorship when filing their reports to their newspapers.

Six years later, when post-Beatle John was in full iconoclastic mood, he would spill the beans to *Rolling Stone* about the determined young groupies who would turn up in every city the Beatles visited. He may have been overselling his case when he said Beatles tours were 'like Fellini's *Satyricon* . . . When we hit town, we hit it . . . Wherever we were, there was a whole scene going.' But it wasn't all exaggeration.

Yet, at the time, not a hint of inappropriate sexual behaviour appeared in the press. The wholesome image that Brian had wanted the Beatles to adopt was the official line and what happened on tour stayed secret. In John's eyes, the accompanying journalists were all part of the Beatles' feelgood party bubble and no one wanted to pop it – perhaps in case they got kicked off the tour. That's possible: there may have been some self-interest involved.

But in those times, when the tabloids were less intrusive, blind eyes in show business were not unusual – every Hollywood star knew that. Besides, the Beatles were now seen as personifications of a new youthful excitement and a mood of happy optimism among the world's baby-boomers. No one wanted to spoil that party.

Midway through the tour a meeting took place that would have a profound effect on John's songwriting. After appearing at the Forest

Hills Tennis Stadium in Queens, New York, the Beatles were visited in their hotel by Bob Dylan. By now, not many artists fazed John, but Dylan was one of them, and the Beatle was, he would later say, 'dumbfounded' when they met. A *New York Post* journalist friend of Dylan's, Al Aronowitz, arranged the meeting, of which John would later have just two main memories. The first was that Dylan was surprised when the Beatles coyly admitted that they had never smoked marijuana. As there was very little pot around in Britain at the time, that was less surprising than it now sounds. But it astonished Dylan because he thought the Beatles had been singing *'I get high, I get high, I get high'* in 'I Want To Hold Your Hand'.

'No,' they said. The lyrics had, in fact, been *'I can't hide, I can't hide, I can't hide'*.

Everyone was amused by the misunderstanding, but the omission in the Beatles' rock and roll rites of passage was soon corrected when one of Dylan's companions quickly rolled a joint and passed it around.

John, Al Aronowitz would remember, was usually the first to experiment with anything new, but he would only try the joint after Ringo, like a medieval royal taster, had taken a few puffs. 'Soon, Ringo got the giggles,' Aronowitz wrote years later, 'and the rest of us started laughing hysterically at the way Ringo was laughing hysterically.'

The other memory was less agreeable, and John would often tell how Dylan kept telling him, 'Listen to the words, man. Listen to the words,' as they played one of his records.

Feeling embarrassed about some of the lyrics of his own songs, John muttered lamely, 'I don't listen to the words.'

Actually, that wasn't even true any more. What John would describe as the 'professional songwriters' attitude . . . a certain style of song for a single' that he and Paul had so far pursued was now giving way to more personal pieces. Paul would still often write little stories in his songs, but John would increasingly 'try to express what I felt about myself'. A typical example would be 'I'm A Loser', which had been recorded just before the US tour had begun.

*'I'm a loser, and I'm not what I appear to be . . .'* went the lyrics. Could that possibly be true? John would sometimes think so. 'Part of me suspects I'm a loser . . . and part of me thinks I'm God Almighty,' he would sometimes reflect.

Certainly, he had periods of bleak introspection. Was he as clever as he wanted to be? Was Dylan cleverer? Musically, he appreciated that

George was a better guitarist, and he would say that he never played lead guitar on any of his songs when he thought George could do a better job. He could live with that. But was Paul a better songwriter than he was? That was more difficult for him. He'd certainly liked one of Paul's newer songs, 'Things We Said Today'. It sounded rather like one of his own, slightly foreboding and built around a bass riff. Had he felt a slight prick of envy when he'd first heard it? If he had, it wouldn't have been the first time that envy and admiration had come together when it came to Paul. Other doubts still lingered, too. Was Paul better-looking than he was? Did girls fancy Paul more than they did him? He'd already realised that they did – the younger ones anyway. But did Paul have a better voice as well?

'Paul has a *high* voice,' he once snapped when I mentioned to him that Paul had a 'good voice'.

And, knowing the trickery that could be done in the studio, he was soon asking George Martin to disguise his voice, no matter how much the producer would tell him, honestly, how much he liked the way he sang.

Then there was his marriage. Had he trapped himself? By the autumn of 1964 John might have been one of the most famous young men in the world, but behind the mask that he wore when he laughed and acted 'like a clown', which he mentions in 'I'm A Loser', there were more than a few insecurities. There always would be.

When the Beatles left America in late September, they had nothing but praise for the experience. 'It's been fantastic,' John said. 'We'll probably never do another tour like it. It could never be the same.'

In private, however, all four would have their grumbles. Although they would joke that they didn't mind the screaming, because it covered up their mistakes, with John fibbing that sometimes he didn't even bother to sing but simply mimed because no one could hear him anyway, they had been virtual prisoners the whole time they'd been in the US. Moving from one hotel room in a city to a stage and then on to another hotel room in another city and so on to another city and stage, playing Monopoly or cards to pass the waiting time, life had soon become stultifying.

On top of that, so determined to meet them had been local mayors, dignitaries and police chiefs, many of whom would be accompanied by their wives and children, as well as disc jockeys, journalists and fans, all four Beatles would regularly retreat behind the locked door of a hotel bathroom to unwind in each other's company. Only they knew what it was like to be at the centre of the howling hurricane of attention that they themselves were stoking, and only they, in their comradeship, could help each other get through it. 'It must have been impossible to be Elvis,' John would say. 'He was on his own.'

# 31

*'We were like Kings of the Jungle . . . like Caesars'*

Once again, they returned home to a grateful, amused nation like celebrated conquerors, as with every week that passed Britain seemed to become a younger and more fun country to be living in. It was now the mid-Sixties, and the cultural revolution of style, colour and pop music that soon would be described by *Time* magazine as 'Swinging London' could already be seen on the streets. As models' skirts became ever shorter and photographers turned into stars, and as op-art and pop-art duelled for attention in fashion, the Beatles personified the moment. More than that: by providing the musical accompaniment to the time they had become the locomotive drawing the whole Sixties cavalcade behind them.

And yet Brian couldn't let his boys rest. Within two weeks they were back on television, and the day after that, off they went on a month's tour of the UK. Quite why Brian worked them so hard – and the frenetic pace would continue for three more years – has never been clear. Perhaps in his inexperience he didn't know what else to do other than to ensure their continuous maximum exposure. And the Beatles didn't complain as they squeezed in enough recording sessions between appearances to finish a second album and fourth new single of the year.

In fact, John would say that those years were the ones he enjoyed most during his Beatles career. London nightlife for rock stars was beginning to flourish, with late-night celebrity clubs like the Bag O'Nails, the Ad-Lib and the Scotch of St James staying open until the early hours. And there, away from the fans, the Beatles would meet and talk with members of other groups, such as the Animals and Rolling Stones. For a year the tabloid newspapers had been trying to create a competition between them and whichever new group came along behind them. At first it had been the Dave Clark Five with their hit '(Feeling) Glad All Over' (which had mischievously become known as 'feeling Glad all over') and now it was the bluesy Rolling Stones. But, though John enjoyed their company and their records, he never seriously considered them as arch-rivals. No one was. As he would say: 'We were like Kings of the Jungle . . . like Caesars.'

By this time the Lennons had given up living in South Kensington. Convenient though it might have been, it was too handy for the fans whose enthusiasm was putting Cynthia and baby Julian under siege. The Lennons needed a house, but somewhere the fans could be kept at a distance.

Never having bought a home before, and knowing little of London, none of the Beatles had any idea where to look, so they asked Brian's accountants for their recommendations. The result was that John and Cynthia chose Kenwood, a large mock Tudor mansion in the wooded, private St George's Hill Estate near Weybridge in Surrey. A few months later, Ringo found another, smaller house up the road, while George moved, with girlfriend Pattie Boyd, into a more modern but equally exclusive bungalow a few miles away, near Esher.

For a wealthy family man – an accountant, perhaps, who enjoyed playing golf – Kenwood would have been idyllic. But for a mouthy rock star, aged twenty-four, who enjoyed the urgency of city life, it wasn't. Although John spent £25,000 buying the property and the same amount again on renovations and having a pool installed, he was never very happy there; and on his days off he would frequently be driven into London for the night life. Paul would make a better choice when he bought an early Victorian detached mansion in the heart of London's St John's Wood, just a few minutes' walk from the Abbey Road studios.

And it was at Abbey Road that the Beatles' legend continued to be built. Their 1964 Christmas single, 'I Feel Fine', a cheery pop song that John put together around a riff and some accidental feedback from his favourite Rickenbacker guitar, was immediately a worldwide hit. But it was a surprising choice, when Paul's 'Eight Days A Week' was ready and waiting and then relegated to being a track on the new, otherwise rather weak, *Beatles For Sale* album. There had been a disagreement over which song to release and John had won that little battle, although later 'Eight Days A Week' would be a number one in the US where Capitol Records released more singles.

A more interesting track than either song was the new album's opener 'No Reply', in which John's lyrics speak of how a girl the singer loves won't see him or talk to him. This was John anguishing to himself again. He always did anguish very well.

Not very long before, the Beatles had been outsiders from Liverpool, seeing London's bright lights like urchins peering in through a frosted window. But now doors were opening for them right across the arts and show business circles. And when John, always restless to try something new, appeared three times with Peter Cook and Dudley Moore on the BBC2 programme *Not Only . . . But Also*, he was flattered to be treated as an equal by the nation's chief satirists – one Cambridge educated, the other Oxford. For Cynthia it was more difficult. To her, such people seemed 'so effortlessly perfect'.

Singer Alma Cogan, who was known as 'the girl with a laugh in her voice', had been a big British star when the Beatles had been schoolboys, when John had derided her singing. She was only eight years older than he was, but to him she'd represented everything that was wrong with British music, old-fashioned and unhip, from the voluminously wide skirts she wore to the cute little songs she sang. But after the Beatles met her on *Ready Steady Go!*, and were then invited, with Brian, to one of her champagne parties at her swish apartment on Kensington High Street, where the famous sat on floor cushions like atolls, he discovered he had some reassessing to do.

As Cynthia would recall, the other guests read like a gossip column of the currently famous, so John, with his built-in prejudices against glitzy London show business, shouldn't really have fitted in. But he did. Cynthia, on the other hand, was made aware of her own lack of sophistication, seeing herself as 'a naïve girl who had simply got lucky and didn't deserve' to be there.

Nor did it help that, much as she liked the bubbly Alma Cogan, she couldn't help but wonder if the singer was flirting with her husband. Did the two have an affair, as has been suggested by Alma's younger sister, Sandra Caron? John never said, and as he usually told someone something, generally his Woolton pal Pete, they probably didn't. Cynthia never asked.

When it came to other women, she never would, not even when a few months later John brazenly began to sing, in front of her, a new song he was writing that started, '*I once had a girl, or should I say, she once had me . . .*' It was the first line to 'Norwegian Wood' and the Lennons were on a skiing holiday in St Moritz with George Martin and his assistant (soon to be his second wife) Judy Lockhart Smith. The producer was astonished, because it was obvious to him that the song was about what John would later describe as 'a little affair' he'd been having with the wife of a photographer friend. But, either because Cynthia wasn't listening to the words or didn't understand their confessional element, she didn't react.

Nor did she ask questions when, one evening, photographer Robert Freeman suddenly turned up at Kenwood with his tearful wife, Sonny. Robert was very angry, asking to speak privately to John, and they were taken by him into the dining room. Cynthia was not included in the ensuing conversation. When the couple left about half an hour later, John gave no explanation, but simply went upstairs to the little studio he'd had made at the top of the house. The incident was never mentioned again. When Robert and Sonny later divorced, Cynthia would write that she 'couldn't escape the conclusion' that John and Sonny must have had an affair, 'although I never had any proof'.

There were other women, too, a journalist friend and an actress, but Cynthia never knew for sure. She didn't want to know. In her autobiography, she wrote: 'I knew that John might have had the odd fling with a girl when the Beatles were on tour . . . If any of them [the Beatles] had the odd lapse, well, they were only human and it meant little.'

It wasn't the odd lapse for John, but that was the way that Cynthia coped with it.


John had never had any real money, but when it arrived he never took the slightest interest in where it came from or where it went to. He'd always been casual about it, going back to when he'd borrowed from friends at art college and forgotten to repay them, and now he was content to let financial experts take care of his wealth for him. He just couldn't be bothered. 'Money flows in and it flows out,' he would tell me, and, rarely carrying much cash, he was usually able to sign for everything.

Mimi's attitude was that he was naïve about money. 'He just never had any idea of its worth,' she would fret, before adding her usual snipe, 'probably because he never had to work hard for it like some people. He was a soft touch. He would listen to a sob-story and then just give his money away to some hanger-on who had spun him a yarn.'

Once she had been the provider, but now John supported her, despite her still regularly criticising him. He'd never liked Cynthia's mother, Lil – nor had Mimi, who considered her to be intellectually and socially her inferior. But, anything for a quiet life; John rented his mother-in-law a house near where he and Cynthia lived, and gave her a monthly allowance, too.

Around his new home at Kenwood his behaviour at first was like that of a lottery winner. To go with the grand house he bought a black Rolls-Royce (although it was second hand), then a Ferrari as well as a Mini Cooper, with black windows and black wheels (prompting Paul to tease that he was 'going to buy a bicycle with black windows'). But even after he passed his driving test in February 1965, John rarely drove any of his cars – or showed much interest in the Volkswagen Beetle he'd bought for Cynthia, or the Porsche that replaced it. With his terrible eyesight, he was hopeless when behind the wheel, and he mainly left the driving to a former Welsh guardsman, Les Anthony. The only cars he did enjoy driving, if only for a little while, were the model ones that he would race around a vastly extended track made up of three Scalextric sets laid out across two empty bedrooms in the attic.

Whenever John got a craze he would throw himself completely into it, before suddenly forgetting it and moving on. When Ringo came to live nearby, the drummer had a go-kart track built in his garden as well as a pool room in his house, so John would go there occasionally. As the drummer so eloquently told me: 'Sometimes I go to John's house to play with his toys, and sometimes he comes to my house to play with mine.'

It was inevitable that at that time the Beatles' closest friends would be their colleagues in the band. Apart from Neil Aspinall, who was now their assistant, and Mal Evans, who was his, nearly everyone else they knew would by now have been awkward in their company. Brian was close, of course, but, at his lavish new apartment in Belgravia, he was a manager first and a friend second. He with his companions, and the Beatles with each other.

It might have been better for Brian had the Beatles been closer to him. Because, alone in London, without a regular partner, he was prone to not always mixing with the safest people, and would get into trouble. But, whatever scrapes he found himself in with badly chosen boys and his newfound interest in drugs, he tried very hard to make sure the Beatles didn't find out.

Since, musically, John and Paul were so closely linked as songwriters it might have been expected that they would have been the closest of friends. They weren't. John always got on with Ringo. Everyone did. He was something of a cheery melding factor in the group. And he usually got on with George, too. His relationship with Paul, however, could be edgier. Paul wouldn't just turn up at Kenwood, as once he would cycle round to Mendips. His visits were professional. Driving down the A3 to Surrey in his Aston Martin, he would wait while John had his Rice Krispies breakfast while reading the newspapers, and then they would spend three hours working together.

'All those songs, like "Help!", "Eleanor Rigby" and "Norwegian Wood", came directly out of the collaboration,' Paul would later reminisce to me. 'And never once did we come away empty-handed. We were both good. If he got stuck, I could always help him. Always. I never failed to help him. And if I got stuck he never failed to help me.' Most of the songs for the film *Help!* were written face-to-face in this way. And when that wasn't possible, they would do it over the phone, John with a guitar in his hands, Paul, perhaps, at his piano.

The Lennons had fled London to get away from the fans and the press, but, although they had a housekeeper in Dot Jarlett, and a driver and gardener, they were still just a young married couple with a little boy who found themselves in extraordinary circumstances. Occasionally Cynthia might go up to London to meet John and the other Beatles after a recording session, and go on to a club. But the general rule was that, as rebuilding work on the house went on around them, they didn't go out to dinner together very often, and ate and drank pretty much the same things they would have done when they were living in Brian's flat in Liverpool. That meant nothing 'fancy' for John, as he liked steak and chips and chip butties, and glasses of milk or beer rather than wine.

Very occasionally they would have guests, with Bob Dylan inviting himself on one occasion and Joan Baez on another, but the most regular caller was John's old friend Pete Shotton, whose career in the police hadn't prospered. Now the owner of a small supermarket in Hayling Island, Sussex, which had been financed for him by John, Pete was only just over an hour's drive away. Mimi would tell John that his friend was a 'cadger', but John knew better. He insisted on helping Pete in any way he could. Pete knew him better than anyone else, much better than Cynthia, and didn't see him as a famous

Beatle. On his own, John could be lonely. When not working with the Beatles and at home with his family at Kenwood, there was a hole in his life that needed to be filled. Pete was always made welcome. Cynthia might have been a wife, but she wasn't a pal who could share in his zany ideas.

And nor would she be at John's side when he was driven into London in his black Mini Cooper, where he would sometimes get wasted, see what turned up, and be driven home in the early hours. Cynthia might have wanted to be there with him, but John was King of the Home as well as a King of the Jungle, and if he didn't want his wife with him, he would have an excuse, and she wouldn't go. So she and Julian would go to bed in their big millionaire's home and John would come back when he felt like it, and then lie in bed all the following morning.

Cynthia might have been living a privileged, luxurious life with money to buy whatever she wanted and to pay the cosmetic surgeon to fix the bump in her nose that she'd always hated, but she was hardly enjoying a normal family life. And though John might sometimes hate himself and wish he could be more of a family man and not get cross with Julian when the little boy splashed his food around the room, he couldn't. He was the way he was and domestic life bored him.

Meanwhile the business of being the Beatles had to go on. New songs for the next Beatles film, *Help!*, were needed, as well as a new single – for which John wrote 'Ticket To Ride'. It was a miserable piece that not everyone thought was strong enough, and that included Mimi, who still always had an opinion on everything. John's own criticism was of the flip side, 'Yes It Is'. A lament for a previous lover, against whom the current one couldn't compare, 'Yes It Is' received some thoughtful reviews when released. John, however, seemed to delight in trashing his own work, especially when he thought it had been the subject of undeserved genuflection by the growing number of Beatles cognoscenti. Casually, he would later dismiss it to me as him 'trying to write "This Boy" again. Same harmony, same chords and double-dutch words. It's embarrassing. *"If you wear red tonight . . ."* Jesus Christ!'

Nor did his derision end there. Another of his songs on the *Help!* album was 'It's Only Love'. 'That was the most embarrassing song

I ever wrote,' he told me. 'Everything rhymed. Disgusting lyrics . . . Even then I was so ashamed of the lyrics I could hardly sing them. That was one song I really wished I'd never written above all else.' Then he paused. 'Well, you can say that about a few of them.' At the other extreme, he was proud of 'You've Got To Hide Your Love Away', which, with only acoustic instruments, was almost folkie. It was, he would say, his 'Afro-Dylan days', a singing style that annoyed Paul. 'Why are you trying to sound like Dylan?' McCartney asked during the session.

When it was released, various theories would be gossiped about the lyrics of 'You've Got To Hide Your Love Away' – that it was a song about homosexuality, and perhaps a message of understanding to Brian Epstein. But if it was, that was something John doesn't seem to have ever mentioned, and it's likely that he would have done.

The movie *Help!* was shot during March and April 1965 in, for tax reasons, the Bahamas, and then Austria. The use of black and white film had given *A Hard Day's Night* a topical newsreel reality feel, but, with more money to spend this time, *Help!* was filmed in the glamorous unreality of Technicolor and Cinemascope. And with a silly script that relied mainly on visual gags, it wasn't nearly as good . . . nor were the Beatles as well behaved on the set. There was a reason for this. In the six months since Bob Dylan introduced them to pot it had become a mainstay in their daily lives.

'We were smoking marijuana for breakfast during that period,' John said. 'Nobody could communicate with us. It was all glazed eyes and giggling all the time.'

Paul confirmed that: 'We showed up a bit stoned, smiled a lot and hoped we'd get through it.'

They did get through it, sort of, and the film was another huge hit, but it's the title song that is best remembered. When John wrote it, with Paul's help for the tempo and the counter melody, he believed he was just writing a bouncy rock and roll number, which is how it was received by the rest of the group and the public. Only five years later, when he went into therapy and was encouraged to read through the lyrics to all his songs, did he reach the conclusion that '*won't you please, please help me*' had been more personal than he'd known.

'That was my "fat Elvis" period,' he would tell me. 'I didn't realise it at the time . . . but later, I knew that I was crying out for help. The real meaning of the song was lost because we needed a single and it had to be fast. I get very emotional when I'm singing the lyrics . . . Whatever I'm singing, I don't piss about . . . It was a bit poetic. I was in a hell of a state when I wrote it . . .' Then, by way of explanation, he added: 'The whole Beatle thing was just beyond comprehension. I was eating and drinking like a pig, and I was as fat as a pig . . . dissatisfied with myself.'

That would be hindsight. At the *Help!* stage in his life, John never admitted to any weaknesses. Paul put it very well when interviewed for *The Beatles Anthology*: 'The thing about John was that he was all upfront. You never saw [the real] John. Only through a few chinks in his armour did I ever see him, because his armour was so tough. On the surface, John was tough, tough, tough.'

Whatever its shortcomings, *Help!* was released to worldwide delight and box office success in the summer of 1965 just a few days after John's second book *A Spaniard In The Works* was published, to rather less excitement. Having run out of his *Mersey Beat* archive he'd been forced to work harder this time, and had even bought James Joyce's *Finnegans Wake* and a book by Edward Lear, to discover what it was that, according to some critics of *In His Own Write*, had influenced him. 'I couldn't see any resemblance to any of them,' he told a BBC literary interviewer, Wilfred De'Ath. He'd never even heard of Edward Lear.

For his new book, once again the critics had much praise, if not quite so effusive. But when asked why he wrote such short mini-pieces, his reply was scornful. 'To you they're *mini-pieces*,' he said. 'To me they're *marathons*.'

As for the lower sales, he really didn't care. 'Okay, it didn't do as well as the first, but then what follow-up book ever does?' he would later tell *Rolling Stone*. 'I had a lot of the stories bottled up in my system and it did me good to get rid of them . . . The plain, unvarnished fact is that I like writing, and I'd go on writing even if there wasn't any publisher daft enough to publish them.'

What he did care about, although he would try to conceal it for several years, was his reaction to the penultimate track on the *Help!* album. It was 'Yesterday', a song Paul had been playing on the piano for over a year, having woken up one morning with it running through his head. Had he dreamed it? He didn't know, and he would go around playing the melody to friends to see if they recognised it, in case he was accidentally copying something he might have heard somewhere. Only when he was convinced that it was a true McCartney original, and had settled on some lyrics – which concern loss, and which some believe to have been a reflection on the death of his mother when he was fourteen, did he think about recording it.

This presented two problems. One was that George Martin couldn't see how a rock and roll band like the Beatles could back Paul without spoiling the song. So he suggested a string quartet as an accompaniment. It was the first time any of the Beatles had sung on record without the others providing the backing, and the first time that John had found himself left out. He had to give his permission. That was the easy bit. The problem was that John hadn't contributed to any of the lyrics either, meaning that 'Yesterday' was a 100 per cent McCartney original. Someone at EMI suggested that it should perhaps be released as a Paul McCartney solo, but no one wanted that. In the end, 'Yesterday' went on to the *Help!* album as a Beatles track and wasn't even released in the UK as a single – although it became a number one hit in America.

Reflecting on this, John suggested that Paul should hang on to all the royalties for the song instead of sharing them. Paul thanked him for the thought, and refused. That would have been against the spirit of the songwriting relationship they'd always had. So, everything was amicably agreed.

The difficulty for John was coming to terms with the fact that Paul had come up with a classic. No matter how much he admired the shape and lyrics of the song, and he did, that familiar little itch of jealousy couldn't help but nag at him, as over the years and everywhere in the world he would hear it – probably the most loved Beatles song of them all – and know that he'd had nothing to do with it.

He was always vague about many things, like dates and times and money, but he would have perfect recall for some details of his life, and one of those was the first time he took LSD. It was one evening around the time of the filming of *Help!* and he and Cynthia had been invited out to dinner along with George and Pattie. 'It was at the flat of some trendy, swinger dentist, you know the sort of people who George hangs out with . . .' he would recall disparagingly to me. 'His wife chose the bunnies for the Playboy Club or something . . . Anyway, we're all there and he slipped it into our coffee without telling us.'

John had heard about LSD, how its full name was lysergic acid diethylamide, and how it was commonly known as 'acid', a psychedelic consciousness-distorting, laboratory-made narcotic. George, at the time, was less informed. Quickly John realised that the coffee had been spiked and became angry. He liked to be the one to decide when he took drugs and to know what he was taking. As soon as they realised what had happened the four guests wanted to go.

Aware that the drug might take thirty minutes to take effect, and not knowing what its effects might be, the dentist kept saying, 'I advise you not to leave.'

But, John would tell me, 'We thought he was trying to keep us for an orgy or something in his house and we didn't want to know.' So they got into George's car and set off to see their friend from Hamburg, Klaus Voorman, who was appearing in the trio Paddy, Klaus and Gibson at the Pickwick Club. By the time they got there, however, the hallucinogenic effects of the LSD had begun, and, going on from there to another club, the Ad Lib, where very bright lights were flashing, they emerged into the club shouting, 'The lift's on fire.'

'It was insane, terrifying, but exciting,' was John's verdict. Cynthia hated it and would later say that she thought she was going mad as everything was changing into nonsensical shapes around her. Pattie, meanwhile, found herself banging on shop windows for no apparent reason.

With George driving very slowly they made their way home to his house in Esher, where eventually they fell asleep. It took Cynthia all night to come down. John, however, was intrigued by the experience. Soon he would be taking LSD again and again. The Preludin and alcohol that had fortified him during the long Hamburg club nights had recently been replaced by pot. But now he'd tried a drug of an altogether different dimension, and he'd enjoyed what it did for him with its *Alice In Wonderland* perception-changing distortions. It would take a little while, but over the following year, LSD would become a potent new diversion. And it would irritate and disappoint that Cynthia, who wouldn't take it again, would regret that it had ever entered their lives.

# 32

*'Once you plug in and the noise starts, you're just a group who could be playing anywhere . . . You forget that you're the Beatles'*

The original plan when the Beatles played Shea Stadium, New York, on 15 August 1965 was that they should arrive by helicopter and descend as if from heaven into the very midst of the 55,000 waiting fans. That, Brian felt, would be the kind of theatricality that only the Beatles deserved as they became the first group ever to play a stadium of such vast proportions. And although, in the event, that wasn't allowed to happen, as, before reaching the stadium, they had to be transferred to a Wells Fargo security van, the day would go down in rock history as the peak of their touring days.

They'd just finished a two-week European tour when, in what looked like natty little toy soldier uniforms, they made their way to the stage at the centre of the ground and looked around in astonishment at the multitude. Before the show they'd all been nervous, but, out there on a little island stage of musical technology, the realisation of how far they were from the audience had the effect of drawing them closer together. In moments like this, when nerves could get to them, it would always be John, the comic, who would lead. He was never much of a keyboard player and didn't play piano on their records, but now he found himself attacking the organ with antic disposition as Paul sang 'I'm Down'. It made no difference that John only knew a handful of chords, or that he attacked the keys with his elbow. Fifty yards away, the fans couldn't hear or see that. John's job was to be the leader of the band, and the best way to lead was to amuse the other members at what they could all see had become the absurdity of Beatles concerts. 'Once you plug in and the noise starts, you're just a group who could be playing anywhere . . . You forget that you're the Beatles,' he said about an afternoon he'd loved.

Some fans – Linda Eastman, who was yet to meet Paul, her future husband, among them – were upset that they couldn't hear the music. But on this day the Beatles didn't care. The fans had come to *see* them, not to *hear* them, which would be the case everywhere as they began their latest traverse of North America. 'We could send out four waxwork dummies of ourselves and that would satisfy the crowds,' was John's opinion. 'Beatles concerts are nothing to do with music any more.'

What they *were* to do with was more difficult to define. In the delirium that their appearances provoked, parallels would be drawn with religious frenzy and mass political communion. That such mob excitement was being sparked by four young men who sang popular songs mainly about the emotional vagaries of adolescents had no precursor on this scale. It was the by-product of twentieth-century communications. When girl fans had screamed in smaller numbers, although with equal intensity, for Elvis, it could be pointed out that he would purposely be sexually provocative when on stage. But the Beatles had always made a point of not being sexy in their performances. John could be funny, Ringo was lovable, and George and Paul looked romantic.

But no one ever called the Beatles' performances sexy. If sex was involved, it didn't emanate from them, so much as it was inevitably everywhere in their hormonally charged, excited teenage audiences. The Beatles on stage were the trigger, as one scream led to ten thousand or fifty thousand more, and in this way the audience became part of the show, an audience primed to react by radio and television, like no other audience in history. The Beatles, and Beatlemania, and their audiences, were all products of their time.

There's an unwritten rule in entertainment that says you should never meet your idols – because nine times out of ten they will disappoint you. For John, Elvis Presley had already disappointed by appearing in vapid beach-boy movies since he'd left the US Army in 1960, and by making some mediocre records. All the same, although Hollywood stars had flocked to the Beatles when they'd first arrived in America, Elvis was, as John said, 'the only person in the United States we really wanted to meet . . . though, I'm not sure that he wanted to meet us'.

So when, during a break in Los Angeles halfway through the tour, a young English journalist called Chris Hutchins engineered a summit between the Beatles and their one-time hero at Elvis's home in Bel Air, the mood was tentative. Elvis had only agreed to it because the Colonel pushed him into it, believing that it would be good publicity. Now, however, he was no longer the twenty-one-year-old rule-breaking and ground-breaking rebel who had inspired them almost a decade earlier.

No photographers were permitted to record the meeting, but if a picture had been taken it would show Elvis in a red shirt and black jerkin, his hair dyed black and lacquered like a helmet, being stared at by the four silent, shampooed, shaggy-haired English usurpers of his throne, John and Paul on either side of him on a horseshoe-shaped settee. Across his large sitting room were Priscilla Presley and some of her girlfriends, all overdressed for the occasion in party attire, who, in turn, gazed at the Beatles. Elvis was then thirty and John approaching his twenty-fifth birthday. But in the way the two men looked, and in their attitudes, there could have been a two-decade difference in age.

Uncomfortable with the awed silence, Elvis finally joked, 'Well, if you guys are just going to stare at me, I'm going to bed.'

The ice was partly broken. But while Paul tried to get a conversation going about the bass guitar, as Elvis was nervously playing a Fender along to Charlie Rich's 'Mohair Sam' that was on his jukebox, John began to speak in a mock Peter Sellers-type German accent. He was trying to be funny, but such was the awkwardness of the situation it's unlikely that Elvis realised. George, meanwhile, had been stoned before he got there, and took little part in any conversation, while Ringo went off to play pool with some of Elvis's Memphis Mafia entourage. For Paul the most memorable part of the evening was that Elvis had the first TV remote he'd ever seen.

It wasn't an unpleasant evening, and John would later say he enjoyed it, but the immediate rapport that had occurred at his meeting with Bob Dylan the previous year was not repeated. Things got better when guitars were passed around and plugged in so that some ensemble versions of rock and roll riffs were played, without much singing. After which Paul ventured to tell Elvis how much they'd all liked his early rock records. To which Elvis replied that he was thinking of recording some more songs in similar vein. Had they not been overawed by the occasion, John and Paul should at that point have offered to write a song for their host. They had the magic touch of the moment and were regularly handing out songs to their friends, some of which became very big hits. But no suggestion was made and the moment passed with John's slightly brusque retort: 'Oh, good. We'll buy them when you do,' which sounded ruder than intended. Years later, Elvis would include 'Get Back' and 'Yesterday' in his stage act, but 1965 was when he really needed a little Lennon and McCartney magic.

As the Beatles left that night, inviting Elvis to visit their rented home in Beverly Glen for a party the following evening – an invitation that was not taken up – John, now quite drunk, returned to his German accent and said: 'Sanks for ze muzik, Elvis. Long live ze King!' It probably sounded as though he was being sarcastic, but he meant it. As he would tell some of Elvis's pals who did attend the Beatles' party the next night: 'Without Elvis I would have been nothing.' He meant that, too.

'It was a nice meeting,' he would say later. 'But he wasn't articulate, that's all . . . He did some good stuff after the army, but it was never quite the same. It was like something happened to him psychologically.' On a crueller day, though, looking for a laugh, he would say that meeting Elvis had been 'just like meeting Engelbert Humperdinck'. His habit of changing his mind was a constant in his life.

The rest of the US tour was the same screaming bedlam the Beatles had come to expect and by the time they returned to England in September the euphoria they'd felt at Shea Stadium was quickly dissolving. But it wasn't so much the fans who bothered them: 'They've paid for a good show and they can go potty if they like,' he said.

What irritated them was having to talk to people they didn't want to meet. Today, rock stars are surrounded by small armies of security men to barricade them against outside demands. But the Beatles travelled with the same little unit they'd always had, with Brian managing, Neil and Mal acting as road managers and security and Tony Barrow looking after the demands of the press. All of which meant that local officials, promoters and police could easily get to them.

The most difficult moments would be when invalids in wheelchairs would be lined up for them as though the Beatles were faith healers. The suspicion was that some of the nurses and carers only brought the patients because they saw it as a way that they could get to meet the Beatles themselves.

It had been at John's insistence that Mimi leave Liverpool and move closer to him in the south of England. She still worried about him, but he worried about her, too, aware of and feeling slightly guilty about the constant disruption to her life from the fans who made pilgrimages to Mendips. So, one day while she'd been staying at Kenwood, he decided to take her by Rolls-Royce on a tour of houses on the south coast where she thought she might like to live. Estate agents had already provided details of four possibilities, but Mimi had grumpily dismissed the first three. Then she'd seen a white bungalow by the beach at Sandbanks at Poole in Dorset, and John had made up her mind for her. 'If you don't have it, Mimi,' he said, 'I will.'

'There were still people living in it,' Mimi would recall, 'so I didn't want to go in, but John did.' She was embarrassed because he was wearing his old jeans and what she described as 'a silly cap'. But he was 'as bold as brass'. It cost him £25,000 – which was the amount he'd paid for his own home, Kenwood. But it was by the sea and had a beautiful view in the richest corner of England outside London.

Mimi had hoped that living less than a hundred miles away would mean that she would see more of Julian, but Cynthia would only remember one visit to Sandbanks, on a sunny summer's day. Putting a picnic together they paddled and sunbathed, with John hiding under a large hat so that no one would recognise him. They didn't.

'It was heaven,' Cynthia would tell me. 'Beautiful. The one moment when we sat as a little family and made sand castles with Julian's buckets and spades. We planned to do it again. But we never did.'

The autumn of 1965 was mainly spent recording at Abbey Road, but there was a break in the sessions when in October all four Beatles were driven through the gates of Buckingham Palace to be awarded with their medals as Members of the British Empire, an honour promoted by Prime Minister Harold Wilson, and bestowed on them by the Queen. Traditionally the Queen's biannual honours had usually gone to establishment figures, such as long-serving civil servants, Members of Parliament, heads of major businesses and charities, and former members of the armed forces. So when the honour for the Beatles had been announced in the summer there had been much amusement in the press, and some outrage, that a mere pop group should be worthy of such decoration. Some retired generals were said to have even threatened to send their own honours back if standards were to be lowered so far. It seems unlikely that any did.

Harold Wilson had been clever. The honour wasn't for the Beatles' contribution to music, it was for their part in boosting the nation's exports. At first there had been some disagreement among the group as to whether they should accept the award. Though Ringo liked the idea, John, a vague republican, wasn't so sure. But he was flattered, too, and putting aside his argument that they would be selling out even further, he got up early ('I couldn't believe that such a time existed') and went off to meet the Queen.

He would later boast that before the investiture, the Beatles smoked pot in the Palace toilets, but that was just John fibbing for the fun of it. They were, the others agreed, too nervous to have done that. As rituals go it was all straightforward enough, with the Beatles waiting in a line for their names to be called, then having to walk forward, bow, and then step further forward. John was first, as usual.

'It's a pleasure giving this to you. Have you been working hard recently?' the Queen asked as she hooked the MBE medal on to his lapel.

Mimi hadn't brought John up to make small talk with the Queen, and John's mind went blank. He *had* been working very hard recording, but for some reason he said, 'No, we've been having a holiday.'

Then, stepping back he bowed again, and, turning, walked away, leaving the Queen to honour his friends. Usually recipients were proud to have been honoured by the Queen, but John quickly sent his medal to Mimi, who put it on her mantelpiece in her new home. At least she was proud of it.

# 33

*'I was sitting trying to think of a song, and I thought of myself sitting there, doing nothing, getting nowhere . . . Then I thought of myself as Nowhere Man, sitting in his nowhere land . . .'*

By 1965, rock music had grown up and changed beyond recognition from the sounds that had seduced John in the Fifties. For the manufacturers of guitars it was a boom period, but for singer-songwriters it was better than that. It was a moment of graduation as rock became the dominant popular music form of the Western world.

No one recognised this better than Lennon and McCartney. But the rivalry wasn't now just between the two of them. There were competitors all around, and, thus challenged, over a four-week autumn period they recorded what many believe were several of their most accomplished songs for the album *Rubber Soul*.

For John, the first would be 'Norwegian Wood', the song he'd begun writing about an affair a year earlier – although in the song the anticipated adultery doesn't quite happen. All kinds of explanation for the title have been proffered over the years, the most popular being that it might have pointed to the nationality of the lady involved. But, as Paul was also heavily involved in the song's lyrics and arrangement, it seems just as likely that the title simply referred, as Paul has suggested, to the wooden strips that were used to clad his little studio in his St John's Wood home.

The last lines of the song, however, are pure John. Having been led on by this flirty young woman, but then told to sleep in the bath, the disappointed suitor then sets fire to her flat. Arson being an unusual subject for a pop song, it was an echo of the black comedy of several of the short stories from *In His Own Write*.

Everything about the recording was interesting. An old Irish folk song in shape, the adding of a sitar that George Harrison had recently acquired brought a spiky atmosphere to the story, suggesting musically that something exotic but naughty might have been in the offing.

It was always one of John's favourites, as was 'Girl', which had a definite Eastern European Jewish feel to it, and on which he asked the sound engineer to make sure to capture his intake of breath before he sang '*Girl . . . girl . . .*' All young men understand the feeling that sigh evoked, and John would talk about how the subject was an idealised dream girl, and not based on anyone he knew. It was also the song on which the Beatles sang the disguised words 'tit . . . tit . . . tit' in the background to fox the BBC and any other would-be censors.

'In My Life' was unblushingly autobiographical. The lyrics had started out one day at Kenwood when John was thinking about the bus journey from his childhood home in Menlove Avenue into the centre of Liverpool, mentioning every place that he could remember. It was before the Beatles had recorded 'Penny Lane', but it included 'Penny Lane, Strawberry Fields and tram sheds,' he said later. Unfortunately, he added, 'it was the most boring sort of "What I Did In My Holidays" bus trip song, and it wasn't working at all. But then, I lay back and the lyrics started coming to me. It was pretty truthful. No psychedelia. No gobbledegook . . .' – just memories of places and people he'd known and loved.

Paul wrote the middle-eight melody on a little Mellotron organ, which became an instrumental break when George Martin went into the studio early one day before John and Paul got there. Playing it on an electric piano, he then speeded up the tape until it sounded like a harpsichord. In that way a moment of baroque music found its way on to a Beatles album.

And then there was 'Nowhere Man', which, as a single, became a big American hit. Usually, and working in an opposite way to Paul, John thought of the lyrics to his songs first, and then searched for the chords to put them to – often writing little pieces of a song before finding a way of joining the fragments together. In the case of 'Nowhere Man', he would remember the chain of thoughts as the song came out almost fully formed. With the dates for the session having been set, 'I was sitting trying to think of a song, and I thought of myself sitting there, doing nothing, getting nowhere . . . Then I thought of myself as Nowhere Man, sitting in his nowhere land . . .'

It could have applied to anyone, but for John it was about him, and the ennui he was increasingly feeling. '*Isn't he a bit like you and me,*' went the lyrics. Living out there in a rich, pleasant estate in Surrey he was a nowhere suburban man, with a pleasant suburban wife, and surrounded by, as he saw them, nowhere suburban neighbours.

Obviously, by this stage the Beatles were no longer expected to record an album in a day, or a single in a three-hour session. So grateful were EMI for the worldwide income that was accruing to the company from the sales of Beatles records they had been virtually given the freedom of Abbey Road studios as their playground. Always experimenting when they were there, they would discover abandoned instruments left behind in the band room and wonder how they could be incorporated into their songs.

Meanwhile, they soaked up George Martin's musical and technical expertise. He'd once been their boss. Now he was their colleague and their teacher. The roles hadn't been reversed. It was still his job to get the recordings fit for release, and his influence on those recordings was massive. He wrote music himself, but although he didn't have the gift for original composition that John and Paul had, he could show them how to best express their gift. Until the recording of 'Yesterday' the previous summer, Martin had been limited mainly to helping them inside the basic rock formula. But with *Rubber Soul*, he, as much as the Beatles, could see that the musical possibilities were, if not infinite, certainly far wider than any of them had previously imagined.

At the same *Rubber Soul* sessions Paul came in with 'Michelle', some of the lyrics having been translated into French by the teacher wife of Paul's school friend Ivan Vaughan – the boy who had introduced Paul to John all those years ago. Then there was 'I'm Looking Through You', a curiously angry song about the breakdown of a relationship, which sounds more like a song John might have written, and 'We Can Work It Out', which was so good and instantly commercial that it was left off the album and became one side of the Beatles' next Christmas single.

It was also another occasion when John and Paul came up with different sections of the same song, Paul writing the verse and John the middle eight – a conversation in music that typified its two writers. 'Paul came to my house,' John would remember, 'with the first bit, and then I came up with "Life is very short and there's no time . . ."' As John saw it, Paul was the optimist, wanting to work things out, while he was impatient, always in a hurry.

It's common to think of Lennon and McCartney as a song-writing team, but that doesn't get near to describing their working relationship. Most music-writing duos, such as George and Ira Gershwin, or Rodgers and Hammerstein, are built on one member being the composer and the other the lyricist. But both John and Paul were complete songwriters in themselves, each often writing both the melody and the lyric to a song, before playing and singing it to the other and inviting suggestions for improvement.

How much Paul contributed to 'Day Tripper' is less certain. One of the quickie rock and roll songs that John would come up with when a new single was due, the title was his hint that he was tripping on LSD now. The lyrics were about a girl, any girl, who was a prick-teaser, although, to avoid being banned by radio stations, she became a 'big teaser'.

When *Rubber Soul* was released at Christmas 1965 it quickly became known as the Beatles' 'pot album'. There's no doubt marijuana was much around when the songs were being written. It was now a constant companion for the Beatles, except, they said, when they were recording. George Martin had become irritated by the giggling during the *Help!* sessions so, in deference to him, pot was less in evidence when they were recording *Rubber Soul*. That being said, the cover of the LP gave the game away, when the Beatles chose a much-distorted image that photographer Robert Freeman had accidentally taken of them. For those who liked clues, and over the following years a virtual academic discipline was invented for the interpretation of possible cryptography in Beatles lyrics, this would be a first no one could miss.

*Rubber Soul* was a ground-breaking record, but perhaps most importantly it finally ushered in the predominance of the album over the single. In 1963, Beatles fans had been largely teenyboppers. Now the songs were more complicated and the fans were older. *Rubber Soul* took the Beatles to another level, and in so doing inspired other groups to match them. In America Brian Wilson of the Beach Boys thought: 'I want to make an album like that.' It was, he said, 'like a collection of folk songs. We did *Pet Sounds* after that . . .'

A new rivalry had begun.

To no one's surprise, John's father, Freddie, hadn't been able to fade back into obscurity after getting into contact with his son again, and one day he turned up at Kenwood. Answering the front door, Cynthia found herself looking 'at a tiny man with lank grey hair, balding on top . . . He looked as unkempt and down at heel as a tramp . . . but, alarmingly,' she said, 'he had John's face.' For some reason, John had never told her that he'd met his father again.

Freddie explained that he needed to talk to his son. John was out at the time, but expected home soon, so Cynthia invited Freddie inside where she made him a cup of tea and some cheese on toast. Then, as they waited, the two had an awkward conversation, until Freddie happened to mention that he knew his hair looked a mess. Immediately, Cynthia, who often cut her mother's hair, offered to reshape it for him, and, getting out a comb and scissors, set about giving her father-in-law a haircut. As often happened, John didn't come home when expected, and eventually Freddie grew tired of waiting and wandered off again.

When he got back, John was not pleased to learn about the visitor. But he was even angrier when, just before Christmas 1965, Freddie recorded a self-written vaguely autobiographical song, 'That's My Life'. It was not a success, but when the tabloid newspapers featured more stories about the singer, John was torn. Whatever he might think of Freddie – and Mimi never softened in her warnings about him – the fellow was, after all, his father.

The past could never be just the past while John was a famous multi-millionaire and his father, living just a few miles away in the Greyhound Pub at Hampton Court, was a usually out-of-work dishwasher.

# 34

*'Christianity will go. It will vanish and sink . . .*
We're *more popular than Jesus now'*

The first months of 1966 were spent lolling around his house, read-ing, writing and seeing his Beatle neighbours. There was no one else John wanted to see down there in Surrey. So, when Maureen Cleave of the London *Evening Standard* rang asking for an interview, he im-mediately invited her to Kenwood. Maureen, an attractive, intelligent interviewer in her early thirties, was a good friend – good enough for him to have lent her his copy of Elvis's first album, when he'd realised how little she knew about rock and roll. Considering how much he treasured it, that was friendship – and when she forgot to give it back he hadn't even pursued her for it. She would, she now told him, soon be giving up her job, and it would turn out to be not only the last time they would meet, but an interview that would have extraordinary consequences.

Mainly, John spent the day amusing Maureen as, carrying a Sia-mese cat, and followed everywhere by three-year-old Julian, he led her around his mansion with its fitted carpets and panelled walls. The Beatles thought she was very grand, with her smart accent and piercing questions, and her subsequent article would clearly suggest that a mock-Tudor house among wealthy stockbrokers wasn't right for the individualist John Lennon. But John had already reached the same conclusion, as he pointed out the expensive bits and pieces that sudden wealth had allowed him to buy and then to carelessly forget: the five televisions – most people only had one at that time; the three cars; phones everywhere – the numbers of which he didn't know; the purple sitting room; the fruit machine and the now abandoned Scalextric room.

For a lifelong keen reader there was also a whole room lined with books, from the *Just William* series beloved from his childhood to hurriedly bought leather-bound editions of Tolstoy, which, as there are only so many hours in the day, would have been still unread, as would the volumes of Swift and Tennyson. The Orwell and Aldous Huxley books might, though, have been looked at.

Like Paul, he too had his own music room at the top of the house, with six interconnected tape recorders, to go with all his other electrical toys, few of which he could make work. All of that might have been expected in any rock star, and it was only when they reached his eccentricities that his merry sense of the absurd appeared, with the purposeless eight little green boxes with winking red lights, the suit of armour, the pair of crutches that George had given him as a present – which was, it might be assumed, a sick joke about John's spazzie act, which he had now thankfully given up – and a gorilla suit.

A gorilla suit?

'I thought I might need one. But I've only worn it twice . . . I thought I might pop it on in the summer and drive around in the Ferrari . . .' He'd also thought that the other Beatles might buy gorilla suits too, so that they could go about together in them, four Beatles dressed as gorillas. For some reason none of the others had, so he'd come up with another idea. 'If I didn't wear the head it would make an amazing fur coat – with legs . . .' Then he added: 'It's the only suit that fits me.'

There was also a very large bible and a crucifix that looked as though it might have belonged on the altar in a Catholic church. From his few weeks as a choirboy in Woolton, right through school, religion was in those days a constant in a Liverpool boy's background. At Quarry Bank he'd amused his friends by drawing a cartoon of Jesus on the cross with a pair of carpet slippers waiting underneath, while at college he'd taken his mockery several steps further by depicting the figure of Christ on the cross sporting an erection.

So, religion was always lurking for him and an ever-easy target, and, as he and Maureen chatted, he gave her his views on the subject. 'Christianity will go,' he proclaimed. 'It will vanish and sink. I needn't argue about that. I'm right. And will be proved right. *We're* more popular than Jesus now. I don't know which will go first, rock and roll or Christianity. Jesus was all right, but his disciples were thick and ordinary. It's them twisting it that ruins it for me.'

At the time, and in the circumstances, his views on Christianity didn't seem particularly outrageous, and as they moved on around the house the two soon began discussing other subjects. One was that Maureen thought he was 'probably the laziest person in England', something Mimi had chided him about when she'd been trying to get him to mow the lawn at Mendips. '*Physically* lazy,' he corrected her. 'I don't mind writing, or reading, or watching or speaking, but sex is the only physical thing I can be bothered with any more.'

When the two had met three years earlier, his ambition, he'd said, had been to get rich. Now he was, in his words, 'famous and loaded . . . They keep telling me I'm all right for money. But then I think I may have spent it all by the time I'm forty, so I keep going.'

But going where? the journalist wanted to know. He became more serious. Living at Kenwood in this 'Hansel and Gretel house' wouldn't do at all, he said. 'I'll get my real house when I know what I want. There's something else I'm going to do, something I *must* do – only I don't know what it is. That's why I go around painting and taping and drawing and writing . . . because it may be one of them. All I know is, this isn't *it* for me.'

*This isn't it for me . . .* The restlessness was growing.

But, if being a Beatle wasn't enough for him, what would be?

What John probably didn't tell Maureen Cleave was that he was currently reading a loose translation of the ancient Buddhist *Tibetan Book of the Dead*. He'd learned about it the previous summer when, during the Beatles' second US tour, he'd had his second LSD trip at their Beverly Hills retreat, along with David Crosby and Jim McGuinn from the Byrds, and film actor Peter Fonda.

The original book, which John never read, was a collection of traditional prayers to be recited at funerals, with the belief that they would ease the consciousness of a person through death and on to rebirth. In California in 1966 that had been taken up and rewritten by followers of Timothy Leary as he proselytised LSD and the psychedelic experience – and which included what the author described as a 'psychological stripping away and a rebirth of the personality'. As such, Leary's *The Psychedelic Experience: A Manual Based on the Tibetan Book of the Dead* had become a guide for those keen to embrace an alternative lifestyle, which also promoted the taking of the consciousness-swerving drug LSD. John Dunbar, the husband of singer Marianne Faithfull, who had set up the small Indica Gallery for avant-garde artists in London's West End, had given John a copy.

To John, ever dissatisfied with the way things were, the idea of a spiritual rebirth, a starting again, was always attractive. He liked to joke that 'reality leaves a lot to the imagination', and, mesmerised by the colours, images and thoughts that bled into his brain when he took LSD, it was exciting that surrealism now came on demand in a sugar lump, which was how LSD was often taken. His taking acid 'went on for years', he would tell *Rolling Stone*. 'I must have had a thousand trips . . . I used to eat it all the time.'

Even assuming that to be a wild exaggeration, and though he never took acid while recording – not intentionally, anyway – its influence on his songs was immediately evident at the very first session for the *Revolver* album in April 1966. '*Turn off your mind, relax and float downstream,*' he sang, the first line of a new song called 'The Void' – later to be retitled 'Tomorrow Never Knows'. With lyrics suggested by the Leary interpretation of *The Tibetan Book of the Dead*, it was a radical divergence from anything the Beatles, or any other band, had done before. And, although melodically little more than a dirge, it set the style for experimentation in Indian and other kinds of music. No idea was now off-limits at Abbey Road, as George Martin puzzled about how to fulfil John's direction that the song's accompaniment should sound like 'thousands of monks chanting'.

Once again, the Beatles were ahead of the moment. Doctors writing in newspapers might be warning that LSD could fry the brain, but as well as John and George, Brian, too, now, regularly took acid trips. It was fashionable in their circle. The effects would wear off after a few hours, and they would say that when it was good, it was fun.

But it wasn't always good, or fun, as John would later regret to *Rolling Stone*. 'I was reading that stupid book of Leary's . . . and I got a message on acid that you should destroy your ego, and I did . . . I let people do what they wanted . . . I was just nothing.' By 'people' it would be fair to assume that he was mainly referring to Paul.

But, a convert to LSD, that was the state he was in when he recorded most of the tracks of *Revolver*. *Rubber Soul* had contained some of his best songs, but *Revolver* was a step back, his main contributions being 'I'm Only Sleeping', an activity that was becoming increasingly an escape for him, and 'She Said She Said', an account of the Los Angeles acid trip when Peter Fonda had kept saying, 'I know what it's like to be dead,' until told to shut up.

Paul, on the other hand, was on a hot streak, going into Abbey

Road with 'Here, There And Everywhere', 'Good Day Sunshine', 'For No One', 'Got To Get You Into My Life' and the sublime 'Eleanor Rigby'. On top of that he was the main skipper behind 'Yellow Submarine', and also came up with the next Beatles hit single 'Paperback Writer' – not that it was one of their best.

'Eleanor Rigby' had grown from an idea about a spinster called Daisy Hawkins, during an evening at Kenwood. Fed up with watching television, John had left the women and led Paul, George, Ringo and Pete Shotton up to his studio, where everyone pitched in with a line or a thought. Quite why Daisy Hawkins became Eleanor Rigby would become one of those puzzles that Beatles fans love, when it became known that there is an old gravestone bearing the name Eleanor Rigby in St Peter's churchyard at Woolton. Did John or Paul subconsciously remember it from childhood?

Maybe. But the line *'wearing a face that she keeps in a jar by the door'* certainly wasn't written on a gravestone. It has the stamp of John Lennon all over it. As for the theme and melody, they are pure McCartney, with an octet arranged by George Martin giving it a touch of Vivaldi – a combined operation. A few years later, John's hazy memory would impel him to tell me that he had contributed 70 per cent of the lyrics to that song, but it was likely to have been somewhat fewer, with Ringo, George and Pete adding some, too.

At the time, John was supportive of Paul's songs, and he praised 'Here, There And Everywhere', and loved 'For No One' – 'that was one of Paul's good ones . . . all his semi-classical ones are his best, actually.' But later he would sometimes struggle to control the little green-eyed monster that would nibble away spitefully when he saw excessive praise for his old friend.

The recording of *Revolver* was completed by mid-June 1966. It had taken nearly three months, and had needed two guitars, one bass, one set of drums, trumpets, trombones, an organ, a sitar, a tabla, a tambura, a cowbell, two cellos, two violas, four violins, a clavichord, a tambourine, a French horn, a piano and some maracas. And then, of course, there were legions of tape-loops, some double tracking equipment and various different microphones. As John saw it, the guy singing 'Tomorrow Never Knows' shouldn't sound like the fellow who used to sing 'She Loves You'.

With a cover especially drawn by Klaus Voorman, it was by far the most ambitious project the Beatles had attempted, and, in general, they were pleased with the results. It presented a problem, however. There was no way that the music they were now creating in the studio could be recreated on stage. But a summer tour, taking in Germany and then the Far East, to be followed by yet another across the US, was due to start in a few days.

What, they were increasingly beginning to ask themselves, was the point of touring?

# 35

*'It's like we're four freaks being wheeled out to be seen,
shake our hair about and get back in our cage afterwards'*

Even before the touring began, John was unhappy. In those days
Capitol Records in the US issued shorter albums than did Parlophone
in the UK, and, in June, an eleven-track LP, *The Beatles: Yesterday and
Today*, went on sale in America with a few songs from *Rubber Soul* and
others from *Revolver*. The tracks were fine, but the sleeve photograph,
which showed the Beatles dressed in white butchers' coats with
lumps of raw meat draped across their knees and bodies, and Paul
holding a headless baby doll to his shoulder, caused outrage, with
American retailers refusing to stock it.

It was an extraordinary error of judgement by Brian in choosing
that photograph for an album cover. But it also revealed discord
within the Beatles. George hated the photograph. He thought it was
'gross and stupid' and was disgusted 'by the baby dolls with their
heads cut off'. John didn't see it that way at all. Feeling humiliated
by the phoney mop-top Beatles' public face, he saw the photograph
as surrealism and had pushed for it.

'I would say I was a lot of the force behind it going out . . . just to
break the image of the Beatles,' he said. It was one of his first acts as
a Beatles iconoclast. For Brian it was the Beatles' first public relations
disaster, and, what's more, the Beatles were falling out among themselves over it. Within a few days Capitol had withdrawn the album.

Until recently, playing to live audiences had been fun and the Beatles had rarely complained about it. But that had been when they
could hear what they were playing. Now it bored them. 'It's like we're
four freaks being wheeled out to be seen, shake our hair about and get
back in our cage afterwards,' John said. 'Only someone who was very
silly would have enjoyed it,' George would remember of this period.

For Brian, however, touring was the only part of the Beatles' career
where he still felt like a hands-on manager. As the group now spent

so much time working in the studio, it was inevitable that they had become closer to George Martin than to him, and Brian was beginning to worry that he was losing influence with them. In addition, while his reputation for brilliance as a manager was still widely believed, it worried him that the Beatles were getting to know about some very naïve business deals he'd made on their behalf, which had already cost them tens of millions of pounds. George and Paul were more bothered about this than John, but it was, inevitably, outspoken John who would hint at it.

On the surface, Brian appeared calm and confident in his multifarious activities – managing Cilla Black, taking a lease on the Saville Theatre in London's West End, setting up his own car company to provide expensive vehicles for the super-rich, and finding the time to keep his other Merseyside groups happy. But everything was built on the Beatles, and the tours were the moments he could relish, weeks when he could get away from London and see how much his all-conquering Beatles still needed him.

So, albeit with bad grace, off the Beatles went in June 1966 on the first leg of their summer tour. The first stop was Germany, with concerts in Munich, Essen and Hamburg. It was the first time that they'd been back to Hamburg as stars, and it wasn't the same. Yes, they met up with Astrid again and their old bouncer pals from the clubs, but the Star-Club had closed down, and they could hardly sneak off to their old haunts in the red-light area accompanied by a German press pack and a thousand fans. Until recently they'd put on a comedy act for reporters, but now they were suspicious and easily irritated.

'How many girls have you had here in Hamburg?' asked one reporter.

'One or two ... How many have you had?' came back Paul uncertainly.

'What do you mean "had"?' snapped John.

'What do you dream about when you sleep?'

'Purple dragons,' replied George.

'What do you think we are?' John bristled. '"What do you dream!" Fuckin' hell ... We're only the same as you, man, only we're rich.'

'Would you be a Beatles fan, if you weren't a Beatle?'

'No,' said John.

So they sang their allotted twelve songs, and moved on to Japan. This was new territory to conquer. But so worried was the Japanese government by a group of nationalists carrying banners saying 'Beatles Go Home' and issuing death threats to the group, whom they saw as representatives of Western decadence, the Beatles were confined by the police to their hotel. As usual they played cards to pass the time.

The stern Japanese discipline did, however, have one welcome side effect. Playing five concerts at the Nikkon Budokan Hall, the Beatles were pleasantly surprised to find that Japanese audiences listened politely before applauding enthusiastically after every song. With a policeman keeping control at the end of every row of the hall, screaming had not yet become a cultural sign of mass approval in Japan. For the first time in a while the Beatles could hear themselves.

The next stop was Manila, the capital of the Philippines, where an estimated 50,000 fans greeted them at the airport, to be followed by a police motorcycle escort as two limousines carried them to their hotel. The itinerary was for them to rest overnight, and then to play two concerts the following day. So Vic Lewis, who was managing the bookings for the tour on behalf of Brian, was surprised to be woken early on the day of the shows and asked by two military policemen to tell them what time the Beatles would be arriving at 'the party'.

'What party?' he asked.

The party was, it transpired, a lunch that Imelda Marcos, wife of despot President Ferdinand Marcos, was giving for three hundred children, and to which the Beatles had been invited.

Lewis knew nothing of any invitation, and nor, Brian insisted, did he, although publicist Tony Barrow remembered an approach from the Philippine government when the Beatles had been in Tokyo, which he had passed to Brian. Whether Brian had replied with regrets or simply forgotten is unknown, but nothing had been done, and the Beatles were unaware of the invitation. However, they would not, Brian told the military police, be attending the party.

A few minutes later, Brian received a telephone call from the British ambassador to the Philippines, telling him that it would be very unwise for the Beatles to insult Mrs Marcos in this way. Brian still refused. Since the incident of Ringo's hair being cut at the British Embassy in Washington he had made a rule of refusing official functions. Whether he was more afraid of the wrath of the Beatles at being dragged from their beds to go to a lunch party, or was simply standing on principle, only he would know. But it was a bigger deal than he realised. Turning on the television, he watched live coverage of Imelda Marcos and her Blue Ladies waiting with three hundred children for the non-arrival of the famous Beatles.

The two concerts at a football stadium went without incident, and it wasn't until the following morning when the group were to leave Manila that the trouble really began. Firstly, sour milk was served for an inedible breakfast. Then the police protection assigned to the Beatles disappeared, while the front page of the morning newspaper ran the headline, in Spanish, 'BEATLES SNUB PRESIDENT'. Television was carrying the same message and showing film of chanting mobs, said to be angry at the insult.

Immediately it was decided to leave the Philippines as quickly as possible. With no hotel porters to help, the entire party hauled their suitcases, instruments and amplifiers out of the hotel and into the limousines they'd hired. With drivers who spoke no English, the journey to the airport was difficult, but it was when they arrived there that the group really became frightened. Hundreds of soldiers with rifles and bayonets were milling about waiting for them, as well as a staged mob of angry chanting Filipinos. Behind the mob, as if to compound the chaos, were hundreds of excited teenage Beatles fans, chanting different messages.

Peter Brown, a friend of Brian's from Liverpool who was travelling with the manager as his new assistant, would describe the scene at the airport as 'truly frightening'. In his memoirs he wrote: 'When our cars stopped outside the terminal, the crowd formed a gauntlet . . . They punched and kicked at us as we rushed by, trying not to panic and break into a run.'

Inside the terminal the escalators, elevators and flight departure boards had all been switched off. People were spitting at them. John said: 'When they started on us at the airport I was petrified. I thought I was going to get hit, so we headed for three nuns and two monks thinking that might stop them.'

'They didn't actually protect us,' said Paul. 'They just stood there looking a bit bemused. But wherever they moved, we moved to the other side of them.'

'At one point,' wrote Peter Brown, 'Mal tried bravely to intervene by putting himself between the soldiers and the Beatles, and the punches started to fly . . . Mal was overwhelmed by six soldiers who punched him and knocked him to the ground . . . and Brian was punched in the back and shoulders several times.'

Eventually they made it on to the waiting KLM airliner that was to take them to New Delhi, only to be told that publicist Tony Barrow had to disembark to have his passport rechecked, the excuse being that there was some dubious question of unpaid tax.

For thirty tense minutes, Brian delayed the pilot from taking off without Barrow, as negotiations went back and forth, with, in the confusion, the local promoter coming on to the plane to talk to Brian. Only when the publicist was back on board did the plane take off. By that time Brian was being physically ill and Vic Lewis was wondering about the whereabouts of the cash they'd been due to earn from the concerts. It would remain John's impression that Brian handed the money over to the local promoter in order to get out of Manila.

It was the bleakest moment in Brian's management of the Beatles. During a couple of days' rest in New Delhi, during which the Beatles agreed that Brian had 'fucked up', John suddenly said: 'No more for me. I say we stop touring.' The others agreed. They gave Brian the news on the flight home to London. After they had finished the forthcoming tour of America, it was decided, there would be no more.

Devastated, hysterical, irrationally unable to see a future for himself, and feeling that he was being rejected, Brian became feverish. An ambulance was waiting for him when the plane landed at Heathrow. Physically, glandular fever was diagnosed. Mentally, a breakdown had been close.

For the first time, the reverse side, the black side, of the outrageous fame that the Beatles had enjoyed had shown its face. It had frightened everyone. And the summer of 1966 wasn't half over yet.

# 36

*'We were on stage . . . our lives had been threatened, then
someone let off a firecracker . . . We each thought
it was the other that had been shot'*

Almost before the newspaper headlines about the snub to Mrs Marcos
had begun to fade, the Beatles were back on the world's front pages.
At least John was, and this time his photograph was appearing alongside those of bonfires of burning Beatles albums.

What he hadn't considered when he'd talked to Maureen Cleave
the previous February was that her interview might be syndicated –
which would make it possible for a little-known American teenage
magazine called *DATEbook* to put his thoughts about Christianity on
its cover. When the article had been published in the UK, and then in
many other countries, there had been no cries of outrage. But when
it appeared in the Bible Belt of the United States, in a totally different
kind of publication from the sophisticated London *Evening Standard*,
and, as a publicity stunt, a disc jockey in Birmingham, Alabama, read
out that John thought the Beatles were 'more popular than Jesus',
the effect was, literally, incendiary.

As across the South preachers rose up in their pulpits and fulmi-
nated against the Beatles, in South Carolina the Grand Dragon of the
Ku Klux Klan nailed Beatles albums to burning crosses and radio
stations began to ban the playing of Beatles records.

Back in England, waiting to fly to America, John was at first mystified by the rumpus. Then he became annoyed. And then worried.
Coming to his aid, Maureen Cleave wrote in the *Evening Standard* that
he 'was not comparing the Beatles with Christ. He was simply observ-
ing that so weak was the state of Christianity, the Beatles were, to
many people, better known. He was deploring rather than approving
this.'

It didn't help much. In Pennsylvania, Republican Senator Robert
Fleming announced that he would try to have the Beatles banned from

the state, while in Cleveland the pastor of a Baptist church threatened to excommunicate any parishioner who attended a Beatles concert.

Brian's first thought was to cancel the tour. But that, he was told, would cost at least a million dollars. The Beatles, and especially John, had no choice but to go to America and explain away the misunderstanding.

The mob hysteria that had created Beatlemania had now turned septic and gone into reverse. Love had turned to anger and local demagogues were using the Beatles as an excuse to attack a younger generation of whose questioning attitudes they disapproved. The vast majority of Americans were bemused by the actions of some of their Christian fundamentalist compatriots – John was only a pop singer, after all. But with his short-sighted stare-in-your face defiance, he made an easy target.

The new tour was due to open in Chicago, and after a media mob descended on John at O'Hare airport when the Beatles landed on 11 August, a more organised press conference took place in Tony Barrow's squashed rooms that night. Those who regularly travelled with John during those days had never before seen him looking so exhausted and defeated. The cheeky bounce was gone as he explained that he hadn't been 'knocking or putting down' religion, or saying that 'we're better or greater or comparing ourselves with Jesus Christ as a person or God as a thing or whatever it is . . .' It was just that he'd been using the name Beatles as a phenomenon that was something separate from himself. 'If I'd said that television is more popular, I might have got away with it.'

'Do you think you're being crucified?' a reporter asked, mischievously trying to put words into his mouth.

John didn't fall for it. 'No. I wouldn't say that at all,' he answered.

On and on the questioning went and on and on the explanations. When on the following day he was told that the Alabama disc jockey who had started the whole affair was now asking for an apology, he smouldered. Swallowing his anger and indignation, he said: 'I still don't quite know what I've done . . . but if you want me to apologise, if that will make you happy, then okay, I'm sorry.' The man whom Cynthia never saw cry in the ten years she was with him was close to tears of frustration.

Eventually the Chicago concert went ahead, and then, though the questions never ceased, the tour moved on to the other cities

– Detroit, Cleveland, Washington, DC, and then on up into Canada, before eventually arriving in Memphis, Tennessee. This was the place the Beatles were most nervous about, a city with a reputation for deaths from gunshots, and where the Ku Klux Klan were making threats again. 'You might just as well paint a target on me,' John said morbidly before the concert.

Everyone was nervous as the Beatles took the stage for two shows at the Mid-South Coliseum. The first went off without incident. Then came the second. Still no problem. Then, halfway through the appearance: 'We were on stage . . .' John would often recount. 'Our lives had been threatened and then someone in the audience let off a firecracker . . . It went *BANG!* And we all looked at each other because we each thought it was the other that had been shot. It was that bad.'

The next day they were on their way to Cincinnati as the tour wound down through New York's Shea Stadium again, where 11,000 seats went unsold, the Dodgers Stadium in Los Angeles and finally Candlestick Park in San Francisco. Up to this point no one outside their immediate circle knew that it would be the end of touring. Brian still hoped they would change their minds. But John and George had had enough.

Before their last appearance they set up a camera with a wide-angle lens on an amplifier. Then, after the last song, Ringo got down from his drums, put the camera on a timer and joined the other three as they all turned their backs on the 25,000 fans in the audience, faced the lens, and a last photograph of them all on stage together was taken. That was it. There was never a shock-horror public announcement. Word just crept out over the following few months.

George would happily have stopped touring a year earlier and had sometimes been quite afraid of the mobs and irrational hysteria wherever they played. But it was John who had led the revolt. 'It was fucking humiliation,' he would often say later. 'One has to completely humiliate oneself to be what the Beatles were . . . I didn't foresee it. It just happened bit by bit until this complete craziness surrounded us.' He had no regrets, except perhaps for fans who hadn't seen them and wished they had.

But the Beatles weren't kids any more. The thousands of live performances that they'd done over their Beatles careers had caught up with them, to the extent that they often felt and looked older than they were. Now they had to find something else to do with their lives.

# 37

*'What if I give you an imaginary five shillings and hammer
in an imaginary nail. Would that be all right?'*

For everybody else in rock music there never was a year like 1966.
From the Mamas & the Papas' 'California Dreaming' and 'Monday,
Monday' to Simon and Garfunkel and 'The Sounds Of Silence' and
the Beach Boys' 'God Only Knows' and 'Good Vibrations' and on to so
many others, all year long the radio stations of the world were ablaze
with melody.

So it was almost ironic that at this point the four Beatles, who
had led the music like Pied Pipers for the past three years, should all
decide to give rock a rest and go off in four different directions when
they got back from America. George took Pattie to India to stay with
Ravi Shankar, immerse himself in Indian culture and create a new
identity for himself, Paul turned to composing the theme music for
the British movie *The Family Way*, and Ringo took a holiday.

John could have done any number of things, because publishers
were offering him contracts to write his autobiography, the National
Theatre was after him to help adapt *In His Own Write* for the stage,
while a greetings card company had an eye on his cartoons. What he
chose to do, however, was something that wouldn't involve him as
the leading creator.

When the Beatles had been touring, Brian had insisted that they
make no public comments on the Vietnam War in case it compromised
their popularity. It was a conflict in which Britain wasn't involved, he
insisted, so Beatle lips should be buttoned. The Beatles hadn't liked
that. It had seemed wrong that they couldn't discuss publicly the
foremost talking point of the day. But, with the last note played at
Candlestick Park, Brian's stricture had ceased to be relevant. And,
just three days after arriving home, John flew off to Germany to begin
filming the anti-war black comedy *How I Won The War* for the director
of both *A Hard Day's Night* and *Help!*, Richard Lester. That there was

so little time between touring and filming might have been due to a shooting schedule beyond his control, but it was typical of John to always race on to the next thing. Neil went, too. John always had to have a pal with him.

On the face of it, the movie's plot, about an absurdist plan to install a cricket pitch behind German enemy lines in the North African desert during the Second World War, was pretty far from the subject of Vietnam. In fact, the movie was really a satire about the jingoism of British war films that John's generation had grown up watching. But, in his role as Musketeer Gripweed, one of the 'poor bloody infantry' whose fate was inevitably to be one of senseless sacrifice, the parallels in futility were there for him to see. From this point forward, he would become an increasingly vocal supporter of anti-war movements.

Lester had flattered him while making *Help!* by telling him he was the most natural actor among the Beatles, so, although his part was rather small, he enthusiastically immersed himself in it. For the first time in his life he was going to pretend to be somebody other than the leader of his gang. Kitted out in an army uniform, given a pair of National Health Service type, round, wire-framed glasses to wear, and his longish wavy hair cut into a 1940s short back and sides style, he looked quite different. Going to Paris for a weekend with Neil, he was thrilled when he found he could go on a bus and wander around a flea market without being recognised. He hadn't been able to do that for years.

As shooting moved from Germany to Almeria in Spain, he took a house with actor Michael Crawford and his wife Gabrielle away from the film crew, from where he would be driven to the location every day in his Rolls-Royce, which had arrived in Spain well stocked with LSD and the other assorted drugs he thought he needed. Soon Cynthia and Julian joined him, together with Ringo and Maureen.

Filming in Spain took six weeks, during which everyone played a lot of Monopoly, and John became not a bad bowler when playing cricket with Michael Crawford – a sport he had mostly avoided when he'd been at school. Most important, though, were the weeks spent sitting cross-legged in his bedroom with his guitar working on a new song. This one didn't come quickly, as had so many of his early hits. It was inspired by the wrought iron gates outside the Spanish mansion where he was living which reminded him of the gates at the entrance to Strawberry Field, the children's home around the corner from

Mendips. So, he added an 's' and called the song 'Strawberry Fields Forever'.

Movie making being a slow, incremental process which involves many hours every day of waiting around, it was not surprising that long before the filming was complete he'd decided that this was not the new direction he'd wondered about. When asked one day by director Lester why he wasn't enjoying himself, he replied with his usual bluntness: 'It's stupid, isn't it . . . boring.'

As a movie, *How I Won The War* wouldn't turn out to be either critically or commercially successful. But there was one aspect for which John would be forever grateful – the little round glasses that he'd worn as Musketeer Gripweed. He'd been wearing contact lenses for three years while on stage, although not always successfully, as he had a habit of dropping them in the dressing room and having to go on stage without them. 'Can you imagine what it's like hearing all that noise and playing and singing and not seeing a bloody thing? It's frightening,' he would say.

But now, at the start of his post-touring days, he no longer believed he had to try to look handsome. He could leave that to Paul and George. It would be far better for him to appear slightly bookish and cerebral. Besides, he rather liked the shape of the wire-framed glasses. They suited him, and he would wear that style happily for the rest of his life. So, from an interesting film, albeit a flop, a new fashion in granny glasses was born.

In later years John would be unable to place exactly the moment when he first heard or read the name Yoko Ono. Was it on a flyer sent to him from the Indica Gallery by John Dunbar? Or had it been that Dunbar had phoned him to mention that a Japanese avant-garde artist from New York called Yoko Ono, who allegedly 'did things in bags which might or might not have included having sex', was putting on an exhibition of her work at the Indica, and John had thought that sounded erotic? Or had John just popped into the Indica, which was next door to the Scotch of St James nightclub, wondering whether he and John Dunbar might amuse themselves by dropping some acid together – and had instead run into Yoko?

John, who had just got back from Spain, couldn't say. What he did remember was that when driver Les Anthony dropped him and a friend, Terry Doran, off at the Indica, he found what he thought at first must be a con as he looked at the items on display and their prices. 'A hundred pounds for a bag of nails? Are you kidding?' he would laugh. 'How much is that apple? Two hundred pounds! Ha!'

Amused, he went downstairs into the basement where he was sure that Dunbar was trying to hustle him into buying something. 'He thinks, "The Millionaire Beatle's coming to buy,"' he was telling himself.

At which point Dunbar introduced him to a very small Japanese lady wearing a black sweater and black trousers, who was peering out from between two curtain folds of long black hair. It was the artist herself, busily preparing her exhibition, 'Unfinished Paintings and Objects by Yoko Ono', which would open the following day. Visiting London with her husband and child, Kyoko, to participate in a symposium called 'The Destruction of Art', she was taking the opportunity to publicise her own work. And few were as single-minded as Yoko when it came to publicity.

To John, it all seemed very silly at first. But he liked silliness, so he went along with it. 'I didn't end up in a bag. I was expecting an orgy, but we met and it was all quiet,' he would often jokily remember. 'Anyway, I'm looking for the action, and I see this thing called *Hammer A Nail*. It's a board with a chain and a hammer hanging on it, and a bunch of nails at the bottom, and I said, "Can I hammer a nail into it?" She said "No", and walked away.'

According to Yoko, she hadn't recognised John. That's possible, although she had, it is believed, insisted to Dunbar that a Beatle be invited. Whatever the explanation, when Dunbar told her who John was, she came back and asked for five shillings. John replied that he didn't have five shillings because he never carried money, but then said: 'What if I give you an imaginary five shillings and hammer in an imaginary nail. Would that be all right?'

Yoko agreed that it would indeed be all right.

John was next intrigued by a ladder leading up to the ceiling with a spyglass hanging there. 'So I went up the ladder and looked through the spyglass at some tiny little writing on the ceiling, and it said "Yes",' he would say. 'At this time all the usual avant-garde bullshit was negative . . . "smash the piano with a hammer" stuff . . . But "Yes" was positive.'

If this scene of the first meeting of John and Yoko was written as a movie script it would almost certainly be acted as a long mutual flirtation and would be a prelude to something else. It was a prelude to very much more, but the story wasn't to be continued for over a year. Shortly afterwards John left the gallery and didn't attend the official opening of the exhibition the next day. The next time he saw Yoko was at a Claes Oldenburg opening, where the two simply made eye-contact but didn't speak.

He didn't know he had met the woman who would change his life. He didn't know anything about her, other than the story of how she was making a short movie, *Bottoms (Film No. 4)*, having put an advertisement in *The Stage* theatrical newspaper for 'intelligent looking bottoms' and then filmed 365 of them. But her zaniness and the idea of the film appealed to him, and when she later contacted him asking for an original music score, he sent her the lyrics of the Beatles song 'The Word'. She had door-stepped Paul first and asked for something, but he'd refused her request.

Yoko had broken into the orbit of the Beatles. She has always claimed that it was purely by accident, and John always gallantly agreed with that. Her detractors, however, and there are many, point to some clever plotting and attention-seeking behaviour on her behalf. What can be said is that, like John, Yoko always had an unwavering belief in herself and her art, as well as an iron will. And in 1966 a little-known avant-garde artist who was wishing to make a name for herself in a new country could do no better than by finding a way of associating with the Beatles, and especially John Lennon, whose every action was newsworthy and who was now rich enough to be a very important patron.

One morning a few weeks after the meeting at the Indica, Yoko arrived without an appointment at the Beatles' office in Mayfair – presumably having been given their address by John Dunbar – and asked to speak to John. She was turned away, but not before she had fallen into conversation with Neil Aspinall and Ringo. What she needed, she explained to the drummer, was financial backing to wrap the huge statues of the lions in Trafalgar Square in canvas. Ringo was nonplussed and told Peter Brown, Brian's assistant, of the meeting, adding the comment that she might just as well have been speaking in Japanese for the little he understood of her plan.

Undeterred, Yoko then sent John a copy of a book of 'instructional poems' she had self-published in Tokyo. It was in Japanese with English translations alongside, and was called *Grapefruit* – of which she had brought a handy boxful from America as a kind of calling card. Everyone she thought might be useful to her was given a signed copy. From the very beginning of her career, she understood the power of networking and self-promotion; especially self-promotion.

Cynthia would say she remembered John reading *Grapefruit* while lying in bed one night. When she asked about it, he dismissed it as something sent by 'that weird artist woman'. But, at the same time, the one-time writer of 'The Daily Howl' couldn't fail to be amused by some of the book's suggestions. For instance: 'Stir inside of your brains with a penis until things are mixed up. Take a walk.' And then: 'Smoke everything you can, including your pubic hair.' These weren't the sort of ideas that Cynthia came up with.

John always liked intelligent, educated women – Eleanor Bron, with whom he had been friendly when she had appeared in *Help!*, had studied at Cambridge and Maureen Cleave had been at Oxford. And Yoko was obviously very bright. He liked older women, too, and Yoko was thirty-three when they met, to his twenty-five. She was also already on to her second marriage. It's unlikely his thoughts about her were, at that point, romantic, or even sexual. If they had been she would have known about it, because he wasn't shy in making his intentions clear. So, if it wasn't sex that first impressed him, what was it? It had to be something altogether less palpable.

This odd little Japanese woman dressed in her black intellectual's uniform, like a pint-sized Juliette Greco, might seem half crazy, but her ideas were unusual. In her presence he felt that she was the star and he the audience. He hadn't felt that way in quite a while. She was an enigma. He'd never met anyone like her before.

But on that day at the Indica that was all he thought. Putting thoughts of her aside, he rejoined Terry Doran, left the gallery and got on with his life.

# 38

*'Strawberry Fields Forever . . . It's about me, and
I was having a hard time'*

Accompanying himself on acoustic guitar, John sang 'Strawberry Fields Forever' on the first day back at Abbey Road in late November 1966, after the longest career break the Beatles had ever taken. The original intention was that their next album would be autobiographical along the lines that 'In My Life' had already begun to explore. But 'Strawberry Fields' was of a quite different order. A stream of consciousness tone poem, it had been generated in equal parts by hallucinogenic drugs and hazy childhood memories.

But which was which? *'No one I know is in my tree, I mean it must be high or low,'* went the lyrics. Was that a memory of a real tree, as in those in which John might once have played hide and seek with Pete Shotton while the Salvation Army band played in the background? Or just a druggy metaphor for alienation and being misunderstood?

When asked to interpret his lyrics, he could occasionally become vague, as I discovered during a discussion of the song. 'That was where I used to go and play . . . a children's home where they had garden parties,' he said. But the meaning? 'It's about me, and I was having a hard time.' Which he followed with stories about how he had always been different, even as a little boy. 'Nobody seems to be as hip as me, is what I'm saying . . . like when I wasn't sure if I was mad or a genius.' Sometimes, as he would explain on another occasion, it didn't do to investigate too closely the meaning in song lyrics.

What was more important to him was the overall dreamlike feel of the song, in the achievement of which all the Beatles and George Martin contributed. The producer arranged the trumpets and cellos, Paul provided the Mellotron flute intro, Ringo draped towels over his drums to muffle their sound and George played his new slide guitar. Normally, while in the studio, John would be in a hurry to finish recording his songs, the opposite of Paul, who would fret over every little detail of the arrangement. But on this occasion, sensing, perhaps, that this was a career-changing moment for him and the Beatles, and possibly even an epochal one for rock music, he was never quite satisfied. And when at last everyone thought the recording was finished, he virtually broke George Martin's heart when he decided he wanted to start all over again.

Even then he was unhappy with the new take and demanded that Martin knit the two different versions together, despite them being in different keys and at different speeds. It would, Martin would say later, be the most difficult task he ever had to do, only achieved by slowing down one version of the song and speeding up the other until they miraculously came together.

Many years later, John and George Martin met in New York, and John talked teasingly about how he would like to record all the Beatles songs again, to which George Martin queried, 'Even "Strawberry Fields"?'

'Especially "Strawberry Fields",' John replied.

Once again, the Beatles had been given the whole of Abbey Road studios to use as a musical workshop, and it took a total of fifty-five hours to record 'Strawberry Fields Forever'.

The next song they turned to could hardly have been more different. It was Paul's 'When I'm Sixty-Four' and was based on a tune that he'd been playing since his Cavern days, now with new lyrics to celebrate his father's sixty-fourth birthday. To Beatle fans it would come as a shock, in that it was a pastiche of Thirties English music hall pop, which might have been written for George Formby. Apart from adding a few odd lines, John's input was minimal.

There were often elements of Paul's work that he would sometimes find twee, but there was nothing twee about his next song, 'Penny Lane'. Melodically it was all Paul, but the title had come from John months earlier when they'd been putting together a series of snapshot images to use in song. Geographically, Penny Lane is a well-known terminus on the outskirts of Liverpool, and was close to home for both of them. The words were just reliving childhood, John would say of the *blue suburban skies* under which they had both grown up, although only in memory was it always a sunny day in often cloudy Liverpool. 'The bank was there, and that was where the tram sheds were . . . and the fire engines were down there, too.' As was the barber's shop, while the *pretty nurse selling poppies from a tray* was

Pete Shotton's girlfriend. Lyrically it was a Lennon and McCartney masterpiece, John and Paul working together at their very best, and confident enough to include a little Liverpool lads' smut with the line *'four of fish and finger pies'*. In fact, it was so good as a song and recording that when the EMI sales department began pleading for something new from the Beatles, George Martin and Brian handed it over along with 'Strawberry Fields Forever' for a double A-side single, deciding at the same time to leave them off the new album.

In that moment, any remaining hope for a Liverpool-inspired album was lost. Instead, the Beatles began making a 'concept album' – a new term then, but one which meant whatever you wanted it to mean. It's possible that the autobiographical element may never have worked, anyway. They had failed to come up with a story when, years earlier, they'd tried to write a play together. So they may well have found the same writer's block on this project. All the same, it was a lost opportunity that it wasn't tried.

But it was never clear why the release of 'Penny Lane' and 'Strawberry Fields Forever' as a single should have precluded the two tracks from also appearing on the album. 'Eleanor Rigby' and 'Yellow Submarine' had both been on *Revolver* as well as being a single. Did the EMI sales department convince Brian and George that a couple of songs released months earlier would hurt the sales of the album when it finally came? All George Martin would tell me was that the decision was the biggest mistake of his professional life.

As recording moved into the New Year, it was already apparent that the songs, and the arrangements with which George Martin was dressing them, were different from anything the Beatles had tried before. And, as if to subconsciously marry with that, the Beatles even looked different, with all four now sporting moustaches – the other three joining Paul who had decided to grow one to cover a top lip that had been cut in a motor-cycle accident.

The new theme for the album that was evolving, mainly in Paul's head, was that the Beatles should subsume their identities in a Victorian-style brass band, the style of which was in permanent collision with the psychedelia of 1967. With the help of a mishearing by road manager Mal Evans, who thought they'd said 'salt and pepper', it eventually became known as *Sgt. Pepper's Lonely Hearts Club Band* – which was to become one of the best-selling albums ever made. With 32 million copies sold to date, it has won several Grammies and dozens of music magazine prizes and other awards.

Whether it deserves the praise it has harvested is debatable. John always had mixed feelings about it, perhaps because he felt it was Paul's project more than his, with Paul's songs 'She's Leaving Home', 'Lovely Rita' and 'When I'm Sixty-Four' being the obvious hits. But though he was probably right to describe his song 'Good Morning Good Morning' as 'a throwaway piece of garbage', the way he used the acts advertised on a Victorian music hall poster he'd picked up in an antiques shop to create 'Being For The Benefit of Mr Kite!' was quite brilliant. Who else would have thought of that, or have been able to put it to music? Who else would have written the later, much copied, 'Lucy In The Sky with Diamonds'?

He disguised his voice again when he sang that, but with its references to *Alice In Wonderland* it might have been regarded as a 'thank you' to Mimi who had first given him the book. Unfortunately, when someone noticed that the initials of 'Lucy', 'Sky' and 'Diamonds' spelled LSD, it was assumed that he was urging Beatles fans to take acid.

He wasn't. His son Julian had come home from infants' school one day with a painting that he'd done, and, when asked to explain it, had simply said, 'It's Lucy in the sky with diamonds' – Lucy being a little girl in his class.

John's reputation had, however, gone before him, and the unintentional connection with LSD became an urban myth, which must have pleased Mimi not at all. There would almost certainly have been LSD at Kenwood when John was working on the song, probably on the chemist's mortar and pestle in which he kept his drugs. He may well have partaken during the writing of the lyrics. But there was no secret message in the song's title, he assured me years after all the fuss had died down and when it really didn't matter if there was or wasn't.

No one wanted to believe that, however, when the album's stand-out track, 'A Day In The Life', had John singing *'I'd love to turn you on'*, which was actually a line that Paul had written. This *was* a song about an acid trip, with its random collection of thoughts, one about a friend, Tara Browne, who had died in a car crash, possibly when he was tripping; another based on a *Daily Mail* headline about four thousand holes in the streets of the town of Blackburn in Lancashire; and a third about 'the English army having won the war', presumably a reference to the film John had just been shooting. Then, between the verses, there was Paul having a routine start to a day on a double-decker bus, until the album comes to a conclusion as a forty-one-piece orchestra goes on an ever-rising crescendo of sound before emoting into a final echoing chord. 'Like the end of the world', was John's instruction to George Martin.

On hearing it and reading the lyrics the BBC had its own instruction about this song. Playing it on the radio was banned.

In many ways, 'A Day In The Life' was a perfect illustration of Lennon and McCartney as mutually supporting songwriters. 'The way we wrote a lot of the time,' John explained, 'one of us would write the good bit, the part that was easy, like "I read the news today" or whatever it was. Then when you got stuck, or whenever it got hard, instead of carrying on you'd just drop it. Then we would meet each other and I would sing half the song and Paul would be inspired to write the next bit, or vice versa.' On this particular track it obviously helped that Paul had taken LSD too, although not with anything like the appetite that John was showing for the drug. Even he, though, prided himself on being professional enough never to take it in the studio – apart, that is, from the occasion when he took it by mistake while working on 'Getting Better'.

'I thought I was taking some uppers to help me stay awake, but began to feel unwell,' he said later. 'That's when it dawned on me that I'd taken some LSD. I told the others, "I can't go on, you'll just have to do it without me and I'll watch."'

Not knowing the reason that John felt ill, George Martin decided that the Beatle probably needed some fresh air. 'I was aware of their smoking pot, sometimes in breaks in the canteen, but I wasn't aware that they did anything serious,' he would remember. 'In fact, I was so innocent that I took John up to the roof of the studio – there being fans waiting outside the front of Abbey Road. If I'd known he'd taken LSD, the roof would have been the last place I would have taken him. There was a small parapet about eighteen inches high, but no railing. It was a wonderful starry night and John went to the edge and looked up at the stars and said, "Aren't they fantastic?" I suppose to him, they would have been especially fantastic, but to me they just looked like stars.'

As usual Lennon and McCartney would get the lion's share of the credit for the album, so it was left to Ringo (who was given 'With A

Little Help From My Friends' to sing) to leaven things out. 'George Martin had really become an integral part of it all,' he told *The Beatles Anthology*. 'We were putting in strings, brass, piano, etc., and George was the only one who could write it all down. He was also brilliant. One of them [John or Paul] would mention that he'd like the violins to go de-de-diddle, or whatever, and George would catch it and put it down. He became part of the band.'

In every way *Sgt. Pepper* was an extraordinary album. George Harrison was disappointed when John and Paul vetoed the inclusion of his song 'Only A Northern Song' after it had been recorded, but then came up with 'Within You Without You', which he recorded separately with a group of Indian musicians; while Ringo learned how to play chess in the long days and nights when he wasn't needed. He may, however, have honestly summed up the opinion of some Beatles fans about the collection when he said, 'I never know what John and Paul are on about half the time.'

Jane Asher would have known very well what Paul was going 'on about'. She was on a tour of North America with the Bristol Old Vic at the time. But it's unlikely that Cynthia had much of a grasp of John's, admittedly more difficult, lyrics, and she never said that he took the time to explain them to her. Perhaps she never asked. Most of the time, however, they got on. 'We had no problems at home. We were two people living in the best way we could under the circumstances,' she would say. 'We really didn't have a cross word.'

John's use of LSD, however, was changing things, she would later tell me, leading him 'towards the destruction of so much that he valued. At home he would be lost in a daydream: present, but absent. I'd talk to him, but he wouldn't hear me.'

Did she ever wonder if drugs had temporarily tilted John's mind? 'He was definitely on a different planet during the making of *Sgt. Pepper*. Although for a time the drugs were part of it . . . I think the drugs destroyed a lot of his creativity.'

As for their marriage, the gap that had been between them on the day they had married was now ever widening.

# 39

*'Did you know, Mick Jagger wears a codpiece
in his underpants when he's on stage?'*

The *Sgt. Pepper* launch party was held at Brian's house in a street just
behind the gardens of Buckingham Palace. How far they all had come!
And, behind his little round glasses, thin, tired and stoned, John
was, for the few journalists present, scarcely recognisable from the
wisecracking 'fat Elvis' Beatle of eighteen months earlier. This was
the new John, the acid-soaked John. He didn't enjoy these enforced
soirées, but his presence had been required by his anxious manager
and record company. So there he begrudgingly was.

With hindsight, *Sgt. Pepper*'s success seems a certainty, but at the
time no one was quite sure how the fans would react to such a change
of direction. It had been a risk, and, having spent an unprecedented
£25,000 (nearly £320,000 in today's money) over the four and a half
months of recording, EMI were taking no chances on it not making
the necessary impact. They'd even splashed out on the cover, em-
ploying pop artist Peter Blake and his then wife, Jann Howarth, to
design a collage of famous faces, against which the Beatles had been
photographed wearing flamboyant pantomime-military uniforms in
a flower-power setting. For four boys who had once bridled about
having to wear suits while on stage, this was quite a change.

John was often grumpy, but he was particularly cross on the
occasion of the launch because Paul had told *Look* magazine a few
days earlier that he had taken LSD. To John, this was a case of Paul
'grabbing the headline', making it look as if he was the most 'tuned in
and dropped out' Beatle, when actually, always more cautious, Paul
had been the last to try acid. That this should bother John may seem
petty, and it was. But in John's mind, *his* role was that of the far-out
bohemian, not straight Paul. The needles of jealousy were always
there.

Not that Paul cared, or probably even noticed. With Jane still on tour he'd spotted a very friendly, sophisticated-looking young American photographer in a blazer and skirt and was enjoying talking to her. Her name was Linda Eastman, and he asked for her New York phone number. She gave it to him.

EMI had worried that sales of *Sgt. Pepper* might be hurt by Paul's drugs controversy, and the banning of three of its tracks by the BBC, but in the event the reverse was the case. Fans just became more curious to know what was on this 'ground-breaking record'.

For the most part, what they found astonished them. Timing is always a factor in entertainment, but somehow, as if through a process of cultural osmosis, the Beatles had once again distilled the moment in music – this time by capturing the vibes of that extraordinary Indian summer of 1967, a half-daft, half-dopey, wholly optimistic time of hippy bells and beads.

With the record released, and the Beatles trying to get on with their lives – John by ordering the painting of his Rolls-Royce in psychedelic yellow with displays of red roses on the sides ('Sacrilege!' cried Rolls enthusiasts), as well as a caravan he'd bought for Julian to play in ('an eyesore', wailed a neighbour) – the legions of the counter-culture now emerged on to the London streets with flowers in their hair, sandals on their feet and cure-all philosophies of love and life on their tongues. It felt as if they had been waiting for a signal only the Beatles as magicians could give.

Everywhere anyone went, all summer long, *Sgt. Pepper* was playing. Every hairdressing salon seemed to have it on, its songs leaked from the open doors of boutiques, while at parties little else made it on to the turntables.

There were other anthems too, of course. Scott McKenzie was directing everyone towards the hippy picnic that was now, apparently, San Francisco, while 'A Whiter Shade Of Pale', which was reigniting interest in Bach, was the year's biggest pop hit. John would play it over and over on the record player he'd had installed in his Rolls-Royce. The sequence of images – 'the sixteen vestal virgins' who were 'leaving for the Coast', the singer wandering through his playing cards, and the girl 'her face at first just ghostly' – obsessed him. Did it make any sense? He didn't know. But he loved the romantic mystery of it.

But it was still only a single. Three minutes or so and it was gone. *Sgt. Pepper* was an album, more than thirty-nine minutes of mood-changing music that was being greeted with almost universal bouquets by rock critics. The Beatles had, it was generally agreed, made the most adventurous, technically brilliant rock album of all time. What the critics would have said had 'Penny Lane' and 'Strawberry Fields Forever' been included defies the imagination. Praise doesn't go that high.

Some, myself included, think that other Beatles albums had a better collection of songs, and that George Martin's arrangements and technical feats bewitched the world into hearing musical and lyrical brilliance where it might not necessarily have been. But, everyone to his or her opinion.

What is undeniable is that with *Sgt. Pepper* the Beatles began a second career, which would be just as big, though less noisy than their first. As the worlds of music, film, art, theatre and fashion bowed and curtsied around them, once again the Beatles were at the very centre of the public's consciousness.

But what was John's opinion of the record? Mixed. 'When you get down to it, it was nothing more than an album called *Sgt. Pepper's* with the tracks stuck together,' he would later tell *Rolling Stone*. 'Actually, I dislike bits of the songs which didn't come out right ... I like "A Day In The Life". It's still not half as nice as I thought it was when we were doing it ...'

This was, of course, John being a contrary old misanthrope for the sake of it, as he often was when interviewed by those he perceived to be unquestioning Beatle fans. While Paul was happy to feel that the album reflected the mood of the time, 'because we ourselves were fitting into the mood of the time', John would become increasingly dismissive of it.

What he and Paul did agree on was that, when necessary, they could write a hit song to order. Which is exactly what they did when the BBC approached Brian and asked him if the Beatles would like to be the British representatives for a global first, a satellite TV link-up of eighteen countries called *Our World*. With the show scheduled to be seen by 350 million viewers across Europe, North America and Australasia, as well as in parts of Asia and Latin America, it was an opportunity without parallel to promote a new single. But what kind of song should they write?

They left it late. Then three weeks before the show, the two sat down and swapped ideas. John's song won for sheer topicality. It was called 'All You Need Is Love' – a slogan for the times. He was always good at the pithy little aphorism. If he hadn't been musical, or become a stand-up comic, and if the Beatles hadn't made it, he might well have had a good living writing catchphrases for advertising.

By Lennon and McCartney standards, 'All You Need Is Love' isn't a great song, the general message being neither profound nor new or true. But it did have simple words which could be easily understood by non-English speaking viewers, and a catchy chorus – '*All you need is love, love, love . . .*' little more than a variation on '*She loves you, yeah, yeah, yeah!*'. According to a droll George Harrison, all the other countries on the show were showing things like 'knitting in Canada, or Irish clog dancing in Venezuela. So, we thought we'd sing "All You Need Is Love" because it's a subtle bit of PR for God.' Soon that PR would sell several million copies at 45 rpm, and begin a fifty-year career as a newspaper headline.

Once again George Martin dressed the song up to make it sound more than it was, giving it a 'Marseillaise' opening to illustrate its internationality; he then tagged on a slice of England by way of 'Greensleeves', and some of America in the shape of a few bars of Glenn Miller's 'In The Mood' as a fade out – unfortunately forgetting to get permission for the use of the latter. The publishers involved were quick to point out the omission. A fee was arranged.

The programme was supposed to be live, as country after country presented its entry, but, with some of the accompaniment pre-recorded, the Beatles were only semi-live. John, in a shiny floral jacket, sang while chewing gum, one hand clasping a headphone to his ear, with Paul alongside and the others sitting on high stools around him. At their feet, between the balloons and flowers, and in celebratory party mood, were Cynthia and Jane, and Pattie and Maureen, as well as Mick Jagger, Marianne Faithfull, Eric Clapton with newly permed hair, Keith Moon, kaftan-clad Keith Richards, Paul's brother Mike McCartney, Graham Nash, Hunter Davies, Brian and some of the Beatles' staff.

'All You Need Is Love' wasn't vintage Beatles, in fact it may even have been one of their weakest singles, but as a slogan it was smack on the pulse of the moment.

So, the silly summer moved on, with stories about hippies and pot and LSD, and pictures of rock stars wearing their psychedelic coats of many colours in the newspapers day after day. Editors usually struggle to fill their pages in the dead days of mid-summer, but in that flower-power year, the favourite musicians of the time were doing all they could to help.

Months earlier, Mick Jagger and Keith Richards had been arrested and charged with the possession of drugs at Richards' country home in West Sussex. When they went for trial at the end of June there was understandably great newspaper interest. By then, however, it wasn't so much the two Rolling Stones who were centre stage in the public mind, it was the lady who had been sitting with them when the bust had taken place. She was Marianne Faithfull – at the time still married to John's friend John Dunbar, he of the Indica Gallery (and, yes, it was a very small world that they all inhabited) – who, the police would say, had been wearing nothing but a white fur rug when her friends had been apprehended.

Marianne hadn't been charged with anything, so she wasn't present at the trial. Not physically, anyway. In spirit, though, she was certainly there, in the shape of an astonishingly febrile rumour that when the police had entered the house they had discovered Mick Jagger eating a Mars Bar that had been lodged in her vagina.

The rumour didn't for a moment sound credible. Nor should it. It wasn't true. Nor, although much was made of Ms Faithfull's nudity under her fur rug, was it mentioned in court. It had no bearing on the case. But John, like the other Beatles, enjoyed a warm glow of schadenfreude to see his chief rival, friendly though he was with Mick Jagger, so embarrassed – laughing as he would when passing on mischievous tit-bits about the Rolling Stone. 'Did you know, Mick Jagger wears a cod-piece in his underpants when he's on stage?' he told me one day. That may not have been true either. But he still passed it on. He always loved gossip.

That so many people wanted to believe (and some probably still do) the unlikely Mars Bar story is because it fitted the carefully manufactured image of the Rolling Stones as long-haired, dissolute rock stars with shameless, free-loving, naked girlfriends, every last one of them high on drugs.

The Beatles, on the other hand, the band who had been honoured by the Queen, were still, somehow, reflected in the cheerful, goody-goody halo that Brian Epstein had insisted shine upon them. They were, it was believed, too big and too much loved by the nation to be the subject of any police drugs investigation – although their pills, pot and LSD were hardly now a secret. All of which meant that the Stones copped it instead.

Where no one was in danger of coming up against an inquisitive policeman was on the high seas, so at the end of July, John, George and Ringo, together with wives and some employees, flew off to the Mediterranean in the company of a relative newcomer to their circle – a young man to whom John had quickly given the nickname Magic Alex. The fellow's real name was Yanni Alexis Mardas, a plausible Greek television repairman by trade, but an electronic inventor of genius in his dreams. John had met him through John Dunbar, with whom Alex lived, and had been immediately excited to hear of the astonishing inventions the repairman was working on – a paint that would make everything invisible, a wallpaper that would work as speakers, and a car paint that would change the colour of your car at the click of a switch.

If it all sounds too good to be true, that's because it was. But, putting his credulity to one side, John immediately bought a Nothing Box from the inventor – that is, a plastic box with randomly blinking lights that went on and off until the battery ran out. Down-to-earth Cynthia never understood the appeal of this toy and nor did she trust Magic Alex Mardas.

But then she wasn't enjoying the same diet as her husband who was completely taken by the zany guy's ideas, so when Alex had suggested that the Beatles should go to Greece to find an island to buy, this was exactly what they did.

John put it this way: 'We're going to live there, perhaps for ever, just coming home for visits. Or it might just be for six months a year. It'll be fantastic . . . all on our own on this island. There are some little houses which we'll do up and knock together and live in communally.'

Years later George took up the story for *The Beatles Anthology*. 'We rented a boat and sailed up and down the coast from Athens, looking at islands . . . It was great. John and I were on acid all the time, sitting on the front of the ship playing ukuleles . . . The sun was shining and we played "Hare Krishna" for hours and hours . . . Eventually we landed on a little beach . . . but it was covered in pebbles. Alex said: "It doesn't matter. We'll have the military come and carry them away."

Then we got back on the boat and sailed away and never thought of the island again.'

This was the state that John was in during the summer of 1967. Boundlessly rich, feted around the world, he was an intelligent man whose eyes were blinkered to the wiles of a charlatan and much else. With his mind frequently addled by LSD, he was bored and spiritually empty, ever ready to pal up with any new friend who might amuse him, or to pursue any new diversion whenever it appeared on the fringes of his life.

# 40

*'I knew we were in trouble then. I didn't really have
any misconceptions about our ability to do anything
other than play music, and I was scared'*

When first invited by George to go and hear the Maharishi Mahesh
Yogi speak, one of John's first thoughts was to make a joke along the
lines of, 'Why would I want to go and listen to some little fakir from
India?' But George, who had been following his own spiritual road for
two years, was seriously interested and hoping to be given a mantra
by the holy man. And, joking aside, John was curious about the yogi.
The result was that three fashionably kaftan-clad Beatles turned up
at the Hilton Hotel on London's Park Lane on the afternoon of 24
August 1967, along with Pattie and a various assemblage of counter-
culture trendies. Ringo was with Maureen awaiting the birth of their
second baby.

That the Maharishi, a diminutive middle-aged man in a white gown
with flowing hair and beard and a squeaky little giggle in his voice,
had chosen this precise moment to bring his 'Spiritual Regeneration
Movement' (of which Pattie was already a member) to London, and
to the very fashionable and expensive Hilton Hotel, was more than
fortuitous. It spoke of shrewd marketing.

The Beatles were impressed, however – with John being fascinated by what sounded like a lecture in 'meditation lite', that is, a way
of rising above the pressures of the world to attain pure awareness
without much effort. You didn't necessarily have to believe in God,
which was handy because John didn't. Meditating alone would calm
the mind. And, best of all, there was no bed of nails involved, or need
to chant for hours, like the monks John had imagined in 'Tomorrow
Never Knows'. Do it the Maharishi way, and meditation would only
take half an hour a day; at an annual tithe of only a week's income,
it sounded like a bargain.

After having a private audience with the Maharishi, all three

Beatles agreed to join the guru and his travelling band of disciples the following day and travel to Bangor on the North Wales coast to spend the August Bank Holiday weekend at a transcendental seminar. For John, it had been an instant conversion.

Like a group of rich hippies, young, carefree partygoers off on a weekend jaunt, the Beatles met the next afternoon at Euston Station to take the train to Bangor. Among them was Mick Jagger, having now been released from jail after just one night in a cell and pending an appeal, and Marianne Faithfull. As it happened, for once Brian had been invited too, but had declined. He had another more temporal kind of weekend in mind.

Naturally the press, presumably alerted by the Maharishi's publicist, were there in force to see the new converts off. Quickly, however, the departure turned into a scrum with the result that Cynthia was left behind with the luggage. She hurried along the platform but could only watch as, with John at a carriage window shouting to her, the train pulled away. Once again she had been left behind, this time in front of a mob of photographers, whose cameras snapped away as she burst into tears. It wasn't just dismay that she'd missed the train that upset her. That moment was symbolic in the rapidly unravelling state of her marriage.

Neil Aspinall, of course, was there to drive her up to Bangor, which she reached not long after the main party had arrived, but John was irritated with her rather than comforting. 'Why are you always last, Cyn?' he chided.

As usual, she swallowed her feelings. She'd been left out of so much of the Beatles' careers for so long, she hadn't known how to fight for her place.

In Bangor it was a bizarre weekend for everyone, finding on arrival that their accommodation was in a hostel at the University College of Wales – which meant two single beds in the rooms. But it was a funny, student-like adventure, too. They enjoyed it.

In fact, so exhilarated were they by the whole transcendental experience that the next day the Beatles put out a public statement renouncing the use of drugs . . . which amused Neil and Mal no end. Not only did it seem unlikely in the extreme that any of them would be able to forsake drugs for very long, it was less than a month since they'd all signed a full-page advertisement in *The Times* calling for the legalisation of marijuana. And which, incidentally, Brian, anxious to be seen to be supporting his boys after Paul's LSD admission, had paid for.

The Maharishi, absolutely thrilled by the massive publicity he was getting, did his stuff by giving everyone a secret individual mantra as a going-home present.

Then on the Sunday lunchtime, the fun came to an end when the pay phone in the college refectory rang. Jane Asher answered it. It was Peter Brown asking if he could speak to Paul. The phone was passed to the Beatle. 'I've got bad news,' Peter said. 'Brian is dead.'

The television news film of John's expression that was broadcast that night showed a washed-out, almost vacant face as a TV reporter tried to get some response from him. 'Where would you be today if it wasn't for Mr Epstein?' the reporter asked.

'I don't know,' John said. What else could he say?

All afternoon details of Brian's death had been reaching him and the others. Brian's alternative plan for the weekend had involved a party at his new country house in Sussex. But when some boys intended as the weekend's entertainment hadn't arrived, he'd become depressed and had driven back to London alone. With his Bentley still parked outside his home in Chapel Street, Belgravia on the Sunday morning, and finding his bedroom door locked, his Spanish butler, Antonio, had telephoned his secretary, Joanne Newfield. Together with Alistair Taylor, who had been on Brian's staff since they'd worked together selling records in Liverpool, the door had been forced. Brian's body was curled up in his bed.

'I understand that the Maharishi comforted you all?' pursued the television reporter. 'Can I ask what advice he offered?'

'He just told us not to be overwhelmed with grief,' John replied, 'and, whatever thoughts we have of Brian to keep them happy, because whatever thoughts we have of him will travel with him, wherever he is.' And, with that, he got into a car to be driven back to London. The unexpected death of those he loved was not a new experience for him.

Pictures of Brian travelled with him in his mind's eye that night on the two-hundred-mile drive home. The Maharishi had called for only positive thoughts, but in these situations conscience plays a disobedient part. Had the Beatles been neglecting Brian since they'd given up touring? Certainly, John had seen little of him during the past year. When the Beatles weren't touring there was no reason why they should meet their manager very often. And he knew, too, from gossip among his staff, that Brian was often unhappy, had terrible problems sleeping, and would disappear for days on druggy benders. But did he also know that Brian's every day was fired by amphetamines, and that he was hooked on a regimen of uppers and downers?

'I didn't watch his deterioration,' John would say later, but he must have known of at least some of it. 'Whenever someone dies, you think, "If only I'd spoken to him he might have been a bit happier,"' he added. But he'd known that Brian had been still in love with him. A few weeks earlier, when Brian had taken an overdose and been confined to the Priory private hospital, he'd sent him some flowers with the message, 'You know I love you . . . I really do. John'. But both of them had also known that John could never love Brian in the way Brian wanted him to.

'I felt guilty because I was close to him earlier,' John said years later. 'But then I was having my own problems, and didn't see him much and had no idea what kind of life he was living.' But another thought was lurking there, too. 'I introduced Brian to pills – which gives me a guilt association with his death.'

Inevitably, though, as the car carrying John and a tearful Cynthia drove through the night, the wound of life without Brian opened deeper as new realities surfaced. What would the band do now? Brian had been the channel through which everything Beatles had gone. Because of him, neither John nor any of the Beatles had ever had to think about anything to do with the business. Perhaps they should have done, because Brian hadn't always given either good advice or done the wisest things for them.

'I knew we were in trouble then,' John would often reflect. 'I didn't really have any misconceptions about our ability to do anything other than play music, and I was scared. I thought: "We're fucked".'

Brian was thirty-two when he died. As their presence would only have summoned a huge mob of fans, none of the Beatles attended his funeral. It was held two days later at Long Lane Jewish Cemetery in Liverpool. Addressing the mourners, Rabbi Samuel Wolfson said: 'Brian Epstein was a symbol of the malaise of our generation . . .'

From the moment his body had been found, broad hints from the tabloid press had suggested that he had committed suicide. So, it was some relief for his family and those who loved him to learn from the inquest that, in the opinion of the coroner, death had been the result of an accidental overdose of a sleeping pill Brian had been taking in excess over many weeks.

Not that suicide hadn't been on his mind a few months earlier. In despair then over yet another blackmail attempt by a boy lover as he had struggled to cope with the financial complexities of his many businesses, while terrified that the Beatles would leave him when they discovered how incompetent he had sometimes been, he had deliberately taken an overdose. There had been a difference on that occasion. In his punctilious way, he had carefully written a suicide note and then left his will alongside it – to be later discovered by his assistant Peter Brown while Brian was recovering in hospital.

But, over that August weekend when he had driven home from Sussex disappointed and alone, wondering perhaps if he should have gone up to Bangor with the Beatles, and then probably dismissing the thought because he knew he wouldn't have fitted in, as he had never fitted in anywhere, no note was written. Nothing had been planned. Desperate for sleep to escape from what he saw as the empty, threatening, disintegrating, abandoned world of his waking life, his death had almost certainly been an accident.

# 41

*'What does it really mean, "I am the egg man"? It could have been the "pudding basin" for all I care. It's not that serious'*

If it all seemed over-hasty, it's because it was. Hardly had Brian been buried than his secrets were being divulged, realisation was dawning, various plans for the future were being suggested and arguments were breaking out as to what to do next.

But first there were things that the Beatles hadn't known about, or hadn't bothered to know about, that had to be confronted, such as the crippling UK tax debt their accountants told them they were facing. Then there was the estimated 100 million dollars they had never had as Brian had accidentally signed away 90 per cent of a merchandising licensing deal for Beatle T-shirts, wigs, lunch boxes, buttons, toys, trinkets (and just about anything else that anyone could stamp the word '*Beatles*' on) when they'd first arrived in America in 1964 and half of that nation had gone Beatle-crazy. It had been the innocent mistake of a young man, who, not much earlier, had been managing a Liverpool record shop and who knew nothing about mass merchandising in America. A streetwise operator had seen him coming.

More disturbing, and especially for John, was the realisation that Brian may have been slightly underhand in not drawing the Beatles' attention to the fact that when they'd re-signed with EMI the previous January for a further ten years at a better royalty rate, NEMS were also still in the deal and would be receiving 25 per cent of their income for another decade. An independent lawyer might have suggested they look more closely at that clause, but they hadn't sought advice outside Brian. 'Brian did a few things that show that he cooked us,' John would later sadly reflect. 'He would say "sign for another ten years". And who got the benefits? Not us. We were the ones who were tied by the balls.'

Once again this was John on an exaggeration rap. Brian had got the best deal he knew how to get out of EMI when the contracts had been renegotiated, so the Beatles had done well. It was just that Brian and NEMS, considering their input, had done even better; as Dick James had done, and would continue to do, far better than Lennon and McCartney out of Northern Songs.

Coming to terms with so much new business information in the days after Brian's death was upsetting. But that turned to joint anger when the Beatles learned of a secret agreement Brian had made with Australian wheeler dealer Robert Stigwood, who had recently joined NEMS and brought with him a new group called the Bee Gees. Exhausted by the demands of his mushrooming show business empire, when the only parts that now interested him were the Beatles and Cilla Black, Brian had agreed an option that gave Stigwood a 51 per cent controlling interest in the company if he could come up with half a million pounds. This meant that, with Brian's death, the Beatles might now be joint-managed by Stigwood and Brian's brother, Clive Epstein, who had no interest in show business and was happy to remain running his family's Merseyside furniture business.

The Beatles may not have been seeing eye to eye on everything any more, but, with their NEMS contract up for renewal that month, one thing they all did agree on was that Robert Stigwood was not going to be their new manager.

But, if it wasn't Stigwood, who was going to manage them?

After consultations with their tax accountants, they held a meeting at Paul's house where they made their decision. They would be their own managers. Their contract with NEMS wouldn't be renewed.

Instead, a new company owned by the Beatles would be formed to take control of the group's earnings. The individual Beatles would no longer be paid directly, as they had been under Brian, but would instead draw their personal expenses from their own company. It was called Apple Corps and had already been set up. Now it would become the centre of their various different interests. Staffed mainly by their friends who had come down with them from Liverpool, it would be headed by Neil Aspinall, their former road manager who had been studying to be an accountant when they'd enticed him away.

The trouble was, as Neil would quickly find, so little had been the Beatles' interest in business, and so total their trust in Brian, not one of them could find a copy of a single contract or document that they had signed. And, instead of having one boss, they now had four . . .

each other. What were the chances of them all agreeing on anything?

For the first time since Brian had come into their lives, the Beatles had to think about something other than music. Whether his deals for them had been good or bad, Brian had represented security. They were all going to miss that. In a business sense they had been or-phaned. 'We just weren't ready for it,' said John.

Ready or not, within a month there would be a nursery of Apple companies, starting with the Apple retail store on London's Baker Street, which sold flamboyant, psychedelic hippy clothes designed by an Anglo-Dutch collective of fashion designers who called themselves The Fool. John's friend Pete Shotton was put in charge. Other projects would soon follow.

In the meantime, the Beatles had to get on with their proper jobs, and, in the absence of any energy from John, Paul had come up with an idea for a television film. It was called *Magical Mystery Tour* and filming was to begin in two weeks' time. While loosely based on the adventures of author Ken Kesey and the Merry Pranksters, who had driven a psychedelically painted school bus across America while high on LSD, Paul's vision was more innocent. His journey would be a mystery tour in a charabanc, like those he'd been taken on to see the Blackpool Illuminations when he was a boy. And, rather than sky-high hippies, his coach would contain a clown, some eccentrics, a fat lady and a dwarf, and, of course, the Beatles, who would sing now and again. Some of the songs had already been recorded.

So, on Monday, 11 September, a large, yellow luxury coach em-blazoned on both sides with psychedelic adornments and the title 'MAGICAL MYSTERY TOUR' set off from London. Picking up Beatles as it made its way towards the west of England, it was followed all the way by a half-mile-long procession of cars containing journalists – including this writer, television crews and, obviously, fans who were getting their last bit of fun before the end of the bizarre 'summer of love' that was 1967.

Throughout the meandering journey, John generally kept out of sight – that is until, on the second day, when the coach became wedged on a narrow Devon bridge over a river on the road to Widde-combe – famous for its fair – and he lost his temper with the following trail of press and fans. Leaping down from the coach he ripped the words 'MAGICAL MYSTERY TOUR' from the sides of the vehicle. Even when the Beatles had first started touring and looking to attract a following, they hadn't made themselves so easy to recognise.

Normally when a star knows he or she is going to be filmed, attempts will be made to look attractive. Paul did, dashing about in a colourful little Fair Isle sleeveless pullover as he played at being the director. But John did the opposite. Wearing what looked like a brown, pinstriped, 1940s 'demob suit', and sometimes a little trilby hat, he resembled nothing so much as a spiv bookie.

Somewhere at the back of Paul's mind, and possibly John's too, there was a good idea for a film. But with no script, few thought-through characters or plotted scenes, no director and no producer, *Magical Mystery Tour* was being made up on the hoof. Its making was, in fact, a perfect example of a hippy pipedream that George Harrison would later sum up very well in *The Beatles Anthology*.

'It was a problem with the hippy period . . . you'd sit around and think of all these great ideas, but nobody actually did anything. Or, if they did do something, then a lot of the time it was a failure. The idea of it was much better than the reality.'

The Beatles knew very little about film-making, but a great deal about music. So, not surprisingly, the songs for *Magical Mystery Tour* were their main interest, one of which, 'I Am The Walrus', would become a Lennon classic.

Its shape had come to him one day that summer as he'd been sitting in his garden with Beatles biographer Hunter Davies, and he'd heard the two-tone siren of a police car passing in a nearby lane. The sound stayed in his mind after the police car had gone, and going to his piano, he played the notes and then recorded them for future reflection. Lyrics then came to him over several weeks as a litany of images, some suggested by LSD flashes, and others scrambled together from memories of childhood rhymes. Finally, he'd taken what had become a song to the studio to play to George Martin, who had then excelled himself by matching the chain of disparate thoughts with extravagant, note-bending orchestrations and abrupt changes of tempo. It was a triumph for the two of them, and John was proud of what he'd achieved – even if there was an element of tongue-in-cheek cunning involved.

He didn't admit it then, but he'd been becoming increasingly amused by the interpretations that Beatles fans were ascribing to his lyrics. A few years later he would let the world into his secret.

'In those days I was writing obscurely à la Dylan . . . where more or less anything can be read into lyrics . . . There has been more said about Dylan's wonderful lyrics than was ever actually in them. Mine, too . . . Dylan got away with murder. I thought, I can write this crap, too. You just thread a few images together and you call it poetry.'

For 'I Am The Walrus' the inspiration had come from *The Walrus And The Carpenter*, the poem that Mimi had read to him when he was a little boy. Little could Mimi have imagined what her attempts to give her young nephew a grounding in English literature might lead to when sauced with LSD.

Ironically, John, unlike the 'intelligentsia' who, he believed, over-interpreted his lyrics, had done the opposite and failed to understand the meaning behind the original story. 'To me, it was a beautiful poem,' he would say. 'It never dawned on me that Lewis Carroll was commenting on the capitalist system. I never went into that bit about what he really meant.' Only after the record had come out did he go back and read the poem again and realise that 'the Walrus was the bad guy in the story and the Carpenter was the good guy . . . But it wouldn't have been the same, would it, "I am the Carpenter . . . "?'

Other people might see depth in them. But not him. 'The words didn't mean anything,' he said. 'People draw so many conclusions and it's ridiculous.' Asked what it really meant when he sang. 'I am the egg man', he would just shrug. 'It could have been the "pudding basin" for all I care. It's not that serious . . . It didn't mean anything.'

All the same he was disappointed when 'I Am The Walrus' was used only as a B-side on the next Beatles single, in favour of Paul's 'Hello, Goodbye'. That was the trouble with being a Beatle, especially with someone as prolific and commercially minded as Paul in the group.

The letter from his father didn't come entirely out of the blue. Despite his promises, Freddie always seemed to be hovering somewhere in the background, with his photograph likely to pop up in a newspaper on any given day. He regretted now that he'd embarrassed his son with his record about his life, and at the urging of his brother, Charlie, he wrote to John asking for an opportunity to explain himself. To his surprise, he got a reply.

'*Dear Freddie, Fred, Dad, Pater, whatever . . .*' John began, wondering how to address the man he hardly knew, and then explained how they would be meeting again very soon. His attitude had softened.

A few weeks later John sent his driver, Les Anthony, to pick up his father from outside Kingston Post Office and bring him to Kenwood, where Freddie stayed for several nights.

Being a Beatle had some disadvantages, but one huge advantage was that it was possible to throw money at almost any problem and solve it. John had fixed Mimi's situation of being under siege from fans in Liverpool by buying her a house in Sandbanks; then, fed up with Cynthia's mother's presence around the house, he'd rented a place for her in nearby Esher. Now he did the same for his father, the staff at Apple being despatched to find a one-bedroom flat, with John instructing his accountants to pay Freddie ten pounds a week – the same amount his father had been earning washing up in the pub. Now, however, he would be living rent-free.

All wasn't quite resolved, however, as Freddie then revealed that he had a nineteen-year-old girlfriend, a student at Exeter University called Pauline Jones, who had nowhere to live, other than going home to her mother. That she didn't want to do. If John was impressed by the idea of his father being able to attract a girl almost thirty-five years his junior, we don't know. But he was a contradictory character and when he was in a welcoming mood, not much stopped him. So, Pauline was quickly engaged as a live-in fan-mail secretary for him at Kenwood. We can only guess what Mimi would have said about all this, if indeed she was ever told.

Without the guidance of Brian, events in the autumn of 1967 progressed at a hectic pace. Having been told by their accountants to invest in new projects rather than give a large part of their money to the government in income tax, an expensive new Busby Berkeley-type scene for the song 'Your Mother Should Know' was added to the self-financed *Magical Mystery Tour*; while the fashion designers The Fool were given a hundred thousand pounds (£1,700,000 in today's money) to set up the Apple boutique, a portion of which was spent on a giant psychedelic mural on the wall outside the shop. Decorated with stars, moons and mystical figures, the mural would draw crowds of sightseers – until Westminster Council ordered it to be painted over. Yet again the Beatles were in the headlines.

'A clothes shop' wasn't, however, exciting enough for John, and soon additional little companies began mushrooming all around the Apple concept. Friend Magic Alex was given Apple Electronics to run, while Jane Asher's brother Peter became the head of Apple Records. Then there was Apple Films, Apple Books and even a company called Apple Hair.

Throughout all this, John was continually being reminded of Yoko Ono, who kept up a pursuit of him by letter. She wanted John to be her sponsor. He was a multi-millionaire rock star with money to burn, and she was a struggling, scarcely known artist, but one whose ego was so dominant she seemed immune to insult or rejection. Finally sufficiently intrigued, John agreed to sponsor one of her installations at London's underground Lisson Gallery in mid-October, a display that consisted of half of everything, a bed, a chair and a room – all painted white. 'I didn't even go to the show,' John would say. 'I was too uptight.' But little by little Yoko was getting under his skin. Not that Cynthia knew yet. And not that anything romantic had occurred between the two of them.

Not everyone around Apple in their temporary offices in London's Wigmore Street was convinced that *Magical Mystery Tour* was going to be the smash hit that the Beatles assumed. Peter Brown, who was now their personal manager, certainly wasn't. But, then again, not many friends and employees were able to tell their four bosses what they really thought, not even after the American TV networks had turned the film down. The emperor's suit of clothing was alive and well at Apple in 1967. And when the BBC bought the film for a prime-time Boxing Day viewing, it seemed that the Beatle nay-sayers had got it wrong again.

When, just before Christmas, Apple threw a lavish fancy dress party at the swish Royal Lancaster Hotel to launch their first project without Brian, confidence was therefore so high that John and Cynthia took Freddie and Pauline in their Rolls-Royce to celebrate with them. John went as a Teddy boy, in a costume more elaborate than any he would have dared wear when he was considered outré at art college, while Freddie, with a joke against himself, dressed as a dustman. Pauline, his teenage girlfriend, wore a gymslip, while Cynthia chose a Victorian-style crinoline and bonnet, which she thought made her look like 'the lady on the front of a Quality Street tin of chocolates'.

John loved the evening. They showed the film, all the guests said they liked it, and he had a great time. The very pretty Pattie Harrison had chosen to go as a belly dancer, and, as the Bonzo Dog Doo-Dah Band played, John, who had always fancied Pattie, made such a point of dancing with her that eventually pint-sized pop singer Lulu, in a Shirley Temple outfit and holding a large lollipop on a stick, berated him.

He should be ashamed of himself for ignoring his wife, Lulu shouted in her broad Glaswegian accent. But he wasn't ashamed. He got drunk, and, according to Cynthia, the evening ended with John and Freddie, father and son, dancing drunkenly together, while she was 'thoroughly miserable. I had been about the only person John hadn't danced with.'

John wasn't insensitive to her feelings. He just didn't care any more.

Freddie and Pauline stayed at Kenwood for Christmas. It may have been the only Christmas John ever spent with his father. Certainly, it was the only one he remembered, and presents were exchanged. Then, like millions of other British families, they all sat around the television on Boxing Day night to watch *Magical Mystery Tour* on the BBC. It was surrealism, something different for Christmas.

It was only the following day, with the rest of the country back at work, when the newspapers published universally lacerating reviews, that the Beatles realised that it was too different. John, who had always been lukewarm about the project, now loyally defended it by saying he loved the film and its dream sequences, only later to admit that it was probably 'the world's most expensive home movie'.

Paul took the setback with a winsome grin. 'I suppose if you look at it from the point of view of good Boxing Day entertainment we goofed really,' he told me that morning.

Actually, the film wasn't as bad as the reviews said. It was simply shown on the wrong day at the wrong time to the wrong audience on the wrong channel. Rock video makers have been making some of the same mistakes ever since. Wanting to see themselves, in their new post-touring world, in the tradition of art school students who had been given a movie camera and a few rolls of film with which to play, off the Beatles had gone into the world of Fellini and Magritte. And, armed only with vague ideas and lots of money, but without expertise or discipline, it hadn't worked.

Had they felt artistically invincible after the overwhelming success of *Sgt. Pepper*? Probably. But now they knew they weren't.

# 42

*'The way George is going he'll be flying on a magic carpet by the time he's forty . . .'*

Freddie and Pauline left Kenwood after Christmas, and John soon arranged for Apple to find them a flat in Brighton well away from any harassment by the press. 'Watch your arse in Brighton,' was John's advice in a letter to his father. There were 'loads of queers' in Brighton. Then, after a week's holiday in Morocco with Cynthia, John was quickly back in the studio recording a new song he'd written, 'Across The Universe'. Once again it utilised the two-tone siren of a police car and he was very proud of it. It was, he told me, 'one of the best songs I ever wrote . . . It's good poetry.'

He'd hoped it might be the next single, but the other Beatles weren't as keen on it as he was, selecting Paul's 'Lady Madonna' instead, which was probably a wise, goodtime rock and roll choice after the bad publicity of the *Magical Mystery Tour* show. But when a new song by George, 'The Inner Light', was chosen as the flip side, John gave up and offered 'Across The Universe' to the World Wildlife Fund for a fund-raising charity album. 'The Beatles didn't make a good record of it. It was a lousy track of a great song and I was so disappointed by it,' he would say. He would be even more disappointed when the World Wildlife Fund failed to realise the song's money-making potential and didn't promote it.

For John to have written a song so fancifully poetic was out of character, but no more so than his continuing fascination with the Maharishi. He hadn't stuck to his renunciation of drugs for long after he'd got back from Bangor, but, having thrown himself into his new craze, he was now a keen proselytiser for transcendental meditation. He had more energy because of meditating, he told David Frost in a television interview, and he was happier, too. Nor did he care if, to a sceptical public, the Beatles were becoming figures of fun for what many newspaper pundits saw as their gullibility. All the answers, he insisted, lay with the Maharishi Mahesh Yogi.

Acting almost on herd instinct, all four Beatles, with their wives and one fiancée – Paul and Jane having become engaged on Christmas Day – had agreed to fly out to join the yogi at Rishikesh in the Indian Himalayas in the middle of February 1968. But before they did, a meeting was arranged with an assistant to the Maharishi at the Spiritual Regeneration's London centre. Cynthia went, too. The moment of their arrival would be etched in her memory for the rest of her life. This is how she described it in her autobiography.

'As we entered the main room I saw, seated in a corner armchair, dressed in black, a small Japanese woman. I guessed immediately that this was Yoko Ono, but what on earth was she doing there? Had John invited her, and, if so, why?'

No explanation was offered. Yoko introduced herself but took no part in the proceedings, sitting silently as John chatted to the Maharishi's assistant and the other Beatles. John even appeared not to notice her. At the end of the meeting things got even odder, when as John and Cynthia left to go to their car, the door of which was being held open by their driver Les Anthony, Yoko climbed in ahead of them. Even John looked surprised, Cynthia wrote. Then he asked Yoko if they could give her a lift anywhere. 'Yes, please,' Yoko said, and gave Anthony her address near Regent's Park. 'Hanover Gate.'

The journey then passed in complete silence. 'Goodbye, thank you,' said Yoko as she was dropped off.

'What was all that about?' Cynthia says she asked John as they set off for home. He told her he didn't know, and offered no further explanation. She knew better than to push him. Obviously he must have known something.

What he didn't tell her was that he'd seen Yoko several times, and had in January invited her to a Beatles session at Abbey Road when they'd been recording 'Hey Bulldog'. She had not, it transpired, been bowled over by what she'd heard. 'Why do you always use that beat all the time?' she'd asked. 'Why don't you do something more complex?' John had been embarrassed, and probably a bit peeved, too, but not too peeved to suggest that the two of them go back to Neil's flat where he'd expected to have sex with her. That was what usually happened when a rock star took a girl back to a flat. But Yoko was different. His approach had seemed crude. She'd turned him down.

The rejection only made her more beguiling and mysterious. By the following month he had decided that when he went to India he would take both Cynthia *and* Yoko with him, but had lost his nerve at the last minute. 'I didn't know how to work it,' he told an interviewer later. 'So, I didn't quite do it.'

Had Yoko still expected to be going to India when she turned up at the Spiritual Regeneration Centre? It would appear so.

A few days later Cynthia came across a typed letter from Yoko among the fan mail at Kenwood, in which Yoko thanked John for his patience, telling him that she was thinking about him and was fearful that she would never see him again. This was more than a fan letter, but, when questioned about it, John again dismissed Yoko as a 'weirdo artist . . . wanting money for all her avant-garde bullshit', or with words to that effect.

It's unlikely that Cynthia was convinced. But for years she'd been believing what she wanted to believe of her husband.

And, with that in mind, John and Cynthia packed their bags and set off to join George and Pattie at Heathrow airport and fly to India and the Maharishi. Paul and Jane and Ringo and Maureen would follow a few days later.

John had little idea of what to expect when, after a drive of two hundred miles by taxi from the airport at New Delhi up into the foothills of the Himalayas, the group arrived at the yogi's ashram in Rishikesh. It was, however, a pleasant surprise. Built on hills that sloped down to the Ganges, while it may have been Third World India outside the walls of the Maharishi's estate, it was never less than comfortable inside. Famous for centuries among Hindus as a holy place of contemplation, the mood there among the hundred or so other visitors was quietly serene.

Naturally the presence of the Beatles, shortly to be followed by Donovan and Mike Love of the Beach Boys, as well as Hollywood's Mia Farrow and her sister Prudence – wherever the Beatles went, others were sure to follow – caused some excitement in the surrounding area. But with journalists and photographers locked out of the centre it was, as the Maharishi had promised, the ideal place to relax and reflect. With no phones and newspapers, external aggravations were kept at bay.

Not that there weren't some internal pressures in what at times would become a kind of spiritual hot-house. One of the first songs that John wrote there was called 'Dear Prudence', after he and George were sent to try to get Mia Farrow's sister to come out of her hut. 'She seemed to go slightly barmy,' John would remember, 'from meditating too long . . . If she'd been in the West, they would have put her away. She'd been locked in for about three weeks [probably much less] and was trying to reach God quicker than anybody else.'

Each one of the Beatles' party probably had a different reason for being in Rishikesh. Usually John was the leader in any new craze, but in matters spiritual it was George who led the way. 'The way George is going he'll be flying on a magic carpet by the time he's forty,' John would joke, but he was scarcely less serious himself, having become convinced that the Maharishi knew some kind of cosmic secret that he was determined to learn. Cynthia, on the other hand, just hoped a stay at Rishikesh might wean her husband off the drugs that she believed were destroying her marriage and his talent; while Paul was simply curious enough to give meditation a try. For straight-talking Ringo and his wife Maureen, it was just a pleasant holiday with friends in a beautiful place, with some light meditation thrown in.

Eating was mainly in a canteen, and there would be communal question-and-answer sessions in the evening, where the guests would sit in rows, everyone now garlanded with chains of orange blossom around their necks, with the women wearing saris. Other than the public meetings, or private discussions with the Maharishi, the rest of the time was free, which proved ideal for John and Paul to work on new songs.

For Cynthia, the bucolic surroundings might have kept John away from drugs and alcohol, but they didn't prove to be the romantic setting that she'd hoped would refresh her marriage. On arrival, she and John had been given a bungalow with a large double bed, but soon John had become increasingly aloof towards her.

'He would get up early every morning and leave our room,' she would later write. 'He spoke to me very little and after a week or two he announced that he wanted to move into a separate room to give himself more space.' It would help him meditate, he said. From then on, he virtually ignored her. She was hurt and upset.

'Our love life had definitely disappeared by then,' she told me. Sex had been replaced by a brother-sister relationship in that, with Cynthia, John was impotent. 'He was having problems, either because of being so high on drugs or whatever. He found it quite difficult with me,' Cynthia remembered, 'although obviously not with someone else. There are many ways of stimulating someone, but I didn't know the tricks.'

She also didn't know letters were arriving several times a week from Yoko Ono to be collected in the ashram post office by John. That was why he'd been getting up and going out so early in the morning.

'Yoko wrote these crazy postcards . . . like "look in the sky. I'm a cloud",' John would say. 'And I'd be looking up trying to see her, and then rushing down to the post office the next morning to get another message. It was driving me mad.'

Yoko kept up the teasing communication throughout the entire time John was in India. She would say later that the idea that she ran after him wasn't true. Some might say that, although they were continents apart, she never left him alone. He wrote back to her, as he wrote to several friends while in India. But although many of his letters to them have been published, those to Yoko haven't. Presumably Yoko still has them.

The value of the Maharishi's lessons in meditating would, for John, ultimately be minimal, but the time in Rishikesh was invaluable to both him and Paul as songwriters. Paul would come home after a couple of weeks with, among others, 'Martha My Dear', 'Blackbird', 'Back In The USSR', 'I Will' and 'Ob-La-Di, Ob-La-Da', while John's Rishikesh songs included 'The Continuing Story of Bungalow Bill', 'Dear Prudence' and 'Yer Blues'. Then there was 'I'm So Tired' with the line *'and curse Sir Walter Raleigh, he was such a stupid get'* for introducing tobacco to England in the late sixteenth century. 'I always liked that. They should have used it for an anti-smoking campaign,' he told me.

Rishikesh had been intended as a spiritual retreat for the Beatles, but for John it proved mainly to be a place to write. 'The experience was worth it, if only for the songs that came out of it,' he would say. 'But it could have been the desert or Ben Nevis . . . It was nice and secure and everyone always smiling . . . up a mountain . . . with baboons stealing your breakfast.

'The funny thing was that although it was very beautiful and I was meditating about eight hours a day, I was writing the most miserable songs on earth. In "Yer Blues", when I wrote *"I'm lonely, want to die"*, I wasn't kidding, that's how I felt. Up there, trying to reach God and feeling suicidal.' He *was* kidding a little, obviously. That was just the italicised way he always talked.

Ringo and Maureen were the first to leave, setting off home after just ten days, missing the children, they said, and not liking the food or the flies. The ashram, Ringo told me on arriving home, 'was just like Butlin's', the holiday camp where he used to play with Rory Storm and the Hurricanes. That was probably a slight exaggeration too.

Paul and Jane left after a month, to be replaced by Magic Alex, after which the serenity of the camp began to fall apart. To Alex, the Maharishi was basically a con-man who was milking the Beatles for fame by association, which was a bit rich, coming from him – the Greek television repairman who had latched on to the tripping and impressionable John with impossible schemes and inventions that never worked.

But when a rumour swept around the camp a few days later saying that the Maharishi had made a sexual pass at an American girl, Magic Alex jumped on it as proof that the yogi wasn't quite the saintly little man he professed to be.

The Maharishi may or may not have been as pure in thought, word and deed as some of his Beatles followers had believed. But no evidence was offered to corroborate the rumour. Not that it mattered. In this now overheated and slightly hysterical closed community, evidence wasn't necessary. Like a scene in the E. M. Forster novel *A Passage To India*, rumour, gossip and possibly cultural differences quickly took over.

Cynthia would later say that, after nine weeks in the ashram, John had told her that he'd already become disenchanted with the Maharishi. For a spiritual man, the yogi was, he'd decided, too interested in money, fame and celebrities – all the charges that had been jokily levelled at the Maharishi by the British press when the Beatles had become so publicly besotted. The possibility that he might be both a good, spiritual man and commercially minded at one and the same time doesn't appear to have been entertained.

George was torn. 'But,' said John, 'when George started thinking it might be true, I thought, "Well, if George is doubting him there must be something in it."' So he decided to leave the ashram, and, as usual in Beatle matters, it became a case of follow-my-leader.

'Why are you going?' the Maharishi asked.

'If you're so *cosmic*, you'll know why,' John snapped back.

With that, amid some irrational and unfounded paranoia that the Maharishi might take steps to prevent them from getting out of the ashram, John's adventure with the 'little fakir' came to an end.

Well, almost . . . The taxi taking John and Cynthia to New Delhi broke down, and when the driver went to try to get help for his vehicle, John stood at the roadside and thumbed a lift from an astonished stranger who, recognising him, then kindly drove the couple to their hotel in New Delhi.

Writers often find ways of wreaking revenge on those they believe to have betrayed them. John's method was that of a songwriter, and already a kind of public revenge on his guru was taking root in his mind. *'Maharishi, what have you done, You made a fool of everyone,'* the lines began, until George, who had been most upset by the experience, managed to convince him to disguise the subject of his attack. So, out went the Maharishi and in came Sexy Sadie. *'Sexy Sadie, oh yes, you'll get yours yet.'* It was spiteful stuff.

Whether anything untoward did happen to the unknown American girl while she was in Rishikesh, no one ever found out, which leads to the suspicion that it probably didn't. George would always feel bad about the way the Maharishi was treated and would later be reconciled with him and the transcendental movement. But the nearest John ever came to an apology was an admission some years after the event that 'We made a mistake there . . . We were waiting for a guru, and along he came . . .'

It's a long flight home from India to London and there are two versions of what happened during it. One tells that John, after weeks of sobriety in Rishikesh, got drunk and made a full confession to Cynthia of the hundreds of girls he'd had sex with before and during their marriage, even naming women she knew, some of whom she'd regarded as good friends.

Cynthia's account of the journey was that she was tearful and upset about the way the Maharishi had been treated, and that the conversation about sex took place a few days after they arrived home, when they were in the kitchen at Kenwood.

'There have been other women, you know, Cyn,' John suddenly said out of the blue. According to her memoir, her response was that she was touched by his honesty. 'That's okay,' she said. At which point he put his arms around her, and told her he still loved her, and asked her if she'd ever had any affairs of her own. She'd told him she hadn't. Nothing had ever gone further than flirting.

Accounts of the chronology of any relationship by the couple involved rarely match completely. But this was how John and Cynthia would remember, or choose to remember, a pivotal moment towards the end of theirs.

# 43

*'I've got something important to tell you.*
*I think I'm Jesus Christ'*

Back in England, John immediately returned to his drug routine. But the juggernaut that had become the Beatles had to go on, and, in the absence of Brian, it would now be driven largely by the energy and idealism of Paul. The Beatles' company Apple would, Paul told me, 'be rather like a Western Communism . . . We want to set up a complete business organisation . . . not just for us but for the general good . . .' And to that end he and John soon began planning a trip to New York to publicly announce their new venture.

Relations between John and Cynthia thawed momentarily after John spent a weekend tripping on LSD with family man Derek Taylor, who was now handling the Beatles' press relations. But when Cynthia asked if she could go with him to New York, the coldness returned. No, John said, she couldn't. This was a business trip and he had a lot of work to do as well as to prepare for the next Beatles album.

So, instead, she accepted an invitation to go on a two-week holiday to Greece with Pattie Boyd's sister Jennie, Donovan and Magic Alex, leaving the care of Julian once more in the hands of housekeeper Dot Jarlett.

John was lying on their bed when she left to catch the plane. 'He was in the almost trance-like state I'd seen many times before and barely turned his head to say goodbye,' she would remember.

In New York, John and Paul had never appeared more business-like. Wearing a suit and clean shaven, John addressed a press conference standing four square alongside Paul in the Apple venture. 'We want to set up a system whereby people who just want to make a film . . . don't have to go down on their knees in somebody's office,' he said. The aim wasn't 'a stack of gold teeth in the bank. And, with that, he invited, through television, citizens of America to fulfil their artistic dreams with a cheque from Apple.

Whether the New York business community listened seriously to the ideas of Western Communism is doubtful. Everyone was too mystified by what sounded like a crazy idea. Nothing John and Paul talked about seemed to have been thought through in a business sense, except perhaps the notion of Apple Records. At the end of their short visit, the only positive step either of them had made seemed to be that Paul had met up once again with the photographer Linda Eastman, who had attracted him a year earlier at the *Sgt. Pepper* launch party.

But when, as a follow-up to the company launch, an advertisement was placed in the London underground newspaper the *International Times* inviting readers to send in their film scripts, songs, poems, tapes, fashion designs, inventions, plays, electronics, novels and recordings, within days the Apple office in Wigmore Street was inundated with thousands of submissions from hopefuls. Not one of them ever got any further.

By that time John was back at Kenwood, and with Cynthia still in Greece he invited Pete Shotton over to stay. No longer managing the Apple boutique, Pete had now become John's personal assistant. Loaded with LSD and smoking joints, the two played together for hours in the attic studio making experimental tapes, before Pete fell asleep. John didn't. The next morning Pete found him in a state of some excitement.

'Pete,' John said, 'I've got something important to tell you.'

'Yes?'

'I think I'm Jesus Christ.'

Pete had heard his pal say some strange things before, but nothing quite like this. But, going along with the fantasy in the druggy mood of the moment, he humoured him by asking if being John Lennon wasn't enough for any man.

No, it wasn't, John said, and immediately decided he had to tell the world, starting with the other Beatles. With Pete driving, the two set off for London where, sitting in the Apple office with his closest associates Paul, George, Ringo, Neil and Derek, John told them of his realisation.

Coolly, they listened, all recognising that John was tripping, and then agreed they would have to think about it. It was, after all, only the drugs talking. Then the new Messiah left to go to lunch with his mate, Pete.

It was evening before the two got home for a dopey top-up. Pete was exhausted, but John was still revving, and at about ten o'clock he started to talk about Yoko. 'I fancy having a woman around, Pete. Do you mind if I get one?' was Pete's published memory of the conversation.

Pete didn't mind. So John got on the phone to Yoko. It was late, she was married and it was a twenty-mile taxi drive out of London for her, but she came anyway, with Pete supplying John with the money to pay the taxi driver. Apparently, her husband, Tony Cox, had taken their five-year-old daughter Kyoko to the south of France for a few days. Dot Jarlett was still taking care of Julian at her home.

In Pete's recollection Yoko seemed shy and nervous when she arrived, and after a few pleasantries he went to bed leaving John to get on with seducing her. 'I didn't know what to do,' John would recall, 'so we went upstairs to my studio and I played her all the tapes that I'd made, all far-out stuff, some comedy and some electronic.'

Evidently she liked what she heard, because after a while, sharing some LSD, they made a recording together. 'It was midnight when we started,' John told *Rolling Stone* – although it must surely have been much later, 'and it was dawn when we finished', and they opened the window to record the sound of the birds' morning chorus as a counterpoint to Yoko's voice. 'And then,' he said, 'we made love at dawn. It was very beautiful.'

Pete got up early that morning and was surprised, when he went downstairs, to find John sitting in his dressing gown eating a boiled egg. 'Have a good time last night?' Pete asked knowingly, as he would have done after his pal had spent the night with any girl.

'Yeah, Pete. It was great,' came back a very serious answer. And then: 'Are you doing anything today?' Pete said he wasn't. In which case, said John, would he go and find a house for him and Yoko to live in. He'd made up his mind to leave Cynthia.

A couple of days later, Cynthia flew back from Greece. While changing planes in Rome, she took the opportunity to phone home and let John know the time she would be back. According to her, his reply was, 'Fine, I'll see you later.'

It was late afternoon when she reached Kenwood. On the flight home, she, Jennie and Alex had talked about going out for dinner that night and had wondered whether John might like to join them. So, on arriving at Kenwood, Cynthia opened the front door for the three of them and went inside. She realised immediately that something was wrong. The porch light was on, and all the curtains were still drawn.

Opening the door to the sun room, she looked inside. This is how she described it in her memoir of life with John.

'John and Yoko were sitting on the floor, cross-legged, and facing each other, beside a table covered in dirty dishes. They were wearing towelling robes we kept in the pool house . . . John was facing me. He looked at me, expressionless, and said, "Oh, hi." Yoko didn't turn around.'

For reasons she would never understand, Cynthia suddenly blurted out that they were all going out to dinner in London and asked John and Yoko: 'Would you like to come?'

She was in shock, made to feel like an interloper in her own home. But the stupidity of the question would haunt her ever after. There was Yoko, wearing her gown, sitting with her husband, having obviously spent the night and day with him, and there she was trying to appear normal. The truth is, she had no idea how to react because it was obvious that they had wanted her to find them like that. 'You had to be in the situation to realise the horror of it,' she told me. 'It was vicious. He knew I'd be coming.'

Rushing upstairs to collect some clothes, passing a pair of Japanese slippers neatly left outside a bedroom, she hurried outside again to the embarrassed Jennie and Magic Alex and was driven away.

# 44

*'I've finally found someone as barmy as I am'*

For months John had been fascinated by Yoko. Now as they talked and talked he was finding out about the many things they had in common, and those they didn't, and how much she had been shaped by her childhood, as he had been by his.

The name 'Yoko', she explained to him, translates as 'the child of one who is overseas and far from home', and, although her childhood, like his, was lived in part against a background of the Second World War, her upbringing could hardly have been more different.

Born in Tokyo in 1933 into a wealthy banking family that claimed a samurai ancestor, her mother was a Buddhist and her father a Christian; her early home schooling meant a governess had, therefore, taken her in Bible reading and Buddhist scripture, as well as calligraphy, music and Japanese culture. The eldest of three children, she explained to me in her first interview with a British newspaper how she'd been 'like a domesticated animal being fed on information'. She'd hated it, as well as the moral code of the time and place. 'God was always watching, and any misdemeanour, or bad thought, had to be confessed to my mother,' she told me. Her mother was, she said, very beautiful, but distant. Her father had wanted to be a concert pianist but had been forced through family pressure into banking. The weight of conformity was all around her. But that conformity didn't extend to sex. As she grew up she would realise that her parents had an open marriage and both took lovers whom she would get to know. That wasn't unusual for her. She would later display a guilt-free and tolerant attitude towards extramarital sex.

Early childhood for Yoko had been spent mainly in the strict but cosseted culture of the Japanese rich, other than for three years when her father was running a Japanese bank in New York, and the family had joined him there. But returning to Japan in 1940, her mid-childhood coincided with the war, when, with her father at a bank in Hanoi, her mother took her children to the country to get away from the bombing of Tokyo. There would be hard times, and in Yoko's version of events, in one instance she had to beg for food. Whether that was strictly true or a slight embellishment – even her best friends would admit that she was never beyond that – is unknown.

Back in a recovering Tokyo after the war, and with her father home from Vietnam where for over a year he had been missing in the chaos of conflict – as John's father had been while at sea – things quickly improved for a highly intelligent, strong-willed child. Soon she was back in school, in the same class, it is said, as the Emperor's son, Prince Yoshi. Then after two terms at university, the family followed her father once again when he was posted back to the US. From her home in the comfortably well-off suburb of Scarsdale, New York, she then enrolled at the educationally permissive, private liberal arts Sarah Lawrence College in Yonkers in 1953.

Already sophisticated, and very intense, she quickly discovered her main interest to be in the avant-garde, and she spent more and more time in New York City and less at college, finally dropping out when she met a young Japanese composer, Toshi Ichiyanagi, who was studying at the Juilliard School. Her parents objected to the relationship, in that Toshi's family were not considered socially elevated enough, but Yoko and Toshi were married in 1956 – the year John was failing his O-levels. She was twenty-two, and was, she would say, a virgin on her wedding night. According to her biographer, Jerry Hopkins, some of those who knew her at the time believe that to have been unlikely.

Renting a loft on New York's Lower West Side the young couple threw themselves into the avant-garde milieu with Yoko attending classes given by the experimental composer John Cage. With money tight, and her parents appalled by her bohemian lifestyle, she sometimes worked as a waitress in a macrobiotic restaurant or taught calligraphy to subsidise the 'events' that she would arrange in their loft.

Yoko's art was highly influenced by the Fluxus group whose Lithuanian leader, George Maciunas, with whom she would later have an affair, described it as 'a fusion of Spike Jones, gags, games, vaudeville, John Cage and Duchamp'. In other words, it was zany and fun, and, in Yoko's style, unfinished, meaning that when somebody witnessed one of her events that person then became part of the happening. She was, she would say, a conceptualist, dreaming up instructions for her pieces, which others might perform. In other words she was a thinker rather than a doer.

If she received any reviews at all they were usually critical, but criticism and rejection never stopped her. Her belief in herself was total. She would always say that she was shy, but 'aloof' or 'impervious' might be better descriptions, and she was always a dedicated self-publicist. Demanding and highly ambitious, if she cared that some people laughed at her, she never showed it. She always had a very formidable hide.

As she told me, she'd been having affairs during her marriage, and in 1961 she and her husband Toshi, whose career was progressing more swiftly than hers, separated. Unsuccessful in her art and with no prospects, she returned to Japan and put on an event in Tokyo. Once again, she failed to ignite any excitement, and soon found herself in a hospital for the mentally disturbed after taking an overdose of sleeping pills. She had been institutionalised by her husband and family.

One person was intrigued by her, however. He was an American sometime film-maker called Tony Cox. Although they had never met, Cox had heard about this strange Japanese artist and sought her out in the hospital. Helping to get her out, Cox went to live with Yoko and Toshi in Tokyo, but when Yoko became pregnant by Cox, Toshi left. 'My first husband was very kind,' she would say. He would go on to have a very successful and honour-laden career in Japan as an avant-garde composer.

After a quick divorce from Toshi, Yoko married Cox. Actually, she married him twice, the first occasion being illegal as, at the time, she was still married to Toshi. Once again, her family were outraged. But, by this time, they had to accept that their eldest daughter was determined to do whatever she felt like doing.

Kyoko, Yoko's daughter with Cox, was born in Tokyo on 8 August 1963. Cox delivered the baby himself at their home, after which Yoko had to be rushed to hospital. At that time in England, in another cultural universe, the storm that would soon become Beatlemania was gathering strength.

Motherhood didn't come naturally to Yoko in that it interrupted her work. So when Kyoko was a baby, Cox found himself doing most of the childcare. Cox was very supportive of his wife in promoting her art, but it was often a tempestuous relationship.

Despite all her efforts and fierce determination, fame as an avant-garde artist eluded her in Japan, so in September 1964 she returned to New York. Cox and Kyoko followed some months later. So far her only real achievement had been the self-publication in Japanese of her book of instructions, *Grapefruit*. Of the few who read the copies she gave away, some thought it was just humorous whimsy.

Her biggest hit was at the Carnegie Recital Hall when she performed her 'Cut Piece'. That involved her appearing alone on stage in a little black dress holding a large pair of scissors, which she gave to members of the audience, who she then invited, one by one, to cut off a piece of her clothing. It took quite a while, but eventually she was left in her bra and pants. Two more cuts severed the halter bra straps, before finally someone cut the holding strap that ran around her back. The bra fell away and Yoko clasped her bare breasts. The event was over.

Proud as she was of the event, there were no reviews in the newspapers. Nor did her next project, 'Bagism', which entailed two people climbing into a very large bag leaving onlookers to surmise what might be happening inside, hit the New York headlines either. What she needed above all else was a patron to support her obsession with her art – someone who was really rich.

Then, out of the blue, she received an invitation to appear at a symposium being held in London entitled 'Destruction in Art'. Cox didn't want to go at first. But Yoko was adamant. London was then the centre of the swinging Sixties cultural world of music, art, fashion, film and theatre. It was the city to be in, the place for her to finally be noticed and taken seriously.

It's unlikely that Yoko told John all these details during their first few weeks together. But even if she did, he wouldn't have been deterred one bit. He was in love. He had, as he told Pete Shotton, 'finally found someone as barmy as I am'.

# 45

*'We've got about two LPs' worth of songs, so get your drums out'*

For a moment, John seemed to stumble in his certainty. When Cynthia returned home after staying with Jennie Boyd and her house mate Magic Alex – who, Cynthia would say, had made an unsuccessful pass at her – there was no sign of Yoko, and John acted as though everything was normal. When Cynthia asked what was happening with her, he simply said, 'Nothing. It's not important,' and avoided any discussion of Yoko. That night, according to Cynthia, they had sex again for the first time in many months.

Soon, however, the coldness returned. A family holiday in Pesaro in Italy with her mother, Julian and an uncle and aunt had been planned for May. She thought about cancelling it, but John pressed her to go. Counting the two months in India, and her break in Greece, it would be her third holiday in three months.

Yoko moved into Kenwood on the day Cynthia went to Italy. She'd left Tony Cox for good, leaving Kyoko in his care. 'We were both so excited about discovering each other, we didn't stop to think about anyone else's feelings,' she later said. 'We just went ahead, gung ho. What we had was more precious than anything else.'

It didn't take long for the new couple to go public. Less than a week later, on 22 May 1968, they took the opportunity to show off their relationship to the press at an afternoon reception at a crowded Aretusa nightclub on Chelsea's King's Road. The event had been planned to publicise the opening of yet another tentacle of the ever-expanding Apple Corps octopus of businesses, Apple Tailoring. But their presence hijacked the event. Yoko clung to John's protective arm throughout, as reporters and photographers mobbed them. John just scowled, as if trying to pretend the press weren't there. Neither answered questions thrown in their direction. But the statement they were making was clear for all to see. While 'John and Cyn' might have been the casual way John had signed postcards to their friends, 'John and Yoko' quickly became a statement that they were something more than an item. They were a brand – *JohnandYoko* – and Yoko had finally got her wish. She was becoming famous.

For the next three and a half years of their lives in Britain – before they moved permanently to New York in 1971 – John and Yoko would practically never be seen apart, with John throwing his energies into not only promoting Yoko and her work, but in publicising his new persona as one half of *JohnandYoko*. With the Beatles he'd always seen himself as the front man, but now he began to subsume his personality into that of Yoko – one of the first artistic enterprises they conducted being to make a film that merged their faces into each other's. It was pure narcissism, but it was also the clearest sign of John beginning to completely reinvent himself. Yoko wasn't now simply giving instructions at her happenings. With John never away from her side, she and he became an event in itself, and soon they would begin to dress accordingly in matching white suits, both parting their long hair down the middle.

For John, it really was a matter of '*I am he as you are he as you are me and we are altogether*', as he'd sung in 'I Am The Walrus'. Tony Barrow, who was no longer acting as the Beatles' publicist since the arrival of Derek Taylor at Apple, would say that from this moment he barely recognised John as the person he'd known for the past five years.

In sunny Pesaro, on the Italian Adriatic coast, Cynthia had been blithely unaware of her husband's public abandonment of her until, returning to her hotel one evening, she found Magic Alex waiting outside. He'd been sent from London with a message from her husband.

'John is going to divorce you, take Julian away from you, and send you back to Hoylake,' she would say he told her.

This time, Cynthia knew her marriage was finished. Yoko had won, and John had once more ducked out of any confrontation by sending a messenger with the bad news. That was what he'd done when he'd sent Nigel Walley to tell Eric Griffiths that he was no longer wanted in the Quarry Men; and what had happened when Brian was given the task of sacking Pete Best. John would always tell how he was the spokesman for the Beatles when they felt they were being badly treated. But when it came to banishing someone from his life, he'd send a messenger.

*

Meanwhile work had already begun on the new Beatles LP – the one we would get to know as the *White Album*, although, as no better title had been agreed, it would be listed simply as *The Beatles*. 'We've got about two LPs' worth of songs, so get your drums out' John had written on a postcard from India to early-leaver Ringo – so hopes were high.

Things, however, had changed. Ever since the Beatles had first gone into Abbey Road, outsiders had been unwelcome when they'd been recording, and that had included Brian Epstein as well as their girlfriends and later wives. But now, as John and Yoko were inseparable, the Beatle's rhythm guitar player insisted that she be with him in the studio at all times.

Paul immediately found Yoko's presence inhibiting. The Beatles had developed a way of working over several years. Any intrusion into this tightly knit team had to be disturbing. And Yoko, who before she'd become involved with John had often opined that she didn't like rock and roll music and believed it to be culturally crude, was not necessarily someone whose advice would be welcomed or valued. For her to immediately believe that she could make suggestions in a field she knew nothing about had to be unsettling.

The major casualty of Yoko's arrival was the Lennon and McCartney writing relationship as Paul now found it difficult in the presence of this arty newcomer. Paul gave a very good example of his frustration at Yoko's presence when he told me: 'If I started to think of a line, I'd begin to get very nervous. I might want to say something like "I love you, girl", but with Yoko watching I always felt that I had to come up with something clever and avant-garde . . . John and I tried writing together a few more times, but I think we both decided it would be easier to work separately.'

At the same time, part of the Beatles' distinctive sound, notably of Paul singing a few lines of a lyric a third above John, was also lost. 'I would love to have sung harmony with John then, and I think he would have liked me to,' Paul went on, 'but I was too embarrassed to ask him.' As he freely admitted, he was annoyed with John, and jealous of Yoko. John now had a new friend to play with in a game that had become dangerously threatening. 'I was afraid about the possibility of a break-up of a great musical partnership,' Paul said. He had good reason to worry.

Whether or not Yoko was welcome at the sessions, the array of new songs to be recorded was evidence of an astonishing outburst of creative energy all round. John had eleven new songs, including 'Glass Onion', 'Happiness Is A Warm Gun' and 'Julia' – which was about his mother. Paul had seven, among them 'Mother Nature's Son' and 'I Will'. While among George's five was one of his best ever, 'While My Guitar Gently Weeps', which was so good he asked his friend, a nervous Eric Clapton, to play lead guitar for him on it.

Not everything that the Beatles began recording that summer would be released on the resulting double LP. Some songs were held over and re-recorded, or even rewritten, for the group's later solo albums. But for John, they represented some of his best work so far. *Sgt. Pepper* might have hit a new peak, but the new songs were less muddied by musical artifice and lyrical gobbledegook than those of the previous year. He was now writing more plainly about himself and his feelings, which was the style he enjoyed most.

He had, however, lost none of his knack of catching the moment in music. By 1968 the world's preoccupation had changed from the love and peace of the previous year to revolt. Chairman Mao was turning China upside down with his Red Guards, in Paris students were taking to the streets in protest, and the Stars and Stripes was being burned on campuses across America in protest at the war in Vietnam. Revolution was in the global air, from Czechoslovakia to Chicago, and 'Revolution', John decided, would be the title of the next Beatles single.

Two different versions were recorded, one for a single and another for the album – not to mention an unreleased ten-minute jam that included a great deal of racket and roar intended to represent the chaos of an actual revolution, and to which Yoko contributed in her own howling way.

John was keen to get the song exactly right. But, although there were minor changes to the lyrics in the different versions, the general theme was less about revolt and more about moderation. *'When you talk about destruction . . . don't you know you can count me out,'* he sang, which hardly sounds like a battle cry.

Some counter-culture movements were disappointed that the great confronter John Lennon didn't want to tear capitalism apart, but John was unimpressed. 'I'm sick of those aggressive hippies or whatever they are,' he said. 'They frighten me . . . a lot of uptight maniacs going around wearing fucking peace symbols.'

The sessions for the *White Album* ran from May until October with only Ringo diplomatically not earning John's ire in his behaviour towards Yoko. Even he, though, couldn't fail to be affected by the strained atmosphere, and in mid-August he walked out, becoming the first Beatle to do so, leaving Paul to play drums on 'Back In the USSR' and 'Dear Prudence'. It was the first split in the Beatles' hitherto solid foundation and came just under a year since the death of Brian Epstein. Ringo returned a week later, to find flowers all around his drum kit, but he had made his point. The fun was going out of being a Beatle.

The days of all four working together as a creative ensemble were passing. With the *White Album*, they were becoming a backing band, with the writer of the song singing and the other three providing the accompaniment. As John would say, the Beatles were now 'just me and a backing group . . . Paul and a backing group . . .'

Things may have been often fraught at Abbey Road, but outside the recording studio the *JohnandYoko* brand was beginning to take off. There was Yoko's event at the Robert Fraser Gallery when 365 white helium balloons were released into the air bearing the message 'You are here'; and then the public showing of a film of a minute of John smiling. Filmed with a very high-speed camera, when shown it was projected at the usual 35 frames a second, which meant it lasted for over half an hour.

It seemed to most critics that such events were no more than Yoko's vanity projects that John was funding, and interest in them was low to non-existent. For *JohnandYoko* to really catch the wider public's imagination they were going to have to do something seriously outrageous.

From a distance, Cynthia would now read about a man she didn't recognise, as her husband dived into what looked to her like a nonsense-filled pool of conceptual art. 'I couldn't believe all the love-ins and the bag-ins he did with Yoko,' she would later tell me. 'This was overwhelmingly a takeover of John's mind and creativity. I think he left his brain behind. It was between his legs for a time.'

# 46

*'My final offer is seventy-five thousand. That's like*
*winning the pools for you . . . You're not worth any more'*

Divorces are rarely happy affairs and so it proved with that of John and Cynthia, and, by any standards, John didn't behave well. His first action was to sue her for divorce citing adultery with a man called Roberto Bassanini, the son of the owners of the hotel in which Cynthia had stayed in Pesaro. His second was to refuse to take Cynthia's phone calls. She, and therefore his son Julian, now aged five, were locked out of his life.

At first John and Yoko had stayed on in Kenwood, Pete Shotton not having found a house for them both, with Cynthia living with her mother in Ringo's spare basement flat in London's Montagu Square. But Yoko was a city person and soon she became bored in the Surrey suburb. So, a house swap was arranged by which John and Yoko went to Montagu Square, and Cynthia, plus mother and son, moved back into Kenwood. Typically, John left most of his clothes and belongings behind when he moved on.

His friend Pete Shotton was soon moving on, too. When asked by John to tidy up the Montagu Square flat because he and Yoko were too busy, he resigned. Yoko had an imperious air about her, and Pete couldn't see how she was busy when all she did was hang around John all day. 'Who the fuck do you think I am?' he would later write that he shouted at John. 'This is Pete Shotton. Do you remember me? I don't clean your fucking house for you. I'm not here to tidy up your underpants and fold your girlfriend's knickers. I've had it. I'm leaving.'

Initially John insisted on all the divorce negotiations being carried out by lawyers, but eventually he agreed to a face-to-face meeting with Cynthia at Kenwood. She assumed it would be just the two of them, but when John arrived, Yoko was with him. Both were dressed entirely in black.

Looking thinner and strained, John came straight to the point. 'What did you want to see me for?' he asked crossly as, like a stranger, he sat down in his own home, Yoko at his side.

'Can't we find a better way to do this?' Cynthia asked. 'I haven't been unfaithful to you. I'm sure you know that.'

'Forget all that bullshit, Cyn. You're no innocent little flower,' John came back, quickly turning defence into attack. Then he questioned her about Bassanini and a young American she'd liked and talked to in Rishikesh. For Cynthia, it was like a flashback to the ferocious jealousies he'd exhibited if she'd so much as talked to another boy when they'd been at college.

At some point in the conversation, Yoko went into the kitchen for a glass of water where she was given a severe ear-bashing by Cynthia's mother, along the lines of, 'Haven't you any shame?' That wasn't the way Yoko saw things.

It wasn't the way John did, either. Abruptly ending the meeting, and calling 'Bye' to Julian, who had been hovering in the kitchen throughout the encounter, he and Yoko got back into the car and were driven away.

Over the next few months the accusation that Cynthia had committed adultery was withdrawn and the divorce went ahead on the grounds of John's uncontested adultery with Yoko. He would speak to his wife only once more before the divorce – on the subject of money.

'My final offer is seventy-five thousand,' Cynthia would say he told her in a phone call. 'That's like winning the pools for you. So, what are you moaning about? You're not worth any more.'

All of us who knew John recognised that he had a callous streak. But, even so, it's difficult to understand why he would speak to the woman he had once loved to distraction in that way, knowing that his abandonment of her was going to change her life and prospects completely.

What was new and confusing to Cynthia was that, for the first time, the generosity he casually lavished on others no longer extended to her. He had never cared about money. Pete Shotton had been given the money to buy, among much else, a small supermarket; a not particularly close friend from college got a house; Magic Alex was given a Jaguar; and Yoko got whatever she wanted and whatever it cost to promote her career. But, although it was John who was breaking up the marriage, Cynthia's lawyers were going to have to fight for her.

In the end they settled for £100,000 (about £1.5 million in today's money) with a further £100,000 to be put into trust for Julian, when he reached the age of twenty-one. It was a lot of money at the time to Cynthia, but it wasn't a huge amount to John.

He had, however, only half arranged the transfer of his affections. Once his divorce was finalised he wanted to marry Yoko. But she was still married to Tony Cox, who was now of the opinion that he'd been shafted.

Cox had encouraged Yoko to pursue John, but only as a patron for her art. He hadn't expected her to run off with the Beatle – although, knowing her as well as he did, perhaps that thought should have crossed his mind.

Dan Richter, who was an old friend of Yoko's and who worked for John and Yoko from 1969 to 1973, explained in his book *The Dream Is Over* how Cox believed that Yoko owed him quite a lot. 'He got her out of the mental hospital in Japan, he kept her going, raised money for her shows . . . went after all the publicity, found backers for her films, borrowed money from banks . . .' And now, it seemed, she was dumping him in favour of a rich, famous fellow who could do so much more for her.

The Coxes' marriage had always been built on Yoko's career, and like that career it had sometimes been shaky, Yoko disarmingly admitting that she saw Cox, in part, as an agent. And it seemed it was the loss of that agent role that vexed the cuckolded Cox most.

The solution lay, as so often, in money. Cox didn't have any, but he did have some very substantial debts, including unpaid rent on Hanover Gate. John, on the other hand, was extremely rich. A transfer from John of £40,000 to Cox, so that the latter could settle his debts, together with airline tickets for him and a new girlfriend to the Virgin Islands, where he could quickly divorce Yoko, did the trick. The divorcing couple also agreed amicably to the joint custody of Kyoko.

All told, replacing one wife with another cost John around £150,000 that year (just under £2.4 million in today's money), but to him it was worth every penny. He was more than merely in love with Yoko. He was mesmerised by her. It didn't matter if the workforce at Apple found her bossy – and they were right, because she certainly was that, one of them remembering her as 'a very pushy broad with not an ounce of humble in her'. Or, indeed, if Paul and George resented her presence in the studio when they were working – and they had every reason to, because whatever talents Yoko had they did not include, at that time, an ability to either understand or make popular music.

None of that concerned John. He saw Yoko as the most intelligent woman he had ever met, who was also very beautiful – looking, he thought, like a cross between himself and his mother, as he wrote to his Aunt Harriet and Uncle Norman – and someone 'who had the same sense of humour as he did'. That was particularly important. Most photographs of the time show Yoko looking glum. But she and John giggled a lot together, as he frequently and fondly teased her. Altogether he saw sides of her to which her detractors were quite blind.

In another relationship, his life was advancing in a contradictory manner. Because, while manoeuvring to get out of his marriage to Cynthia, he was simultaneously helping his now reconciled father, Freddie, into a marriage with Pauline, his student lover. Pauline had become pregnant, and Freddie was anxious to do the decent thing, as John had done with Cynthia, by marrying the girl. But how? Pauline, who was still under the age of twenty-one, had been made a ward of court by her mother who disapproved of Freddie. That meant there was nowhere in England where Pauline could be legally married to the father of her unborn baby.

Nowhere in England, maybe. But Scotland has always kept its judiciary separate from that of English law. If the couple could get to Scotland, they could be legally married. Which is exactly what they did, with John footing the bill for his father and girlfriend to run away romantically to the little village of Gretna Green, just over the border inside Scotland.

What Mimi's comments were when she read of John's part in his father's escapade is not known. What was recorded was her opinion of Yoko when John took his new lover down to Sandbanks to meet her. If Cynthia had been a disappointment, Mimi's initial opinion of Yoko was worse. She was probably polite enough on the day, but later she revealed her true thoughts when she talked, in those less diplomatic times, to journalists.

'I took one look at her,' she told one reporter, 'and I thought, "My God, what's that?" I didn't like the look of her right from the start. She had long black hair, all over the place, and she was small . . . I told John what I felt while she was outside looking across the bay. I said to him, "Who's the poisoned dwarf, John?"'

It's very unlikely that she ever spoke those words to John's face. If she had, she would almost certainly have been shunned henceforth, and she wasn't. But for those who wonder where John learned to exaggerate and speak so caustically and plainly about others, look no further than the woman who raised him.

A little plain speaking from John, or any of the Beatles, to the staff of the Apple boutique in London might conceivably have led to a different outcome. Or maybe not. The whole idea of the store had been a rich hippy whim that was now haemorrhaging money, and the Beatles had already wearied of being shopkeepers. So on 31 July 1968, just eight months after it had been opened, the Apple shop was closed down – by simply opening the doors and giving away all the stock.

The giveaway was, John would say, Yoko's idea – a sort of avant-garde shopping event – and although it cost the Beatles somewhere between £10,000 and £20,000 to, in the lingo of the time, 'liberate the shirts and dresses and coats', he loved it, quickly convincing his colleagues of how cool it was in its wackiness. So, together with their wives and friends, the four Beatles raided the shop the night before the big giveaway and filled their cars with outlandish garments that they would probably never wear, and then watched on the TV news as crowds arrived at what turned into a Beatle feel-good carnival.

John shrugged off the loss. Running a 'fucking shop' just wasn't his thing.

Paul had known Cynthia since his school days and had always liked her. Now he felt sorry for her, and probably more than a little bruised himself, too – Jane Asher having broken off their engagement when, returning home unexpectedly, she'd caught him with another girl. So, at a loose end one day, he drove down to Kenwood to see Cynthia and Julian, finding himself starting to absently sing 'Hey Jules' as he went. Cynthia was grateful for his visit. After John left her, she would discover herself dropped by the other Beatles for many years.

Famously Paul's 'Hey Jules' soon turned into 'Hey Jude', and would become the next Beatles single – pushing 'Revolution', for which John had held so much ambition, on to the flip side. To placate him, the disc was marketed as having two A-sides, but disc jockeys chose to play 'Hey Jude' rather than 'Revolution', and John didn't like that.

But nor, a few weeks later, did Paul like John's insistence that eight minutes and thirty-two seconds of a sound collage of distorted shrieks, fragments of speech, including the unexplained line 'You become naked', and bits of reversed music titled 'Revolution 9' should be included on the *White Album*. It had been partly recorded on the night John and Yoko first made love, and then added to in the studio by a helpful, if bemused, George and Ringo.

Exasperated, Paul would privately tell me that he didn't think a Beatles album was the place for it. He was right. But John was unbending, although even he struggled to fully explain why the track was on the album. 'It's not specifically about anything. It's a set of sounds, like walking down the street is a set of sounds. And I just captured a moment of time, and put it on disc, and it's about that . . . It was maybe to do with the sounds of a revolution . . . so that's the vague story behind it. But apart from that, it's just a set of sounds.'

Which is what it was, a collection of sounds that simply puzzled, then aggravated, the overwhelming majority of fans who bought what was otherwise a dazzling double collection of songs. Perhaps if Brian Epstein had still been alive he could have intervened on the part of common sense. But there was no one who could tell John what to do now . . . other than Yoko.

The marathon recording sessions for the *White Album* ended on 13 October. John had been expecting a rest then, but Apple got a tip-off, through friendly *Daily Mirror* journalist Don Short, that the police drugs squad were planning to raid the Montagu Square flat where he and Yoko were living. Frantically he and Yoko cleared everything druggy they could find from their home. 'I was thinking that Jimi Hendrix had lived there, so God knows what we might find in the carpets,' he told me.

Then on 18 October, the drugs squad of the Metropolitan Police arrived, banging loudly on the basement door and demanding entrance. 'We'd been in bed,' John remembered, 'and our lower regions were uncovered. Yoko ran to the bathroom to get dressed, with her head poking out, so that they wouldn't think she was hiding anything . . .' With his usual panache for melodrama, and probably trying to think of an excuse for his delay in answering the door, John said he told the police: 'We were scared, we thought it was the Kray Brothers trying to get in' – the Kray Brothers being a notorious murdering London gang at the time.

The response of the police was to read a warrant for his and Yoko's arrest through the window and to break open the door so that they could carry out their search, during which their drug-sniffing dog found 200 grams of hashish, a cigarette rolling machine with traces of marijuana, and half a gram of morphine.

The man in charge of the search was Detective Sergeant Pilcher, the same policeman who had arrested Mick Jagger and Keith Richards the previous year, and who was making a name for himself in his targeting of rock stars. He would later nab George and Pattie Harrison on similar charges.

'JOHN LENNON ARRESTED ON DRUGS CHARGES' might have made an eye-catching headline in that night's London *Evening Standard*, but it was hardly a major drugs bust. Pleading guilty, John's fine would be a petty £150 when the offence went before the Marylebone Magistrates Court. He would forever claim that he believed the drugs had been planted, and they may well have been. Detective Pilcher was kicked out of the police and imprisoned for four years in 1972 for attempting to pervert the course of justice in another case.

But the drugs conviction was to become a bane of John's life when a few years later it was used against him in the United States. In one way, however, he'd been very lucky. Without the tip-off he might well have faced a much more serious charge. That of the possession of heroin.

Although amphetamines had become a regular part of his life when the Beatles were in Germany, to be followed by pot when *Rubber Soul* was recorded and then LSD for *Sgt. Pepper*, John had never, until this point, used hard drugs. When he and Yoko got together, however, she told him how when he'd been in India she'd gone to Paris and had been offered heroin at a party, which she'd enjoyed. He had become intrigued. As usual, wanting to experience everything that life had to offer, he became determined to try it for himself, and inevitably he found a way – probably during Yoko's exhibition at the Robert Fraser Gallery that summer. Fraser, the rich, dandy art dealer who had been arrested with Mick Jagger and Keith Richards but who, unlike them, had gone to prison for six months, was a heroin addict. Pushers gravitated to his gallery. Soon John would be hooked, too.

'I never injected,' he would say. 'Just sniffing, you know.' But he rarely did anything he liked by halves. As Paul said, 'he would always go overboard' on a new craze. Before long, heroin would become a problem for him.

# 47

*'I'd never seen my prick on an album*
*or even in a photograph before'*

Getting Yoko appreciated as an artist, making her famous for what he saw as her genius, and presenting her as the other half of his own new personality had by late 1968 become John's paramount aim in life. But how could he best do that? What would be certain to generate the most public attention?

Then he had an idea. It would be cheap and easy to do. Inviting Apple's Tony Bramwell to the Montagu Square flat, he asked him to set up lighting and a camera on a tripod with a time-delay mechanism, and then to leave while he and Yoko took some photographs. The film was then developed in the utmost secrecy.

The resulting black and white photographs, one showing John and Yoko standing together, completely naked, facing the camera, and the other a naked rear view of the couple looking back over their shoulders, would be the images, front and back, of their first LP together, officially titled *Unfinished Music No. 1: Two Virgins.*

Gasps emanated from the other Beatles and staff and friends when the photographs were shown – to be followed by much shaking of heads and not a few giggles. Even John had pause for thought. 'I must admit I was a bit shocked when we got the pictures back,' he said. 'I'd never seen my prick on an album or even in a photograph before. I thought, "What on earth! There's a fella with his prick out."'

It was, though, worth it 'for the howl of protest that went up. It really blew their minds . . . Paul gave me long lectures about it and said, "Is there really any need for this?"' In fact, Paul saw the photographs as another inexplicable act of sabotage of the Beatles' image. But, loyal to the Beatles, he never said that in public.

Of course, most newspapers immediately blamed Yoko, but she had her own explanation as she told me one night at Abbey Road in

October 1968, while in the next suite John and George Martin were busy mixing 'Cry Baby Cry'.

'I know some people may think, "Ah, the bottoms girl, Yoko, has persuaded John into it,"' she said, 'but that wasn't how it was. I don't think my *Bottoms* film inspired him either. I know some people may think I have a bottoms fetish, but when we made the film I was so embarrassed that I was never in the same room as the filming.'

In fact, she didn't think John had even seen the *Bottoms* film. 'He heard one of the tapes of my voice pieces and said, "This should be an LP record", and that if it were made it should have a picture of me naked on the cover. I don't know why he said that. I suppose he just thought it would be effective. He didn't even know me that well at the time.

'Anyway, he sent me a drawing of me naked and I was terribly embarrassed. But when we decided to make a record, we decided that we should both be naked on the sleeve . . . And it's nice. The picture isn't lewd or anything like that. Basically, we're very shy and square people. We'd be the first to be embarrassed if anyone was to invite us to a nude party.'

John can't have been surprised by the general reaction – only perhaps by the ferocity it generated, when Sir Edward Lockwood, the record company chairman, angrily declared that EMI, to whom John with the Beatles was under contract, would absolutely not be releasing or distributing the record with that cover. Lockwood *did* see it as lewd. As for Mimi, she was furious to read how her nephew was 'making an exhibition of himself'.

To those who knew John, the most surprising aspect of it all wasn't so much that he was showing himself naked, but that the sleeve also showed Yoko nude. Because, despite what he might have got up to with many women, sexual jealousy had always governed his serious relationships.

When he and Yoko had first got together, he had made her write down a list of all the men she had slept with before they met. Then, as he told me, he made a list for her of all the serious affairs he'd had, going back to the girls in Liverpool about whom Cynthia had never known.

There was more. 'John wanted me with him all the time,' Yoko told me, even making her go with him to the bathroom at Abbey Road. 'John was scared that if I stayed out in the studio with a lot

'Christianity will go . . . We're more popular than Jesus now,' John told interviewer Maureen Cleave in 1966, in a statement that was wilfully misunderstood by rabble-rousers in the US Bible Belt. Here he apologises to journalists in Chicago before the start of the Beatles' last US tour.

Brian Epstein in 1966 – by this time the most successful music manager in the world.

'John with his son, Julian, then aged five, in the little boy's Kenwood bedroom.

The Beatles and friends with the Maharishi in Rishikesh in the Himalayan foothills in 1968. 'It was nice and secure and everyone always smiling . . . with baboons stealing your breakfast,' was how John would remember the break for meditation.

When John and Yoko got together in 1968 he seemed to consciously merge his personality and his looks with hers.

▲ The last live gig the Beatles ever played was on 30 January 1969, and took place before *Let It Be* film cameras on the roof of their Apple headquarters in London's Savile Row. 'Thank you very much, we hope we passed the audition,' John said as police arrived and the session had to end.

▼ John and Yoko exchange a bag of their recently cut hair with Michael X, a self-styled revolutionary leader, for a pair of bloodstained boxing trunks which had been allegedly worn by Muhammad Ali. Michael X, real name, Michael Malek, was a violent con-man, who would be hanged for murder in Trinidad in 1975.

▲ By December, 1969, when John was in Canada, his appearance was radically different from his mop-top days as he went about tearing down what he saw as the myth of the Beatles.

To promote his new single, 'Instant Karma', John appeared on the BBC's *Top of the Pops*. Yoko, who was blindfolded and knitting, for reasons unexplained, was also in the act.

When John and Yoko moved to New York in 1971, they quickly became involved with protest movements which resulted in his being kept under surveillance by the FBI. John would eventually come to believe that he might have been used by some of the movements' leaders.

John and David Bowie became good friends in 1974,
collaborating on Bowie's hit 'Fame'.

John during the 'Lost Weekend'. Out on the town at the Troubador in
Los Angeles in 1973 with some celebrity drinking buddies who liked to call
themselves the Hollywood Vampires. To the right of John is his friend Harry
Nilsson, then Alice Cooper and Micky Dolenz as well as singer Anne Murray.

▲ John and May Pang – the pretty young assistant who Yoko suggested should have an affair with her husband. 'I'd been trained to believe that men like John . . . never picked women like me . . . We did not have affairs with them,' May would say. Then she ran off with him for eighteen months.

◄ Julian and Sean in 1980.

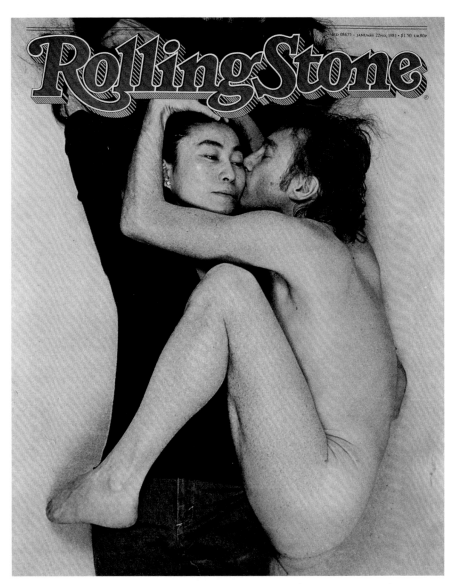

'You've captured our relationship exactly,' John said
to photographer Annie Liebovitz when she took
this photograph of him and Yoko for *Rolling Stone*
magazine shortly before his murder.

of other men, I might run off with one of them,' she joked. Others have suggested there may have been another explanation as to why the two would disappear to the bathroom together during recording sessions. But, be that as it may, why would a man who was by nature jealous and insecure publish a photograph of his lover naked for all the world to see?

Equally puzzling is how he appears not to have anticipated, or even understood, the degree of ill feeling that Yoko was beginning to generate among fans and the general public. To him, 'lost in the glow of love', as he would put it, Yoko was the saviour who had taken him away from the prison that had become his marriage and the Beatles. But to the public she was a disruptive element, a view that was only strengthened when it was admitted in October that, although both were still married to other people, she was pregnant with John's child.

For much of the Sixties the Beatles had reflected a sunny image. They were Britain's most famous export, and millions, from all generations, loved them. 'When I'm Sixty-Four' was already on its way to becoming an anthem in care homes for the elderly, and 'Yellow Submarine' had become a nursery rhyme in kindergartens. Nor were they just any rock group. There were lots of those around. By 1968 they had become the pivot around which much contemporary cultural activity rotated, and the prism through which a whole generation of young Brits saw themselves.

But now they were growing up and growing apart and John had introduced a strange-looking woman into the group, a 'mysterious, crazy, unreadable Japanese lady' who said she was an artist and did things in bags, who had made a film about bottoms and who had stolen John from his wife . . . The fans didn't like what they were reading in the papers and they didn't like Yoko. But, John being John, that meant only one thing. He would now become more resolute than ever in his championing of her.

Throughout the next few weeks of a hypocritical little tabloid morality storm, during which Yoko miscarried the baby she was carrying, John displayed, in a series of interviews, a lofty above-it-all attitude towards the *Two Virgins* cover. 'What we did,' he said, 'was to purposely not have a pretty photograph, not have it lighted so that we looked sexy or good . . . We used the straightest, most unflattering picture just to show that we were human . . . We felt like two virgins because we were in love . . .'

As for the personal attacks on him, he just didn't care. 'People think I'm a perverted crank now, just because of the nude bit. There's no shame in appearing nude . . . I suppose the trouble is I've spoiled my image . . . People just want me to be lovable. But I was never that. Even at school I was just "Lennon!" Nobody ever thought of me as cuddly.'

Despite the fuss, the *Two Virgins* album was on sale in time for Christmas, to some amusement, but not many sales. The independent company Track Records issued it in the UK and a small label called Tetragrammaton put it out in the US, where, although the nude covers were hidden inside brown paper envelopes, twenty thousand copies were seized as 'obscene material' by police in New Jersey. By then, as was his nature, John had pretty well forgotten it.

Once again, EMI had worried that negative publicity about John might hurt sales of the *White Album*. It didn't. Nothing could yet puncture the demand for the Beatles and their music.

Nor was there anything that could temper John's determination to merge his rock and roll career with that of Yoko's avant-garde happenings. The opportunity soon arose when John was asked to appear in mid-December on stage in the Rolling Stones' film *Rock And Roll Circus*. He would only sing, he said, if Yoko could sing too. And so it was agreed. Playing with musicians other than the Beatles for the first time ever in a scratch band of Keith Richards, Eric Clapton, Mitch Mitchell and Israeli violinist Ivry Gitlis, John sang 'Yer Blues', before Yoko made a howling, wailing and incomprehensible rock debut with a song called 'Whole Lotta Yoko'. To those of us in the audience, it was difficult to see the point of the performance.

A week later at an Arts Lab celebration, John joined Yoko inside a large white bag for thirty minutes at the Royal Albert Hall in a piece titled 'The Alchemical Wedding'. If the audience there was equally baffled, they were probably too polite to say so. This was John Lennon, after all. Whatever he did had to be interesting, hadn't it?

By Christmas 1968 the Apple organisation had moved into a splendid Queen Anne house in London's very smart Savile Row. Just five minutes from Piccadilly Circus, it couldn't have been more central – although that was, perhaps, not always to its advantage.

Everyone likes a house-warming celebration, so that was what the Beatles combined with a Christmas party for themselves, their staff and friends and children on 23 December. It was the season of good cheer and, putting quarrels aside, everyone was there, George and Pattie, Ringo and Maureen and children, and Paul with Linda Eastman and her five-year-old daughter Heather. They had both come to live with him during the making of the *White Album*, and Linda was now entrenched as part of the Beatles family. Divorced, and the daughter of a successful New York show business lawyer, Lee Eastman, Linda had brought a new stability to Paul's life. She was friendly, family-oriented and determinedly unglamorous, and Paul and she had become inseparable too – providing a kind of counterbalance to the weight and influence of John and Yoko.

Not that John and Yoko turned up without family support. Julian, aged five, was there in a rare outing with his father, while Yoko brought with her both Kyoko, also five, and her estranged husband, Tony Cox.

As might be expected, it was an extravagant affair, with a set time for eating dinner, before which John and Yoko, to everyone's astonishment, suddenly appeared as Father Christmas and Mother Christmas and began handing out gifts.

Unfortunately, a couple of the guests were feeling pangs of hunger rather than the warmth of goodwill, as they waited to be fed. They were two members of the Oakland Chapter of Hells Angels, Frisco Pete and Billy Tumbleweed – aka Sweet William, who, having bumped into George Harrison in San Francisco, had accepted his invitation to visit Apple if they were ever in London.

Together with their Harley-Davidsons they'd taken the invitation seriously and were now roaming around the new green-carpeted Apple offices wondering oafishly and drunkenly when the food was going to be served 'at this fuckin' party', and getting into an eyeball-to-eyeball confrontation with the bespectacled fellow dressed in a red coat and hood with a cotton wool beard stuck on his face.

'What the fuck's goin' on in this place?' Frisco Pete is said to have demanded. 'We wanna eat . . . And those two fuckin' broads upstairs [presumably the cordon bleu chefs] tell me I've gotta wait until seven . . . There's a forty-three-pound turkey in that fuckin' kitchen and I fuckin' want some of it *now*!' he stormed at Father Christmas. And,

# 48

*'Thank you very much. We hope we passed the audition'*

John just wasn't ready. It was only eleven weeks since they'd finished recording the *White Album* and he hadn't written anything new since then. Yet there the Beatles were on the second day of January 1969, in the chill of Twickenham Film Studios, rehearsing in front of film cameras for yet another album, tentatively titled *Get Back* after a new song from Paul.

Quite why there was such urgency to return to work has never been clear, other than that Paul was a workaholic who believed that a band that played together stayed together. A better plan might have been to have taken six months or a year off and waited for inspiration; or, as George sensibly suggested, going away and doing their own solo albums, and then getting back together later when they were more in the mood to work together. But ever since they'd met Brian Epstein, the emphasis had been on hard work, with a Beatles album, or usually two, every year, and four singles annually. So here they were, back on the daily grind of being Beatles, and therefore being expected to be brilliant and creative whether they felt like it or not, because that was the level they'd set themselves.

All kinds of ideas had been mooted for the coming year. One was that perhaps they should play three nights at the Roundhouse at London's Chalk Farm and be filmed there by the BBC – that certainly appealed to the BBC. Then there were crazy notions about performing in front of the Pyramids in Egypt, or at a torchlit Roman amphitheatre in Tunisia, or on an ocean-going liner. They were the Beatles after all. Anything was possible. 'I'm warming to the idea of doing it in a lunatic asylum,' John would observe wryly.

But, in the meantime, under the directorship of Michael Lindsay-Hogg, they were going to return to being a live band and spend a couple of weeks rehearsing and then recording a new album before the cameras; letting the public see them and their way of happily working together, trying out what new songs they had, and enjoying playing some old rock and roll numbers. The problem was, they *weren't* happy working together. The carefree Beatle days were long gone, as Lindsay-Hogg's fly-on-the-wall filming would show.

Only a fraction of the material shot and recorded by him made its way into the finished film, but at least forty hours of recordings of the sessions, and the conversations between songs, have survived. And from them, it's apparent that for Paul and George, Yoko's ever-presence, with her readiness to voice an opinion about what the Beatles should and shouldn't do, not only when they were recording but in board meetings too, was still a major problem. John had always been the most garrulous of the band, but sometimes it felt that she was now talking for him, as he would just listen and nod.

Walking on eggshells, Paul was now acutely aware of what might happen if he, or either of the others, complained too loudly. 'There are only two things to do,' we hear him reasoning to George. 'One is to fight and try to get the Beatles back to being four people without Yoko, and to ask Yoko to sit down at board meetings. The other is just to accept that she's there because there's no way that John is going to split with Yoko for our sakes. He's going overboard. But he always goes overboard. If it came to the push between Yoko and the Beatles it would be John for Yoko. John would just say to us, "Okay I'll see you then." And, we're not wanting that to happen. But it's going to be a comical thing in fifty years' time if people say that the Beatles broke up because Yoko sat on an amp.'

But it wasn't all about Yoko. Under-prepared, the Beatles argued among themselves about arrangements and songs, with John frequently complaining that Paul hadn't given him enough time to write any. These were, he would later say to journalists, 'the most miserable sessions ever . . . We just couldn't get into it . . . You couldn't make music at eight in the morning in a strange place with people filming you, and coloured lights . . . I was stoned all the time and just didn't give a shit . . .'

That wasn't quite true. He cared enough to launch into George Martin, telling him, 'On this one, George, we don't want any of your production crap. It's going to be an honest album, OK! I don't want any overdubbing, or any of that editing you do.' Which was particularly galling for Martin, as it had been John who had insisted on all the 'production crap' on, for instance, 'Strawberry Fields Forever' in the first place.

He was right about the sessions, though. They were miserable. And Paul, who had already written three of his all-time biggest hits, 'Get Back', 'Let It Be' and 'The Long And Winding Road', for the album was obviously irritated by his colleague's lack of industry.

'Haven't you written anything yet?' we hear him ask John.

'No.'

'We'll be faced with a crisis.'

'When I'm up against the wall, Paul, you'll find me at my best. I think I've got Sunday off,' John comes back.

'I hope you can deliver,' answers Paul.

'I hope was a little rock and roller, Sammy with his mammy,' John says and falls into wordplay.

There was nothing more Paul could say as he watched John return to Yoko's side. 'I think we've been very negative since Mr Epstein passed away,' he rather formally tells George and Ringo. 'We probably *do* need a central daddy figure to say, "Come on, it's nine o'clock. Leave the girls at home, lads."'

But John wasn't going to leave this girl at home. Paul might feel that he knew what was best for the Beatles, and was still convinced that 'the band can improve when we're together', but John, who didn't care about the Lennon/McCartney writing relationship now, was no longer listening.

Paul joked with his old friend about expecting to see him performing 'in a black bag next week' and got on with his work, which included instructing the other Beatles on how he wanted them to play on the songs he'd written.

Eventually this was too much for George and a row blew up on film. Along with Yoko doing, in George's words, 'her screeching number', the lead guitarist had had enough. 'I'll see you around the clubs,' he told the other Beatles, walked out and drove back to Liverpool. For a session and a film that was already struggling, this presented a problem. When Ringo had left the previous year, Paul, who is a decent drummer, had sat in for him. But neither John nor Paul was as good a guitarist as George.

John and George had grown close in the past few years, but although John sympathised with the guitarist's belief that he was considered less equal than the two paramount Beatles songwriters

– 'it's a festering wound,' he tells Yoko. 'It's only this year he's recognised who he is and all the fucking shit we've done to him' – the tapes reveal him to be indifferent to George's absence. 'If George leaves, he leaves,' he says. 'If he comes back, we'll go on as if nothing happened . . . If he doesn't come back by Monday or Tuesday next week, we'll ask Eric Clapton to do it.'

For him, the concept of the Beatles had already changed. 'I don't think the Beatles revolve around just four people,' he says at one point, which was an opinion shared, one suspects, only with Yoko.

The days at Twickenham wandered on. On one of them John and Yoko entertained the film crew by dancing a waltz around the studio, while on another Yoko wailed 'John . . . John . . . John . . . John' like a lost wraith so manically and so insistently that the normally placid Ringo was heard to say bluntly to her and John: 'I think you're both nuts, the pair of you.'

After two weeks they'd all had enough of Twickenham and agreed to return to the Apple headquarters in Savile Row, where George rejoined the group with a new song, 'I Me Mine', telling everyone, 'I don't care if you don't like it.' They told him they liked it very much and that they would record it.

But where would they record it? Magic Alex Mardas had promised, and been paid, to build them a modern state-of-the-art recording studio. But he hadn't, because he didn't know how to. By all accounts what he'd done was to put in an antique oscillator on a few planks of wood with a few small speakers around the walls in a badly sound-proofed basement. At this point the scales must have finally fallen from even John's eyes. Magic Alex had been his man, and John had been led up the garden path once again.

According to George Harrison, the studio 'was the biggest disaster of all time' where Mardas 'would walk around in a white coat like some sort of chemist . . . but didn't have a clue what he was doing'. George Martin was simply astonished.

Magic Alex didn't stay around Apple for much longer. And as EMI technicians from Abbey Road ripped out his equipment and, under Martin's guidance, installed a portable system of their own, the Beatles got back to work, now with keyboard player Billy Preston as a welcome guest at George's invitation.

Making the album took just over a week, with the film crew crowded around the group in the little studio, but no longer would the film be called *Get Back*. Another of Paul's songs, 'Let It Be', seemed, in view of everything, a more appropriate title for the movie. Nor was anyone talking about ending the film in a Roman amphitheatre in Tunisia. For one thing, 'Ringo won't go abroad,' said Paul. For another, all four Beatles just wanted to end the bitter experience as quickly as possible. Then director Michael Lindsay-Hogg had an idea.

The phone calls to the news desk at London's *Evening Standard*, and passed on to me at my desk, started shortly after midday on 30 January 1969. 'A tremendous racket is coming from the roof of a building in Savile Row,' came the first report, to be quickly followed by calls from excited office workers who had identified the sound as that of the Beatles. The band were, it was said, playing on the roof of their heritaged eighteenth-century building, with their guitars and voices carrying right across Mayfair and beyond.

As people leant out of office windows, or left their typewriters to join others who had abandoned shopping in nearby Regent Street and hurried to congregate on the pavement outside 3 Savile Row, far above them the Beatles were giving a free concert. Accompanied by their staff and a few friends, with John wearing a fur coat, George in what looked like an astrakhan rug, Ringo in orange and Paul, now with a full black beard, in a dark suit and open-necked white shirt, the Beatles were playing on a temporarily boarded stage not much larger than that at the Cavern.

They hadn't been particularly keen to play. The day was cold and grey. They were miserable. But Lindsay-Hogg had been persuasive. If the police could leave them alone to disturb the peace for just thirty minutes, he would have enough material to finish the film with some élan, and put an end to this unhappy album and movie that they all regretted having started. And for the first time in months, Yoko wasn't at John's side but tucked away against a chimney. It was the Beatles, just the Beatles, playing together as a band in the way they'd started out.

As Paul sang 'Get Back' and 'One After 909', and John pleaded 'Don't Let Me Down', none of them thought much of the moment, other than hoping to quickly get it finished. But as a reel of film, it would turn out to be one of the most remembered moments of their careers. They didn't realise it at the time, but it would be the last time they would play together in public, too . . . well, in semi-public. 'Thank you very much. We hope we passed the audition,' said John, as the police arrived and the session was ended. It was as good an end-line as you will get. They had indeed passed the audition. He'd always had a way with words.

As for the album they'd been making, with none of the Beatles or George Martin wanting to face wading through the hours of music, all the tapes were handed over to EMI assistant Glyn Johns to see if he could edit together a decent LP from them. There was no hurry. It would take a year to cut the film that was to accompany the record, and who knew where any of them might be by then.

# 49

*'It was Yoko that changed me. She forced me to*
*become avant-garde and take my clothes off,*
*when all I wanted was to become Tom Jones'*

John liked journalists and journalists liked him, because more than anything he liked to talk. In 1969 there weren't barricades of publicists to come between the star and the interviewer, and when fame and success depended to a large extent upon visibility in newspapers and magazines, the world famous would happily make themselves available. John was never less than open and entertaining with writers he trusted. Seeming to talk instinctively in headlines, he may not always have bothered with strict accuracy, but he always made certain that his florid versions of events were quotable.

That had been his mood when, at Twickenham Film Studios, he'd been interviewed by Ray Coleman, the editor of the *Melody Maker*, whom he'd known since the Beatles had come to London in 1963. It had started off as a regular chat about filming, but when asked, almost as an aside, if he was happy with the way things were shaping at Apple, he just couldn't contain himself. It wasn't easy for four musicians with no management experience to run the multi-million-pound, many-tentacled Apple company, he admitted. What's more, they were approaching a cash flow problem.

They hadn't got half the money people thought they had, he said. They needed a businessman's brain to run Apple. 'It's been pie in the sky from the start,' he admitted. 'We did it all wrong . . . It needs a new broom and a lot of people will have to go . . . If it carries on like this, all of us will be broke within the next six months.'

Much of this was true. The Beatles were rich, but Apple money was being lavished daily on prodigious hospitality and expensive projects that never reached fruition. Basically, there was an absence of a powerful management structure at Apple, which might explain how a new Mercedes motor car could have simply disappeared into thin air – which was the rumour in Savile Row in 1969.

On the other hand, one part of Apple, the bit the Beatles knew most about, the record company, was proving extremely successful. While all the tapes sent by hopeful wannabes had by now gone to fill a land tip, Paul's protégée Mary Hopkin had scored a massive hit with 'Those Were The Days', road manager Mal Evans had brought in Badfinger, and Peter Asher had signed James Taylor for his first album. Then there were recordings by the Modern Jazz Quartet, and one of John Tavener's 'The Whale', a suggestion that had come from, of all people, Ringo. All Apple probably needed was a slimmed-down prospectus, a concentration on music, and a prudent, sensible boss whom the four owners of the company could agree upon. They didn't get one. The few possible managers they had approached already had good jobs.

Then, over in New York, a man called Allen Klein read John's interview with the *Melody Maker* and interpreted it as the cry for help for which he had been waiting. He flew immediately to London.

Klein, who already managed the Rolling Stones and had worked with Bobby Darin, Sam Cooke, Connie Francis and the Dave Clark Five, was a very clever lawyer and accountant and to say that he knew the record business was an understatement. At the same time, to say that he was universally liked, or even trusted, would be untrue. He had earlier tried, unsuccessfully, to prise the Beatles from Brian Epstein's grasp, and now, through Mick Jagger, he set up a meeting at London's Dorchester Hotel with John . . . who took Yoko with him.

John liked him on sight and convinced himself that they had things in common. Klein, a small, thickset man, had come up the hard way. Born in New Jersey and sent to an orphanage at four after his mother had died of cancer, he had taken advantage of the GI Bill by volunteering for the US Army after high school and then going on to college to study accountancy. Brilliant with figures, he would impress John by constantly scribbling calculations on a notepad at his side to prove his points as he talked. But what particularly got home to John was that Klein was totally familiar with his songs.

'He not only knew my work, and the lyrics that I'd written, but he also understood them,' John would immediately start telling everyone. 'He knew every damn thing about us . . . He's a fucking sharp man, and anybody that knew me that well, without having met me before, had to be the guy to look after me.'

Once again, John had acted on impulse. He saw Klein as he romantically liked to picture himself, as a working-class, motherless boy who by his own endeavours had raised himself up and taken on the snobbery of the establishment. For Klein it had been by questioning the accounting practices of US record companies, and devising independent recording schemes that would revolutionise the record industry. He had a reputation as a fighter in New York, a guy who made money for his clients, but maybe made too much for himself, too. None of that bothered John. He would, he promised Klein, talk to the other guys the following day.

He did. George and Ringo were interested. Paul was appalled. He'd reached the opinion that Linda's father, the upmarket music lawyer Lee Eastman, should represent the Beatles, together with his son John Eastman. The Eastmans didn't like Klein, and he didn't like them. Socially they were a wide distance apart.

The Beatles now formed two camps, Paul and the Eastmans in one and John, George, Ringo and Klein in another. The wedge that Yoko had driven between John and Paul when she had appeared was now being dug ever deeper into that relationship over the management battle, and both parties had good reasons for their antipathies towards the other's choice of representatives. Paul didn't trust Klein and thought that his asking for 20 per cent of the Beatles income was, now that they were so famous, plain greedy. John, on the other hand, felt that if the Beatles were managed by Paul's girlfriend's father and brother, he, Ringo and George were likely to be less favoured by them than Paul in any internal Beatles dispute.

Both had valid points. In any sensible world, the Beatles would all have stood back and sought an alternative manager to sort out their problems, one that they could all agree upon. But the Beatles' world wasn't always sensible.

For the next few weeks the Eastmans and Klein attempted to work together in a tangled web of conflicting financial interests and affairs that involved NEMS, a company called Triumph Investment, Northern Songs, ATV, EMI, Klein's company ABKCO, the Eastmans, Apple and the Inland Revenue. But soon that became impossible. When Paul was outvoted by the Apple board of directors to make Klein the group's business manager, he only accepted it through gritted teeth. Klein might speak for Apple but not for him, he insisted. Lee Eastman did that.

So, it was hardly surprising that when Paul married Linda Eastman at Marylebone Town Hall on 12 March, none of the other Beatles was invited. He'd hoped to keep it a secret, but that was impossible, and hundreds of fans, the majority being girls and young women, mobbed the event.

To John, who heard about it when he and Yoko were being driven down to Sandbanks to see Mimi, this seemed like a challenge. Whatever Paul could do, so could he, but hopefully without any fans being present. And as Yoko's divorce from Tony Cox had now come through, Peter Brown was immediately put to finding a quiet place for an instant marriage.

Interestingly John, who had only married Cynthia because he felt he had to, was initially keener to marry than Yoko. She enjoyed, and valued, the idea of being an independent woman, and was quite open that she had never really wanted to be married the first two times. Nor, she would say, had she wanted to have a child. Now she was heading for a third marriage. But she did wonder if she needed to get married. 'I didn't particularly like the idea of limiting myself to one man again,' she would tell writer Philip Norman.

John had no such doubts. Whenever his behaviour over that period is questioned, and the spur-of-the-moment decisions he made in everything he did, it has to be seen through the prism of a man who was head over heels in love.

There was something else, too. By marrying Yoko, John would, in his terms, be marrying into the avant-garde intelligentsia. Cynthia had been a not very good illustrator from art school. In John's eyes, Yoko was the real thing. With her, he was no longer just a rock and roll singer, albeit with the most famous group in the world. He was, like her, an *artist*, and he began to use the word constantly in conversation about himself.

In the early days of the Beatles' success he had always been slightly embarrassed about the teenybopper fans. But he now loved that his fans were university students, and he was thrilled to accompany Yoko to Cambridge University to join in one of her events. He had been distracted while at school, playing to the crowd, enjoying being the class clown, and had missed the further academic education that Mimi had wanted him to have. Now Yoko, the Sarah Lawrence-educated artist, the well-read sophisticate from New York, was, by their association, helping him to move, in his eyes, into a social status where his eccentricities would be seen as a manifestation of the genius he believed he was. Of course he wanted to marry her. She was helping him to reinvent himself and his life. He was starting again.

At first, he fancied the idea of being married by the ship's captain on an ocean liner, but on finding there were no cabins available he considered a ceremony on a ferry to France across the English Channel. That wasn't possible either. Finally, Peter Brown came up with the solution. John and Yoko could be married in Gibraltar. Located on the southern tip of the Spanish peninsula, Gibraltar had been a dependency of Great Britain since 1713, and therefore, as it was legally part of the UK, no proof of residency was required.

Yoko, wearing a short white dress, a big hat and large sunglasses, and John in a white suit and tennis shoes, were flown in a private jet to Gibraltar and driven straight to the British Consulate where they were married by the registrar. An hour later they were back on the plane to Paris, a city John had long considered to be romantic.

'Intellectually, of course, we don't believe in getting married. But one doesn't love someone just intellectually,' John told a reporter on arriving. Yoko saw it in a far less romantic way. 'We're going to share many happenings and events together,' she said, 'and this marriage is one of them. We are planning a big happening.' And, after a couple of days in Paris, the newly-weds stepped into John's Rolls-Royce to be driven to Amsterdam's Hilton Hotel, for their honeymoon.

The joke in those days was that honeymooners spent their first week of marriage together in bed, enjoying what had, until then, been forbidden, or at least furtive. But, in the sexual sense, John and Yoko's honeymoon had been months earlier when, as John would say, 'We were either in the studio or in bed.'

Their Amsterdam honeymoon was quite different. For a week the pair sat side by side in bed wearing striped pyjamas, and surrounded by flowers and hand-drawn posters that read 'Bed Peace' and 'Hair Peace', inviting reporters to come and listen to them as they espoused the cause of world peace.

John put it this way: 'Yoko and I decided that whatever we did would be in the papers, so we decided to use the space . . . as a commercial for peace . . .' Marching was fine and dandy for the Thirties, he said, but today different methods were needed. 'It's sell, sell, sell. If you want peace you've got to sell it like soap.' The newspapers were filled with 'war, war, war . . . so let's get some "peace, peace, peace" in the headlines for a change'.

It was a noble sentiment, and he didn't care if people laughed at them. They did. 'Yoko and I are willing to be the world's clowns if it will do some good,' was his reaction.

The following week the Lennons flew to Vienna where a film they had produced was being shown on television. It was called *Rape*, and was a *cinéma-vérité* documentary in which a camera team had picked on a girl in London, seemingly at random, and followed her as she became increasingly afraid. It had echoes of the way the Beatles had been hounded, but it also forecast a world in which the paparazzi could accidentally play a part in hounding a woman to her death. Think only of Princess Diana who was to die twenty-eight years later in a crash in a Paris underpass as the paparazzi raced to keep up with the car in which she was travelling.

It was a good subject for discussion, but for its promotion John and Yoko decided to utilise a Yoko bagism event, and hid inside a very large bag from which, at a press conference, they answered questions. Inevitably it was the bag, not the film or its subject, that grabbed most of the headlines.

At around this time it became not unusual to begin to hear usually sensible commentators privately asking if John had in fact gone mad, so bewildering was some of his behaviour. With his thin, drawn face, white suits and long hair and beard he had taken on a quite different public persona. But when, during an interview one day, I suggested to him that he was now thought of as 'Nutty John', he rather liked it. 'Yes, that's what I am, "Nutty John".'

Mad he may not have been, but he was certainly very angry when he learned that Dick James, who had so astutely spotted the Lennon and McCartney songwriting talent, had decided to quit while he was ahead. Seeing the disintegration of their partnership James had, without warning them, sold his controlling shareholding in Northern Songs to ATV magnate Lew Grade.

John and Paul may have had their differences, but control of their songs, the most important element of their lives' work, united them. For the next six months they would join together to fight to prevent ATV owning their songs. 'I'm not going to be fucked around by men in suits sitting on their fat arses in the City,' was how John put it. In the end he would be.

Ironically, at a moment when in a business sense they couldn't speak without falling out, musically John and Paul were drawn closer together. Coming home from his European honeymoon tour with a new song, 'The Ballad Of John And Yoko', John was insistent that it should be an instant Beatles single – despite the fact that 'Get Back' had only just gone to the top of the charts. And, anxious to build at least one bridge with his old friend, Paul agreed to record it with him.

Neither George nor Ringo was in London at the time, but that didn't stop them. Going to Abbey Road, John sang and played both rhythm and lead guitar, while Paul was on bass, drums, piano and maracas, and then added a harmony. One of them even played a few guitar chords lifted from when 'The Honeymoon Song' had been part of their Cavern act. Altogether, it was almost a more sophisticated version of the sessions the two had enjoyed as teenagers at Paul's father's house in Forthlin Road, Liverpool. One Abbey Road engineer at the time said it was a while since he'd seen John and Paul working so happily together. Yoko wasn't there.

It wasn't a great record, certainly the weakest single the Beatles ever released, but, as a kind of talking blues, it was witty and good-humoured with John even having a joke at his chief tormentors, the tabloid pundits, by singing *'She's gone to his head, they look just like two gurus in drag'*. His great hero, Chuck Berry, would have been proud of that line.

Of course, Yoko *had* gone to his head, and he was glad of it. 'It was Yoko that changed me,' he scoffed to me. 'She forced me to become avant-garde and take my clothes off, when all I wanted was to become Tom Jones. And now look at me. Did you know, "avant-garde" is French for bullshit?'

A week later, returning to the Apple roof, he went through a cere-mony before a Commissioner of Oaths, changing the middle name his mother had given him. Out went John Winston Lennon and in came John Ono Lennon.

For anyone who still doubted his resolve, John hammered it home when he said: 'I'm always John and Yoko. That never stops. We're a twenty-four-hour couple. So, whatever I'm doing as a Beatle, Yoko is sitting on my shoulder like a parrot.'

Which might have been how the other Beatles considered her when they saw that the sleeve of their new single, as it was released in America, portrayed not just the usual four Beatles . . . but Yoko as well.

'Yoko used to sit in on the photos,' Paul would remember. 'And we really didn't know how to tell her to get out . . .'

# 50

*'I think you're daft. I'm leaving the Beatles.*
*I want a divorce . . . like I had from Cynthia'*

Being a Beatle had by now become a part-time job for John, as illustrated when at the end of May 1969 he turned up in Canada with Yoko. He'd wanted to go to the US on the *Queen Elizabeth*, taking with him a two-man film crew. But when he reached the ship at Southampton he discovered that his US visa request had been turned down, because of his UK drugs conviction the previous year. The Bahamas was his next choice, because of its proximity to the US, but then he changed his mind and moved on to Montreal to stage another peace bed-in there. As North American journalists queued up to interview him, he and Yoko talked day after day from their bed in Room 1742 at the Queen Elizabeth Hotel.

Throughout 1969, colleges across America were racked with protests against the Vietnam War, to which John's perhaps surprisingly mild response was that the students should act responsibly and peacefully in their confrontations with the police. 'All I'm saying is give peace a chance,' he would sum up many a conversation.

That should be a song, Yoko told him. Which is what it became a couple of days later in the shape of 'Give Peace A Chance', with a local Canadian record producer, Andre Perry, bringing a recorder and microphones to his hotel room. The recording didn't take long. Helped by Tommy Smothers on another acoustic guitar, someone to open and close a wardrobe door to provide a steady rhythm, and the voices of disc jockey Murray the K, who was up from New York for the occasion, singer Petula Clark, Timothy and Rosemary Leary, various journalists and the Canadian branch of the Radha Krishna Temple, an eight-bar chant was elevated into a classic protest anthem. John, wearing white pyjamas this time, sang from his bed.

The interviews John and Yoko did may have garnered widespread press coverage, but it was 'Give Peace A Chance' that was John's real gift to the peace movement as it became an instant hit, drawing people together to be sung on anti-war marches in many countries. It didn't matter that more voices were later secretly added to those present by the record producer to give it more body; or that the words that John sang between the choruses were gobbledegook; or that one of them was 'masturbation' while 'mastication' was written on the lyric sheet, because the message of the song was too important to risk it being banned by radio stations over a jokey reference to onanism. What mattered was that the song summed up in nine English words and a couple of chords the expression of millions.

Creating a slogan and setting it to the simplest of music – this was where John was brilliant. Released as a single by the Plastic Ono Band, 'Give Peace A Chance' would be his first recorded venture outside the Beatles.

Back in London, meanwhile, a problem had arisen. If Allen Klein was to succeed in his promise to get EMI and Capitol Records in the US to increase the Beatles' royalty rate, he was going to need some new material to dangle in front of their eyes. But the *Let It Be* film and tapes were going to take months more to edit.

It was diplomatic Paul who broke the ice. After talking to John, he rang George Martin and asked if the producer would work with the Beatles again, just like they used to. Martin agreed that he would, but he insisted there could be no messing about as there had been at Twickenham. There wouldn't be, Paul promised, and the Abbey Road studio was booked for the beginning of July.

This gave John just enough time to drive Yoko, together with Julian and Kyoko, up to Liverpool to show them where he had grown up, and then on to Scotland to meet some members of his family. Bizarre as his life had become, he'd always stayed in touch by letter and postcard with his mother's sisters and his cousins.

By all accounts it was a pleasant enough family holiday, despite Yoko's insistence, to Scottish horror, on feeding John a macrobiotic diet. Not long after starting back again, however, John accidentally drove the family saloon he'd hired into a ditch. With his very poor eyesight, he'd never been better than a terrible driver. Fortunately, no one was seriously injured, although both John and Yoko had to have several stitches, as did Kyoko, while Julian was in shock.

Yoko had, however, also suffered a whiplash back injury, which

meant that when John finally reached Abbey Road to begin recording, he was followed by a hobbling Yoko, and then by four porters
who wheeled a bed into the studio. More porters then appeared carrying sheets and blankets and made up the bed, into which Yoko then
climbed, propped up by pillows so that she didn't miss being part of
the session. 'It wasn't the ideal way for making records,' Paul would
remember. George Martin wasn't much amused either, but he would
laugh about it for years afterwards as he told and retold the story.

Apart from that little surprise, this last album that the Beatles would
make together, and which was appropriately given the title *Abbey
Road,* could hardly have gone more smoothly. Because he'd arrived
late, John didn't play on one of George's two stand-out tracks, 'Here
Comes The Sun', although he was on 'Something', and he hated Paul's
song 'Maxwell's Silver Hammer', which he considered twee. And,
while improving John's 'Come Together' with a thumping bass riff,
Paul wondered if his colleague might not be sued for plagiarism for a
line in the lyrics – which he eventually was. But these were everyday
recording differences, and nothing to fall out about. The real problem
was that even with Ringo's 'Octopus's Garden' and John's sexy, bluesy
paean to Yoko 'I Want You (She's So Heavy'), the Beatles didn't have
enough new songs to fill both sides of a twelve-inch record.

At which point George Martin came into his own, encouraging John
and Paul to rummage around in their minds for any unfinished songs
that might be fitted together to create a continuous twenty-minute
piece. Paul leapt at the challenge and quickly delivered 'Golden Slum-
bers', 'She Came In Through The Bathroom Window', 'You Never Give
Me Your Money' and 'Carry That Weight'. While John, less enthusiastically, dug out 'Mean Mr Mustard' and 'Polythene Pam' for which he
used a pronounced Scouse accent and an inimitably Liverpool turn of
phrase – *'You could say she was attractively built'.*

'It was supposed to be about a mythical Liverpool scrubber, dressed
to kill in her jackboots and kilt, like a whore,' was how he described
it to me, before casually, and rather unfairly, dismissing the entire
medley. 'They were just bits of songs that had been forgotten and
should have probably stayed forgotten.' But without them there
would have been no album.

In the year since he'd left Cynthia, John liked to say that he and
Yoko were living out of a suitcase. They'd certainly been a moveable

feast, having shuttled between Kenwood and Montagu Square before ending up at Ringo's house, just down the road from Kenwood, when the drummer and his family moved on to a grander home in Surrey. Now, however, Tittenhurst Park, an estate in Berkshire that John had bought for £350,000 with money owed from US publishing royalties, was just about ready for occupation – if you didn't mind living with the builders. Finally, he and Yoko had a home of their own. It would, John believed, give him the seclusion he needed, and it was quite a place. First built in 1769, with later early nineteenth-century additions, its main building was a graceful white-painted mansion, surrounded by over seventy acres of private parkland, with groves, lodges and protected massive Oriental trees. If John's previous house in St George's Hill Estate had been rich, mock Tudor suburbia, Tittenhurst Park was genuine Georgian/Regency England.

Out in the country, though less than forty miles from London, it should have been ideal for an eccentric millionaire and his new wife. John and Yoko, however, though they spent much of the next two years having walls pulled own, a recording studio built and white carpet imported through Harrods from China and laid throughout their home, never really settled. With the two gardeners, the housekeeper/cook, the two secretaries and Yoko's old friend Dan Richter there to pursue their whims and projects, everything they could have wanted was to hand. They even had a lake dug in the grounds, lined with rubber and stocked with fish, when the whim struck them. But the fish died, and so did their early enthusiasm.

It didn't help that, from the start, John and Yoko were dabbling with heroin again, with Dan Richter, who had a heroin problem himself, acting as an occasional courier for them. As he admits in his memoir, he would leave a little supply outside their bedroom door. When John was in a mean and martyred mood, he would sometimes blame his recourse to drugs on the pain that the other Beatles had inflicted on him and Yoko by their attitude towards her. But that was just an excuse. The truth lay closer to his addictive personality. He liked what drugs did to him. 'I started to smoke at fifteen, though I hated the smell,' he told me one day at Tittenhurst. 'And I started drinking then too. All I did later was mix some stuff in the tobacco and add pills to the drink when I was on tour or working in Hamburg.' Later, along came other drugs. In the world in which he lived, that was hardly unusual.

He would always insist that he never injected, although some friends wonder whether that was true, as days would go by when he and Yoko would be locked in their bedroom that summer, only coming out when they had to. Such a day occurred in August when John joined the other Beatles for their final official photograph together as they all crossed the zebra crossing on Abbey Road for the cover of their last album.

He was still unwell from heroin use when he was present a few weeks later on a cold, late August night as Bob Dylan made a return to live appearances at the Isle of Wight Festival of Pop. It wasn't a great gig, but the atmosphere must have sparked something in John. He'd never appeared at a mass rock festival like Woodstock or Monterey. Was he wondering what it was like? Whatever the reason, he accepted the very next invitation he received, which happened to be a rock and roll peace festival in Toronto, starring Chuck Berry, Little Richard, Fats Domino and Bo Diddley. Hastily ringing around, he put together a band of Eric Clapton on lead guitar, Klaus Voorman on bass and Alan White on drums, met them at London airport, and then decided what they were going to play on the flight over.

It began as a difficult night for him, when he suffered a fit of vomiting backstage which was believed to be a side effect of the heroin battle he was fighting. But the ovation that erupted when his presence was announced both astonished and galvanised him as he and his new friends launched into some formulaic rock and roll standards, before getting to his own songs 'Yer Blues' and 'Give Peace A Chance'. Naturally, Yoko ended the set by doing her wailing thing to John's guitar feedback accompaniment, and, not surprisingly, she wasn't so well received. That didn't matter to John, as he continued to blank out any negativity towards her. What did matter was that he'd loved being back on stage before an adoring crowd. Did he really still need the other Beatles alongside him? 'The buzz was incredible,' he said after the show. 'I never felt so good in my life.'

Then it was straight back to Tittenhurst, where he forced himself to kick heroin, or, as the euphemism went, to go 'cold turkey' and come off the drug. It was, he told me, dreadful and made him desperately unwell, but, more than ever anxious to write from within himself, he turned the experience into a song, 'Cold Turkey'.

*'Thirty-six hours rolling in pain, Praying to someone, free me again,'* he screamed. It was harrowing stuff, and too tough for Paul and George

when he suggested it might make a Beatles single. So, undeterred, and with the help of the ever-faithful Ringo and Klaus Voorman again, he recorded it as another Plastic Ono Band record. It was a flop. The world wasn't ready for a pop record about getting off heroin – if, indeed, the fans even knew that was what it was about. Not every record buyer was familiar with the patois of the drug subculture. In Britain 'cold turkey' was something you ate with the Christmas dinner leftovers on Boxing Day.

And not every fan wanted to see John's penis gradually growing into tumescence and then slowly settling into detumescence either. But that was the subject of a twenty-minute film, titled *Self Portrait*, that he and Yoko had made. Neither John nor Yoko attended the screening at London's Institute of Contemporary Arts, nor, as far as I know, was the film ever shown again. Perhaps even John realised that, this time, he really had gone too far.

Since the appointment of Allen Klein as business manager, the Apple headquarters in Savile Row had ceased to be the merry, day-long cocktail party that it had been in the carefree days of 'Western Communism'. There had been resignations, with Peter Asher having gone and taken James Taylor with him, after finding that the Klein atmosphere was no longer convivial. And there had been sackings, too, most notably that of Ron Kass who was running the Apple record label. More poignant, though, was the firing of a tearful Alistair Taylor who had been a good friend and servant of the group ever since Brian Epstein had requested that he accompany him on that fateful first visit to the Cavern back in 1961. What most hurt, Alistair told me, was that having been told of his sacking by an upset and embarrassed Peter Brown (doing Klein's dirty work for him), he could no longer get John or Paul on the phone.

Not that it was all dirty work that Klein was doing. At a board meeting on 20 September, which was attended by Ringo, John and Yoko, and Paul but not George who had gone to Liverpool to see his mother who was ill, he had some good news to impart. EMI and Capitol Records had agreed to a huge hike in the Beatles' record royalties. Even Paul had to admit that the man he so disliked had done well for them. It was good for Klein, too, of course.

It might have been best if the meeting had broken up at that point. But, instead, ever enthusiastic, Paul then began to suggest ways in which the Beatles might progress in the future. This is how he re-called the afternoon, to me.

'I began to feel that the only way we could get back to playing good music again was to start playing as a band again,' he said. 'But I didn't want to go out and face two hundred thousand fans because I would get nothing from it. So, I thought up this idea of playing surprise one-night stands in unlikely places . . . just letting a hundred or so people into the village hall, so to speak, and then locking the doors. It would have been a great scene for those who saw us and great for us, too.'

When he'd finished speaking, he asked the other Beatles what they thought.

John's reply was: 'I think you're daft.'

Paul asked him what he meant . . . 'after all, he is John Lennon, and I'm a bit afraid of the "rapier wit" we all hear about,' he said.

So, John repeated himself. 'I think you're daft. I'm leaving the Beatles. I want a divorce . . . like I had from Cynthia.'

# 51

*'I used to be a performing flea . . .*
*Now I've become a crutch for the world's social lepers'*

He hadn't planned to say it. When he'd been in Toronto he'd mentioned to Eric Clapton that he was thinking of leaving the Beatles; he'd told Allen Klein, too – only to be asked not to mention it to the other Beatles yet. But when at the meeting Paul had begun outlining his own plans, he just hadn't been able to stop the words tumbling from his mouth. Paul's memory of the day was that he was in total shock. Of all four members of the band, he was the biggest Beatles fan. Other than go to school, being a Beatle was all he'd ever done, and, despite all the warning signs in John's behaviour, he just hadn't seen this coming. Ringo wasn't particularly surprised, and when George was told, all he felt was relief that the break was out in the open.

Except that it wasn't. At Klein's insistence, John's decision to leave wasn't to be made public, not only until after *Abbey Road*'s release a few days later but until the *Let It Be* movie and album came out the following spring. To Paul this seemed like a reprieve because, as he knew well, John regularly contradicted himself and changed his mind. There had to be a good chance that he would have second thoughts. After all, why would anybody want to leave the Beatles? It didn't make sense.

It did to John. Even if no announcement had been made, he was, he now felt, already free of his Beatles responsibilities. And as Paul busied himself promoting *Abbey Road* and disproving a creepy 'Paul is dead' rumour that bubbled up from America and garnered much press coverage, John, with Yoko ever at his side, and working from a large room at Apple, threw himself into a whirlpool of diverse, disconnected and sometimes plainly wrong-headed activities.

There was, for instance, a commission to draw some lithographs depicting Yoko and himself, and overseeing the editing of the film of both his Montreal bed-in and the Toronto peace concert. There was also help to be given to the parents of a man called James Hanratty. Hanratty had been hanged for what had become known as the A6 murder in 1962, and his parents, believing that their son had been innocent, had come to John seeking help in getting an inquiry set up to clear their son's name. Moved by their despair, John agreed to finance a film about what they believed to have been a terrible miscarriage of justice. He, of course, had no more experience of miscarriages of justice than anyone else – and the film would, in the end, never be made. But his fame and fighting spirit were beginning to make him a magnet for the desperate. He put it another way. As pleas for funding or help rained in on him, he told me: 'I used to be a performing flea . . . Now I've become a crutch for the world's social lepers.'

It was a role that appealed to the boy who had 'always wanted to take the side of the underdog', as Mimi had remarked. But for John to really feel free to play the part, he would, he decided, have to divest himself of one of his establishment credentials. That was the medal that had been presented to him as a Member of the British Empire, along with the other Beatles, by the Queen in 1965. He'd been embarrassed by it at the time. Now he saw getting rid of it as a way of announcing a new John Lennon to the world for the approaching Seventies.

Sending Les Anthony, his driver, down to Sandbanks to retrieve the medal from Mimi's mantelpiece, he then wrote a short letter to the Queen. It read:

*Your Majesty*

*I am returning my MBE as a protest against Britain's involvement in the Nigeria-Biafra thing, against our support of America in Vietnam and against 'Cold Turkey' slipping down the charts.*
*With love*

*John Lennon*

Then, after instructing Anthony to drive to Buckingham Palace in his Rolls-Royce and deliver the letter and medal, much amused, he rang me at the *Evening Standard* to report news of his stunt. The story just caught the last edition of the day for commuters to read on their journey home that night.

As John had anticipated on the phone, his protest was not well received. The Queen didn't comment – she never does – but newspaper pundits railed against the Beatle's act of disrespect, not just towards the monarch, but towards the honour itself. In truth, it really wasn't John's finest moment. To equate, in a bad taste joke, the terrible civil war then raging between Nigeria and its breakaway province of Biafra with the poor sales for his latest record was uncomprehendingly insensitive. Years later he would regret the wording of the letter. But he never regretted sending back his MBE.

There was something else that began during those last months of 1969 that he would come to regret – a burgeoning relationship with a self-proclaimed and, to everyone but John, dubious British Black Power leader. The man's name was Michael de Freitas, aka Michael Abdul Malik, once known as a pimp and bully-boy for a London slum racketeer but who was now presenting himself as a reformed, saintly character. Going under the protest name of Michael X, de Freitas had a plan to open a black cultural centre, the Black House, in the Holloway Road, a poor area of North London. And John, attracted by what seemed an excellent cause, had money to spare for it. De Freitas, who was a con-man, among much else, played him well, as he had other rich benefactors. John's intentions were good, but he was gullible and unquestioning. Having decided that he was anti-establishment, he was welcoming of others in whom he saw the romance of the rebel. In the case of Michael de Freitas, it would all end terribly.

As he was already considering the Beatles 'to be part of history', a sense reinforced when it became clear that there was no hope of stopping ATV owning Northern Songs, John had little interest in the new Beatles single, 'Something'. It was the first time that the Lennon–McCartney axis had allowed a George Harrison song to be the A-side of a record. And, although his 'Come Together', on the flip side, got equal billing, his focus was on a new John and Yoko experimental album, *Unfinished Music No. 2: Life With The Lions*. The title was a jokey reference to the BBC radio family show that he had enjoyed as a boy. The contents of the album, the sales of which were tiny, included a recording of the heartbeat of the unborn baby that Yoko had miscarried.

It followed a pattern. Everything John and Yoko now did was

seen through the window of their mutual self-obsession – although John wouldn't have seen it that way. To him, he and Yoko were 'Mr and Mrs Peace'. And, following an appearance at a UNICEF benefit concert alongside Delaney & Bonnie and Friends in London in mid-December, when George Harrison, Eric Clapton and Keith Moon joined him on stage in what was really a supergroup jam session, the couple launched a Christmas 'War Is Over' peace campaign. It involved identical large white billboards being posted up in the centres of major cities in twelve countries around the world – all carrying the message in massive black print 'WAR IS OVER', and in smaller print 'Happy Christmas, John and Yoko'.

Whether the billboards had any influence on the promotion of peace was unknowable, but, in John's mind, like the bed-ins, they set up a conversation that he hoped would be discussed by newspaper columnists and radio and TV presenters in the run-up to Christmas.

He hadn't known much about Ronnie Hawkins until he'd met him at the Rock and Roll Toronto Peace Festival, other than that he was an early rocker of Elvis's vintage from Arkansas 'who used to waggle his arse', and that, now based in Canada, his band, the Hawks, had eventually become The Band. But that was enough for John, and when Ronnie offered his home for the Lennons to use as their Canadian headquarters, he quickly accepted. Ronnie, his wife Wanda and their children hadn't realised what would hit them.

There they'd been, ready to celebrate Christmas, with a little spruce tree and a few flashing lights, in their roomy house and grounds out in the snow-covered fields of Ontario. Then, within hours, a van had arrived from Capitol Records and unloaded the biggest, whitest, most synthetic, gingham-draped Christmas tree they'd ever seen, together with a gilded cage bearing two pure white un-cooing doves. Then came the telephone company to install half a dozen new lines, a macrobiotic cook was hired together with his Zen cookbook, and a young woman was chauffeured in to do the extra washing-up.

That was only the beginning. Soon after the arrival of their guests, for whom Ronnie and Wanda vacated their double bed, and who were accompanied by their assistant, art critic Anthony Fawcett and this writer, an art publisher turned up from Paris bearing with him five hundred lithographs in a limited edition recently drawn by former art student John, for personal autographing.

Nor did the interruptions stop there. As posters shouting 'WAR IS OVER' appeared on the Hawkins' sideboards and sofas (and one or two saying 'BRITAIN KILLED HANRATTY', which puzzled everyone apart from the guests), next came television producers from both Canadian and American networks, together with their soundmen, cameramen and interviewers, to be followed by radio reporters with their tape recorders and newspaper reporters with their notebooks.

John was in his element. Hour after hour he and Yoko – but mainly John, because he was the one everyone wanted to talk to – would chat to radio shows all over the US and Canada, before breaking off to get something to eat and do a bout of lithograph signing, scribbling his name under drawings he'd made of the sex life of his wife and himself. He'd been working on them for months in the privacy of his home. Now he wanted the world to see them. The intimacy depicted in the prints came as a surprise.

'Why do you draw so much cunnilingus?' I asked the artist as I passed him sheet after sheet to sign.

'Because I like it,' John grinned merrily.

Standing to one side, Yoko watched without expression.

A few years earlier John had said to Maureen Cleave, 'I hope I grow out of being sex mad.' Then, when she pressed him on the joys of marital fidelity, he had added comically: 'Do you mean to say I might be missing something?'

Now infidelity was never in his mind. 'We're not immune to sex, you know,' he said. 'We're always sussing each other out. But you have to weigh up whether or not it's worth it. There's a difference between fancying other people and having sexual fantasies about them. We wouldn't mind going to see a sex show . . . you know, being voyeurs. But we wouldn't want to join in. Our main trouble is finding people who are like us, who get the same kicks as us.'

'We're very jealous people,' came in Yoko at that point.

'I'm jealous of the mirror,' said John.

'I think I'll go and change soon,' said Yoko a few minutes later.

'Oh good, I'll come and watch,' came back John, putting down his signing pen.

As to whether his drawings were good or not, he had no idea. Nor did he care. 'They won't be taken seriously anyway,' he said. He had just read and laughed over an article in the *Daily Mirror* in which he'd been named as 'Clown of the Year'. He wasn't offended. He liked to read about himself, whatever was written.

But watching him that weekend in Canada, when he was away from the down-to-earth teasing retorts of the other Beatles and his Apple colleagues, not to mention the impertinently cynical British press who had known him for a long time, was to see him basking in a reverence that he didn't get in his own country. While one New York art dealer, who, admittedly, may have had one eye on the marketing of the lithographs, was telling him that he should be nominated for the Nobel Peace Prize, a local Toronto rabbi was declaring John and Yoko to be the 'finest people' he'd ever met. Then there was comedian Dick Gregory and poet Allen Ginsberg arriving in Canada to offer their support, followed by an invitation to the Toronto home of media intellectual Marshall McLuhan, and, to top it all, an audience with Canadian Prime Minister Pierre Trudeau in Ottawa.

John had to be flattered. He was certainly in as good a mood as he'd been in months, as, wearing a balaclava and the sergeant's jacket he'd bought in an Army and Navy store, he even went skidooing across the snow around Ronnie Hawkins' fields. Being a Beatle had given him the fame to be listened to, but his own country was, for the most part, deaf to anything he had to say. 'I have the hardest time in Britain,' he complained to a Canadian reporter. 'They don't take anything we do or say seriously. It's a continual put down.'

But for the best part of a week in Canada, he'd found himself viewed as something quite different – an intelligent, free-thinking advocate of protest; or, as he saw it, 'an ambassador for peace'. That made him feel good about himself. He wasn't just thought of as a rock star any more. Perhaps that was why, back at the Hawkins' house, he decided to let me in on his big secret . . . that he'd left the Beatles. He giggled as he told me.

But I wasn't laughing. I was dismayed. I was a Beatle fan. Like Paul, I really hoped he'd change his mind.

John and Yoko were back at home at Tittenhurst Park for Christmas in time for John to learn that the heavyweight BBC television programme *24 Hours* had chosen him as its 'Man of the Decade'. He was surprised and pleased. Yet the restlessness in his spirit was digging in again. The Sixties was the past. Whatever happened next was what interested him now.

# 52

### 'Free means free'

The Lennons spent a family New Year at a rented farmhouse at Aalborg in northern Denmark with Yoko's former husband, Tony Cox, his new wife, Melinda, and Kyoko, who was in Cox's care. They must have enjoyed some of their time there because they stayed for over three weeks, but later they never talked much about it, other than to tell funny stories about the people they'd met there who believed in flying saucers.

Since they'd last seen him, Cox had 'found God' and become opposed to drugs, alcohol and cigarettes – which must have made it a New Year of some sobriety for John – and was now involved with a group who called themselves the Harbingers. One of the Harbingers talked John into being hypnotised in an effort to give up smoking, but it didn't work. Nor did an attempt to get John to remember a past life. What did work was a pair of scissors applied by a local Danish girl in a barn, who made short work of his long hair, and Yoko's too. In the world of *JohnandYoko*, what one did the other had to do as well. In a ritualistic sense, it seemed that they were both being shriven to begin the new decade. John looked better with his hair cropped, Yoko not so good. That bothered her.

While they'd been in Toronto the previous September, John had been in discussions about a free Peace Rock Festival to be held there the following July. But when the organisers flew to Denmark for further talks and John realised that the project wouldn't be completely free, as tickets would cost a dollar each, he got angry. 'Free means *free*,' he insisted, worrying now that profit rather than peace might have been lingering at the back of the minds of some of the organisers. And when the Harbingers then talked about how they would fly John and Yoko to the festival in a psychic-powered car and that flying saucers would be landing at the event . . . that was enough. 'He said he'd been on a flying saucer,' John would relate, beaming. 'But we wondered . . . if he was so spiritual, why was he so fat?'

He withdrew his name from the project, and he and Yoko returned to England carrying their shorn hair in a white plastic bag. Kyoko stayed with her father, Tony Cox, who was now loath to hand her over into the care of a couple who took drugs.

A January spent lying low in Denmark might have had some weird moments, but at least it meant that he wasn't in England when an exhibition of his lithographs opened at the London Arts Gallery in Bond Street, Mayfair. It didn't stay open for very long. After officers in plain clothes had mingled with the guests at an evening champagne reception, uniformed police arrived the next morning and spent three hours examining the drawings, before confiscating eight of them, including one depicting Yoko masturbating. They then charged the owners of the gallery under the Obscene Publications Act. Not surprisingly there was a rumpus in the press, which, although the charges were later withdrawn, did wonders for the value of the drawings. Originally on sale at £41 ($100) each, today they fetch up to £10,000 ($14,500) at auction.

John remained indifferent to the fuss and the fact that the police had 'arrested some pieces of paper . . . It's a laugh,' he said. Ignoring the press ridicule, he decided it was time for a new single from the Plastic Ono Band. He called it 'Instant Karma!' and he wrote and recorded it in a single day, with George Harrison on lead guitar and Phil Spector, an old friend of Allen Klein's, acting as producer. It wasn't classic Lennon, although it did involve a very similar chord progression to 'All You Need Is Love'. But it was joyous, had a Fifties-style echo and thumping bass and drums, and a chorus for everyone to sing along to. It would sell over a million copies in the US and John would promote it in the UK by singing live on BBC-TV's *Top Of The Pops* as Yoko sat blindfolded and knitting – the significance of which was not immediately apparent.

But then, nor was the significance of John handing the bag of his and Yoko's hair clippings over to Michael de Freitas at the Black House in return for an alleged pair of Muhammad Ali's blood-smeared trunks. To those of us present it all seemed eerily phoney.

The shadow of heroin was lingering again, too. Yoko was pregnant, and, suffering complications, she was admitted to the private London Clinic in Harley Street, where John was given his own bed in her room. One winter's Saturday afternoon while I was visiting, Michael de Freitas and a friend turned up with a large suitcase, inside of which was a gift of a large plastic bag full of marijuana. Even John was surprised by the amount.

But then de Freitas had reason to be grateful to him. He was awaiting trial on a charge of robbery and demanding money with menaces, with John having provided the bail money. Since only a couple of years earlier de Freitas had been in jail for eight months on another charge, his future probably looked precarious, and it hardly came as a surprise when a few months later he abandoned the Black House, jumped bail and took a flight to Trinidad.

That might have been the last John ever heard of the man who dreamed of being a revolutionary leader and called himself Michael X. That was not to be the case.

But for me that afternoon in the London Clinic was memorable for something other than the visit by de Freitas and his pal. John was always very careful not to admit to the use of hard drugs by either himself or Yoko outside the circle of people whom he knew were also doing drugs. I hadn't known. So it was a surprise when, before de Freitas arrived, a nurse had been giving Yoko an injection, and John had suddenly exclaimed to the nurse: 'She's a junkie, you know.' Anxious for Yoko, the protective cloak he always held around her, and her reputation, had momentarily slipped.

For months Paul had been absent, partly at the hideaway farm he'd bought himself on the Mull of Kintyre in Scotland, kicking his heels, staying away from Apple and shunning the other Beatles whom he felt had betrayed him. His hope was that eventually he would get a call from John saying that he was ready to go back to work. But the call had never come.

'I was bored,' Paul told me. 'I like to work. I'm an active person . . . I'd just got a new recording machine in my house and I found that I liked working alone.' So over the winter of 1969–70 he wrote and recorded a whole album on his own, playing all the instruments himself.

But there was a snag. Following his successful work on 'Instant Karma!', Phil Spector had been asked by Allen Klein if he could salvage the *Let It Be* tapes that had been lying unreleased for over a year. Even back then, Phil Spector, who would later be imprisoned for murder, was often thought to be unhinged. But as a record producer, in his day, he was gifted, giving every song he touched the 'Phil Spec-tor treatment', be it one by the Ronettes like 'Be My Baby' or the Righteous Brothers' 'You've Lost That Lovin' Feelin''. Working that way he'd had a lot of hits.

Now, given a Beatles album to remix and re-produce, he found himself able to take over two of Paul's best songs, 'Let It Be' and 'The Long And Winding Road', and apply the Spector treatment to them, too – without having to ask the singer-songwriter's permission.

This would be something new for Paul but by the spring of 1970 he had his solo album, *McCartney*, finished and ready for release, and Spector had fashioned the *Let It Be* tapes into a good Beatles album. The problem was Klein and John, not to mention United Artists, the distributors of the film of *Let It Be,* wanted the Beatles album released in March, and Paul wanted his album out then, too. It didn't make sense for the two albums to be released almost together and therefore to be in competition with one another. But with emotions running as high as they were, sense didn't always come into it.

At around this point, Paul was sent a remixed version of what Spector had done to 'The Long And Winding Road'. He was horrified. 'I couldn't believe it,' he told me. 'I would *never* have women's voices on a Beatles record.' When he complained to Klein he got a note back saying it was too late to make any further changes. 'It's no good me sitting here and thinking I'm in control,' Paul raged, 'because I'm obviously not.'

Heels were dug in. Looking for a way out of the impasse, John and George decided to send Ringo, who had never fallen out with any of the other Beatles, to Paul's house with a letter from them. It read: 'We're sorry it turned out like this. It's nothing personal. Love, John and George (Hare Krishna).'

For Paul it could hardly have been more personal. It seemed every-one was against him. John had wrecked the Beatles, then he'd brought in Allen Klein, whom Paul didn't want, who had then brought in Phil Spector, whom Paul also did not want, who had then gone on to ruin one of his best songs. And now they were telling him he couldn't release his solo album when he wanted to.

Screaming at Ringo, the inoffensive messenger, he threw him out of his house. At that, the other Beatles gave in. If it meant so much to Paul, they would let his album come out three weeks before the launch of the *Let It Be* album and film.

A week before the release of *McCartney*, Paul issued an ambiguous question-and-answer statement in which he admitted that he was neither planning a new Beatles album or single, nor could be foresee a time when he and John would become an active songwriting partnership again.

What he didn't say was that he had 'left' the Beatles. He didn't have to. The *Daily Mirror*, to whom the statement had been leaked, said it for him. 'PAUL QUITS BEATLES' ran the front-page headline on 10 April. At which point the world fell in around his head.

The questions and answers had been devised and intended as a clever piece of publicity for his solo album. But, unintentionally, it labelled Paul, who had done more than anyone to keep the Beatles alive, their destroyer. It was very ironic. Millions of fans around the world were aghast. How could Paul have done such a thing?

Nor was it only Beatles fans who were upset. Down at Tittenhurst Park, John was fuming. As he had started the Beatles, he had always assumed that he would be the one to finish them. He'd wanted to do it the previous September, but had been talked out of it by Allen Klein. Now Paul had grabbed the glory, as he saw it.

'Why didn't you write it when I told you in Canada at Christmas?' he asked me that day.

'You asked me not to,' I replied.

'You're the journalist, Connolly, not me,' he stabbed back.

Had Paul been a much-loved king who had abdicated, the convulsions of disappointment and accusations of betrayal that ran around the world that day couldn't have been angrier. Paul's nice-guy image was shattered. Quickly he tried to row back against the stream of vitriol. 'It was all a misunderstanding,' he told me. 'I thought "Christ, what have I done? Now we're for it," and my stomach started churning up. I never intended the statement to mean "Paul McCartney quits Beatles".' But, whether he intended it or not, and John was convinced that he had, that was how it was perceived, and would be for many years.

There was now no going back. But with the break-up out in the open, all four could get on with the rest of their careers independently of each other if they so desired, leaving the unravelling of their interests to their legions of lawyers. That process would take years, during which John's attitude towards Paul would be ever-changing.

For instance, while he was irritated that *The Times* music critic William Mann ('that fucking idiot that wrote about Aeolian cadences') gave Paul's album *McCartney* a glowing review, John would also tell the ingratiating writer of a pop music paper who had criticised 'Let It Be' that it was 'the best song in the charts'. It was, it seemed, all right for him to criticise Paul, but that was not always the case for anyone else. Equally, while occasionally amusing reporters by saying Paul's records were like those of Engelbert Humperdinck, he would also often quickly point out that he had only ever chosen two people to work with, one was Yoko and the other was Paul, so 'I can't have been a bad judge of talent'. And when he felt that there was too much praise for George Harrison's songs, he would angrily say to me, 'Paul and me were the Beatles. We wrote the songs.' A love-hate relationship doesn't begin to describe how John felt about Paul. They'd been together for half their lives by the time the Beatles finally broke up. A mass collision of emotions was inevitably involved on both sides.

None of the Beatles attended the premiere of *Let It Be* on 8 May. They just couldn't face the hoopla, and it was a bleak and unhappy spring for John and Yoko at Tittenhurst Park. According to the staff, the only excitement they had one week was when the donkeys they kept had escaped from the meadow. By this time, with most of the building work finished, the house was becoming more of a home, though one that was barely lived in. Life revolved around a huge kitchen and living area on the ground floor, manned by a cook, while secretaries, Sally and Diana, tried to keep up with the eccentricities of their employers. Elsewhere rooms were left empty or littered with records, rails of coats and bags of clothes, recording equipment, books, tapes, posters and instruments, dumped there by the removal men and never sorted by their owners. A rarely used pool table occupied another room that was lined with the unread leather-bound books that John had presumably claimed from Kenwood when his marriage to Cynthia had ended, while a white grand piano and stool would soon be the only furniture in one stately but otherwise empty sitting room.

A spiral staircase led from the kitchen to a landing, at the end of which was John and Yoko's large all-purpose bedroom. There two giant stereo speakers, one of which had a framed copy of the *Two Virgins* photograph on top, stood sentinel at either side of a huge bed, at the foot of which was a large television that was rarely turned off or the sound turned on. It would be here that John and Yoko would spend much of their time.

They weren't alone on their estate, with Yoko's old friend Dan Richter and his wife Jill and their little boy Sacha living in one of the cottages, but whenever I visited it was impossible to escape the feeling that they might be lonely. John would always deny this, saying, 'How can I be lonely when I've got Yoko?' But then he would admit that they didn't have many friends. His friends had been the Beatles and Neil and Mal, but they were the people he'd worked with, he would say.

There had been another problem with heroin that spring, John's third, which he had overcome, and on sunny days he and Yoko would take a trip round the estate on a little electric golf cart, the two of them wearing ex-Royal Air Force greatcoats with the insignia torn off. John liked that look. 'I always wanted to be an eccentric millionaire and now I am one,' he told me one day, with a smile of satisfaction, as he looked back at his house and everything he owned.

What he needed, though, was some new inspiration. Then one day a parcel arrived from Apple. Among the constant legal papers that he was obliged to read was an advanced copy of a book called *The Primal Scream* by Los Angeles-based psychotherapist Arthur Janov.

Janov had insisted to his New York publishers 'that as John was the most famous person in the world' they should try to get a quote from him for the book's jacket. It was a long shot, but it came off and Janov would end up with a lot more than a quote. No sooner had the book made its way to Tittenhurst Park than John became obsessed with it, as, over four hundred pages, Janov explored his theories on the root of neurosis through what he called primal therapy.

John hadn't only found a new craze, but a new vocabulary, too. As Yoko had encouraged him to talk about himself as an 'artist', now Janov gave him a word to describe his feelings – 'pain'. Through primal therapy – that is, by reaching into the child inside the adult to the point at which the patient is screaming in emotional anguish at uncovered memories – the secrets of neurosis could be unlocked. That was primal scream.

At John's request, Yoko, who always manned the phones in the Lennon household, made a call to California. John needed to talk to this Arthur Janov.

# 53

*'I might just as well have been a comedian
getting egg thrown in my face'*

By his looks alone, with his thick, iron-grey, curly hair and permanent suntan, as shown in the author's photograph on the back of his book, Arthur Janov, at forty-six, was born to be a West Hollywood psychotherapist. He reminded John of Jeff Chandler, and he had a charismatic, some might say overbearing, personality to match.

Within a couple of phone conversations John was hooked. But, as he was still banned from the US, he couldn't yet visit Janov in California for a consultation. So Janov, knowing that he had landed the big one, came to him, bringing his wife Vivian, who was also a psychotherapist, and their children. Put up at the swish Inn on the Park hotel on London's Park Lane, the two were then ferried every day to Tittenhurst Park for sessions, John with Janov in the recording studio that was still being built at the back of the house, and Yoko in their bedroom. Once again, whatever John did, Yoko did too.

Basically, Janov's technique was to get his patients to regress to childhood to relive the emotional pain, be it of loss, rejection, separation, lack of love or whatever, which his theory said was the cause of neurosis. Therapy like this could have been invented with John in mind. Not only had he been abandoned by his father, and then, in Mimi's account, asked to choose between his parents, he'd then been given away by his mother, while the uncle whom he'd loved had died. After that had come the death of his mother, to be followed a few years later by that of his best friend Stuart. Then there was his guilt at having introduced Brian Epstein to pills, then watched as his manager had lost control of his life through drugs.

John certainly had a lot to talk to Janov about and, being John, he wouldn't have held anything back. Did he talk about his sex life, about his confused adolescent sexual feelings about his mother, who behaved like a girlfriend with him, about the bar girls and strippers in Hamburg, the Beatles' groupies and his affairs after he was married? Did he mention Brian when he talked about sex, or his impotence with Cynthia towards the end of their marriage, or his ferocious jealousies and any conflictions he might have felt when he decided to publish his erotic lithographs of Yoko? Forty pages in Janov's book were devoted to sex, and we can be sure that John read that chapter very carefully, after which he would have moved on to the sections on 'Fear and Anger' and 'Drugs and Addictions' that followed. Without ever having met him, Janov had almost come up with the John Lennon Playbook. Little wonder that John gave me a copy. As with all his enthusiasms, he wanted to share it.

The initial treatment in London lasted for just three weeks, but Janov had clients to attend to in Los Angeles and couldn't neglect them for much longer. John, however, needed more therapy. Fame with money often talks. Through his lawyers, John was able to get a temporary US visa on 'health grounds', and, in July 1970, renting a home in Bel Air, he and Yoko flew out to continue the sessions in Janov's Los Angeles consulting rooms.

Everything continued to go well there at first, but gradually, as the Lennons were asked to take part in group therapy sessions, the gloss on Janov began to fade. And when the psychotherapist requested that the two be filmed during group therapy, John withdrew. The last thing he needed was to be filmed lying on a psychotherapist's floor screaming his head off.

Like the Maharishi before him, or even Magic Alex, Janov, whom John had believed would resolve his neuroses, was now seen to be yet another false prophet – maybe even 'a flake'. And with the time limit on his visa having overrun, John, with Yoko at his side, headed back to England. Janov felt that his most famous client needed more months of therapy. John thought he'd had enough. He'd got what he needed.

When he arrived home, John didn't at first want to talk too much about what had taken place, 'because everyone will say, "he's off again, he's found something else"', but the Janov influence on him just kept leaking out as he described 'screaming for hours' during sessions. It had, he was sure, been a useful experience in that, as Janov had convinced him, he'd grown up blocking his true feelings, and, as that was now no longer the case, he felt freed from his past.

That had to be good, and just as he had used his stay with the Maharishi to write songs for the *White Album*, he now produced a collection of eleven songs that he'd been writing during and after therapy. He recorded them in the late summer of 1970 at Abbey Road, with Phil Spector as producer.

The new album was, as he put it, 'my insight into myself'. With no catchy hit single on it, the songs were sometimes angry, self-pitying and accusatory, and accompanied only by Ringo, Klaus Voorman on bass and sometimes either Spector or Billy Preston on piano, the sound was harsh and spare. Simply titled *Plastic Ono Band*, John was as proud of it as anything he would ever record, because it was so autobiographical. 'I wasn't trying to make a bloody variety show,' he told me when he first played it to me.

The very first track was called 'Mother', and straight away his parents got it in the neck for what he now perceived to have been their neglect of him as a little boy. '*Mother, you had me, but I never had you . . .*' he sang of the once-worshipped Julia, before in the second line he turned the anger on his father.

'I'm writing this way now because it's the way I feel,' he said as we listened together. 'I used to say I wouldn't be singing "She Loves You" when I was thirty, but I didn't know I'd be singing about my mother . . . I was going through my life in therapy and so I wrote about the most important things that happened . . . Just like any artist. When I was a teenager I wrote poetry, a lot of which was gobbledegook, because I was hiding it from Mimi or perhaps hiding my emotions from myself.'

Another song was given the ironic title of 'Working Class Hero', which was how, now unshaven and usually wearing a working man's bibbed denim dungarees, he liked to see himself. With his menacing acoustic guitar throbbing as he sang, he attacked the very stairway to success that he had followed. '*As soon as you're born they make you feel small*,' he began. And the struggle through life could only get worse, he explained.

I was thinking about all the pain and torture that you go through on stage to get love from the audience. You go up there like Aunt Sally having things thrown at you . . . I might just as well have been a comedian getting egg thrown in my face . . . How often do you think the Beatles enjoyed a show? All this about gigs and clubs is a dream . . . Actually, more like a nightmare. One show in thirty would give us any real satisfaction and you'd go through all kinds of hell to get that.

I know I perform of my own choice, but that's the game. I set myself up to get knocked down . . . It's like performing for your parents all the time. All people like me start off with this appalling need for love . . .

It was now over a year since, in his mind, the Beatles had ceased to exist, and it was time to say goodbye to them in music. So, to (almost) end the album was a song called 'God', in which he renounced all idols and myths in a litany that went from the Bible to Buddha, and on to I-Ching, Kennedy, Elvis, Dylan . . . ending with 'I don't believe in Beatles . . . Yoko and me, that's reality . . .' The dream, he said, was over. He'd been the dream weaver and the Walrus, but now he was just John.

'I'm not a tough guy,' he explained. 'I've had a facade of being tough to protect me from whatever was going on as a kid or a teenager or a Beatle. But I'm not like that. I'm not going to waste my life as I was before . . . which was running at 20,000 miles an hour. I have to learn how not to do that, because I don't want to die when I'm forty.'

Arthur Janov's primal therapy had, it seemed, helped him close a door on a part of his past. It had, however, savagely wrenched open another.

For the past two years John's father, Freddie, had been living with his young wife Pauline and their eighteen-month-old son David in a town house in Brighton. Pauline worked as a translator and John paid for the rent on the house and gave a stipend to his father. Although John hadn't been in touch recently, Freddie had no reason to believe that they were not still on the good terms they'd been when his son had cheered him on to Gretna Green with Pauline.

So, with this in mind, and hoping to raise some money of his own, Freddie wrote to John wondering how he would feel if he were to write his autobiography. A reply from a secretary at Tittenhurst Park came within days, summoning Freddie and Pauline to a meeting.

It was the first time the two had been invited to the house, and, as it was on John's thirtieth birthday, they'd bought a birthday card and a bottle of aftershave as a present.

John, however, hadn't been planning a birthday party. Having kept them waiting in the kitchen, sitting at the large wooden table there, John suddenly hurried down the spiral staircase and, as Pauline would narrate in her book *Daddy, Come Home*, sat down facing his now puzzled father.

'I want you out of the house and I'm cutting off your money,' he spat at Freddie. 'Get out of my life and get off my back.' He was, Pauline wrote, unrecognisable from the friendly Beatle she'd last seen two Christmases ago.

Trying to defend himself, Freddie pointed out that he hadn't asked for any money, that it was John who had insisted on giving it to him, at which point John erupted at the way Freddie had abandoned him twenty-five years earlier. Hardly letting Freddie in again, he screamed that both his father and mother had abandoned him, even calling his mother, Julia, 'a whore'.

Then, reaching across the table, he grabbed his father by the lapels and told him that he was never to write anything without his approval. 'And if you tell anyone what happened here today, I'll have you killed . . . I'll have you cased up in a box and dumped out at sea right in the middle of the ocean . . . twenty, fifty, or, perhaps, you'd prefer a hundred fathoms deep.'

Anyone who knew John well would have recognised that he was out of control on a rant that was almost certainly fuelled by whatever drug he'd chosen to take that day, and that his mouth was running away with him. When he got in a state like this, there was no telling what he might say.

But Freddie didn't know his son very well and he was frightened and upset. In his anger, John said that he was insane, and, witnessing his son's behaviour, Freddie thought it quite possible. So, when Freddie received a letter from Allen Klein's new regime at Apple telling him to get out of his home or start paying rent to John, he went to see a solicitor. There he lodged an account of the meeting with his son, detailing the threats that John had made, and including melodramatic instructions that, were he to 'disappear or die an unnatural death', it should be made public.

He would never attempt to see John again.

A few days after John's tirade I happened to be down at Tittenhurst

Park and, knowing nothing of the meeting, wondered aloud whether John thought his father might be upset at the lyrics about him on the forthcoming album.

John fixed me with an uncompromising glare. 'If he is, too bad. What did he do for me? He didn't turn up until I was famous. I should get upset. The first time I saw him was on the front page of the *Daily Express* and he was washing dishes. He left me. I didn't leave him. Anyway, he was down here last week. I showed him the door.'

The album was released in December 1970 to good reviews, but, for an ex-Beatle, not record-breaking sales. George Harrison's three-disc solo album *All Things Must Pass* – which partly comprised new recordings of songs that John and Paul had turned down for the Beatles, and included the huge hit 'My Sweet Lord' – had been re-leased two weeks earlier and sold better. Not altogether surprisingly, John couldn't hide a little shard of jealousy that the reviewer in *Time* had called George a 'philosopher'. That was the role he thought he should play. Nor did he like it that George had been complaining in interviews that he and Paul had kept him in the background. 'I never stopped encouraging George,' he insisted incredulously to me in late 1970. 'When we began he could hardly open his mouth to sing. I kept telling him, "Open your fucking mouth . . ." And the reason we didn't do more of his songs is because they just weren't good enough. When they got better later on, we did them . . . So he must have learned something working all those years with Paul and me.'

He might have got his divorce from the Beatles, but, as in any marriage, what his former partners – and in this marriage there had been three – did or said, or what was even written about them, could quickly touch an unguarded nerve.

Yoko had recently suffered another miscarriage and John was showing a caring side to his nature. At the time, several newspaper writers and some of the Apple staff, not to mention millions of fans, struggled to see what he could see 'in this crazy Japanese woman'. She had bewitched him with her mysterious Oriental ways, went one theory. But, really, it was much more basic than that. She was a pal, and they amused and supported each other.

One afternoon, John contrasted, probably without realising it, the relationship he had with Yoko with the one he'd had with Cynthia.

'Normally an artist has someone from whom he can suck completely,' he said. 'He says, "I'm the artist. Where's my dinner?" And the other person has to be passive and quiet. But Yoko's an artist, too, so she helps me in another way.'

She was unconventional, intelligent, egotistical and just plain different. But she didn't mind being teased, and she made him laugh. They shared drugs, too. And then there was the sex – and other people to cook the dinner.

# 54

*'The radicalism was phoney, really, because it was out of guilt. I always felt guilty that I made money, so I had to give it away or lose it'*

When it came to returning favours, John remembered his friends, and he owed a big 'thank you' to Jann Wenner, the publisher of *Rolling Stone*, who had backed him loyally throughout the journalistic feeding frenzies of the *Two Virgins* and the Beatles break-up. So the beginning of December 1970 saw him and Yoko in New York publicising his new album – lawyers having found a reason for him to be granted another temporary US visa – and doing a long interview with *Rolling Stone*, including a photo session with the young Annie Leibovitz. Some of what he said that day he'd often expressed privately with 'not for publication' requests. But with *Rolling Stone* the prohibitions came off as he went on a long iconoclastic rant.

Of course, as was his nature, he exaggerated a lot. Not even he could have had sex with, as he boasted, 'a million chicks'; and did he honestly believe that 'Yoko's bottoms thing' was 'as important as *Sgt. Pepper*'? But that was John. When he was in an album-selling mood, the hyperbole bubbled, and, to give *Rolling Stone* its due, there had never before been such a lifting of the lid on any rock group. In a realpolitik sense, John wanted to find headlines in the world's newspapers when the next edition of *Rolling Stone* was published. And he got them.

There was, however, a selfish side to his outburst. That he confessed to his behaviour during Beatles tours as part of his destruction of their legend might, in his new desire for honesty, have been conscience-salving for him. But when he talked of 'orgies' and of tours being 'like Fellini's *Satyricon*', he wasn't just talking about himself. If the wives and partners of any of the other Beatles and their lieutenants had been in any doubt as to what might have happened when their boys were away, they weren't now. Did he ever pause to think about the wounds he might be opening? Or had his heroin use blunted his sensitivities, as he would later claim?

Apart from his visits with the Beatles, it was his first time in New York, the city that he called Yoko's 'old stomping ground', and he immediately felt at home, but slightly sheepish, as she showed him around Greenwich Village and introduced him to her old avant-garde friends. In London, it would be mainly John who would make the introductions, but in New York it was Yoko who led the way into the 'hip art world'. As Dan Richter, their assistant, expressed it: 'John wanted to be cool and accepted . . . as something more than a rock star. Yoko was his guide, his entrée . . . He was constantly trying to become more sophisticated.'

One of the routes to this was, John began to believe, in film-making. Yoko's *Bottoms* film had been a minor cause célèbre, so the two now planned to do a sequel. It was entitled *Up Your Legs Forever*, for which Allen Klein's most junior member of staff, a twenty-year-old called May Pang, contacted as many celebrities of the couple and friends as she could, and asked them to meet in a small studio where they would have their bare legs filmed. She found 364.5 pairs in all – Andy Warhol having agreed to join the project encouraging others, including actor George Segal, writer Tom Wolfe, Klein himself and someone with an artificial leg. The point of the film was never really apparent, but it amused John no end.

Yoko had been an early feminist, and now at her side (rather than Yoko being at his side), John would increasingly display the zeal of the convert about the exploitation of women – which was something that might, but evidently didn't, conflict with the plans he and Yoko had for another film they made called *Fly*. The idea for that movie was to follow in extreme close-up a fly walking around the naked body of a young woman. Several models were considered, the chosen one going professionally by the name of Virginia Lust – who appeared to be completely stoned throughout the filming. Presumably, Yoko believed that the viewers of the film would be so interested in the perambulations of the fly that they might not at first notice its location. Well, maybe . . .

It was, it seems, a difficult shoot. First the young woman's body was painted with honey to attract the fly, and discourage it from flying away. But when that didn't work it was decided to spray the insect with carbon monoxide, in the hope that when it woke it would start walking around. It didn't. Understudy flies came and went. As John watched, ever loyal to his wife, Yoko insisted that the fly be placed on the woman's toe. Then on her breast. Then on her . . .

At which point the cameraman, Steve Gebhardt, backed off. 'I can't do that,' he said. So Yoko put it there.

Dan Richter described the shooting of the scene in his book *The Dream Is Over*. 'For almost 24 hours . . . drugged flies . . . were staggering around Virginia Lust's naked body . . . from the hills of her breasts to the dark valley of her vagina.'

They had been married for almost two years when in January 1971, John and Yoko flew to Japan where the ex-Beatle was introduced to his wife's very conservative parents, who had now retired there. By arriving wearing a modish surplus military outfit, John didn't immediately endear himself to Mr Ono, but he had always got on with older women and Mrs Ono was soon charmed.

The couple, however, didn't stay long in Japan. Returning to England after just one week, John's next ventures would show him to be in almost faux revolutionary mood. As a performer, he needed the 'straight press' to reach the fans, but the youthful rebelliousness of the underground newspapers, with their small circulations, had always appealed to the romantic anarchist in him. And when the Oxford-educated writer and activist Tariq Ali, together with academic Robin Blackburn, asked to interview him for the far-left newspaper *Red Mole*, he was flattered.

He wasn't, however, particularly truthful. He would later refer to himself as 'a chameleon', although detractors might describe him as more of a 'cushion', in that he would, in this period of his life, increasingly begin to wear the imprint of the last person who sat on him – be it the Maharishi, Janov or Yoko. And it's impossible not to draw the conclusion that at least some of the things he said in the interview with *Red Mole* were said to impress what he saw as his intellectual interviewers with his underground political credibility, rather than give an honest account of his childhood.

For example, this assertion: 'It's pretty basic when you're brought up, like I was, to hate and fear the police as a natural enemy and to despise the army as something that takes everybody away and leaves them dead somewhere. I mean it's just a basic working-class thing . . .'

That was just baloney. He hadn't been brought up in a working-class home, and neither had Mimi raised him to regard the police as enemies. Nor was that a typical reflection of how most working-class British people viewed the police or the army. When, at an early gig, the Quarry Men had been frightened by a gang of Teddy boys, it had been a friendly, protective police constable who had escorted them safely to the bus stop so that they could make a getaway.

The truth was sometimes inconvenient, but John's revised version of his life would always go unchallenged by interviewers. Perhaps, on reflection, he realised that he'd gone too far in cosying up to his interviewers, because when he was put on the spot by Tariq Ali and asked how he thought 'we could destroy the capitalist system here in Britain', his response was simply to talk the talk and then make a new record.

It was called 'Power To The People' and released just a month after 'Instant Karma!', with a picture sleeve that showed him making a fist salute and wearing one of the white hard hats that the Japanese leftist Zengakuren protestors wore during anti-American demonstrations. It would be his least successful solo single so far.

Nearly a decade later, after a couple more self-reinventions, he would be honest enough to be dismissive of the way he'd been at that time. 'The radicalism was phoney, really, because it was out of guilt. I always felt guilty that I made money, so I had to give it away or lose it. I don't mean I was a hypocrite. When I believe, I believe right down to the roots. But, being a chameleon, I became whoever I was with.'

To another journalist he said: 'Tariq Ali kept coming around asking for money for *Red Mole* . . . I was rich . . . Any time anybody said anything like that, I would fork out. I wrote "Power To The People" as a sort of guilt song.'

Might another explanation have been that, with his own battles won, he found himself repeatedly welcoming the struggles of others in order to reinforce his own image of himself as being someone in permanent rebellion?

'What are you rebelling against, Johnny?' the Marlon Brando character is asked in the movie *The Wild One*.

To which he replies: 'Whaddya got?'

There was an echo in this line of John Lennon at this stage in his career?

*

Another kind of guilt, certainly a worry, may have been preying on Yoko's mind at that time. She'd had another miscarriage the previous summer, and perhaps that loss had brought home to her the fact that she already had a child, Kyoko, who was now seven, and whom she rarely saw. Finding herself unable to get in touch with her daughter, she discovered that Tony Cox had taken the little girl to the Mediterranean island of Majorca where he had enrolled on (coincidentally) a Maharishi meditation course.

In his eccentric way, Cox appears to have been a good father, and had always had more time to spend with Kyoko than had Yoko. But, now anxious to renew her access to her child, Yoko flew with John and a Spanish lawyer to Majorca where, without asking, they took Kyoko from the kindergarten where Cox had left her and returned with her to their hotel.

When Cox found out, he called the police, who arrested John and Yoko and took Kyoko into care. As the British newspapers caught up with the 'tug-of-love' story, and wrote that John and Yoko had been arrested for kidnap, Kyoko was handed back to her father, and it was agreed that the whole matter would be decided by the court the following month.

But when Yoko and John returned to Majorca a month later, clutching documents from Yoko's Virgin Islands divorce from Cox that stipulated 'shared custody', they found that Cox and the child were no longer there.

So it would go on, in a chase and search that would never end, as Tony Cox and Kyoko went back to America and disappeared.

John was never the kind of star to hang out in showbiz circles, mixing with Hollywood actors, glamorous actresses and hanger-on celebrities. In fact, throughout his career he avoided and mocked the tinsel and fake tan of fame. But when his and Yoko's film *Fly* was shown out of competition during the Cannes Film Festival in May, he broke the habit of a lifetime and flew down to the South of France.

John was long used to applause simply for existing, but the screening did not turn out to be an unalloyed happy experience. Dan Richter believed it had gone well, but others reported that European cineastes greeted it with catcalls and whistles, despite it having been cut by over an hour to just twenty-five minutes. Virginia Lust's zonked patience and the various flies' travails had, it seemed, been in vain.

John just shrugged. Once again, his money and fame hadn't result-ed in recognition for Yoko – whom he liked to call 'the world's most famous unknown artist' – so he would just keep on trying. Yoko, he insisted, was a genius. One day, he was determined, the world would know her as such.

When Michael de Freitas had jumped bail and avoided British justice by disappearing to Trinidad, John had given his wife Desiree and their children free lodging in the gatehouse at Tittenhurst Park. Now with the family reunited in Trinidad, John and Yoko flew to the island to visit them. By this time, John had to have been aware of de Freitas's violent reputation. But something inside him refused to believe it. Within a couple of years he would find himself forced to accept the truth.

# 55

*'"Imagine" is anti-religious, anti-conventional and anti-capitalist, but because it's sugar-coated, it's accepted'*

Sessions for *Imagine* began at the almost completed recording studios at Tittenhurst Park in June 1971. Yoko, as well as John, would be credited as one of the producers, along with Phil Spector – who brought the (very stoned) film star Dennis Hopper along with him on the first day. Being a producer was quite a promotion for Yoko, as her experience in the studio was minimal. That, however, didn't prevent her from sometimes telling very experienced musicians how they should play. George Harrison had agreed to be lead guitar for the basic band, and would turn up when necessary, and Alan White, who was soon to join Yes, was on drums. Klaus Voorman was again on bass, with top session player Nicky Hopkins at the keyboards.

Only ten tracks long, some of the songs that John chose for this second solo album had been around for some time, 'Jealous Guy' being a rewrite of a song he'd composed while in India, while 'Gimme Some Truth' had been tried at a Beatles *Let It Be* session. Altogether it was a mix of styles, and this time he *was* 'trying to make a bloody variety show', or at least something that would be popular. Although 'Oh Yoko!' was considered by EMI for a single, controversy would later rage around just two of the other songs. One was a soul number called 'How Do You Sleep?'

Relations with Paul had worsened since his former songwriting colleague's decision to ask the High Court to wind up the Beatles a few months earlier, and John had not taken well some silly digs about him and Yoko on Paul's album *Ram*. *'Too many people going underground . . . too many people preaching practices,'* Paul had sung. It was silly, but it was no big deal.

John's response was, however, vicious. Playing 'How Do You Sleep?' on the piano he was grinning with delight as he sang the words to George Harrison, as captured on the promotional documentary *Gimme*

*Some Truth: The Making of John Lennon's Imagine Album.* 'This is a nasty song,' we see him say. 'Think nasty.'

It was an unkind song. *'A pretty face may last a year or two, but pretty soon they'll see what you can do'* was one line, while another suggested that the only song of value that Paul had written alone was 'Yesterday'. There was much more, and Paul was understandably upset when he heard it. It could, however, have been a lot worse, had Allen Klein not explained that John was laying himself wide open to a very damaging libel action if he didn't change one of the lines. He did.

Not only was it unpleasant, it was also a self-revelatory own goal, demonstrating as it did John's continuing jealousy of Paul's good looks, as well as his prevailing envy of the younger man's gift for melody. While a gratuitous dig at Linda, suggesting that she wore the trousers in the McCartney house, was deeply ironic. If any of the Beatles had a demanding wife, it was John himself.

Nine years later, he regretted the lyrics – 'they just came out of my mouth', he would say. 'I wasn't really feeling that vicious . . . I used my resentment and withdrawing from the Beatles and the relationship with Paul to write a song.' It was a pretty lame excuse. Had the title song of the album not been one of his most commercial ever, 'How Do You Sleep?' might have been the album's most memorable track. Nothing, however, could top 'Imagine'. With a litany of suggestions for brotherly love, it captured the moment that year and for many more to come. The music and words had come quickly, and had been inspired, John said, by 'instructions' that Yoko had written in her book *Grapefruit* which began with the word 'imagine . . .'.

'Imagine letting a goldfish swim across the sky . . .' was one of them. From this John fashioned *'Imagine there's no heaven, it's easy if you try . . .'* The song was, in his words, 'anti-religious, anti-conventional and anti-capitalist, but because it's sugar-coated, it's accepted'. By sugar-coated he meant that it had a pretty tune and an almost churchy piano feel. It was recorded quickly in just three takes, the second version being chosen for release.

He knew when he wrote it that he'd come up with something special. But it was always good to get an outsider's opinion. So, a few weeks later, just after the album was completed, he took me to his and Yoko's bedroom and played me some of the tracks on an acetate he'd had cut.

He began with 'Gimme Some Truth'. 'This,' he said, 'will be the new single.'

I tried to hide it, but I wasn't very impressed. It sounded like a rant to me, rather than a hit. 'What's on the other side?' I asked.

Then John turned the acetate over and played me 'Imagine'.

'Surely that should be the A-side,' I said as it ended.

John looked across at Yoko who was sitting on the bed. 'Yoko, Ray thinks "Imagine" should be the single.'

'Oh, good,' she said. 'I like that one, too.'

Neither gave so much as a hint that they'd known all along what the A-side of the single was going to be, and that *Imagine* would be the name of the album. Presumably John had wanted to test his own opinion on someone who hadn't been involved in the recording.

The film that was made during the sessions is both cringe-making, in that it includes some staged sections of John and Yoko in matador hats and cloaks running around the gardens pretending in pop video fashion that they have lost each other, and fascinating in that it reveals several facets of John's character. There's his quickness while at work in the studio, his unpleasant impatience when the engineer screws up, and, in contrast, his patience with Yoko's interruptions.

But there is something else in the film that hadn't been planned but which, in retrospect, would look significantly ominous. In a break during recording a young American hippy in a sheepskin coat turned up at the door wanting to talk to John about the messages in the Beatles' lyrics. Normally he would have been kept well away by Mal Evans, who was there acting as a minder, but John wasn't opposed to meeting the young man.

It was a touching moment caught on film, as the scruffy and lonely young man asked John if he was thinking of anyone in particular when he wrote 'Carry That Weight'.

That song, John explained, had been written by Paul. But even if it hadn't . . . 'I'm just a guy who writes songs . . . Don't confuse the songs with your own life.' If the songs meant something to other people that was good, but he was only writing about himself, his feelings and his own experiences.

Disappointment and confusion washed over the young man's face as he was told bluntly by the man he idolised that he had been wasting his time. He couldn't answer.

'Are you hungry?' John asked finally.

The reply was inaudible.

'Let's get him something to eat,' John said, and led the young, confused stranger into his house.

Those weeks during and after the recording of *Imagine* were as cosy a time as there would ever be at Tittenhurst Park, and one day when a Hare Krishna group turned up they were given a cottage in which to live, and the job of painting a little temple on the estate.

'They're all ex-druggies, but they're all right,' John told me when I asked about them.

At first everything went well and the lodgers would ghost around the grounds chanting 'Peace, man', 'Hare Krishna', 'Peace', whenever they passed anyone.

Then, suddenly, they were gone. 'What happened to the Hare Krishna people?' I asked the next time I was there.

John grinned. 'Oh, I had to show them the door. They were driving me mad with all that chanting of "Hare Krishna" and "Peace" all the time. I couldn't get any peace.'

A new Saturday night TV chat show, hosted by Michael Parkinson, started that summer on BBC1, and because I knew Parkinson I was asked if I might help with suggestions for guests. I suggested John and Yoko.

Parkinson was keen but, illustrating how far John had slipped in mainstream public interest in Britain, the producer was worried. Three years earlier he would have gone down on his knees to get John Lennon on a chat show. But now? 'What if they both get into a bag and won't come out?' he fretted. Or if they just want to talk about peace or beddism or turn up in their pyjamas or do some crazy avant-garde thing like taking their clothes off . . . ?

I assured him that wouldn't be the case and that John could be very funny when he wanted to be.

Finally, the go-ahead was given.

My assumption had been that the whole show should be given over to a John and Yoko interview. But at the last minute the producer decided that he daren't risk it. Film actor Trevor Howard was booked for the second half of the show, presumably on the basis that if John and Yoko did do something too zany their interview could be quickly terminated. So, John became the warm-up act instead of the main attraction. Now, that *was* crazy!

As I expected, John was on top form, and kept the studio audience laughing throughout. So, it was with some chagrin that halfway through the programme host Michael Parkinson had to apologise that they had run out of time, thank John and Yoko for coming and promise that they would have more time on another occasion.

There never would be another occasion.

By 1971 satellite television had shrunk the world. And when a new and bloody conflict erupted in what had been East Pakistan but was now struggling to be born as the new country of Bangladesh amid a terrible cyclone which added floods, starvation and a mass exodus, its showing on the TV news every night pricked consciences. Conflicted geopolitical interests stayed the hands of the nations who might have helped most, but music was non-political. So when Bengali sitarist Ravi Shankar telephoned his friend George Harrison and asked if there was anything he could do to help, a new movement was begun as George found himself arranging the biggest concentration of rock stars ever to appear on stage together on behalf of the Bangladeshi victims. It was the most laudable of aims, and would be copied several more times during the next forty years.

The plan was that two concerts would be held in New York at Madison Square Garden on 1 August 1971, and, naturally enough, one of the first friends George invited to join him was John. Thinking it might turn into a Beatles reunion, which was the last thing he wanted, John was unsure at first. But when word came that Paul would definitely not be there, John agreed to appear alongside Bob Dylan, Ringo Starr, Eric Clapton, Leon Russell, Badfinger, Billy Preston, Ravi Shankar and George himself.

As plans were rapidly put into place for the concerts, John was staying with Yoko in the Park Lane Hotel on Central Park South, with Yoko's sister, Setsuko, flying over from university in Switzerland to join them there. Everyone was excited. But then, it all went wrong. George had invited only John to appear on stage. He didn't want Yoko's style of music in his charity show. He didn't like it. It wouldn't fit. The concert was billed as 'George Harrison and Friends'. He didn't consider Yoko to be one of his friends.

Yoko, however, had always assumed that she would be included;

and that the all-powerful John Lennon would persuade George to let her sing. John was torn. He wanted to be loyal to his wife, but he could see George's point of view, too. Inevitably he and George fell out over it and John returned to his suite to give Yoko the bad news. She erupted. She was a strong woman and she didn't take defeat easily. John, she felt, hadn't fought hard enough for her.

They rowed for hours, with John throwing furniture around, before, unable to face the situation any longer, he simply walked away from it. Calling a taxi, he went to the airport and caught the first plane to Paris, leaving Yoko, who still believed that George would back down, behind.

Only the next afternoon did Yoko admit defeat. On Allen Klein's advice, she flew back to London. The following day, she and John, now both back at Tittenhurst Park, were reconciled, and put out a story that they had always intended to be in England for the British publication of Yoko's book *Grapefruit* the following week. No mention of the row was made by either. They decided upon a story and stuck to it, although they both knew that it wasn't true. The rewriting of history would always be a feature of their relationship. Having settled on a version of events that best suited them and the way they told their lives as a perfect, if unconventional, love story, they would stick to it, with any blemishes or inconsistencies painted out.

It was a pity that John missed George's Concert for Bangla Desh. He would have enjoyed it and his presence would have enhanced it. But it was better for George that he wasn't there. It was a momentous moment when rock music found a new and benevolent purpose, and when George, for so long a junior partner in the Beatles, finally came of age. Had John been beside him on stage, he might once again have been eclipsed.

John and Yoko stayed at Tittenhurst Park for only a few more weeks. Despite the mountain of money John had spent on the house and gardens, the two had never really settled. Yoko was bored there as she'd been bored when they'd lived together at Kenwood. She was a metropolitan woman. And John, too, always liked to be where the action was.

In August 1971, he and Yoko returned to New York. That was the place to be, the city Yoko thought of as home. By leaving England

# 56

*'America is the Roman Empire and New York
is Rome itself. New York is at my speed'*

From the moment he and Yoko moved into their several suites on the seventeenth floor of the St Regis Hotel on East 55th Street, John was in love with New York. He loved the constant rattle of the city, the energy, the mix of peoples, the architecture and basically the whole twenty-four-hours-a-day feel to the place, where television never closed down. As he would often say: 'If I'd lived in Roman times, I'd have lived in Rome. Where else? Today America is the Roman Empire and New York is Rome itself. New York is at my speed.'

And, with the *Imagine* album released on 9 September, and the single already on the disc jockeys' playlists, he found, almost as he had in 1964 when the Beatles had first arrived in America, that his voice was once again all over the radio stations. It was a terrific way to be welcomed to his new home and for him to start a new life.

'It was Yoko who sold me on New York,' he would later romanticise. 'She'd been poor here and she knew every inch. She made me walk around the streets and parks and squares and examine every nook and cranny. In fact, you could say I fell in love with New York on a street corner.'

He was exaggerating again. Although they bought a couple of bikes to get around on, John and Yoko were never far away from a limousine. Nevertheless, he was hooked on New York as he had never been on London, and straight away he and Yoko set about establishing themselves, not as a rock star and his arty wife, but as an avant-garde film-making couple.

As the trunks began arriving from Tittenhurst Park, the extra suites they'd taken in the St Regis started to fill with newspapers, magazines, bundles of fan mail and posters, as well as film editing and video equipment and a copying machine. Soon staff were hired to stage-manage their various projects, and, as John luxuriated in

America's openness to them, other guests in the hotel, such as film stars Fred Astaire and Jack Palance, agreed to make fleeting appearances in their films. 'Look at this,' he said to me as he picked up a letter off the pile. 'A university in Tennessee is offering me sixty thousand dollars just to talk. *Just to talk!* I don't even have to bother singing. It's unbelievable. Invitations like this come every day.'

One such invitation, for Yoko, actually – although he knew that he was the real draw – had already been accepted. It was for a retrospective of her work called *This Is Not Here*, to be mounted at the Everson Art Museum at Syracuse in upstate New York. There was a problem, however. Most of Yoko's art had been in the form of 'instructions' and 'happenings', like bagism, where a few people would sit around and watch as she got into a bag. There had been a few films, admittedly, but not all of them were suitable to be shown to the general public. Her *Bottoms* movie might be all right but John's penis in *Self Portrait* was unlikely to get past the artistic board at the museum. How best, then, to fill the massive amount of space being offered by the museum?

As she told me, 'You don't need to be an artist to make art . . . it's just a frame of mind', the solution was to write to every famous person John and Yoko knew and invite them to make an offering as a guest artist in what were described as 'water pieces'. John himself set the pace with a joke – a plastic bag filled with water that he entitled *Napoleon's Bladder*; George Harrison sent a milk bottle and Bob Dylan a copy of his *Nashville Skyline* album in a fish tank. There were, of course, some of Yoko's greatest hits, too – her *Eternal Clock*, which had no hands, and an all-white and therefore unplayable chess set.

But mostly there was a lot of water, and, on the day the exhibition opened, thousands of students, most of whom had probably never been to an art exhibition in their lives before, invaded the gallery hoping to see a Beatle. They did. John, on his thirty-first birthday, was everywhere promoting his wife.

'I've bet Yoko a thousand dollars that before the end of this year somebody somewhere will write an article which really understands her work,' he told me. 'I don't mean any of that intellectual bullshit that I've had about my albums by people who like them but don't understand them. I mean an article by someone who really knows what he or she is talking about. If nobody writes it, I'll have to write it myself.'

To watch him that day, hurrying about mingling with students, was to see the needy side of him. No longer was he John Lennon the famous rock star. He was John the would-be intellectual, hustling for his wife, almost ingratiating himself as academics from the University of Syracuse hung about hoping to catch his Beatle eye.

Only Yoko could judge whether or not the exhibition was the success she'd hoped – but it probably wasn't. With so much water sloshing about on the floor, a lot of people got wet, and some of the fans, in student guise, couldn't help but take home some of the guest artists' entries as souvenirs of the day that John Lennon went to Syracuse.

The following day, putting on his protest hat, and followed by a caravan of TV, radio and print media, John insisted on visiting a tiny Native American reservation of the Onondaga Nation who, he'd been told, were fighting plans to build an extra lane to a highway that ran through their land. It may have sounded a little patronising when, as he was buying up the village shop of souvenirs, he told his surprised hosts that as a boy he'd 'always pretended to be an Indian' when he'd played Cowboys and Indians in the back garden in Menlove Avenue. But he really had, as Mimi remembered.

He may not have got the Onondaga on to *The Dick Cavett Show* as he wanted, but his visit didn't hurt. The extra lane on the highway was never built. If there was one thing John knew a lot about, it was the power of publicity.

He could hardly have done more to promote Yoko's career and to be seen to be loving with her in public, but she knew about the sharp side of his tongue, too. While the St Regis Hotel was a useful base for a couple of months, what the couple really needed was a proper home in New York. So, hearing that there might be an apartment available in the stately Dakota building on Central Park West, John put on a suit and tie in order to be interviewed by the reputedly stuffy co-op board of directors who decided who could live there.

Yoko, unfortunately, didn't know about their conservatism. As John and I were talking while he waited for her to get ready, she suddenly emerged from the bedroom wearing a pair of floral hot pants and a blouse with the top three buttons undone.

John exploded. 'You look like a tart, a fucking whore,' he raged, his temper out of all proportion to the situation. And then, since I had a friend who lived in the same block and knew the nature of the place, he turned to me for support. 'Tell her, Ray.'

She didn't need telling. Without a word, or indeed a change of expression, she went back into the bedroom to return a few minutes later wearing a demurely long skirt.

They didn't find a new home at the Dakota that day, and they would soon move down to the West Village where they rented a sparsely furnished apartment on Bank Street from one of the Lovin' Spoonful. But a volatile side to their relationship had been exposed. John had lost none of the temper with which he used to upset Cynthia. But Yoko, though she may have got the dress code wrong, knew how to handle it.


Astonishingly, although 'Imagine' was the biggest solo hit of his career, John was so bound up with his new life in New York he wasn't aware that it hadn't even been released as a single in the UK. A decade earlier, getting into the charts had been his greatest ambition. Now, Britain was history for him.

What he did want was a Christmas hit with a peace message, so, casually borrowing the off-the-shelf melody of the eighteenth-century folk song 'Stewball', he wrote 'Happy Xmas (War Is Over)', which he recorded with Yoko and the children of the Harlem Community Choir. It wasn't one of his best songs, and it wasn't the hit in the US that he'd hoped for, but for well over four decades it would be a December staple in supermarkets and shopping malls. It would, however, mark a turning point for him. With the exception of 'Imagine', which would be finally released as a single in the UK in 1975, four years after he'd recorded it, 'Happy Xmas (War Is Over)' would, in 1971, be the last hit he would have in Britain in his lifetime. It wasn't just that as he lost interest in Britain, British fans began to lose interest in him. In popular songwriting terms he was, as Cynthia would say, 'losing his mojo'.

Why? Was it because tastes were changing? Or was his mind not on the day job any more, as he spent less time with musicians and more with others in New York who had attached themselves? With the Beatles, and even afterwards, there had been the stimulus of his old pals – musicians he trusted who weren't afraid to tell him what they thought, and who, by their very presence in the studio, acted as editors of his work, as Paul had done par excellence. For years he'd turned to Ringo after each vocal take, or after he'd run through a new song, to get the drummer's opinion. He would always insist that Yoko was a brilliant musical partner – 'Why should I work with Paul McCartney when I have Yoko to work with?' he would always tell me. But, whatever her talents in other fields, Yoko couldn't begin to fill the void in John's creative life that had opened when he'd ripped apart the band he'd started.

Nor could any of his new American friends. There were several, from David Peel, a Lower East Side street entertainer who would amuse with an album that John produced called *The Pope Smokes Dope*, to avant-garde film-maker Jonas Mekas. While at the other end of the social spectrum was Dick Cavett, who would later become a useful ally.

From the day John and Yoko made New York their base, noisiest of all their new pals were Abbie Hoffman and Jerry Rubin, a couple of sometimes jokey counterculture Yippie activists who had achieved nationwide notoriety during the anti-war demonstration at the Democratic National Convention in Chicago in 1968. Like Robin Blackburn and Tariq Ali before them, they saw John as a useful rallying tool for their anti-establishment programme, and, as others had found, John could be easily led when flattered.

He'd always liked to reminisce about when he'd been at art college in Liverpool, but, at that stage in his life, student politics and political revolt had largely passed him by as his total focus then had been on music. Now, as Hoffman and Rubin successfully tapped into the inner rebel on the seventeenth floor of the St Regis Hotel, or when playing at being a bohemian down in the Village, he would take to the streets as he had never felt able to do in London.

It was all radical chic, but soon, with him and Yoko wearing black berets, he was taking part in a freedom rally, and writing and singing a song about a guy called John Sinclair who had been given a three-year jail sentence for possession of marijuana. 'It ain't fair, John Sinclair,' the ex-Beatle sang. It wasn't fair. Sinclair was released three days later.

A riot at Attica State Prison near Buffalo, New York, that had left twenty-nine prisoners and ten guards dead was his next theme, which he sang about on David Frost's TV show. He was the sermonising darling of the moment in New York and he was relishing it. So, when he was approached by the Northern Aid Committee in the US, more usually known as NORAID, which he believed raised money for the widows and orphans of Republicans involved in the Troubles in Northern Ireland, his instinct was, as always, to give.

It was a mistake. It was now 1972, and by getting involved in Northern Ireland he was treading on blood and uncertain ground. The sectarian bombings, murders and reprisals between militant republicans and equally militant unionist paramilitary groups were complicated and growing ever more violent. According to the BBC, in that year alone 470 ordinary people would be killed and almost 5,000 injured in 1,382 terrorist bomb explosions.

John, who still wore his pacifist colours loudly and proudly, would say that he was told that no money he gave to NORAID would go to the IRA to buy guns and explosives. That might well have been the case. But how could he be sure? He couldn't. He got a roasting from the British press when the story got out.

It was another example of John's naivety, of his being a soft touch and leading with his heart rather than his head. Ireland has a special place in the collective memory of many Liverpudlians, and, like many people in that city, John had Irish ancestors. But he had followed his emotions without taking the time to fully understand the complexity of the situation. In the event, when he was asked to do a benefit show for Republicans in Dublin, he scrambled for impartial ground and replied that he would do one only if he could do another the following week for the Unionist side. After that the idea didn't go any further and he would say nothing more publicly about Ireland.

Nor did he have much to say when he learned that Michael de Freitas, for whom he had put up bail money in London but who had slipped away to Trinidad before his trial, had now been arrested there for a murder. Before de Freitas had left the UK, his Black House project had been gutted by fire. When his new commune in Trinidad had also been set alight, police investigated and discovered two freshly dug graves in the grounds. One contained the body of an associate of de Freitas, Michael Skerritt, and the other that of a young English woman, Gale Ann Benson, the daughter of a Conservative MP. They had both been hacked to death, with Benson, who was in a relationship with a cousin of de Freitas, an American called Hakim Jamal, having been buried while she was still breathing. By the time the police arrived, Michael de Freitas had escaped to Guyana, but he was soon captured and returned to Trinidad to face trial. Despite the enormity of the alleged crimes, John would loyally, but quietly, pay the fees of the defence lawyer.

Back in New York, John had something closer to home to engage his thoughts. His phone was being tapped. When he first mentioned it to me in 1972, I thought he was being paranoid. He sometimes was, but not this time. Richard Nixon's government, however, were. Abbie Hoffman and Jerry Rubin had been high on the FBI watch list for four years, and, with a new Presidential election due in 1972, the last thing the Nixon administration wanted was John Lennon going across the country whipping up dissent among students and young people. And, importantly, the 1972 election would include eighteen-year-olds for the first time – not a naturally pro-Nixon age group.

So, when the rumour got around that a huge anti-war demonstration was being planned for the Republican Convention to be held in San Diego that summer, and that a performance by John was to be the magnet, it worried the FBI. It didn't matter that John had no intention of appearing there, let alone of whipping up a demo crowd, it was time for the FBI to start surveillance on him with a view to having him deported. Pushed by H. R. Haldeman, an assistant to Nixon at the White House, and right-wing Republican senator Strom Thurmond, the FBI tried, but they couldn't do it.

With the help of a clever and expensive immigration lawyer called Leon Wildes, John and Yoko always got the necessary extensions to their visas. And, as they sat through several Immigration and Naturalization Service hearings and Wildes would tell again and again how they needed to be in America in order to find Yoko's missing daughter Kyoko, it began to occur to them that what they really needed was permanent residence in the US.

John had always been good at getting the public on his side through the media. So, when Dick Cavett gave his whole show on ABC over to him and Yoko, it was the perfect opportunity to speak directly to the public.

'I felt followed everywhere by government agents,' he told Cavett in his half-jokey, conversational style. 'Every time I picked up the phone, there was a lot of noise [a sign that the call was being overheard] . . . I'd open the door and there'd be guys standing on the other side of the street. I'd get in the car and they'd be following me and not hiding . . . They wanted me to see that I was being followed . . .'

Of course, Cavett wanted him to sing as well as talk, so John promptly surprised a goodly section of the watching audience by singing 'Woman Is The Nigger Of The World'. It was a song based on a quote given by Yoko to women's magazine *Nova* in the UK in 1968, and knowing how controversial it would be, John neatly prefaced it by explaining that Irish republican James Connolly had once said 'the female worker is the slave of the slave'.

Before the show ABC had been worried about the use of the 'N' word. But there were no protests about it. When the song had been released as a single a couple of months earlier it had been banned from most radio stations and hadn't sold. So now John was hoping that it would be given a second chance when it became the lead song on his new album *Some Time In New York City*.

Again he was to be disappointed. The new album, a hastily concocted collection of the protest songs he'd written and recorded while living in New York, was savaged by the critics, who found the lyrics mostly trite. It would sell just a tenth as many copies in its first year of release as *Imagine* had. Ironically the best song and easily the best track was 'Woman Is the Nigger Of The World', with its second-line lyric *'if you don't believe me, just look at the one you're with'*. But it would remain a song that would be rarely heard.

It was a setback. John would later deride the songs of that period as 'journalism' when what he did best was 'poetry', but he'd never really known failure in records before. It hurt.

For the first time in his career, he began to feel alone and unsure. He still kept in touch with Neil and Mal, but Apple in the UK had become little more than a collecting house for royalties. His main contact with the record world was now Allen Klein at his ABKCO office in New York. But Klein, the man he'd championed as the saviour of the Beatles' finances and to whom he'd given his psychedelically painted Rolls-Royce, didn't seem so attractive any more. Although the manager had undoubtedly improved the Beatles' royalty deals, there was disquiet among all four of them about how much Klein was paying himself out of their earnings. And George was now fretting about income from his Bangladesh concert that had gone Klein's way in expenses. Law suits would inevitably soon follow.

As the FBI surveillance continued, John began drawing away from Hoffman and Rubin as he realised that he was more valuable to them than they were to him. As he would admit a few years later, they had been pretty well the first people to get in touch with him when he'd first gone to live in New York, after which he'd become swept up in their enthusiasm. It was time to end the relationship, but not before attending one last party at Jerry Rubin's apartment on the night of Nixon's re-election landslide victory on 7 November 1972.

It was a bitter evening for everyone there. The enemy had won. And then, after drinking far too much, and already high on cocaine, John lost control of his behaviour.

# 57

*'Listen, Phil, if you're going to kill me, kill me.
But don't fuck with my ears. I need them'*

John got very drunk at the party. There was a girl there. He took her into a room and had sex with her. Everyone knew what was going on. It was the room where all the coats had been left on the bed. It was late. People wanted to go home, but they couldn't get their coats. That, in a nutshell, was what Yoko told me some time later, in a call from New York. 'It was,' she said, 'very embarrassing.'

'Embarrassing' wasn't the word that most wives would have chosen to describe the situation. But most wives aren't Yoko. She'd long known that when John got drunk he would begin to behave irrationally and could be sometimes violent, and for this reason she always limited the amount of alcohol in their apartment. But there was no limit on drinks and drugs at the party in the Village. Other partygoers that night would say that they tried to calm John down, that he was blabbering and shouting and pushing them off, before he disappeared into the bedroom with the young lady. Exactly what Yoko was feeling, other than embarrassment and probably anger, is impossible to say. While she would always be happily indiscreet about events in her life that others might have tried to hide about their own lives, she rarely explained her emotions. When I sympathised, the most she would say to me was: 'John can be very hard to live with sometimes.' Cynthia had known all about that.

The following day John was full of remorse. But a line had been crossed. After nearly five years together – literally together, night and day – the myth of perfect love that the two had woven around themselves, 'like Cathy and Heathcliff' as Yoko liked to say, had been shattered.

But what were they going to do about it? They didn't know. The allure of being a bohemian living in the East Village had gone for John. Becoming involved in that scene had been largely at Yoko's behest. The area had always appealed more to her than it had to him. Anyway, the apartment on Bank Street was too small. Nor did John want to hang out with Rubin and Hoffman and their friends any more.

Since the scattering of the Apple staff upon Allen Klein's arrival in London, Brian Epstein's former right-hand man Peter Brown was now living in New York and working for impresario Robert Stigwood. Invited to Peter's apartment on Central Park West one afternoon, John and Yoko enthused at the view it provided. That, John decided on the spot, was the view they should have.

There were no apartments available in the block in which Peter Brown lived. But one was available in the building next door, the huge, brooding, gargoyle-adorned building on the corner of West 72nd Street – the Dakota, the late-nineteenth-century mansion block they'd first visited eighteen months earlier. With Leonard Bernstein, the critic Rex Reed and Gloria Swanson as neighbours, and a guard on the door to keep the fans at bay, it was one of the most fashionable and secure addresses in New York. They set up home in the Dakota in February 1973 – just a few weeks after the incident at the party. They would be happy there, they thought.

They were wrong. The problem was within themselves. John would spend hours sleeping or staring mutely at the TV, or tinkering list-lessly with his guitar, wondering why he wasn't able to function in the way he used to. Even Yoko was losing interest in her projects, closing down a film she had planned with her friend Dan Richter. The visa problem didn't help, and, though it might seem impossible to believe considering the millions the Beatles had generated, there were money problems, too. Since Paul had taken the other Beatles to court in 1970 to break up their legal relationship, the band's joint income had been frozen in the hands of a receiver nominated by the court. That meant that vast sums from royalties were mounting up for all four, but it wasn't money they could get their hands on. John was rich, for sure, but until the legal differences were resolved, and they were numerous, he had a cash-flow problem – at least, if he wanted to spend cash in the way he, and especially Yoko, liked.

That was irksome enough for someone who was used to never con-sidering the cost of anything. But the real problem for the two was that the dazzle had gone out of their lives, their marriage and their sex. They were suffocating each other.

They talked about their marital problems, about the girl at the party and John's unsated sex drive. Yoko would say later that she suggested that perhaps he should go out with other women, if that was what he wanted. She would understand. John felt he needed to get away, but he couldn't go alone. He always had to have someone at his side. So they discussed who he might go away with. Mal Evans, the faithful roadie whom John never criticised, was now living in Los Angeles, so he was a suggestion.

But Yoko had a better idea. What about May? May Pang, the pretty young woman they'd met when she worked for Allen Klein, but who now worked full time for them at the Dakota? John liked May, Yoko pointed out. Everyone liked May. Twenty-two years old in her jeans, T-shirt and big round glasses, she was always busy, cheerful and willing, as bright as a button and, as Paul would say, 'the voice of common sense'. She was also very efficient. What she wasn't, having been brought up in a Chinese immigrant family, was an expensively educated, sophisticated, elite posh girl.

John was excited by the suggestion, but he left it to Yoko to make the first move on May. At the time, John was writing songs for a new album, which would become *Mind Games*, and May had been delegated by Yoko to help him.

Then one morning, as May would record in her memoir *Loving John*, Yoko made her suggestion. According to May, the conversation, which might sound like a scene from a movie, but which tallies very closely with what Yoko told me, went like this. 'Listen, May, John and I are not getting along . . . John will probably start going out with other people. Who knows who he will go out with? I know he likes you a lot. So . . . ?'

May would write later that she was stunned by the proposal. She was out of her depth. It seemed wrong. John was her boss, and he was married. Unwittingly she'd become caught up in the games of this older, much more experienced, worldly wise couple: 'I'd been trained to believe that men like John, men who were talented and famous, never picked women like me. We worked for men like John. We did not have affairs with them,' she would say.

She batted back the proposition. But, she says, Yoko persisted. To her it seemed a logical, happy solution that the two should get together.

'Don't worry about a thing,' Yoko told the assistant. 'It's cool. I'll take care of everything.'

A few nights later, at Yoko's continued encouragement, May went to the studio with John and, when recording was over, allowed him to go back with her to her apartment and went to bed with him.

Yoko was so delighted with the arrangement that, shortly after John's album was delivered to Capitol Records and she had to go to a feminist convention in Chicago for a few days, she suggested that May move into the Dakota while she was away. It would be more convenient for her and John, she told the young assistant.

In the event, it turned out to be more convenient for the new lovers to run away to Los Angeles, John's excuse to himself being that he was going to help Ringo with an album. From that moment John and May would be together for the best part of the next eighteen months.

That Yoko had so casually arranged for her husband to take a mistress astonished not only May. But for Yoko, it made perfect sense. Some upper-class wives in Japan, as in many other cultures, had traditionally welcomed a mistress into the family home. Yoko might be a feminist, but she was now following a long tradition. If the pain of John's escape to California with May hurt her, it wasn't something she ever admitted. On the contrary, she would always say that it was she who sent John and May to Los Angeles. That was what she told me.

That isn't how May remembers the episode. But then, much of what happened during the following year and a half is murky. It depends upon whose interpretation of events, and the motivations of the principal players in the ménage, we want to believe. In May's eyes, Yoko's pride couldn't abide that word might get around that she'd been abandoned by her husband for a pretty younger woman. It was important to her that she was seen to be in control.

As for John, he'd been given permission to enjoy himself. He was off the leash. He'd been married for virtually all his adult life. Now he felt like a teenager again, with a girl, actually not long out of her teens, who liked nothing so much as to talk about and listen to rock and roll music.

In fact, as May soon began to realise, he wasn't off the leash at all. As she and John settled into the Los Angeles rock and roll lifestyle, Yoko would phone regularly, morning and night, sometimes over a dozen times a day, reminding May that her job was to make John happy, to take care of him and keep a careful watch so that he didn't get into any trouble. That was how Yoko saw the affair. May was just doing a job.

Yoko would say that John phoned her a lot, too. Quite what he thought Yoko's motivations might have been for suggesting his relationship with May is uncertain. He knew that she had a crush on a guitarist with whom she had been working. Was she secretly thinking that if she and John had an open marriage she could have an affair of her own? That was what he implied in a phone conversation with his old friend Pete Shotton.

At first, John enjoyed a holiday in Los Angeles with May, living in an apartment owned by his lawyer, Harold Seider, but soon he wanted to get back to work. With the release of the movie *American Graffiti* a rock and roll revival was taking place, and he wanted to be a part of it. Reverting to his old life as a rock and roller, a new album of the kind of songs he'd started out playing in Liverpool seemed to be the way in. And who better to produce the album than the most famous rock producer of them all, Phil Spector?

When Yoko was told of Spector's involvement, she was immediately, and not without cause, alarmed. May was worried too, and didn't like the guy. 'Into the jaws of the dragon,' John joked as he and May first visited Spector's house. But, although he would secretly call Spector 'the Vampire', and Yoko continued to warn him against the producer, he insisted on working with him and gave him 'total control' over the album. He liked what Spector had done with *Imagine*. He wanted another hit like that.

However, no sooner had recording begun than things started to go wrong. Beatle sessions under George Martin had been closed affairs of hard work, but with Spector, on his home patch of Los Angeles, the studio soon became open house. Star friends like Cher, or Joni Mitchell who turned up one night with Warren Beatty and on another with Jack Nicholson, would drop by to chat, and of course to meet John Lennon. Once the place where Charlie Chaplin had made his films, the studio at A&M Records was set up to take only eight musicians, but at one time May counted twenty-seven – including Steve Cropper from Memphis, Leon Russell and virtuoso guitarist Jesse Ed Davis. And with Phil Spector displaying every facet of his hysterical megalomania, the drink never stopped flowing.

Now May was to discover the Jekyll and Hyde effect that drink could have on her lover-boss. Angry that every song was taking so long to record as Spector demanded take after take of the musicians, the longer John waited to sing, the drunker he got. One night after becoming involved in a heated argument with the producer, he drank so much he was in no fit state to record.

With the help of a bodyguard, Spector got John into a car and drove him to the Bel Air house of another rock producer, Lou Adler, where John and May were living while Adler was away. The argument then turned into a fight before Spector and the bodyguard settled it by dragging John up to the bedroom, tying him up hand and foot, taking off his glasses and leaving, telling May not to release him until he was sober. Inevitably John broke free, and, as May ran down the lane to the nearby Bel Air Hotel seeking help, he trashed the house, pulling down and smashing platinum albums from Lou Adler's walls. 'Taking his glasses off was the worst thing they could have done,' May remembers. 'He was blind without them and in the dark, too.'

The following morning he was mortified, frighteningly unable to remember what he'd done. When Yoko learned what had happened she blamed May for not doing her job properly and letting John drink. But how could May have stopped him? Yoko had been right about Spector's malign influence. When John had recorded with him in England, it had been at his home where he had been in control.

The sessions struggled on. It bothered May that Spector wore a gun in a shoulder holster, but John was convinced that the bullets in it were blank. Then one night, a provoked Spector pulled out the gun, waved it above his head and pulled the trigger. Bang! The bullet had been real, and it lodged in the ceiling. Shaken, John tried to make a joke of it. 'Listen, Phil, if you're going to kill me, kill me. But don't fuck with my ears. I need them.'

With Yoko on the phone from New York more and more often demanding progress reports – or, in Yoko's version of events, John calling her frequently for reassurance – his behaviour continued to be unpredictable. As fond as he was of May, and even Yoko never denied that, on one occasion he had sex with a groupie and ordered May back to New York. Deeply upset, she went, but when she arrived there Yoko took her out to dinner and asked her to return to Los Angeles to take care of her husband. He needed her to nurse him through these moments, Yoko insisted. So May, looking more like a

Californian rock chick with every day that passed, was now a nurse as well as an assistant and girlfriend.

May did as she was told. She was in love with John. It was, she would later reflect, a crazy lifestyle in which she didn't know from one moment to the next where she stood.

The sessions continued but soon there would be headlines about how a drunken John had been thrown out of the Troubadour nightclub with a sanitary towel strapped to his forehead. This was followed by more stories about how he ruined a Smothers Brothers comeback performance by constant heckling with his friend Harry Nilsson. He would be embarrassed to see the *Los Angeles Times* the next day.

Usually, John's anger would be directed towards others, but at lunch one day when he thought May had been flirting with David Cassidy, he violently berated her. She denied it, but, enraged with the jealousy that was never far away, he accused her of being with him only because she wanted his money, ending a tirade of abuse by smashing her glasses and telling her that their relationship was over, and that they must go back to New York. May wouldn't have known it, but it was almost a rerun of how he had verbally threatened and thrown his father out of the home he had provided for him three years earlier.

Twenty-four hours later John and May were in New York again, only for John to change his mind, ask forgiveness and for the two of them to get back on a plane to Los Angeles.

# 58

*'To finish off . . . we thought we'd do a number
by an old estranged fiancé of mine called Paul'*

As inexplicable and self-destructive as was some of John's behaviour, his time with May wasn't just eighteen months on the razzle. By no means. He worked hard, writing, recording and producing for most of the time, with the loyal May always at his side. Only his violent aberrations made the headlines. When *Mind Games* was released – the cover of which features a miniature John looking like a Lilliputian walking away from a prone Gulliver-like giant Yoko – he made himself available to all the US rock magazines, and even made a jokey video for TV. Unfortunately, the album was another setback with justifiably poor reviews, and, by John's standards, modest sales. There was, however, an upside. Through the promotion he became good friends with Elton John. Both had started their careers having their songs published by Dick James, with whom both had later fallen out. They had a lot to talk about.

At May's instigation, he also spent time at Disneyland with his son Julian, now aged ten, whom he hadn't seen in the two years that he'd lived in America. The boy hadn't been invited to New York to see his father because his presence in the Lennons' household would have reminded Yoko of the loss of her daughter Kyoko, whom she still hadn't been able to find.

With work on his *Rock 'n' Roll* album coming to a halt when Phil Spector suddenly disappeared, taking the already recorded tracks with him, John was at a loss as to what to do next. Then his friend and drinking partner Harry Nilsson came up with an answer. Nilsson liked golden oldies too, so John agreed to produce an album for him. It was called *Pussy Cats*, and, hearing about the project, Ringo flew in to join the team, as did another drummer, Keith Moon.

On the first night of recording, who should turn up at the studio door but Paul and Linda. It was the first time since the Beatles had broken up that John and Paul had been in the same room. Would there be an almighty row? Absolutely not. When musicians get together and conversation runs out or gets awkward, they do what they always do. They play. With Paul on drums, in the absence of Ringo and Keith Moon that night, and John picking up his guitar, soon to be joined by Stevie Wonder, they went into a jam of 'Midnight Special'. It was a song John and Paul hadn't played together since they'd been at the Cavern. It was an icebreaker. As the evening ended, John invited Paul and Linda to come to the house he and May, along with Ringo, Nilsson and Moon, had just moved into, on the beach just north of Santa Monica, the following day.

The McCartneys arrived, bringing their children with them, and were given a tour of the house. John and May delighted in showing every visitor their bedroom, which was said to be the one in which Marilyn Monroe had entertained either Bobby or Jack Kennedy, or perhaps both, at different times – no one was sure. But John did love his gossip. After the tour, Paul went to the piano downstairs and began to play, as he did wherever he went. At that time he was going through a hot spell professionally, with the success of 'Live And Let Die' and the album *Band On The Run*. If John was jealous, and he probably was, he didn't show it.

Before Paul left that day, he had a surprise for his former partner. Taking John aside, he told him that when Yoko had been in London recently, where she'd taken John's place on the Apple board, she'd told him that if her husband wanted to get back with her, he would 'have to work at it'. So here was Paul acting as the mediator between John and the woman who had so often infuriated him and who had helped break up the Beatles. Life, John must have thought, is full of ironies.

As much as John admired Harry Nilsson's voice, the sessions didn't go as well as he'd expected. The problem was partly that Harry was ruining his voice with alcohol and drugs, and eventually he began coughing up blood. But it wasn't only that. Harry, Ringo and Keith Moon wanted to party every night, leading May to sometimes think that she was living in 'an asylum for the insane'. Paul had thought it was 'crazed'.

Soon, John began to realise that ruin lay ahead. And, as he was producing the album, he was responsible. 'I just woke up in the middle of it and thought, "There's something wrong here. I'd better straighten myself out.'" He did, and took Harry and the tapes back to New York and remixed the album there.

Was it that the visit from the successful solo Paul had brought back the old competitive spirit in him, seeing himself as Paul would have done, an old friend going nowhere, throwing his talent away in the modern land of the lotus eaters? Or was it that Yoko was said to be thinking about finding a divorce lawyer?

Back in New York, he went to live a few blocks away from the Dakota at the Pierre Hotel, where May joined him. Soon Yoko would suggest that the two move to another apartment in the Dakota that had become vacant, but John chose instead to rent a place for May and himself in Sutton Place on East 52nd Street.

Yoko was happy with that. And when, after sloping off for a night with a girl he'd met, he got Yoko to tell May that he'd stayed the night in a spare room at the Dakota, she was even amused. It's a bizarre situation when a wife lies to her husband's mistress when he is being unfaithful to that mistress.

John had always liked New York, and, once back, he was soon in the recording studio making a new album. He called it *Walls And Bridges,* and for its sleeve he asked Aunt Mimi to send him some illustrations he'd done at school when he was eleven. One showed a game of football, and another was a scene of two Hollywood-style Red Indians on horses galloping towards the artist. His past never left him. Whenever he called Mimi, she always wanted to know when she would be seeing him again. But he could never say. While the visa problem was still rumbling on, he daren't leave the US in case he could never get back in. When he asked her to come and visit him, her answer was always that she wasn't 'going to any country where the police had guns'. She probably just didn't want to go. She was still a stubborn woman.

*Walls And Bridges* would be a big improvement on *Mind Games*, although John's self-absorbed, self-pitying attitude lingered in songs like 'Nobody Loves You (When You're Down And Out)' and 'Scared' – good as they were. Playing the songs to Elton John one night before recording them, however, Elton asked if he could be on one of the tracks and chose 'Whatever Gets You Thru The Night', on which he played organ and sang harmony. It was John's least favourite song on the album, but by that time Elton knew more about the current US record market than he did, and insisted that it would be a number one. Should that happen, John promised that he would appear on stage alongside Elton, never thinking it was even likely. The single failed completely in the UK, but it became a million seller in the US, John's first since 'Imagine' in 1971.

Not everyone rejoiced at the success of the album, and the lacerating that John gave Allen Klein in 'Steel And Glass' was vicious. The five-year contract that John had pushed George and Ringo to sign had now run its course and would not be renewed, and, feeling that Klein had cheated him in some way, John went after him in the only way he knew how. *'You leave your smell like an alley cat,'* he sang.

Klein didn't like it, but he had bigger fish to fry. For four years, teams of lawyers had been working in London and New York on finding a way to dissolve the Beatles' partnership and were now inching towards a settlement. And, as John was now prepared to agree with Paul that hiring Klein had been a mistake, a separate suit against the American manager was also in progress. Naturally, by way of protecting himself and his business, Klein was, in return, suing the Beatles.

Paul was right when he said that the legal fees involved in the Beatles' dissolution must have put many lawyers' kids through college, because lawyers were everywhere. Just as one team had reached an agreement for John and Paul with ATV Music about Northern Songs, a new problem appeared for other lawyers to sort out. The new dispute referred back to the Beatles' recording of 'Come Together', when John had ignored Paul's caution and borrowed a line from a Chuck Berry song. This being music publishing, inevitably the head of the company who owned the song had noticed, and equally inevitably he wanted some form of compensation.

The man was Maurice Levy, who was a tough guy in the record world with Mafia links. To John, it seemed that the easiest way to satisfy him was to record three songs for his *Rock 'n' Roll* album that Levy published. As the tapes for the album that Phil Spector had spirited away had finally been retrieved by, yes, more lawyers at Capitol Records, he was now keen to finish it.

Despite all the warnings about Levy, John took a shine to the fellow. Sometimes his naivety knew no limits. Levy was a character, he said. He was certainly that. After recording the necessary additional songs, John was so pleased to finish the album he sent Levy an unmixed copy of all the tapes. That was another big mistake.

*

By this time, he and Yoko had been apart for fifteen months. According to May, John said that when Yoko had suggested divorce, he agreed to it, only for Yoko to decide, upon returning from a disastrous solo singing tour in Japan, that the stars weren't right – she was now heavily into astrology. Yoko had talked vaguely about divorce on the phone to me, too, but how serious either she or John was on the subject is impossible to say, so adept were they at playing games with each other, floating ideas and then withdrawing them. How much May could believe what they each told her is difficult to judge too.

A new John, however, was emerging in the East River apartment where he and May were now living. He was at his most friendly and sociable in years, as he welcomed guests to his home. Small though it was, with Greta Garbo living in the same block they were hardly slumming it, and Paul and Linda turned up on their first night there. 'We spent two or three nights together,' John would later say, 'talking about the old days. It was cool seeing what each other remembered from Hamburg and Liverpool.' Mick Jagger came round too. He found it easier, he would tell May, now that he didn't have to negotiate Yoko first, and he would always bring a bottle of good wine with him. One weekend he took John and May to stay the night at Andy Warhol's house, which he and his then wife Bianca were renting at Montauk on Long Island. Elton was a visitor too. John had never been so welcoming.

Then one Friday night, stepping out on to the roof terrace, John saw a UFO over the East River. He called May to come and see this 'black, grey object . . . with flashing lights' as it passed the UN Building, and moved on down the river. She saw it too. So convinced were they by what they had seen that John was happy to be interviewed the next day by a TV news team, wearing his flat cap and pointing at the sky as he happily recounted the experience. He knew that, with his reputation for taking mind-altering drugs, some people might not be surprised to hear that he believed in flying saucers. He certainly hadn't when the Harbingers had talked about them when he'd been in Denmark in 1970. But seeing is believing. He wasn't stoned, he insisted. Whatever it was, he remained convinced for the rest of his life that he had seen something that he couldn't explain.

Thanksgiving 1974 was the night Elton, in the middle of a US tour, chose for John to fulfil his promise about 'Whatever Gets You Thru

The Night', and join him on stage at Madison Square Garden. He didn't force the issue. John could back out if he felt he wasn't up to it. But John wanted to do it.

Foolishly, though, he'd mixed champagne and cocaine the previous night, so he was still feeling unwell as he put on a black suit for the show, together with a jewelled pendant that Elton had bought him as a gift. He and May travelled to the Garden with Elton in his limousine, to find, when they arrived, that Yoko had sent both singers a large white gardenia. John attached his to his lapel. Then, as the show started and Elton began going through his hits, John and May waited in the wings for Elton to make his announcement.

At this point, memories of the evening, and the events that followed, begin to diverge. Yoko would say later that John had no idea that she was attending the show, and John would agree. But May remembers things differently, because, she says, she'd been asked by Yoko to make sure there were tickets for her and her date for the night, her friend, guitarist David Spinozza, and that John knew very well she would be there.

Rumours had been flying around among the concert-goers all day, so when at last Elton turned to the audience and said, 'Seeing as its Thanksgiving, we thought we'd make tonight a little bit of a joyous occasion by inviting someone up with us on stage . . .' and John walked on, the auditorium was primed to explode. John was surprised at the reaction. 'It was just like Beatlemania . . . I hadn't heard it since the Beatles,' he would later tell David Sheff at *Newsweek*.

Immediately John and Elton went into 'Whatever Gets You Thru The Night' and then came 'Lucy In The Sky With Diamonds'. But the biggest response was yet to come. 'We tried to think of a number to finish off with so I can get out of here and be sick,' John joked, 'and we thought we'd do a number by an old estranged fiancé of mine called Paul . . . It's an old Beatle number, and we just about know it.' And then, with a little tease as Elton's lead guitarist played the intro to 'I Feel Fine', he and Elton went into 'I Saw Her Standing There'.

It was a clever choice. Elton had suggested 'Imagine', but, as John would later say, 'I didn't want to come on like Dean Martin doing my classic hits. I wanted to have some fun and play some rock and roll.' So a song that Paul had written virtually alone was chosen. It was the first time John had ever sung lead on it, but now Elton was taking the harmony he used to sing, and John was laying the foundations of a bridge back to Paul. Whether that bridge would ever be completed, he didn't know.

Sitting in the audience, Yoko would later say that she thought John looked lonely. But standing in the wings, May thought he was amazing, believing that the night would be the start of something new.

John took May to a reception at the Pierre Hotel after the show. Yoko was there, and in the truncated version of events that she and John would later agree upon, they looked into each other's eyes and that was that. Romance was rekindled and they were together again.

Actually, it wasn't and they weren't . . .

John did some table hopping at the party, chatted to Yoko for a while, and was intrigued as Uri Geller did some spoon bending. Then he took May home to their apartment in Sutton Place.

*'What would you think if I began writing with Paul again?'*

Christmas 1974 was a good time for John. His appearance with Elton John had been a big success, he had a hit album and a single high in the charts, he was seeing Paul again and he had a mid-town Manhattan home life where he lived with a girlfriend who adored him. He possibly didn't love her as much as she loved him, but he'd been with her for a year and a half, and had, despite other distractions, always quickly come back to her. So, their relationship, which was cosy, with no interfering staff, and in which May always did the hiring of cars and then the driving, the booking of appointments and the social arrangements with their friends, must have had quite a lot going for it.

His life was, however, as complicated as ever, when he suddenly found that four different issues from his past were simultaneously converging on him. The first was the Beatles dissolution problem. It had taken four years and five different legal teams, but now, as his lawyers showed him the terms while he and May sat in bed, John and Yoko style, he wanted more time to think about it. It was important for tax reasons that the papers were signed before the end of the year, but still John hesitated.

The second issue, more of a blessing than a problem, was that his son, Julian, about whom he had felt guilty for years, was coming to stay with him and May for Christmas.

But then there was Yoko. Was she really 'thinking of taking him back', as she'd now told May? He didn't know. He didn't know if he wanted to go back. He was as happy now as he'd been in years.

Finally there was George. He certainly wasn't happy. He was on a forty-city US tour, but there had been poor reviews and the thinning audiences resented having to listen to forty minutes of Ravi Shankar's Indian music before the ex-Beatle came on stage. So George had looked to John for help and not found it. Then, as the tour had reached New York just before Christmas, John sent a message to George, offering to do anything he could to help. For George it was too late.

Hadn't he done everything John had asked for years, George asked bitterly – and that included agreeing with John to appoint Allen Klein as their manager. But where had John been when he'd needed him? Once again George's long-held resentment at feeling himself a second-class Beatle had bubbled up. John understood. No one other than the four Beatles could understand what they'd lived through. It was almost a family row, because in so many ways the Beatles had been a family. Now George was feeling abandoned. He'd started this tour by himself and he would finish it by himself, he told John bitterly.

Then, on the night when Paul, George and John were to meet at the Plaza Hotel and sign the dissolution documents, John didn't turn up. He was lying in bed in his flat in Sutton Place. 'I didn't sign it because my astrologer told me it wasn't the right day,' he would say later. This was the first anyone had ever heard of him having an astrologer. But Yoko had one. In the end he sent a white balloon. Paul and George were livid.

With such bad feelings around him, it must have been a relief to take May and Julian down to Florida to visit Disney World, where his girlfriend watched as, in their bedroom in the Polynesian Hotel, John finally succumbed to common sense and signed the dissolution agreement. Thus, in this Mickey Mouse world, the Beatles' career of almost two decades, and their thirteen-year legal partnership, formally came to an end.

The tension had been lifted. Everyone was happy, and back home in Sutton Place, John, May and Julian had a regular Christmas with a tree and presents. Then there was a trip to Montauk to show Julian a house John had seen while he'd been with Mick Jagger that he was thinking of buying. That was where Julian would be staying next year, he told his son. And it got even better when, with Julian returning to London, Paul and Linda invited John and May out and ended up at a David Bowie studio mixing session, during which Bowie and John turned a jam session into the song 'Fame'.

Almost immediately, however, a new problem arose when it became known that Maurice Levy, the man whom John thought was a 'character', had decided to show that character by distributing the unmixed *Rock 'n' Roll* tapes that John had sent him as a cheap TV mail order album. John had been warned. His judgement of people had never been his strongest suit.

Once again lawyers had to be called in, although this time at Capitol's expense, as it was their album that Levy was ripping off. Quickly, an injunction was slapped on Levy, making it pretty well impossible for him to sell his version of the album, which he was calling *Roots*.

John, working out of his Lennono Music office at Capitol Records on the Avenue of the Americas, with May at his side, began his final mix of the material. He was in a busy, jubilant mood, May remembers. And even before he'd finished *Rock 'n' Roll*, he began compiling material for a new album, playing the songs to May as he went. Then came a call from Paul. He was going down to New Orleans to record his next album. Did John and May want to come down too? Paul asked.

Did he? In his new social whirl, he was tempted enough to tell Art Garfunkel over dinner about the invitation. Garfunkel thought he should go, and that if Paul wanted him to join in the recording he should do that, too. Still toying with the idea, John asked May: 'What would you think if I began writing with Paul again?'

'Are you kidding?' said May, delighted.

Not as frequent a letter writer as he had been, John still liked to haphazardly keep in touch with old friends, and in one typical letter to Derek Taylor, who had now ceased to be the press officer at Apple, he typed: 'Bowies cutting "universe" (Let It Beatle). Am a gonna be there (by request of courset). Then possibley down to New Orleans to see the McCartknees.'

To this day May remains convinced that had John joined Paul in New Orleans they would not have been able to resist working together again. She was excited.

Then Yoko rang.

She had, she said, found a new way of giving up smoking, and it was very effective. It was by hypnotism. Since John had been getting through two packets of his loosely packed French cigarettes a day for more years than he knew, he was keen to try the cure. The hypnotism would, said Yoko, take place at the Dakota. May asked to go too, to see the cure for herself, but John refused her.

For two weeks Yoko repeatedly changed the time of the appointment, May would later write, sometimes because the stars weren't right. So John carried on writing his next album. One song that May liked particularly was called 'Tennessee'.

Then, on Friday, 31 January 1975, Yoko called to say that the stars were in their right places.

'I'll call you later,' John told May, and set off for the Dakota to be hypnotised.

# 60

*'I feel I've been on Sinbad's voyage and
I've battled all the monsters'*

When John hadn't returned from the Dakota by ten o'clock, May became worried and phoned Yoko, asking to speak to him. John was sleeping, Yoko replied. 'The cure was very difficult.' He would call her back the following day. He didn't. So, on the Saturday, May called Yoko again. John was exhausted and still sleeping, Yoko told her this time.

Sunday came and went with no word from John. May could see the picture that was emerging. It was the one that she had feared.

On the Monday morning she had to attend a check-up at the dentist. She'd booked sequential appointments for both herself and John, and, as she left the dentist's surgery, she found him waiting to go in. She hung round until he came out. Then together they walked back to their apartment.

When they got there, and were in private, he told her what she'd already guessed. Yoko had 'allowed' him to go home, he said. He'd just come back to pick up a few belongings. 'It wasn't anybody's fault. It just happened,' he explained. Then he lit a cigarette. The cure obviously hadn't worked.

As May tells it, he looked 'dazed' and 'disoriented'. Was he just trying to hide his embarrassment, and perhaps some shame or guilt, at a difficult moment? Or was there, as May believes, some other reason? It's impossible to know.

'Tell me about the cure,' she said as, between tears, she watched him pack.

'It was horrible,' he said. 'Just like primal therapy . . . I was throwing up all the time. Kept throwing my guts out. I kept falling asleep, and, when I woke up, they would do it to me again.'

For a man who had so much to say on virtually every aspect of his life, John never said anything publicly about what happened to him when he underwent hypnosis. He never revealed anything about the hypnotist, what his or her qualifications might have been, or the method that was used. Since he became so ill during the process, presumably some kind of aversion therapy was included.

There was still some final work to do preparing *Rock 'n' Roll* for release, so May continued her work as his assistant, after which they would go back to the apartment and go to bed. Then John would shower before he went home to Yoko. Although he told May that Yoko had said that it would be all right for him to continue to keep her as his mistress, his wife would soon change her mind about that, and his assignations with his lover would become increasingly furtive. In public John and Yoko would present themselves as a reconciled couple and very much in love. But in private he would slip away to see May occasionally for a further eighteen months, using visits to a hospitalised friend as a cover. He never did go down to New Orleans to see Paul, however.

May had reasoned at the very beginning that famous men like John never chose women like her or had affairs with them. Well, she'd had an affair with him, but now she was being cast aside as, over the next few years, their meetings became fewer.

But why *did* John suddenly go back to Yoko when everything seemed to be going so well, when he was looking at an entirely different kind of future that might well have involved working with Paul again? Had he become bored with his young lover? Obviously not, as he continued to see her in secret. Or had a part of him been in love with Yoko all along? That was the line that he and Yoko would take as he joked about the affair being an eighteen-month 'Lost Weekend', after the Billy Wilder movie about an alcoholic that he'd seen on television. 'The separation failed,' he would say. That's possible.

Perhaps, though, there is a further explanation. Was John running away from the demons within himself, which, when they'd lived in California, neither he nor May had sometimes been able to handle? It was all very well for Yoko to tell May to look after her husband and keep him out of trouble when she chose her as his mistress, but on occasions it had been an impossible task. May didn't do drugs nor did she drink much, and she knew that alcohol and cocaine had a devastating effect on the behaviour of her lover-boss. But when he made up his mind, she couldn't stop him mixing them.

Had John come to realise that, as pleasant and cosy as things had become in New York with May, there would be other times when he might not be so happy or so social, when, as he had earlier worried, he might be 'fucked up'? Had his song 'Scared' on *Walls And Bridges* reflected his fear of himself? Did he feel he needed someone with an iron will at his side? No one ever questioned the strength of Yoko's will, or the length to which she would go when she wanted something. When he was with the Beatles he'd written the song 'I Want You (She's So Heavy)' for the *Abbey Road* album. It had been about Yoko and had been purposely misunderstood and mocked by some who were of a mind to criticise. But John had known what he was saying. He had seen Yoko as being 'heavy' in the metaphorical sense of being both intellectually and artistically substantial. She was also, by nature, extraordinarily controlling of the environment she inhabited.

But there may have been something else, too. When John had found himself back at the Dakota for the hypnosis weekend, did he look around at the large, rich, swanky seventh-floor apartment with the fashionable address of 1 West 72nd Street that he owned, a place that contained nearly all his belongings, the bits and pieces of his life's work? Did he feel that it was time to cease his wanderings and come home to the orderly life of the mother ship? Was it simply easier that way? Did he sense that in her eccentric, manipulative way, Yoko was the person who could offer him what he needed most – security? Was that the attraction? Had Yoko somehow convinced him, having convinced herself, that only she could protect him? Had the life he'd been living and the strain of being so famous for so long mentally exhausted him? 'I feel I've been on Sinbad's voyage and I've battled all the monsters,' was how he expressed it to writer Pete Hamill a few days after returning home.

It hadn't been all battling monsters while he'd been on his Long Weekend. May had been good for him, and he'd been very busy, very creative and done a lot of work. Unfortunately, it had been his occasional inner demons that had captured the headlines. And there had always been an impermanence about it.

With the Beatles negotiations settled, and the visa problem looking less worrying now that Nixon had resigned and the White House had been cleared of his motley crew, was John looking for a nest for himself, a place where, without any worries, he could curl up and rest?

Yoko was demanding and could be difficult, but, so long as he didn't upset her or question her enormous ego and desire for equal fame with him, she was capable of taking care of everything – policing the phones and directing the staff. All the time John had been with May he had stressed that he didn't want to do anything to hurt Yoko. That didn't suggest he still necessarily felt romantic love for his wife, but a more dutiful regard and respect for her in what had really always been a symbiotic relationship. She had needed him for his fame and the cachet it gave her, for his money and the limousines. And he had been drawn to her for her zany intelligence and the entrée she appeared to give him to the avant-garde. She made him feel clever, not just a rock and roller. And, now, as she ran the Dakota apartment and staff, and sat in his place on the Apple board, she seemed to offer to bring order to his life. With Yoko in charge, arranging all the stuff he couldn't be bothered to do, he would never have to worry. He could rest. She was more than a wife to him. She was more like a mother. Perhaps that was why he began to call her Mother.

When *Rock 'n' Roll* was released that spring, John knew it would be a disappointment to his fans. It was a disappointment to him. By disguising his voice with too much reverb and echo, and with the backings far too fussy, between them, he and Phil Spector had failed to capture the excitement in the simplicity of the original hits that they had once both enjoyed so much. A cover version of Gene Vincent's 'Be-Bop-A-Lula' was good enough, although taken too fast, but, other than when paying homage to the first songwriter who influenced him with Buddy Holly's 'Peggy Sue', the whole album sounded as though he'd simply tried too hard. He'd done a better job of rock classics when he'd sung 'Money' and 'Please Mr Postman' back in 1963 with the Beatles.

# 61

### 'I'm blessed with a second chance'

John dropped out. It was as simple as that. It was fashionable for a student to drop out of college to join a rock and roll band. But John turned that on its head. He dropped out of rock and roll and his two dozen guitars to stay at home and become a dad. Dr Winston O'Boogie, as he'd whimsically referred to himself during his Lost Weekend, had been banished, to be replaced by the reborn *JohnandYoko*. Once more John was changing his life, starting again, even referring to his pre-Dakota life as his 'previous incarnation'. And, to go with his new life, he would soon have some new crazes, too.

'Dear Ray,' Yoko wrote to me on a postcard that spring of 1975, 'Here's a hard one for you to take – John and Yoko have not only come back together, but they're having a baby – due October!'

That *was* a surprise . . . to John, as well. He'd told Cynthia at one of their rare meetings a couple of years earlier that he didn't believe he would be able to father any more children, because his procreativity had been wrecked by the many drugs he'd enjoyed. He'd been wrong. But for Yoko there would be problems.

'She'd had too many miscarriages,' John would explain. 'When she was a young girl there was no Pill, so there were lots of abortions and miscarriages. Her stomach must be like Kew Gardens in London . . . But this Chinese acupuncturist in San Francisco said, "You behave yourself, no drugs, eat well, no drink. You have child . . ."'

Yoko put a romantic spin on the conception. 'When John came back, we had great sex and I got pregnant,' she smiled to an interviewer, which John confidently dated as occurring on 6 February, six days after he left May. Like his father, he, too, was confident that he knew the exact moment of his son's start in life.

Years later Yoko would admit that initially, at the age of forty-two, she wasn't sure whether she wanted a baby and had considered another abortion – only deciding to continue with the pregnancy when she saw how keen John was to be a father again.

And he *was* thrilled. He'd been halfway through writing the songs for his next album, but when the pregnancy was confirmed, he put them to one side. Fatherhood was an experience that he'd largely missed with Julian, occurring as it did at the height of Beatlemania. 'I've already "lost" one family to produce, what . . . *Sgt. Pepper*?' he wrote dismissively of the Beatles' most famous album. This time it would be different. 'I'm blessed with a second chance,' he said. And, with no outside obligations, he threw himself into fatherhood with the fervour he would always adopt when beginning any new project. That meant, as instructed by Yoko, cleansing his body of alcohol and going on a macrobiotic diet, and also hanging up his guitar. If he ever needed a shot of rock and roll as a reminder he could only find it in what he and Yoko called the Black Room in their Dakota apartment, the place where he kept his jukebox stuffed with mainly Fifties rock and roll records. Mostly, though, he didn't need it. He cancelled his subscription to *Billboard* magazine, didn't try to keep up with the pop charts any more, although he followed the Bee Gees, Bowie and Elton John, and tuned the radio in the kitchen to a middle-of-the-road easy listening station. Actually, he was probably more likely to hear Beatles records there, too.

He'd written a log while he'd been away from Yoko with May, outlining his everyday life of 'waking up in strange places, or reading about myself in the papers doing extraordinary things, half of which I'd done and half of which I hadn't'. Now the two of them ceremonially burned the log as they reaffirmed their marriage vows. Then, as he was starting a new life while waiting for the baby to arrive, he began a morbidly personal new journal, noting everything he did or thought during each day. He often wished, he would write, that he and Yoko weren't famous any more and that they could 'enjoy a really private life'. But he knew that was a futile desire – and he certainly enjoyed the financial perks of world fame, as did Yoko, to an even greater extent. What he did do, however, was to avoid giving any interviews for the next four years.

He'd always been a letter writer, so with no audience outside his home to amuse, he began to write dozens of letters (typing them, actually, because he worried that his handwriting was illegible) to family and friends at home in the UK. Generally just chatty and jokey, some of them would also unpeel a John Lennon quite different from that of his recent public image, someone who cared enough about his relatives to ask them to send him recent photographs of themselves and their children. Mimi got a request too, to send him his old school tie. Although he liked to say that the past was behind him, that only the present and future mattered, his childhood never left him.

His cousin Liela had always been his favourite relative. She was now a doctor, and when she criticised his lifestyle in a letter he was quick to fondly tell her, 'old bossy boots', that she may have been 'a little naive' in judging him, before going on to have a bit of a grouse about Mimi. He was, he wrote, thinking of taking piano lessons, because he could 'only play with eight fingers . . . self-taught and lousy . . . Mimi would never let me have a piano in the house . . . said it was common' – adding that his aunt still believed that he had 'no talent' and that he'd simply 'got lucky'. Actually, Mimi didn't think that at all, but the bruises of his fights with her, which the whole family had known about, were still there. 'She always wanted to castrate everyone (male and female) and put their "balls" in an apple pie!' was his merry end to that particular little complaint.

One person to whom John probably didn't write was Michael de Freitas, who was still known to the newspapers by his chosen 'revolutionary' name of Michael X. He did, however, add his signature to a petition calling for clemency, after de Freitas was found guilty in court in Trinidad, and sentenced to death for murder. John, a long-time opponent of the death penalty, didn't desert the man he had once trusted and whom he believed to be reformed, but who had conned him out of thousands of pounds before going on to murder. Clemency was not granted. De Freitas was hanged in Port of Spain on 16 May 1975.

Yoko had a difficult pregnancy, and during it John revealed his caring side as, on doctor's orders, she had to spend much of the time in bed. And when in late September she was taken into New York Hospital two weeks early, he went with her, 'sleeping on the floor', John would tell his half-sister Julia.

His US visa problem had by this time been going through the legal process for over four years, as he had dug in ever deeper and refused to be extradited. Then, in October, while at the hospital, he received some good news. By a margin of two to one, the US Court of Appeals had ruled that his 1968 conviction for cannabis possession in London had been unfair by the standards of US law, and it recommended that the Immigration and Naturalization Service use its discretion regarding his visa. For the first time he could see a happy ending on the horizon.

In the immediate future was Yoko's baby. There are various conflicting theories about why Sean Ono Taro Lennon came to be born by Caesarean section the following day, 9 October, John's birthday. Was it because Yoko believed, as did some people in Japan and the Far East, that a son born on the same day as his father would inherit the soul of his father after he had died? John would later deny that that had been the reason, but Yoko was no stranger to some bizarre beliefs, and neither John's word nor hers was always to be trusted on personal matters. Whatever the explanation, the baby would be in intensive care for two weeks, before Yoko could take him home. Coupled with the good news from Leon Wildes, John's visa lawyer, it was time for a double celebration. Elton John was named as the baby's godfather, chosen, John would joke, because Elton didn't have any children (at the time), so Sean could inherit all of his money too.

The Lennons didn't have a nanny at first, John would tell half-sister Julia – which must have brought a wry smile back in Liverpool, where few people could afford a nanny; Cynthia certainly hadn't when she'd had Julian. But, though he grumbled that he was losing sleep when Yoko was breastfeeding and he needed to be at her side every four hours, he was actually rejoicing in his new role.

Before Sean had been born, Yoko had put it to him that, when she had the baby, the division of labour in their home would be reversed from the usual practice. As Tony Cox, her second husband, had found when he'd had to look after Kyoko, John was going to have to do the child rearing too. In return, Yoko, it was decided, could, in the absence now of Allen Klein or indeed anyone else, take more of an interest in John's business affairs. She had no experience of business. But she had never lacked for self-confidence. Eventually she would become his manager and take control of his finances. It wasn't as if he was planning to have an active career anyway. 'It's irrelevant to me whether I ever record again,' he would write in 1978. And, now that the Apple funds had been released, he wouldn't need to, as money flooded in from his song and record royalties.

So, while Yoko issued instructions to her ever-growing Dakota staff from the groundfloor office she called Studio One, John happily retreated into his letter writing, catching up with people from his past, the jokes still sparkling. In a letter to me that autumn he referred to Beatle George as 'George (I'm with God) Harrisong' who was in New York and about to have 'the unmitigated honor' of meeting the 'incredibly beautiful and intelligent Sean Ono Lennon' before signing off with: 'P.S. The Bay City Rollers are gay (scoop) except one who's pretending. What's the world coming to, I says.'

Another letter, earlier in the year, had been to the Beatles' former road manager Mal Evans. Mal planned to write a memoir based on diaries he'd kept while working for the group, but he wanted John's blessing before he started. John was all for it. 'Make a buck but don't fuck it . . .' was his advice.

He'd always been very close to Mal, who at nearly six foot four and heavy with it had been the Beatles' gentle giant and bodyguard when needed, his sheer size, friendly manner and horn-rimmed glasses keeping at bay most of those who would do them harm. Like Neil Aspinall, Mal had been at every gig and every recording session. He'd been an employee, but, more than that, a trusted friend. Never taking sides, he was always willing and available, to the extent that when Allen Klein fired him, he found himself reinstated in his job by the Beatles the following day.

Not that there had been much for him to do when the Beatles broke up. So Mal, who was no longer involved with Badfinger, the group he'd discovered, had decided to leave and make it on his own as a songwriter and record producer. In his own quiet way, he wanted some of the glory. John's attitude had been to encourage the roadie to make the break.

It probably wasn't the best advice. Mal on his own, without the Beatles, was rudderless. Separating from his wife Lil, and leaving her and their two children behind in England, he was seduced away to California. Badfinger had hit the US top ten with a song that he'd produced, but there would be no more hits for him.

On 4 January 1976, two years to the day after leaving his wife and children, Mal became depressed in his Los Angeles apartment and picked up an air rifle that he used for taking pot shots at lizards. On seeing the gun, the girlfriend with whom he was living called the police, saying, it was alleged: 'My old man has a gun and has taken Valium and is totally screwed up.'

When the police arrived, they told Mal to put the weapon down.

Mal responded, the Los Angeles Police Department would later say, by pointing the gun at them.

He was shot dead instantly, four bullets hitting him. He was forty. Only afterwards did the police discover that the gun was an air rifle and wasn't even loaded.

John, like all the Beatles, was devastated. Mal had been the most inoffensive of men, the bodyguard who had never had a fight; the former Post Office telephone engineer who had only become involved with the Beatles because, going back to work after eating his sandwiches for his lunch at the Pier Head in Liverpool one day, he'd heard music that 'sounded like Elvis' coming from a basement in a back street. From that moment his fate had been sealed.

Mal's body was cremated in Los Angeles three days later. No one from his family was present, although Harry Nilsson attended the brief ceremony, after which his ashes were sent back to his wife, Lil, in England.

She never received them. They got lost in the post. John's response when he heard that was the saddest of unhappy quips he ever made. 'Have they tried looking in the lost letter department?' he asked bitterly.


John's record contract with EMI and Capitol came to an end in February 1976, and, although he was asked to renew it, he declined. Not even a better offer from Columbia could tempt him. He no longer wanted to be encumbered with obligations to make music. As he watched as Paul made album after album, busy as ever, he felt no desire to join in the race any more. The muse had dried up when he'd returned to the Dakota. He always claimed that he wrote best when he was under pressure, but now he had removed himself from that possibility. No pressure: no muse.

But, and it's easily forgotten, for a singer-songwriter an album takes at least a year out of a musician's life, from writing the songs, to their recording, and then there is the necessary promotion that follows. John was bored with all that. Instead, always aware that in not having been to university he was less educated than he would like to have been, he began to read widely, usually having several books open at the same time. Then there was time to take Sean for walks in his pram in Central Park across the road, and to concentrate on the macrobiotic, no-sugar diet that he had now adopted.

Towards the end of the previous year he'd asked Neil at Apple in London to try to make contact with his father, to whom he'd behaved so brutally when he'd summoned him to Tittenhurst Park in 1971. Having long regretted his behaviour on that day, he now wished to make amends.

But Freddie didn't take up the offer of a reconciliation that Neil offered. He didn't want anything more to do with his son. There was an irony there. John, he felt, had abandoned him.

Then, early in 1976, Freddie's wife Pauline phoned Apple. Freddie had been diagnosed with stomach cancer. He would now like to talk to his son again. The next day John phoned his father in hospital and they made their peace. Not knowing how ill his father was, John told him he looked forward to getting him over to New York when Freddie felt better. But, following surgery, Freddie died a few weeks later.

Apart from Pauline there was only one other person at Freddie's funeral, the publicist who had encouraged him to make a record. He would remember a bouquet of flowers being delivered that was almost bigger than the grave. It was 'from John, Yoko and Sean'.

A few days later, Pauline sent John an unpublished autobiography that Freddie had written, outlining his version of the events leading up to his desertion, as Mimi had always told it, of his five-year-old son. It hadn't been all his fault, he maintained. John had by now probably already realised that.

At lawyer Leon Wildes' suggestion, John had carefully burnished his image during the past year by enthusiastically taking part in charity events, and even singing 'Imagine' on stage at a TV tribute to honour Lew Grade, the chairman of ATV Music, whose company now owned Northern Songs. It had worked. After the phone-tapping, FBI surveillance and snooping, court appearances, statements, appeals, extensions and depositions by high-profile character witnesses, the long struggle for him to solve his US visa problems was finally ended in a small room on the fourteenth floor of the Immigration and Naturalization Service in New York on 27 July 1976. John, or at least his legal team, had won. He could now apply for a Green Card. His residency in the United States was secure.

'It's great to be legal again,' John smiled to waiting reporters and cameras on leaving the building. But then, safe in the US at last, he couldn't resist having a last sarcastic snap back at his former tormentors. 'And I would like to thank the Immigration Service for finally seeing the light of day.' That was John, always wanting the last word.

# 62

*'I never stop wanting to make music'*

For the best part of the next four years, John was rarely seen in public, or even by many of his old friends. As Yoko spent more and more time in her office running the business, he would, in theory, look after Sean. He did enjoy his time with the child, but when he found that was all too much of a chore he would hand him back to the governess Yoko had hired and hide away in his bedroom reading and watching TV. This was not new behaviour: he'd *always* spent a lot of time in his bedroom, scribbling notes to himself, drawing cartoons or writing little stories or lyrics, and, sometimes, just getting quietly stoned – a practice he still kept up. This was the way he put it in a letter to Derek Taylor: 'I myself have decided to be or not to be for a couple of years . . . Boredoms set in. How many backbeats are there, I ask myself.'

What was new was that, apart from walking a block or so down to a Japanese restaurant or La Fortuna coffee shop on Columbus Avenue, he rarely ventured very far outside his home. For a man who had previously packed so much into his every day, this 'suspended animation', as his Dakota assistant Fred Seaman would later describe his boss's new existence, was incomprehensible. It was also liable to induce depression.

Business bored him, but with Yoko running everything and everyone from her office, it was going on all around him, all the time. As his Dakota apartments – and there were now several – became the centre of his domestic, professional and financial interests, cooks, masseurs, cleaners, acupuncturists, accountants, lawyers, builders, psychics, interior designers, art dealers and decorators, together with a bodyguard for Sean, but not one for John, would compete for his wife's attention and instructions.

Yoko wasn't *only* John's manager, however. Seeming also to view herself in the role of his guardian, within a year of his moving back in with her she had become the drawbridge between him and the outside world. With an assistant on a switchboard filtering incoming calls to him through her, she decided upon those to whom he might or might not want to speak.

Inevitably, as the years passed, with few signs of him in public, a rumour got around that he was turning into a hermit, locked away in the grim-looking towers of the Dakota, seeing no one other than Yoko and Sean, and refusing to come out and play with his old friends when they phoned. This sounded silly to him, but there was an element of truth in it. Although Paul and Linda visited a couple of times, as did John's rascal of an old school friend Pete Shotton, even Mick Jagger would complain that he could never be put through to John when he phoned, and he soon gave up trying. And those who might tempt him back into mischievous ways, Keith Moon and Harry Nilsson for instance, were simply not welcome in his life any more. 'Yoko has him all locked up,' Mick Jagger would say. But to believe that was to miss the point. There was nothing keeping John in the Dakota. He could go out any time he wanted to. The difficulty was, since he'd given up his Lennono Music office at Capitol Records, and had retired from music, he had nothing to do, nowhere to go and no one to see. Apart from famously learning to bake bread, and watching a lot of *Dumbo* cartoons with Sean as the baby grew into a little boy, John's ambition had evaporated, as May would notice during his increasingly rare secret meetings with her.

A few years later he would describe this time as his 'househusband period'. But this was just an excuse. He was a multi-millionaire with a legion of staff at his beck and call to do the househusband tasks. Stuck there in the Dakota, looking down at the cars passing outside, he was really just passing the time. Worrying about his diet – photographs show that he had become anorexic-thin – convinced that the FBI were still listening in to his calls, he would spend his days sending out assistants to buy books and records and expensive liver for his three cats. Like Mimi, he loved his cats, Sasha, Misha and Charo. But it was as though he'd escaped from one life that had perhaps sometimes frightened him during his Lost Weekend, without finding a fulfilling alternative. Many people who retire too early from exciting jobs show similar symptoms of depression. But they aren't usually still in their mid-thirties.

Yoko had long had an interest in the occult and tarot numerology, a branch of which meant that she would plan not only her and John's daily lives according to the various constellations of the planets, but that her business affairs were also ordered around her astrological readings. It's difficult not to imagine a younger, more cynical Liverpudlian John Lennon mockingly rejecting this as hocus pocus, but he now went along with whatever Yoko said. Did he believe in it? He must have done . . . to an extent . . . when he wanted to. He'd believed in Magic Alex and the Maharishi, too.

Once again he was wearing the imprint of the last forceful person who sat on him. And Yoko had the strongest personality of anyone he'd ever met.

For years he'd been telling Mimi that as soon as his Green Card came through he would take Sean and Yoko to the UK to introduce the little boy to her and his family. But he didn't. His first trip out of the US was to Hong Kong by himself under instructions from Yoko and her tarot cards. It was the first time he'd been anywhere on his own since he'd flown back to Liverpool from Hamburg in 1960. The purpose of the trip seems to have been . . . simply that he made the trip.

The following year, after attending an eight-week intensive Berlitz Language School course in Japanese, he took Yoko and Sean, plus a small retinue of governess and assistants, on a three-month holiday to Japan to meet Yoko's extended family. He didn't much enjoy it. Although Japan offered a relative anonymity he couldn't have expected in the UK or US, he got bored, and soon Yoko requested that her friend Elliot Mintz join them. It was in Japan that John learned that Elvis Presley had been found dead at his home in Memphis, aged forty-two. That gave him pause for thought. At least *he* wasn't spending his time in a white suit in Las Vegas singing his old hits. What he *was* going to do, he didn't know.

He was glad when it was time to go home, but he had reckoned without another of Yoko's interpretations of her cards. Apparently, while the numbers said it was good for her to fly back from Tokyo to New York eastwards, John's numbers meant that he and the rest of the retinue, including Sean and his governess, had to continue westward to Hong Kong, on to Dubai and then home to the US via Frankfurt. Some husbands might have thought this was a wild goose chase, but John seems to have simply accepted it as one of 'Mother's' regular little eccentricities. And, with no job to go to when he got back to New York, it wasn't as if he was pushed for time.

*

So, the late Seventies passed bizarrely, if relatively uneventfully, as John watched Sean grow into a toddler, pulling at his reins, and then into a little boy at nursery school, with more holidays in Japan with the child's cousins. By any standards Sean was being raised in a most peculiar household in which on one occasion his father chose not to speak for ten days, and at other times was decidedly druggy; while his mother regularly relied on the advice of psychics. Money, however, was no object. 'Whatever Sean wants, he gets,' was Yoko's order to her staff. And chastisement was rare.

One Christmas, Sean's half-brother Julian, now aged fifteen, came to stay when the Lennons went down to Palm Beach in Florida. The older boy couldn't help but notice how Sean was the centre of his father's devotion in a way that he had never been. That had to hurt. On another occasion, the couple whom Yoko would call 'John's in-laws', Paul and Linda, turned up at the door singing Christmas carols. But if Paul had been vaguely hoping for a Lennon and McCartney rapprochement, as Linda always was, it wasn't to be. That moment had been passed when John had returned to Yoko.

As for Yoko herself, it seemed that she had found her metier in life as, with a telephone rarely out of her hand, she ran the busy Lennon empire, where the astrological phrase 'Mercury is in retrograde' was as likely to be heard as 'avant-garde' used to be. She was, she thought, good at business, perhaps because her father had spent a lifetime in banking, and sister Setsuko was making a career for herself in the World Bank. An alternative view was that she was lucky, and had a never-ending income stream from song and record royalties with which to play.

Dabbling in art, even buying a Renoir, she also became obsessed with ancient Egyptian artefacts, which meant that she and John flew to Cairo – causing John to joke to his cousin Liela, whose father had been Egyptian, 'I might dig up some of your father's relatives'. Her shrewdest purchases, however, were in property. As Mark Twain had advised a century earlier: 'Buy land. They're not making it any more.' And that held true in the late twentieth century more than ever. So she added to their Dakota apartments with farms in upstate New York, a herd of Holstein Friesian cows, and eventually a house by the sea on the north shore of Long Island called Cannon Hill.

*

John would later tell interviewers how much he had enjoyed his years being a househusband, but the frequency with which his frustrations over small, everyday aggravations would cause him to explode into temper would suggest that this long period of self-enforced idleness wasn't suiting him. On the occasions he'd spent time with May, who always welcomed him back, he seemed anxious and fragile. He would talk about music with her. May was a fan as well as a lover in a way that Yoko had never been, and one day in December 1978 she asked him if he wanted to record again.

'Of course I do. I never stop wanting to make music,' he told her. But he did nothing about it.

At home he didn't get very far with the book he intended to write, *The Ballad Of John And Yoko*, which he'd once considered might become a Broadway show; and, presumably because he wasn't satisfied with some of the short stories that would be included in his posthumous book *Skywriting By Word Of Mouth*, they weren't, at the time, even offered to a publisher. He kept up with a new post-May journal he was writing, and he even began talking into a cassette machine about his earliest memories from Liverpool, but his days mainly seemed to be lived on the fringes of a world that Yoko was running without him. His songs were the great provider for all the activity he saw around him in his home, but sometimes his own presence there must have felt like an irrelevance.

Then in 1980 a change began to take shape, and, almost by design, it seemed to involve Paul. In January of that year Paul was arrested at Tokyo airport on a charge of possessing drugs, when he, Linda, their children and his band Wings were entering Japan to play a concert tour. Since many a fan loves a conspiracy, a rumour immediately surfaced that Yoko must have wickedly tipped off the Japanese authorities that Paul had some very potent marijuana in his suitcase. It was nonsense, of course – the tip-off, not the pot. Not even Yoko, with or without her tarot cards, could have engineered that kind of intervention. But the whole episode of Paul's short incarceration put John into a merry state of schadenfreude about his old friend, and amused him enormously – although he sent him a Good Luck card. More importantly, it put Paul firmly back in his mind. And when, a few weeks later, he heard Paul's new single 'Coming Up', he was intrigued, sending an assistant out to buy the album it was on. To this day, Paul believes that the success of 'Coming Up', a huge hit, may have triggered John's return to music, in that it helped reawaken his competitive spirit.

Yoko had a problem at the time. She had developed a heroin habit, as she admitted to writer Philip Norman. Needing some time alone to secretly go cold turkey and cope with withdrawal symptoms, she packed John, Sean, his Japanese governess, and assistant Fred Seaman off to their beach house, Cannon Hill.

The house had a splendid view of the ocean, which for John was a magnet. Perhaps because he'd grown up in a port, with a father and grandfather who'd gone to sea, water had always held a fascination. And, after mucking about in a dinghy with an outboard engine with his assistant Seaman, he decided to buy a yacht and learn to sail. Quickly mastering the basics of that, he then decided, as he did with all new enthusiasms, that he needed a bigger challenge; a real sea voyage, for instance. Accordingly, a 43-foot schooner, the *Megan Jaye*, at Newport, Rhode Island, was chartered for July, and preparations were begun.

Meanwhile, Yoko, having recovered from her heroin problem, had a new idea for him too. It was time for him to take another trip, and she instructed that he fly to South Africa. It might have seemed to some that she was always trying to get rid of him, but he did as he was told, putting in a call to May, whom he hadn't seen for over a year, when he arrived in Cape Town. He was apologetic at first for not having called for so long, but, he said, he'd hidden his secret book of phone numbers somewhere and had forgotten where he'd left it. After that, they talked about music, as they always did, and planned to meet again in New York at some later unspecified date. Then, after talking for an hour and a half and making a vague future plan, he went home to New York again, to join the waiting *Megan Jaye*.

A crew of four had been assembled for the voyage, all experienced sailors, so now the only question to be asked was, where should they go? John rather fancifully liked the idea of sailing across the Atlantic to England and then up the Thames or the Mersey, but that was impractical. As usual Yoko consulted her tarot cards. The answer the cards gave was that south-east was John's best direction of travel. The only place south-east of Newport was Bermuda. So that became the destination. It seemed an impulsively difficult venture to undertake, but for John it was at last a chance for adventure after years of mental suffocation. And on 4 June 1980, he kissed Sean goodbye and set off on the 630-mile ocean voyage.

As the least experienced member of the crew, and no doubt considered by the real yachtsmen as merely a rich passenger, the most useful contribution John could make was in the galley making up meals for his companions. But, under supervision, he was given turns at the wheel, too. For two days it was beautiful summer sailing weather, and he loved it, amusing the crew with funny stories about his life with the Beatles, and asking about theirs. Then the weather reports began predicting something very different – a Force 8 gale.

Soon everyone except John and the captain, a grizzled rock of a guy and a former rock promoter called Hank Halstead, were ill with seasickness and had taken to their bunks. With John at his side, Halstead stayed at the wheel through the gale for forty-eight hours until, too exhausted to continue, he insisted that the inexperienced cook/passenger would have to take over.

Terrified, but lashed to the rails, John did. This was how he would later describe the experience to *Playboy*.

> I was there driving the boat for six hours, keeping it on course. I was buried under water . . . smashed in the face by waves for six solid hours. It won't go away. You can't change your mind. It's like being on stage; once you're on, there's no getting off. A couple of the waves had me on my knees. I was just hanging on with my hands on the wheel . . . and I was having the time of my life. I was screaming sea shanties and shouting at the gods! I felt like a Viking . . . or Jason and the Golden Fleece.

By the time they reached Hamilton, Bermuda, after seven days at sea, Halstead and the rest of the crew had revised their opinion of their celebrity passenger. It had never been intended that he would be left in charge of the boat, but he'd performed astonishingly well.

More importantly, John had revised his opinion of himself. He'd enjoyed the control he'd felt in his arms as he'd crashed through the waves and gale. He could do it. For years he had depended on others to do everything for him, for May to be at his side day and night, and for Yoko to direct all those who worked for him. But he'd been in charge; dependent on no one; completely his own man again. Seven days at sea had done more for his self-confidence and his sense of his own worth than five years hiding from the world in the Dakota.

Exultant, as soon as he landed he phoned New York and asked assistant Fred Seaman to bring him his guitar down to Bermuda. He had work to do.

For the first time in five years, John Lennon was ready to start writing and recording again.

# 63

*'It was amazing. I was there on the beach . . .*
*just playing guitar and singing'*

His head, he would say, was suddenly full of songs, and he loved Bermuda. When Seaman reached the island he found a changed man. The pale, indoors New York pallor was gone. John was, he would write, 'exuding health and vitality', and happier than he'd ever seen him.

Yoko had stayed behind in New York, but Sean and his governess had accompanied Seaman down to Bermuda. Soon a large house, Villa Undercliff, was found for the family. With polite, discreet tourists and reggae on the radio, the carefree ambience of this sub-tropical little British dependency was the perfect environment to undam the creativity that had been suppressed for so long. After playing with Sean on the beach, John would go to work in the afternoons and evenings, and, using some basic recording equipment he'd bought in a local store, would make demo copies on cassettes of the music that was now bubbling out of him again. One of the first was the reggae-styled 'Living On Borrowed Time'.

'It was amazing. I was there on the beach taping songs . . . just playing guitar and singing,' he would delight in telling interviewers. Luckily the Villa Undercliff had a piano, and recording got even better when a computerised drum machine was quickly sent down to him from New York.

He'd always had odds and ends of songs, some half-written and others half-recorded on cassettes that he'd been working on at the Dakota, and when he'd been with May he'd been working on a song with the working title of 'Tennessee'. That title and the original lyrics had now been replaced with 'Watching The Wheels', a riposte to those who thought he'd been crazy while sitting in the Dakota and no longer 'riding on the merry-go-round' of fame. It was as good as anything on the *Imagine* album. Then there was the witty 'Nobody

Told Me', with its mention of the UFO he and May had seen. 'Beautiful Boy (Darling Boy)' was a hymn of devotion that every parent could sing to a child, complete with the rueful line about life being what happens to a person while 'you're busy making other plans'. That thought wasn't original to John. He'd read it in a magazine, but, by borrowing it, he took authorship of it in the public mind. Another 'steal' was the line 'Grow old along with me, the best is yet to be', which he lifted from the poet Robert Browning for the song usually known as 'God Bless Our Love'. If he was going to steal, at least he stole from the best, and, unlike Chuck Berry lyrics, Browning's lines were long out of copyright. And then there was 'Woman', ostensibly a guilty 'thank you' to Yoko for teaching him 'the meaning of success', but which, like all his best work, had a universality about it.

Eventually, after several changes of plan, Yoko visited him in Bermuda, but she only stayed for the weekend. John was upset and angry, Fred Seaman told me. John had looked forward to her coming, and to playing his new songs to her. It was important to him that she liked the songs. He always needed approval. But she had business to attend to and she soon left. Whether there was anything else, or anyone, that kept her in New York during those weeks is only speculation and rumour. But, as John would later admit, when he couldn't get her on the phone one day, his response had been to sit at the piano in Bermuda and write the bluesy song 'I'm Losing You'. Yoko might have shown that she was immune to romantic anxiety and sexual jealousy when she had set him up with May, but he wasn't.

He left Bermuda and returned to New York on 29 July, on a direction and timetable that Yoko's tarot cards decreed were positive. Already he had the title of his new album. It would be called *Double Fantasy* after a yellow freesia he'd seen while walking with Sean in the Botanical Gardens in Bermuda.

Originally he had planned his comeback album to be a solo affair, and he certainly had enough songs for one, but Yoko had convinced him that she should be on it too, with one of her songs always following one of his, like a conversation. He knew that wouldn't be what any record company would want. But that was what Yoko wanted, so, in the end, he wanted it too.

After rehearsing the musicians chosen for the new sessions at the Dakota for a couple of nights, recording began with producer Jack

Douglas at the Hit Factory in midtown Manhattan on 8 August. It took just nine days to record twenty-two songs, with fourteen chosen for *Double Fantasy*, seven of John's and seven of Yoko's. John worked quickly on his songs, having worked out in his head all the arrangements beforehand. Yoko took longer with hers. Never having been a professional musician or singer, it was more difficult for her.

In order to maintain total control of the project, John paid all the costs of production, and only when recording was finished was a record company sought to press and distribute the album. That was Yoko's job, and the company chosen was a new one owned by David Geffen, the former manager of Crosby, Stills and Nash and many other big rock names. It is believed that Geffen agreed the deal without hearing any of the tracks.

'Yoko's a tough customer. One never really knows what's on her mind,' Seaman overheard Geffen telling John.

Other label chiefs had, it was rumoured, lost some of their enthusiasm when told that only half the tracks on the album would be by John, but he hadn't been prepared to consider reducing the number of Yoko's tracks in favour of more of his own. Was that because he knew there would be ructions at home? Or was it simply loyalty to his wife? Ever since they'd met, Yoko had been in love with the idea of performing on stage as a rock star. When she'd tried doing it in New York and then Japan while John was with May, she'd failed. Now he was going to help her, even though he knew that her presence on the album would mean that many fans would simply lift up the pick-up when a Yoko song came on and move it to the next one by John. To say that he and Yoko by this stage had a complicated, sometimes contradictory, often incomprehensible relationship would be an understatement.

For years John had idealised their love affair in song, but Seaman, who would overhear their rows, would observe that reality was very different. It was, however, a difference that they never revealed or explained in the rash of interviews they did together to promote the album, as soon as the record deal had been signed.

'It's a teacher-pupil relationship,' John told *Playboy*. 'She's the teacher and I'm the pupil.' While to *Newsweek* he said: 'Being with Yoko makes me whole. I don't want to sing if she's not there.' There was no mention of any tensions in the marriage. For them the point of all interviews was to sell records, and to do that they would fall back on the public idyll that had been created of *JohnandYoko*, an enduring love story.

While they waited for the album to be released, John turned forty on 9 October, with Sean becoming five on the same day. To celebrate the two birthdays, Yoko organised a sky-writing bi-plane to smoke-write 'Happy Birthday John and Sean. Love Yoko' in the clear blue afternoon sky above Central Park. Sean was very excited and watched from the roof of the Dakota along with his governess and some other members of staff. John wasn't interested in public birthday celebrations and went to bed for a sleep instead. Yoko didn't watch either.

A single from the new album, '(Just Like) Starting Over', was released as a teaser during the last week of October. Purposely in the style of an 'Elvis/Orbison song', according to John, it was selected not because it was the strongest track – it wasn't – but because its title and theme captured the moment of reincarnation for John's career. Although it was an instant top ten hit, it was not received without some disappointment. Nor was the album, when that followed three weeks later.

John cared more about the sales than the tepid reviews. Yoko, too, and she decided that action was needed if there was to be sufficient interest in her first single, 'Walking On Thin Ice', a disco track that John was producing. So, to accompany the record, she planned a promotional video that was filmed on 26 November at a studio in SoHo where photographers Allan Tannenbaum and Ethan Russell had cameras waiting on a set that consisted of a divan bed by a window, through which fake sunlight was streaming.

Nudity had worked earlier for Yoko in generating publicity. Now it would be called upon again. After taking off the kimonos that they were wearing, she and John lay naked on the bed and pretended to make love for the next four hours, with Yoko helping dictate the camera angles. Talking to *Playboy*, a few weeks earlier, John had scoffed at the idea that 'John and Yoko would do anything for publicity'. The 'Walking On Thin Ice' video would seem to suggest otherwise. Whether John enjoyed the filming, or knew before he arrived at the studio what he was expected to do in it, is uncertain. But he went along with it anyway.

With Christmas approaching, Yoko's single to be completed, and albums to be sold, it was a busy time, but John was particularly pleased when on Saturday, 6 December, British disc jockey Andy Peebles and a BBC team arrived at the Hit Factory studios for a radio interview. John had been living in the United States for nine years and despite his promises to Liela and Mimi, whom he'd phoned that morning, he hadn't been back to the United Kingdom once in all that time. Nor had either of them, or indeed any of his family, other than Julian, been to see him. Mimi would later blame herself for not having gone to New York, but Seaman had gathered the impression that for John and Yoko the timing had never been quite right when she'd brought it up.

It is difficult to understand why John hadn't been back for a visit. Most likely he was too proud. He didn't want to go home as a has-been curiosity from the Sixties. When he did go, he wanted it to be on the back of a number one hit record. Hence the visit from the BBC and the opportunity to promote the album.

The interview lasted for three hours, with John happily remembering the people he'd worked with when the Beatles had performed live dozens of times on BBC radio in their early days. He was in good spirits, recounting how when old friends from England asked why he wasn't homesick, he joked about how he would tell them that England wasn't going to vanish, that it would still be there when he decided go back. Then, to finish the interview, he explained how it had been Yoko who had sold him on New York, having left London when he'd felt it was difficult to go out because of the intense public interest in the Beatles. Of course, being John, he exaggerated it a bit.

'We couldn't walk around the block . . . couldn't go to a restaurant . . .' he said. 'Yoko told me, "You will be able to walk here . . . you can walk on the street." But I would be walking around, tense like, waiting for somebody to say something, or jump on me, and it took two years to unwind . . . I can go right out of this door now and go in a restaurant . . . I mean people come and ask for an autograph or say "hi", but they don't bug you, you know.'

John went down to La Fortuna on Columbus Avenue for his breakfast on Monday morning, 8 December, after which he had his hair cut. He'd had it longish, Beatles 1966 style, for the past few weeks, having gone through periods of either a pony tail or long hair and beard disguises over the past few years. Now he wanted it cut almost 'schoolboy, 1958' short, for when Annie Leibovitz arrived later that morning to photograph him for *Rolling Stone*.

While that was taking place, Yoko was phoning me in London, insisting I fly over immediately to do an interview for the *Sunday Times* that I'd called about a few weeks earlier. It was agreed that I would take an early flight the very next morning.

Having heard about the nude session that John and Yoko had done for the pop video twelve days earlier, Annie Leibovitz already had an idea in mind for her photograph when she arrived at the Dakota. Putting it to John, he happily undressed for her, but, for some reason, Yoko was now reluctant to take off her clothes. So Leibovitz simply asked her to leave everything on, which was a pair of black pants and black sweater. Then the naked John curled up and wrapped himself around his impassive wife on their bed, as though he was an overgrown baby hanging on to its mother, whose eyes were almost closed. It was an unsettling photograph, perhaps more so when John exclaimed to the photographer, 'You've captured our relationship exactly.'

The interviews were still coming thick and fast, and, after talking to RKO Radio, John and Yoko left the Dakota later that afternoon to go to the Record Plant for John to do more work on Yoko's new single.

As they left the side entrance of the building on West 72nd Street there was the usual scattering of fans hanging around hoping to catch a glimpse of him. The new album had put him back in the public eye, so there were a few more there than was usual.

As John was crossing the pavement, a plump young man in glasses held out a copy of *Double Fantasy* to be autographed.

John signed, murmuring words to the effect of: 'This what you want?' Then, getting into the RKO Radio team's car that was giving him and Yoko a lift to the Record Plant, he was driven away from the smiling fan.

Mixing the record took most of the evening. Yoko was thrilled about it and wondering why it couldn't be released immediately, but David Geffen, who popped in to see them, was insistent that it must wait until January. It was too close to Christmas now to put it out.

They finished work at around ten thirty. John was in good spirits, pleased with the work he'd done. After reminding producer Jack Douglas to be there 'bright and early' the following day to complete the mixing, and deciding not to get something to eat before going home, he and Yoko got into their waiting limousine and were driven back up Central Park West.

It was around 10.54 as the vehicle pulled up at the kerbside outside the Dakota. Getting out of the car, he and Yoko walked the few paces towards the security officer's cubicle in the bridged carriageway entrance to the building. Yoko was slightly ahead, when John, who was carrying some cassettes of the evening's work, heard a voice call to him from a few feet behind. 'Mr Lennon . . . ?'

Still walking, he half-turned to see who it was. At that moment four bullets ripped into his back. His walk became a stagger as he strived to reach the Dakota's security cubicle, before dropping the cassettes and collapsing inside it. Yoko was screaming. The young security officer on duty was pressing the alarm to call the police. As he lay on the floor of the cubicle, blood was pouring from John's mouth and chest.

Outside on the Dakota forecourt the plump young man for whom John had earlier autographed a copy of *Double Fantasy* dropped his gun. Making no attempt to escape, he hung around; then, taking out a paperback copy of J. D. Salinger's novel *The Catcher In The Rye,* he began to read.

His name was Mark Chapman, and he had just fulfilled his ambition. He had made himself famous.

# 64

*'I don't believe in dead heroes'*

There was blood everywhere. Although a patrolling police car was at the Dakota within a couple of minutes, the bullet wounds in John had done devastating damage. As more police arrived to arrest the gunman, John was being carried by two police officers to their car and rushed to nearby Roosevelt Hospital. 'Do you know who you are?' asked one of the officers. Half the world knew who he was.

The doctors in the resuscitation emergency department had been alerted and were waiting as John was rushed in. But there was nothing anyone could have done. John was pronounced dead at 11.15. The official cause of death was given as shock as a result of massive haemorrhaging. John had bled to death.

Yoko, who had been taken to the hospital in a following police car, was told immediately, and David Geffen was summoned to the hospital to be with her. Then Yoko was driven back alone to the Dakota, where she was let into the building by a side entrance.

By then, as news of John's murder was being told and retold all night on radio and television stations, crowds were emerging on to streets around the Dakota. In London it was already early morning on 9 December, and I was cancelling my flight to New York, and sitting down to write the obituary John had enquired about a decade earlier. It seemed heartless at the time, and it was difficult. But that's what a journalist does.

Yoko would tell how she phoned Mimi to tell her. But Paul, who had become accustomed to turning off his telephone at night, didn't hear until Linda arrived back at their home in Sussex after having driven their children to school, having been told by other mothers at the school gate. Cynthia was staying with Ringo's ex-wife Maureen when she heard. Yoko asked her not to go to New York. She understood. But both Julian and Ringo went.

Nearly everyone who is old enough can remember where they

were when they heard the news. It wasn't simply that a famous rock star had died. John was more than that. He had become symbolic of his time, of the music, of the Sixties, of saying what he thought, and of his generation. At that time, America had become, sadly, familiar with political assassinations following the killings of President Kennedy, his brother Robert Kennedy, Martin Luther King and Malcolm X. But those had all been, in some part, politically motivated murders. John, as the world would come to know during the next few days, had been killed simply because of how famous he was.

For days the Dakota was under siege from thousands of fans, as radio stations around the world played records by John and the Beatles, newspapers published special supplements, and television stations quickly assembled documentaries. And, as is the nature of these things, *Double Fantasy* shot to the top of the charts, and 'Imagine' was re-released.

There was no funeral for him and there would be no gravestone. Thirty-six hours after his death, John's body was driven in a hearse to Hartsdale Crematorium in New York State and swiftly, and privately, cremated. When Yoko returned to the Dakota she asked Julian, who had recently arrived, if he would like to hold the still warm urn containing the ashes of his father.

The following Sunday there would be vigils in Liverpool, where fans chorused 'We love you, yeah, yeah, yeah', and another across the road from the Dakota in New York's Central Park, in the area now known as Strawberry Fields. Yoko watched from a window as a message from her to the fans was read out, in which she said John had prayed for everyone.

She no doubt meant well, but, for those who knew him, it's difficult to imagine John in prayer for humanity. But, as if to satisfy some emotional demand, his image was already being whitewashed, and his memory canonised. In life he'd been a joker and a rebel. In death he was already being seen as a martyr. There was irony in that. From his very emergence onto the world stage, he'd made no secret of the fact that he didn't believe in the veneration of dead stars. 'I don't believe in dead heroes,' he once told me, repeated to *Playboy* just a few weeks before his death: 'I don't appreciate worship of dead Sid Vicious, or of dead James Dean, or of dead John Wayne . . . It's garbage to me. I worship the people who survive.' He wouldn't have appreciated the worship of dead John Lennon either, but that was what he got.

Though millions who didn't know him loved him, sometimes those who knew him well didn't always like him. A natural leader, who could so easily be led and who saw himself as a chameleon, he was at various times a clever, witty, angry, funny, sharp-tongued, far-sighted, impetuous, talented, guilt-laden, preaching, sardonic, exaggerating, gullible, aggressive, unfaithful, obsessive, self-absorbed, outspoken, jealous, sometimes cruel but often generous man. He was certainly no saint, but, to his friends, he was hard not to like. Above all, he was absolutely a one-off.

# AFTERWORD

*'I couldn't shoot him like that. I wanted to get his autograph'*
– Mark Chapman

What kind of person could have committed so senseless a crime? Only a mad man. The story of how Mark Chapman became, at twenty-five, one of the twentieth century's most infamous killers is impossible to be viewed in any other way. For almost five years, until just before his murder, John had lived a private life. But one of Mark Chapman's motives was to achieve the exact opposite for himself. He would say later that he thought that by killing John he could take some of his fame and have it for himself – the fame that John had often found a burden.

Chapman had been a Beatles fan as a teenager, but then, after becoming a born-again Christian, he took exception to the song 'Imagine' and the line 'Imagine there's no heaven, it's easy if you try'. The song was intended, and interpreted by most people, as being about peace and against violence, about a world without hate caused by religion or politics. But Chapman misunderstood the message. So he performed an act of total violence on a man who had famously preached non-violence.

But who was Mark Chapman before his crime? Apparently, he was fairly bright as a child, but soon became troubled. Born in 1955 in Texas, where his father was in the US Air Force, but brought up in Georgia, he was just nine when Beatlemania hit America. He loved the Beatles and he also loved watching *The Wizard Of Oz* on TV. But at fourteen he began taking drugs . . . 'Everything apart from heroin,' he would admit later.

Then at sixteen he suddenly changed and became a born-again Christian, angry now that John Lennon could ever have said, in that much misunderstood interview, that the Beatles were 'more popular than Jesus now'.

By the time he was twenty he was working for the YMCA, and spent some time in Beirut before being repatriated to the US when civil war broke out in Lebanon. For a time, he was a success. Working with Vietnamese refugees, he was caring and popular. However, as that job finished, and a girlfriend left him, depression overcame him. He stopped studying and took a job as an armed security guard. He was a very good shot. But thoughts of suicide preyed on his mind.

Then, once again, he changed his life. In 1977 he went to Hawaii, where he spent hours on the phone to the equivalent there of the Samaritans who talked him out of suicide. On one occasion he actually did attempt to take his own life, but, on failing, he went on a world trip to the Far East, then India, Iran and Switzerland.

When he got back to Hawaii he married his travel agent, Gloria Abe, a Japanese American. They should have been happy together, but by the summer of 1980 he was becoming increasingly disturbed. He wanted to change his name to Holden Caulfield, the fictional character from *The Catcher In The Rye*. On at least one occasion he signed himself 'John Lennon'.

By now he was, it's been reported, sometimes sitting naked at his tape recorder and mixing together his reasons for killing John Lennon from Beatles lyrics, *The Wizard Of Oz* and lines from *The Catcher In The Rye*. He wanted, he would say, to rid the world of what Holden Caulfield called 'phony people'.

With a five-thousand-dollar loan from his father-in-law it was a short step to the gunshop in Honolulu where he legally bought a .38 revolver. Then he took a plane to New York where he did a thorough recce of the outside of the Dakota and the streets around that part of Central Park. But he had no bullets for his gun, and couldn't buy them in New York. Flying down to Georgia he got hold of five hollowed-point cartridges, the kind which expand as they pass through the target, and thus cause maximum damage.

Back in New York he still hadn't determined completely that John would be his victim. John might, he thought, be too difficult a target. But if that turned out to be the case he had a list of other targets, too, Jackie Kennedy and the actor George C. Scott among them.

Then he changed his mind again. God, he said, spoke to him. John had been granted a reprieve. Going back to Honolulu, Chapman told his wife what his intentions had been and said he'd thrown the gun into a river.

That was a lie. By 6 December he was back in New York outside the Dakota. Staying that night at the YMCA, he left the next morning, sickened, he would say later, by the sounds of gay sex in the next room. Checking into the nearby Sheraton Hotel, he bought a copy of *Double Fantasy*. Then, because that was what Holden Caulfield had done in *The Catcher In The Rye*, he called an escort service and invited a prostitute to his hotel room, just to talk. When she left at 3 a.m., a hundred and ninety dollars better off, she hadn't taken off her clothes.

Before he left his room the following morning he laid out an old letter from a superior with the YMCA praising his work in the refugee camp, together with photographs of himself with Vietnamese children, placing behind them a poster of Judy Garland as Dorothy with the Cowardly Lion from *The Wizard Of Oz*. They were meant to be found.

Then he set up watch outside the Lennons' apartment, his loaded gun in his pocket, the album and the copy of *The Catcher In The Rye* in his hands. In mid-afternoon he met John for the first time as he and Yoko left the apartment building, and pushed the record into his hand. John duly signed it.

'I was on Cloud Nine,' Chapman would say later in his prison cell. 'There was a little bit of me going "why don't you shoot him?" But I couldn't shoot him like that . . . I wanted to get his autograph.'

By the time John and Yoko returned from the studio, Chapman had been waiting outside their apartment for over twelve hours. His moment had come. He took aim and fired at point-blank range.

As John was raced away to hospital, Chapman waited to be arrested. 'I'm sorry I gave all you guys this trouble,' he apologized to the police when he was handcuffed. 'Don't hurt me. Please don't hurt me.'

At the time of writing he is still in Attica State Prison, thirty-eight years after his crime.

# AFTER JOHN DIED, WHAT HAPPENED TO . . .

**YOKO ONO LENNON:** John once described his wife as 'the world's most famous unknown artist: everybody knows her name, but nobody knows what she does'. Having moved into dance records with the last song John produced for her, 'Walking On Thin Ice', Yoko continues to record and has had several number one hits on the US Dance Chart. In 2015 New York's Museum of Modern Art held a retrospective exhibition of her avant-garde early work. After John's death she began an eight-year relationship with her interior designer, Hungarian Sam Havadboy. She has never remarried. Losing touch with her daughter, Kyoko, in 1971, when her second husband, Tony Cox, absconded with the eight-year-old child, Yoko did not see her again until 1994 when Kyoko got in touch. The two are now reconciled.

**SEAN LENNON:** Partly privately educated in Switzerland, Sean later dropped out of Columbia University to focus on his avant-garde music. A singer/songwriter, he plays guitar, drums, piano and keyboards, and lives with his girlfriend Charlotte Kemp Mulh in New York.

**JULIAN LENNON:** An avid collector of Beatle memorabilia, after first making a career as a singer/songwriter, Julian is now more interested in photography and documentary film-making. He lives in Monaco.

**CYNTHIA LENNON:** Life wasn't always easy for Cynthia following her divorce from John, and after several business failures she had to auction many mementoes of her years with him. Married a further three times, she died at her home in Majorca in 2013 with her fourth husband, Noel, and her son Julian at her bedside. She was seventy-five.

**MIMI SMITH:** A few days before he was murdered, John called his aunt, telling her that he was homesick and looking forward to coming back to England. After his death Mimi was upset to discover that the house John had bought her in Sandbanks, Dorset, had still been in his name and had therefore become the property of Yoko Ono. She died there in 1991, after which the house was quickly sold and demolished.

**SIR PAUL MCCARTNEY:** Paul is one of the most successful song-writers of all time, as he continues to write, record and tour the world. Three times married and the father of five children, his first wife, Linda, died of breast cancer in 1998.

**GEORGE HARRISON:** All his life George loved to make music, and following the break-up of the Beatles he had a successful solo career before co-founding the Traveling Wilburys in 1988 with Jeff Lynne, Roy Orbison, Bob Dylan and Tom Petty. After George and his wife Pattie divorced in 1977, he married Olivia Arias the following year, with whom he had a son, Dhani. George died of lung cancer in 2001, aged fifty-eight.

**RINGO STARR:** The only Beatle with whom all the other three played in their later careers, Ringo overcame a problem with alcohol in the Eighties and has since forged a second career as Ringo Starr and His All-Starr Band. Divorced from his first wife Maureen, who died in 1994, aged forty-eight, and with whom he'd had three children, he now lives in California with his second wife, actress Barbara Bach.

**PETE BEST:** Sacked by the Beatles in 1962, Pete didn't see or speak to any of the other Beatles for forty-five years. In the mid-Sixties, in a deep depression, he tried to commit suicide. His brother, Rory, and mother, Mona, found him, after which she gave him 'the most angry and sensible talking to I've ever had in my life'. Following that he worked for twenty years as a civil servant in Liverpool, before return-ing to drumming in 1988, and occasionally touring with the Pete Best Band.

**MAY PANG:** After John left her in 1975, May remained in touch with Paul McCartney and her friends Cynthia Lennon and Freda

Kelly, the Beatles' fan club secretary. Married to record producer Tony Visconti in 1989, the couple divorced in 2000. They had two children. May now lives in New York.

**NEIL ASPINALL:** Having started out as their road manager, Neil stayed with the Beatles through a variety of roles before becoming the chief executive of their company Apple Corps from which he retired in 2007. He died of lung cancer in 2008.

**SIR GEORGE MARTIN:** Continuing to work into his eighties, George also produced the group America, Celine Dion, Neil Sedaka, Cheap Trick, Elton John and hundreds of other artists. During his career he won six Grammies and an Oscar. He died, aged ninety, in 2016.

**PETE SHOTTON:** After falling out with John over Yoko's demands, Pete co-founded the Fatty Arbuckle diner chain in the UK, eventually selling his share for £5 million. In 1997 he joined the reformed Quarry Men with whom he still enjoyed playing the washboard – as well as a guitar. He died of a heart attack in 2017. He was seventy-six.

**HARRY NILSSON:** A multi-talented man, from early computer programmer to a singer-songwriter with a three-and-a-half-octave range, Nilsson never had the success and fame his brilliance deserved. Profoundly affected by the death of John, he later joined the Coalition to Stop Gun Violence and made appearances for gun control fund-raising, donating record royalties to that cause. His lyrics to the song '1941' were the inspiration for the film *That'll Be The Day*. Married three times, and with a total of seven children, he died of a heart attack in 1994.

**PHIL SPECTOR**: Brilliantly successful record producer though he might have been, Phil Spector had a dark side. And in 2009 he was sentenced to 'nineteen years to life in prison' for 'using a firearm in the commission of a criminal act', after actress Lana Clarkson was found shot dead at his Los Angeles home.

# JOHN LENNON'S BEST RECORDINGS

John Lennon recorded over 400 songs during his career, over 300 of which were with the Beatles. Of those, more than 150 credited both Lennon and McCartney as the writers, although sometimes only one of the two might have done the writing. Almost invariably, however, the songwriter who had conceived the basic idea of the song would sing it. For the Beatles records listed below, John was the lead vocalist. As a solo artist John went on to record over seventy of his own compositions, and fifteen covers of hits by other people.

Please Please Me
From Me To You
There's A Place
Baby It's You (a Beatles cover of a Shirelles record)
She Loves You
You Really Got A Hold On Me (a Beatles cover of a Miracles record)
Money (a Beatles cover of a Barrett Strong record)
Please Mr Postman (a Beatles cover of a Marvelettes record)
It Won't Be Long
Not A Second Time
To Know Her Is To Love Her (BBC version – a Beatles cover of a Teddy
    Bears song written by Phil Spector)
I Want To Hold Your Hand
This Boy
You Can't Do That
I Should Have Known Better
If I Fell
I Call Your Name
A Hard Day's Night
I'm A Loser
Every Little Thing
No Reply

I Feel Fine
Rock And Roll Music (a Beatles cover of a Chuck Berry record)
Ticket To Ride
You've Got To Hide Your Love Away
Help!
Norwegian Wood
Day Tripper
In My Life
Nowhere Man
Girl
And Your Bird Can Sing
I'm Only Sleeping
Strawberry Fields Forever
A Day In The Life
Being For The Benefit of Mr Kite!
Lucy In The Sky With Diamonds
All You Need Is Love
I Am The Walrus
Across The Universe
Revolution
Julia
Cry Baby Cry
Sexy Sadie
Yer Blues
Glass Onion
Happiness Is A Warm Gun
I'm So Tired
The Continuing Story Of Bungalow Bill
I Want You (She's So Heavy)
Come Together
Instant Karma
Mother
Working Class Hero
God
Love
Look At Me
Imagine
Crippled Inside
Jealous Guy

Oh My Love
How?
Woman Is The Nigger Of The World
Scared
Nobody Loves You (When You're Down And Out)
I'm Losing You
Watching The Wheels
Woman
Nobody Told Me There'd Be Days Like These
Grow Old With Me (also known as God Bless Our Love) – a cassette
    demo version that hadn't been professionally recorded at the time
    of his death, but has been much covered by other artists since.

# BIBLIOGRAPHY

Aronowitz, Al: *Dylan and the Beatles*, AuthorHouse, Indiana, 2004

Badman, Keith: *The Beatles Off The Record*, Omnibus Press, 2008

Baird, Julia and Giuliano, Geoffrey: *John Lennon – My Brother*, Grafton Books, London, 1988

Barrow, Tony: *John, Paul, George, Ringo And Me,*. Andre Deutsch, London, 2011

Beatles, The: *The Beatles Anthology*, Cassell, London, 2000

Braun, Michael: *Love Me Do – The Beatles' Progress*, Penguin Books, London, 1964

Brown, Peter and Gaines, Steven: *The Love You Make*, New American Library, New York, 1983

Burger, Jeff: *Lennon On Lennon*, Chicago Review Press, 2017

Coleman, Ray: *John Winston Lennon*, Sidgwick & Jackson, London, 1984

Coleman, Ray: *John Ono Lennon*, Sidgwick & Jackson, 1985

Connolly, Ray: *The Ray Connolly Beatles Archive*, Plumray Books, London, 2016

Davies, Hunter: *The Beatles – The Authorised Biography*, William Heinemann, London, 1968

Davies, Hunter: *The Quarrymen*, Omnibus Press, UK, 2001

Davies, Hunter: *The John Lennon Letters*, Weidenfeld & Nicolson, London, 2012

DiLello, Richard: *The Longest Cocktail Party*, Alfred Music, USA, 2014

Doggett, Peter: *You Never Give Me Your Money*, The Bodley Head, London, 2009

Epstein, Brian: *A Cellarful of Noise*, New English Library, London, 1998

Fawcett, Anthony: *One Day At A Time*, New English Library, 1977

Giuliano, Geoffrey and Giuliano, Brenda: *The Lost Beatles Interviews*, Virgin Books, London, 1995

Giuliano, Geoffrey, *Lennon In America*, Robson Books, London, 2000

Goldman, Albert: *The Lives Of John Lennon*, Chicago Review Press, 1988

Graustark, Barbara: 'The Real John Lennon', interview for *Newsweek*, 1980

Hamill, Pete: 'Long Night's Journey Into Day', *Rolling Stone*, 1975

Harry, Bill: *The Encyclopaedia Of Beatles People*, Blandford, London, 1997

Henke, James: *Lennon Legend*, Weidenfeld & Nicolson, London, 2003

Hopkins, Jerry: *Yoko Ono*, Sidgwick & Jackson, London, 1987

Hutchins, Chris and Thompson, Peter: *Elvis Meets the Beatles*, Neville Ness, London, 2016

Lennon, Cynthia: *A Twist Of Lennon*, Star, London, 1978

Lennon, Cynthia: *John*, Hodder & Stoughton, London, 2005

Lennon, John: *In His Own Write*, Jonathan Cape, London, 1964

Lennon, Pauline: *Daddy, Come Home*, Angus & Robertson, London, 1990

Lennon, Yoko Ono: *Grapefruit*, Simon and Schuster, New York, 1970

Lewisohn, Mark: *The Complete Beatles Recording Sessions*, Hamlyn, 1988

Lewisohn, Mark: *The Beatles – All These Years – Vol 1, Tune In*, Little, Brown and Co., London, 2013

Macdonald, Ian: *Revolution In The Head*, Fourth Estate, London, 1994

Miles, Barry: *John Lennon – In His Own Words*, W. H. Allen, London, 1981

Miles, Barry: *Paul McCartney – Many Years From Now*, Secker and Warburg, London, 1997

Norman, Philip: *John Lennon*, HarperCollins, London, 2008

Norman, Philip: *Paul McCartney*, Weidenfeld & Nicolson, 2016

O'Dell, Chris with Ketcham, Katherine: *Miss O'Dell*, Touchstone, New York, 2009

Pang, May and Edwards, Henry: *Loving John*, Corgi Books, London, 1983

Peebles, Andy: *The Lennon Tapes*, BBC, London, 1981

Richter, Dan: *The Dream Is Over*, Quartet Books, London, 2012

Riley, Tim: *Lennon*, Virgin Books, 2011

Rosen, Robert: *Nowhere Man*, Soft Skull Press, USA, 2000

Seaman, Frederic: *Living On Borrowed Time*, Xanadu, 1991

Shotton, Pete and Schaffner, Nicholas: *John Lennon/In My Life*, Gronet, London, 1983.

Spitz, Bob: *The Beatles – The Biography*, Little, Brown and Co., New York, 2005

Taylor, Derek: *As Time Goes By*, Faber & Faber, London, 1973

Taylor, Derek: *It Was Twenty Years Ago Today*, Bantam Press, London, 1987

Turner, Steve: *Beatles '66 – The Revolutionary Year*, Ecco, London, 2016

Wenner, Jann: *Lennon Remembers*, Talmy, Franklin Ltd, UK, by arrangement with Straight Arrow Publishers Inc, 1972

William, Allan and Marshall, William: *The Man Who Gave The Beatles Away*, Coronet, London, 1975

Womack, Kenneth: *Maximum Volume, The Life of Beatles Producer George Martin, Vol. 1*, Chicago Review Press, 2017

# ACKNOWLEDGEMENTS

This biography is the end result of many decades writing about the Beatles as a journalist, and I owe a debt of gratitude to many people who helped me along the way. They include Pete Best, Tony Bramwell, Peter Brown, Tony Calder, Maureen Cleave, Rod Davis, Hunter Davies, Lil Evans, Anthony Fawcett, Bill Harry, Ronnie Hawkins, Freda Kelly, Mark Lewisohn, Mike McCartney, Sir Paul McCartney, Thelma McGough, Barbara O'Donnell, Yoko Ono, May Pang, Dan Richter, Fred Seaman, 'Mimi' Smith, Ringo Starr and Pauline Sutcliffe. Sadly, some are no longer with us, but all are fondly remembered. They include Neil Aspinall, Tony Barrow, Ray Coleman, Mal Evans, Dick James, Cynthia Lennon, Linda McCartney, Sir George Martin, Harry Nilsson, Derek Taylor and, of course, John Lennon.

# NOTES

## Chapter One:

p1 'Conceived on the kitchen floor'. From *Daddy, Come Home* by Pauline Lennon based on Freddie Lennon's unpublished memoir.

p1-3 Courtship details of John's parents. *The Beatles Authorised Biography* by Hunter Davies.

p5 'His story differed from hers'. Letter from John's uncle Charlie Lennon to this author, 1982.

p6 'No "tug-of-love" scene and "no raised voices"'. *The Beatles – Tune In* by Mark Lewisohn.

p6 'Every child has a right to a safe and happy home life'. Aunt 'Mimi' Smith in *The Beatles Authorised Biography*.

p7 'I've done a very wicked thing'. Allegedly said by Mimi Smith and recounted to this author by Cynthia Lennon in 2005.

## Chapter Two:

p9 'I was a nice, clean suburban boy'. John in *The Beatles Authorised Biography*, later, in variations, to this author and several other interviewers.

p12 'As bright as a button and quick in his movements'. Mimi Smith to this author.

p13 'I was passionate about *Alice In Wonderland*'. John in *The Beatles Authorised Biography*, and to this author and others.

p13 'I used to think about becoming a journalist . . .' John to this author.

p14 'One of the great moments of my life . . . first harmonica . . .' John in Ken Zelig interview.

p14 'He wasn't a sit-in-the-corner quiet Harry'. Jimmy Tarbuck in the *Guardian*, 2009.

p15 'I was aggressive because I wanted to be popular'. John in *The Beatles Authorised Biography*.

## Chapter Three:

p16 'John desperately needed the supportive presence of whoever he felt closest to at the time . . .' Pete Shotton in *John Lennon In My Life*.

p17 'The sort of gang I led went in for things like shoplifting'. John in *The Beatles Authorised Biography*.

p17 'He was known in the neighbourhood as "that John Lennon!!"' Rod Davis to this author.

p18 'That was typical of John . . . supporting the underdog . . .' Mimi Smith to this author.

p18 'I can see him now in the garden, dancing around Pete Shotton who was tied up to a tree . . .' Mimi Smith in *John Lennon* by Ray Coleman.

p19 'The Stanley sisters . . . five strong women'. John to this author.

p20 'Freddie had "made a shambles" of his life . . .' Freddie Lennon's recollection of Mimi's letter to him, from *Daddy, Come Home*.

## Chapter Four:

p23 'I'm either a genius or I'm mad'. John to this author (London *Evening Standard*) and many other interviewers.

p23 'On the road to Damascus a burning pie . . .' John's own memory of a school essay in *The Beatles Authorised Biography*.

p24 'I've been proved right. They were wrong and I was right'. John on school memories to this author *(Evening Standard)* and other interviewers.

p24 'He would get what we used to call "black marks" all the time . . .' Rod Davis to this author.

p27 'I've had a lot of death in my life'. John Lennon to this author (*Evening Standard*).

## Chapter Five:

p31 'He showed me the name "Elvis Presley" in the charts in the *New Musical Express* . . .' *Ibid.*

p32 'I thought about it for days at school, about the labels on the records . . .' *Ibid.*

p33 'Nobody was fighting and dancing in the aisles . . .' John Lennon to this author, *Ibid.*

p33 'I was a very insecure male . . .' John to *Playboy*, 1980.

## Chapter Six:

p37 'I was never really a street kid or tough guy'. John to *Rolling Stone* magazine and reprinted in *Lennon Remembers* by Jann Wenner.

p38 'I couldn't take my eyes off him . . .' Mimi Smith in *John Lennon* (Ray

Coleman).

p40 'I learned a lot from Paul . . .' John to this author *(Sunday Times Magazine)*.

p41 'So, what are you going to do with him?' Mimi in *The Beatles Authorised Biography*.

p42 'He has been a trouble spot for many years in discipline . . .' Quarry Bank headmaster in *The Beatles Authorised Biography*.

## Chapter Seven:

p45 John arrived at art college looking like a Teddy boy . . . Bill Harry and Thelma McGough to this author.

p47 'He was very simple, yet complex . . .' Mike McCartney to this author.

p50 Account of Barbara, his on-off girl-friend . . . *John Lennon* (Philip Norman).

p50 'What's so sad about the past, is that it's passed . . .' John to Howard Cosell, ABC Radio.

p50 Account of an early girlfriend. *Ibid.*

p50 'I wonder who's kissing her now'. Title and first line of a popular song, written in 1909 by Will M. Hayes and Frank R. Adams.

## Chapter Eight:

p52 'We asked George to join us because he knew more chords . . .' John to this author.

p52 'George looked even younger than Paul, and Paul looked about ten with his baby face . . .' *Ibid.*

p52 'Your little friend's here, John'. Paul McCartney's recollection to Barry Miles in *Many Years From Now*.

p53 'But for your mum to be actually living somewhere else . . .' *Ibid.*

p55 Account of Mimi and Michael Fishwick's relationship from *The Beatles – Tune In* by Mark Lewisohn.

p55 John's account of accidentally catching his mother with Bobby Dykins from *John Lennon: In My Life* (Pete Shotton and Nicolas Shaffner).

p56 'I was never neat. They might as well have put me in sky-diving for the use I was at lettering . . . ' John to *Rolling Stone* and other interviewers.

p56 'Some blokes will do anything to get out of the army'. John, as remembered by Thelma McGough and told to this author.

p57 'In the front room of some guy's house that he called a recording studio . . .' John to *Rolling Stone*.

## Chapter Nine:

p60 'I turned to see her body flying through the air . . .' Nigel Walley in *The Beatles – Tune In.*

p60 'The copper came to the door . . . asking if I was her son . . .' John in *The Beatles Authorised Biography.*

p61 Julia's daughters were told their mother was in hospital. *John Lennon – My Brother* by Julia Baird and Geoffrey Giuliano.

p61 'I couldn't leave John now. He had nobody'. Mimi in *John Lennon* (Ray Coleman).

## Chapter Ten:

p62 'The underlying chip on my shoulder that I already had, got really big then . . .' *Rolling Stone.*

p62 'Don't take it out on me because your mum's dead'. Thelma McGough quoting John to this author.

p63 'Even though it wasn't my stop, I collected my drums, left the bus, and left them'. Colin Hanton quoted in *The Quarrymen* by Hunter Davies.

p65 Stuart was 'the nicest of all John's friends'. Mimi Smith in *John Lennon* (Ray Coleman).

p66 'That was the big occasion, to watch his fingers . . .' Paul in *Paul McCartney: Many Years from Now* by Barry Miles.

## Chapter Eleven:

p69 'No dirty jokes in front of Miss Powell . . .' John quoted in *A Twist of Lennon* by Cynthia Lennon.

p71 'There was something wrong with me . . .' John in *The Beatles Authorised Biography.*

p91 'It was terrible. I couldn't stand being without her . . .' John in *The Beatles Authorised Biography,*

p72 'Was I to blame for being unfair?' A lyric from 'I Call Your Name' by John Lennon and Paul McCartney.

p72 'John wasn't the best, but he wasn't the worst'. Cynthia Lennon to this author, *Daily Mail.*

p72 Mimi 'didn't think any girl was good enough for her boy . . .' *Ibid.*

## Chapter Twelve:

p75 'Paul could have gone to university . . .' John to this author.

p76 'Anyone can play the bass. It's only got four fucking strings'. *Ibid.*

p76 'I decided to spell it BEAtles to make it look like beat music as a joke

. . .' To this author and other interviewers.

p78 'George and I were always slightly jealous of John's other friendships. He was the older fella . . . and . . . when Stuart came in . . . we had to take a bit of a back seat'. Paul McCartney in *Many Years From Now*.

p79 'We looked at the group. "One in every four" . . .' Paul McCartney in *Many Years From Now*.

p80 'We'd tell Stu he couldn't sit with us . . .' John to *Rolling Stone* and several interviewers.

## Chapter Thirteen:

p83 'That's very nice, John. So, what are you going to do now?' Mimi Smith in *John Lennon* (Ray Coleman).

p84 'He could keep one beat going for long enough . . .' John talking about Pete Best to *Rolling Stone*.

## Chapter Fourteen:

p88 'We'd have to eat and drink on stage'. John in *The Authorised Beatles Biography* and to many interviewers.

p90 'I might have been born in Liverpool, but I grew up in Hamburg . . .' John to *Rolling Stone* and in other interviews.

p91 'The sexiest letters this side of Henry Miller'. John in *The Authorised Beatles Biography*.

## Chapter Fifteen:

p93 'Women should be obscene and not heard'. John, joking in many interviews.

p94 'I thought I could chat him up . . . kid him on we could get him some birds'. In *The Authorised Beatles Biography*, and variations in other interviews.

## Chapter Sixteen:

p97 'Is this what I want to do? Night clubs? Seedy scenes?' John to Yoko's friend Elliot Mintz in 1976.

p97 '. . . spent his money on a gangster's moll . . .' from *John* by Cynthia Lennon.

p98 The Beatles at Litherland Town Hall on 27 December, 1960 – as remembered in *The Beatles* by Bill Harry.

p100 Stuart beaten up. From various accounts, including Pauline Sutcliffe to this author, *The Beatles Authorised Biography*, *John Lennon* (Philip

Norman) and *The Beatles – Tune In*.

p102 'Being a Short Diversion on the Dubious Origins of the Beatles' – headline in *Mersey Beat*.

## Chapter Seventeen:

p105 'There was a certain type . . . you'd call them groupies now'. John to *Rolling Stone*.

p106 'It was terrible . . . It was just Tony Sheridan singing with us banging in the background. It could have been anyone'. John in *John Lennon* (Ray Coleman)

p107 'I really got lumbered [with the bass]'. Paul McCartney in *Many Years From Now*.

## Chapter Eighteen:

p110 'Paris . . . all the kissing and holding . . . it was so romantic'. John to *Playboy* in 1980.

p111 'They'd have more chance with the bohemian beauties on the Left Bank . . .' Jürgen Vollmer in *The Beatles – Tune In*.

## Chapter Nineteen:

p112 'Brian Epstein looked efficient and rich. We were in a daydream till he came along'. John to *Rolling Stone*.

p115 'Late. But very clean'. George Harrison in *The Beatles Authorised Biography*.

p115 'It was a choice of making it, or still eating chicken on stage'. John in *Rolling Stone*.

p115 'Paul has the glamour. John has the command'. Brian Epstein in *A Cellarful Of Noise*, his autobiography.

p115 On becoming 'a performing flea'. John to this author (*Evening Standard*).

p116 'I thought the only place John was going was the Labour Exchange'. Mimi Smith in *John Lennon* (Ray Coleman).

## Chapter Twenty

p120 Cynthia told to stay away from the Cavern . . . Told to this author.

p121 '. . . what John would call his "spazzie" act . . .' George Harrison in *The Beatles Anthology*.

p121 'I'm sure Brian was in love with John . . .' Paul in *Many Years From Now*.

p122 'I was the closest to Brian . . .' John to *Rolling Stone.*

p123 'You have a good record business in Liverpool . . .' Allegedly Dick Rowe of Decca to Brian Epstein, quoted in *The Beatles Authorised Biography.*

p123 'Brian would come back from London and he couldn't face us . . .' John in *John Lennon* (Ray Coleman) and with variations to other journalists.

p124 'I asked whether they had been published . . .' Ardmore and Beechwood employee Jim Foy to Mark Lewisohn in 1987 (*The Beatles – Tune In*).

**Chapter Twenty-one:**

p126 'I looked up to Stu. I depended on him to tell me the truth . . .' John in *The Beatles Authorised Biography.*

p127 'You have to decide if you want to die or go on living'. John to Astrid Kirchherr, in *John Lennon* (Ray Coleman).

p127 John wrote 'pornographic' love letters . . . Cynthia Lennon to this author.

p128 George Martin's background. Interview with this author, *Daily Mail*

p128 'Rock and roll was alien to me . . .' *Ibid.*

**Chapter Twenty-two:**

p132. 'They were charismatic . . .' George Martin to this author, *Ibid.*

p133 'We'll have to get married . . .' John in *John* (Cynthia Lennon).

p134 'I've got some bad news for you . . .' Pete Best to this author about being sacked, *Daily Mail.*

p134 'We were cowards . . .' John to this author re. Pete Best.

p135 Description of her wedding – from *John* (Cynthia Lennon).

**Chapter Twenty-three:**

p138 'John was seeing a girl who I knew and I was dying to tell her that he was married . . .' Freda Kelly to this author.

p139 'When the dirty work came . . .' in *Rolling Stone.*

p139 'When you write something as good as that song, I'll let you record it'. George Martin to this author, *Daily Mail.*

p140 Brian Epstein was to act as their songwriting agent and would take 20 per cent of their royalties. *You Never Give Me Your Money* by Peter Doggett.

p141 'I used to scream at him to open his mouth and *sing* . . .' John to this author.

p141 'Brian used to bring rock stars who were not making it any more . . .'
John to *Rolling Stone*.

p143 'Please, lend your little ear to my pleas'. Lyrics to popular song
'Please', written in 1933 by Ralph Rainer and Leo Robin.

p143 'We were the best bloody band there was . . .' John to this author,
*Radio Times*.

p144 Dick James's background from conversations with this author.

## Chapter Twenty-four:

p148 'Not for a minute'. George Martin when asked if he'd ever
thought 'Please Please Me' was a song about sex to this author,
*Daily Mail*.

p149 Helen Shapiro 'just had to carry on singing and smiling her way
through it all' Fan Plum Balmforth, 1963.

p151 'If they were lousy we gave them to George or Ringo'. John to this
author.

p151 'It nearly killed me . . . Every time I swallowed it was like sandpaper'.
John to various reporters.

p152 'We'd sung for twelve hours, almost non-stop . . .' John in many
interviews.

p152 'From Me To You': 'We nearly didn't do it, because it was too bluesy'.
John to this author, *Sunday Times Magazine*.

## Chapter Twenty-five:

p156 'I watched Brian picking up boys and I liked playing it a bit faggy'.
John to *Rolling Stone*.

p157 'What about that then, Pete? Fancy swapping wives?' John quoted in
Pete Shotton's memoirs, *John Lennon: In My Life*.

p158 'I must have had a fear that maybe I was homosexual to attack him
[Bob Wooler] like that'. John to Andy Peebles, BBC radio, 1980.

## Chapter Twenty-six:

p162 'One more ciggy, and I'm going to hit the sack'. The Beatles talking in
*Love Me Do – The Beatles' Progress* by Michael Braun.

p166 'We were downstairs in the cellar . . . and we had the line, "Oh you, got
that something"'. John to this author, *Sunday Times Magazine*.

p167 '. . . their flat, submediant key switches . . . chains of pandiatonic
clusters'. From a review of the Beatles' music in *The Times* by music
critic William Mann, 1963.

**Chapter Twenty-seven:**

p169 'This isn't show business. It's something else'. John about Beatlemania in press reports.

p171 'It just seemed ridiculous . . . It was just something you could never
do . . .' John to *Playboy*, 1965.

p171 'The bread rolls were shaped like penises and the soup was served out
of chamber pots'. George Harrison in *The Beatles Anthology*.

**Chapter Twenty-eight:**

p173 'Everyone in Liverpool thinks they're a comedian'. George Harrison in
*The Beatles Anthology*.

p174 'Never in a million years did we think anything like this'. John in
press reports on the Beatles' welcome in America in 1964.

p175 'Come on now, do your stuff'. Press reports of party at British
Embassy in Washington.

p175 'Then some bloody animal cut Ringo's hair . . .' John years later to
this author.

**Chapter Twenty-nine:**

p178 'I can't help my feelings I go out of my mind . . .' A lyric from 'You
Can't Do That' by John Lennon and Paul McCartney.

p178 'It was a comic strip version . . .' John in *Rolling Stone*.

p179 'It wasn't what you would call a happy reunion . . .' when John met
his father. Reporter Don Short to this author.

p180 'If I hadn't been a Beatle I wouldn't have thought of having the stuff
published . . .' To Cliff Michelmore on *Tonight*, BBC, 18 June, 1965.

p181 'It's about nothing. If you like it, you like it. If you don't, you don't'.
*Ibid.*

**Chapter Thirty:**

p186 'The idea of being a rock and roll musician sort of suited my talents
and my mentality . . .' John, with variations, to many reporters.

p186 'It was like Fellini's *Satyricon* . . .' John to *Rolling Stone*.

p187 The Beatles meet Dylan. From *Bob Dylan And The Beatles* by Al
Aronowitz.

p187 'Part of me suspects I'm a loser . . .' John to this author.

p188 'Paul has a *high* voice'. Indignant John to this author.

## Chapter Thirty-one:

p191 'We were like Kings of the Jungle . . . like Caesars . . .' John to *Rolling Stone*.

p192 Such people seemed 'so effortlessly perfect'. Cynthia Lennon on meeting Dudley Moore and Peter Cook in *John*.

p192 'a naïve girl who had simply got lucky and didn't deserve' to be there. *Ibid*.

p193 'It was obvious that the song ('Norwegian Wood') was about what John would later describe as "a little affair".' George Martin to this author.

p193 'Money flows in and it flows out'. John to this author.

p193 'Probably because he never had to work hard for it like some people . . .' Mimi in *John Lennon* (Ray Coleman).

p194 'Sometimes I go to John's house to play with his toys . . .' Ringo to this author, *Evening Standard*.

p195 'And never once did we come away empty-handed . . .' Paul to this author, *Daily Telegraph*.

p196 The song 'Yes It Is': 'Same harmony, same chords and double-dutch words . . .' John to this author, *Sunday Times Magazine*.

p197 The song 'Help!': 'That was my "fat Elvis" period . . .' John to this author, *Evening Standard*.

p198 'On the surface, John was tough, tough, tough'. Paul to Barry Miles, *Many Years From Now*.

p199 'It was at the flat of some trendy, swinger dentist, you know the sort of people who George hangs out with . . .' John to this author.

## Chapter Thirty-two:

p201 'Once you plug in and the noise starts, you're just a group who could be playing anywhere . . .' John to reporters after the Beatles' appearance at Shea Stadium.

p202 'We could send out four waxwork dummies of ourselves and that would satisfy the crowds . . .' John to *Rolling Stone*.

p202 'The only person in the United States we really wanted to meet'. John to Chris Hutchins and other reporters about Elvis.

p203 Details of the Beatles meeting Elvis. From *Elvis Meets The Beatles* by Chris Hutchins. Also Paul McCartney to this author.

p205 'It was heaven'. Cynthia Lennon to this author of the only picnic she had with John and Julian.

**Chapter Thirty-three:**

p208 'Girl' – on which the Beatles sang the disguised words 'tit . . . tit . . .
    tit'. John to this author, *Sunday Times Magazine*.

p208 'In My Life': 'It was pretty truthful. No psychedelia. No gobbledegook
    . . .' John to this author, *Ibid*.

p209 'We Can Work It Out': Paul was the optimist, wanting to work things
    out, while he was impatient, always in a hurry – John's view of the
    difference between him and Paul to this author.

p211 'A tiny man with lank grey hair, balding on top . . .' Cynthia's first
    view of Freddie Lennon in her biography *John*.

**Chapter Thirty-four:**

p213 *'We're* more popular than Jesus now'. John to Maureen Cleave,
    *Evening Standard*.

p214 'Sex is the only physical thing I can be bothered with any more'. *Ibid*.

p215 'Reality leaves a lot to the imagination . . .' One of John's frequent
    jokes about drugs.

p216 'For No One': 'That was one of Paul's good ones . . . all his semi-
    classical ones are his best . . .' John to this author, *Sunday Times
    Magazine*.

**Chapter Thirty-five:**

p218 'It's like we're four freaks being wheeled out to be seen, shake our hair
    about and get back in our cage afterwards'. John to *Rolling Stone*, 1970.

p218 'Only someone who was very silly would have enjoyed it'. George
    Harrison in *The Beatles Anthology*.

p221 'They punched and kicked at us as we rushed by . . .' Accounts
    of scare at Manila airport by Peter Brown and Tony Barrow to this
    author.

**Chapter Thirty-six**

p223 'He was not comparing the Beatles with Christ . . .' Maureen Cleave,
    *Evening Standard*.

p224 'If you want me to apologise, if that will make you happy, then okay,
    I'm sorry'. John at Chicago news conference, 1966.

p225 'Our lives had been threatened and then someone in the audience let
    off a firecracker . . . It went *BANG!*' John to *Rolling Stone*.

p225 'One has to completely humiliate oneself to be what the Beatles were
    . . .' John to this author (*Evening Standard*) and also *Rolling Stone*.

## Chapter Thirty-seven:

p229 'I was expecting an orgy, but we met and it was all quiet'. *Ibid.*

p229 'What if I give you an imaginary five shillings . . .' John to this author and many other journalists about his first meeting with Yoko Ono.

p230 'Stir inside of your brains with a penis until things are mixed up . . .' An instruction in Yoko Ono's book *Grapefruit.*

## Chapter Thirty-eight:

p232 'Strawberry Fields Forever' 'is about me, and I was having a hard time'. John to this author, *Sunday Times Magazine.*

p234 '. . . the biggest mistake of my professional life'. George Martin to this author on leaving 'Penny Lane' and 'Strawberry Fields Forever' off the *Sgt. Pepper* album.

p235 'Lucy In The Sky With Diamonds': 'No secret message'. John to this author, *Sunday Times Magazine.*

p236 'In fact, I was so innocent [about LSD] that I took John up to the roof of the studio'. George Martin to this author.

p237 'I never know what John and Paul are on about half the time'. Ringo to this author, *Evening Standard.*

p237 'We had no problems at home. We were two people living in the best way we could under the circumstances'. Cynthia Lennon to this author.

## Chapter Thirty-nine:

p241 '"All You Need Is Love" . . . a subtle bit of PR for God . . .' George Harrison in *The Beatles Anthology.*

p242 'Did you know, Mick Jagger wears a codpiece . . . ?' John in wicked mood to this author.

## Chapter Forty:

p248 John sent Brian some flowers with the message 'You know I love you . . . I really do'. From *The Love You Make*, Peter Brown's memoir.

p248 'I introduced Brian to pills – which gives me a guilt association with his death'. John to *Rolling Stone.*

p248 'I knew we were in trouble then'. John, reflecting years later to this author on the death of Brian Epstein

## Chapter Forty-one

p251 Not one of them could find a copy of a single contract or document that they had signed. Peter Brown in *The Love You Make* and *You Never Give Me Your Money* by Peter Doggett.

p252 Filming of *Magical Mystery Tour*, as witnessed by this author for the *Evening Standard*.

p254 'I Am The Walrus': 'It could have been the "pudding basin" for all I care. It's not that serious . . .' John to Andy Peebles, BBC radio.

p257 'I had been about the only person John hadn't danced with'. Cynthia Lennon in her autobiography *John*.

p257 'From the point of view of good Boxing Day entertainment we goofed really'. Paul to this author, *Evening Standard*.

**Chapter Forty-two:**

p258 'Watch your arse in Brighton . . .' John joking in a letter to his father in *The John Lennon Letters* (Hunter Davies).

p258 'Across The Universe' was 'one of the best songs I ever wrote . . . It's good poetry'. To this author, *Sunday Times Magazine*.

p259 'As we entered the main room I saw . . .' Cynthia Lennon in *John*.

p261 'He would get up early every morning and leave our room . . .' *Ibid*.

p262 'Yoko wrote these crazy postcards . . .' John to this author.

p262 'I'm So Tired': they 'should have used it for an anti-smoking campaign'. To this author, *Sunday Times Magazine*.

p263 Rishikesh 'was just like Butlin's . . .' Ringo to this author, *Evening Standard*.

p263 '. . . if George is doubting him there must be something in it'. John to this author and others.

p264 'There have been other women, you know . . .' From *John* by Cynthia Lennon.

**Chapter Forty-three:**

p267 'I think I'm Jesus Christ'. John in *John Lennon In My Life*.

p268 'I fancy having a woman around, Pete. Do you mind if I get one?' *Ibid*.

p269 'You had to be in the situation to realise the horror of it . . .' Cynthia Lennon to this author.

**Chapter Forty-four:**

p270 Biographical details of Yoko Ono told by her to this author *(Evening Standard)*, and also from Jerry Hopkins' book *Yoko Ono*.

p270 'God was always watching . . .' Yoko Ono to this author, *Evening Standard*.

p272 'My first husband was very kind . . .' *Ibid*.

p273 Cox had once been 'kept prisoner in his bath'. From *Yoko Ono* by Jerry Hopkins and *The Lives Of John Lennon* by Albert Goldman.

## Chapter Forty-five:

p274 'We were both so excited about discovering each other . . .' Yoko in *John Lennon* (Philip Norman).

p275 He barely recognised John as the person he'd known for the past five years. Tony Barrow in conversation with this author.

p276 'We've got about two LPs' worth of songs . . .' John in postcard to Ringo.

p276 'If I started to think of a line . . .' Paul McCartney to this author, *Evening Standard*.

p276 'I was afraid about the possibility of a break-up of a great musical partnership'. *Ibid*.

p277 'I'm sick of those aggressive hippies or whatever they are'. John to *Rolling Stone*.

## Chapter Forty-six:

p279. 'I'm not here to tidy up your underpants and fold your girlfriend's knickers'. Pete Shotton in *John Lennon: In My Life*.

p280 'I haven't been unfaithful to you. I'm sure you know that'. Cynthia to John, as recounted in *John*.

p282 Freddie was anxious to marry Pauline. From *Daddy, Come Home*.

p282 'I took one look at her . . .' Mimi on seeing Yoko, *Liverpool Echo*.

p284 'It's not specifically about anything'. John on 'Revolution 9' in *John Lennon* (Ray Coleman).

p284 'I was thinking that Jimi Hendrix had lived there, so God knows what we might find in the carpets'. John to this author.

p285 'She told him how when he'd been in India she'd gone to Paris and had been offered heroin . . .' From *Yoko Ono* by Jerry Hopkins.

p285 'I never injected . . . Just sniffing, you know . . .' John to *Rolling Stone*.

## Chapter Forty-seven

p287 'I must admit I was a bit shocked . . .' in *Rolling Stone*.

p288 'Ah, the bottoms girl, Yoko, has persuaded John into it'. Yoko to this author, *Evening Standard*.

p288 'Making an exhibition of himself'. Mimi Smith to this author.

p288 John wrote down a list of all the women with whom he had slept. John to this author.

p289 'John was scared that if I stayed in the studio out with a lot of other men . . .' Yoko joking to this author.

p289 'What we did was to purposely not have a pretty photograph'. John to *Rolling Stone*.

p290 'People just want me to be lovable. But I was never that. Even at school I was just "Lennon!"'. John to this author and variously to other interviewers.

p291 'There's a forty-three-pound turkey . . .' From *John Lennon* (Philip Norman).

## Chapter Forty-eight:

p293 'I'm warming to the idea of doing it in a lunatic asylum'. John in an out-take of the film *Let It Be*.

p294 'There are only two things to do . . .' Paul McCartney recorded during filming of *Let It Be – The Ray Connolly Beatles Archive*.

p294 *Let It Be* . . . 'the most miserable sessions ever . . .' – John to this author. *Ibid.*

p294 'On this one, George, we don't want any of your production crap . . .' John to George Martin – who told this author, *Daily Mail*.

p295 'Haven't you written anything yet?' Paul on the soundtrack of *Let It Be – The Ray Connolly Beatles Archive*.

p295 'We probably *do* need a central daddy figure . . .' On an unused out-take of the film *Let It Be, Ibid.*

p296 'I think you're both nuts, the pair of you'. Ringo, *Ibid.*

p297 'Thank you very much. We hope we passed the audition'. John on the *Let It Be* soundtrack.

## Chapter Forty-nine

p299. 'It's been pie in the sky from the start . . .' John in *John Lennon* (Ray Coleman).

p300 Allen Klein 'not only knew my work, and the lyrics . . . he also understood them . . .' John to this author and other journalists.

p302 But she did wonder if she needed to get married. From *John Lennon* (Philip Norman).

p303 'It's sell, sell, sell. If you want peace you've got to sell it like soap . . .' John to this author, *Evening Standard*.

p305 'It was Yoko that changed me. She forced me to become avant-garde . . .' John to this author, *Evening Standard*.

## Chapter Fifty

p309 A bed brought into Abbey Road studio for Yoko. Told to this author by George Martin – *The Ray Connolly Beatles Archive*.

p310 John and Yoko were dabbling with heroin. Dan Richter in *The Dream Is Over*.

p310 'I started to smoke at fifteen, though I hated the smell . . . ' John to this author, *Evening Standard*.

p313 'I began to feel that the only way we could get back to playing good music again . . .' Paul McCartney to this author, *Evening Standard*.

## Chapter Fifty-one:

p315 'Now I've become a crutch for the world's social lepers . . .' John to this author, *(Evening Standard)*.

p315 'Your Majesty, I am returning my MBE as a protest . . .' John reading his letter to the Queen in a phone call to this author, *Ibid*.

p317 John and Yoko in Canada. This author's account of accompanying them, *Ibid*.

p319 'I've left the Beatles . . .' John tells this author – *The Ray Connolly Beatles Archive*.

## Chapter Fifty-two:

p321 'He said he'd been on a flying saucer . . .' John to this author.

p322 'She's a junkie, you know'. John on Yoko in the London Clinic. This author's account.

p323 'I would *never* have women's voices on a Beatles record . . .' Paul McCartney to this author, *Evening Standard*.

p324 'You're the journalist, Connolly, not me'. John to this author, *The Ray Connolly Beatles Archive*.

p325 'Paul and me were the Beatles. We wrote the songs'. John to this author, *Ibid*.

p326 'I always wanted to be an eccentric millionaire and now I am one'. John to this author, *Evening Standard*.

## Chapter Fifty-three:

p327 John and Yoko and Arthur Janov. John to this author (*Evening Standard*) and more from *John Lennon* (Philip Norman) and *Rolling Stone*.

p328 The last thing he needed was to be filmed lying on a psychother-apist's couch screaming . . . John to this author.

p329 *Plastic Ono Band* album is 'my insight into myself'. John to this author, *Evening Standard*.

p329 'I used to say I wouldn't be singing "She Loves You" when I was thirty . . .' *Ibid.*

p330 'I don't want to die when I'm forty'. *Ibid.*

p330 Freddie Lennon summoned to Tittenhurst Park. From *Daddy, Come Home*.

p331 'I want you out of the house and I'm cutting off your money . . .' *Ibid.*

p332 'He left me. I didn't leave him'. John about his father to this author, *Evening Standard*.

## Chapter Fifty-four:

p335 'John wanted to be cool and accepted'. *The Dream Is Over* by Dan Richter.

p335 Filming of *Fly*. Dan Richter's, May Pang's and Jerry Hopkins' accounts.

p336 'It's pretty basic . . . to hate and fear the police as a natural enemy . . .' Interview in *Red Mole* with Tariq Ali and Robin Blackburn.

p337 'The radicalism was phoney, really, because it was out of guilt . . . [I'm] a chameleon'. – John to David Sheff (*Playboy*).

p338 Kidnapping/tug-of-love of Kyoko. Press reports and Dan Richter's account.

## Chapter Fifty-five:

p340 Recording of *Imagine*. From Dan Richter's account in *The Dream Is Over*. Further details from the documentary film *The Making Of Imagine*, and conversations with John when he played the album to this author.

p342 'I'm just a guy who writes songs . . .' John in *The Making Of Imagine*.

p343 'I couldn't get any peace . . .' To this author, *The Ray Connolly Beatles Archive*.

p345 John was torn. Row in New York over the Bangla Desh concert. From Philip Norman's *John Lennon*, Jerry Hopkins' *Yoko Ono* and May Pang to this author.

## Chapter Fifty-six

p347 'America is the Roman Empire and New York is Rome itself . . .' John to this author (*Evening Standard*) and other interviewers.

p348. 'I don't even have to bother singing . . . Invitations like this come every day'. John to this author, *Ibid.*

p348 Yoko's exhibition in Syracuse. This author was present. *Ibid.*

p349 'You look like a tart, a fucking whore . . .' *Ibid.*

p351 'Why should I work with Paul McCartney when I have Yoko . . .' John to this author, *The Ray Connolly Beatles Archive*.

p353 FBI tapping Lennons' phones. This author first told in phone conversation with John.

p353 Immigration Service battles from Philip Norman's *John Lennon*, Bob Spitz's *The Beatles*, *The Dick Cavett Show* and press reports.

**Chapter Fifty-seven:**

p356 John got very drunk at the party. There was a girl there . . . Yoko Ono in telephone conversation with this author.

p358 'John and I are not getting along . . .' Yoko to May Pang. Told to this author by Yoko Ono. Further details from *Loving John* by May Pang, and in conversation with May Pang.

p358 'I'd been trained to believe that men like John . . . never picked women like me'. From *Loving John* (May Pang) and in conversation with this author.

p359 John's Eighteen-month 'Lost Weekend'. From press reports, *John Lennon* (Ray Coleman), David Sheff of *Newsweek*.

p360 'Into the jaws of the dragon . . .' From *Loving John* (May Pang).

p361 'Listen, Phil, if you're going to kill me . . .' *Ibid.*

**Chapter Fifty-eight:**

p364 'He has to work at it . . .' Paul McCartney on getting John back with Yoko. From *Many Years From Now* (Barry Miles).

p364 'I just woke up in the middle of it and thought . . .' John to *Newsweek*.

p368 'It's an old Beatles number . . .' John on stage with Elton John at Madison Square Garden.

**Chapter Fifty-nine:**

p370 Was Yoko really 'thinking of taking him back'? May Pang in *Loving John*.

p372 'What would you think if I began writing with Paul again?' John to May Pang, in *Loving John*.

p372 'Bowies cutting "universe" (Let It Beatle)'. In letter from John to Derek Taylor, *The John Lennon Letters*.

p373 Yoko called to say the stars were in their right places for John to undergo hypnotism to stop smoking. From *Loving John* (May Pang).

**Chapter Sixty:**

p374 'The cure was very difficult . . .' Yoko to May Pang (*Loving John*).

p374 'It wasn't anybody's fault. It just happened . . .' John to May Pang, *Ibid*.

p374 'It was horrible. Just like primal therapy . . .' John to May Pang re. hypnotism, *Ibid*.

p376 'I've been on Sinbad's voyage . . .' John to Pete Hamill (*Rolling Stone*).

**Chapter Sixty-one:**

p378 'John and Yoko have not only come back together . . .' Postcard from Yoko Ono to this author.

p378 'She'd had too many miscarriages . . .' John to *Playboy*, 1980.

p378 'When John came back, we had great sex and I got pregnant . . .' Yoko in *John Lennon* by Philip Norman.

p379 'Waking up in strange places, or reading about myself in the papers . . .' Pete Hamill in *Rolling Stone*.

p382 'My old man has a gun . . .' Death of Mal Evans. From newspaper reports, conversations with Neil Aspinall and author's interview with Lil Evans, *Daily Mail*.

p382 'The unmitigated honor . . .' John's letter to this author, *The John Lennon Letters*.

p384 Freddie diagnosed with stomach cancer . . . From *Daddy, Come Home*.

p385 'I would like to thank the Immigration Service . . .' John to press, 1976.

**Chapter Sixty-two:**

p386 'I myself have decided to be or not to be . . .' Letter to Derek Taylor, *The John Lennon Letters*.

p387 'Yoko has him all locked up', Mick Jagger quoted in the *Observer*.

p389 Buys Long Island house. From *Living On Borrowed Time* by Fred Seaman.

p390 'I never stop wanting to make music'. John to May Pang in *Loving John*.

p391 Phones May Pang from South Africa. From *Loving John*.

p392 'I felt like a Viking . . . or Jason and the Golden Fleece . . .' John to *Playboy*, 1980.

## Chapter Sixty-three:

p394 'It was amazing. I was there on the beach . . . just playing guitar and
   singing . . .' John to *Playboy*, and in variations to *Newsweek*, the BBC
   and others.

p395 'Grow old along with me . . .' Lines borrowed from poet Robert
   Browning for the song 'Grow Old With Me'.

p396 'Yoko's a tough customer . . .' David Geffen overheard talking to John
   by Fred Seaman. *Living On Borrowed Time*.

p396 'It's a teacher-pupil relationship . . .' John to *Playboy*.

p398 'Yoko told me, "you will be able to walk here [in New York]"'. John
   to Andy Peebles, BBC radio, 1980.

p399 'You've captured our relationship exactly'. John to Annie Liebovitz,
   *Rolling Stone*.

p399 'This what you want?' John's alleged comment to his assassin Mark
   Chapman on giving him his autograph (press reports).

## Chapter Sixty-four:

p401 Paul McCartney didn't hear of the murder until Linda returned
   from the school run the following morning. Paul to this author, *Daily
   Telegraph*.

p402 'I don't believe in dead heroes . . .' John to this author, *The Ray
   Connolly Beatles Archive*.

p000 'I don't appreciate worship of dead Sid Vicious . . .' John to *Playboy*.

## Afterword:

p404 Mark Chapman's background. Various *Press* reports.

p406 'I couldn't shoot him like that . . . I wanted to get his autograph . . .'
   Mark Chapman to the police.

p406 'I'm sorry I gave all you guys this trouble . . .' *Ibid.*

# PICTURE CREDITS

# INDEX